LEGAL PRACTICE AND CULTURAL DIVERSITY

AF839993

Cultural Diversity and Law

Series Editor:
Prakash Shah, School of Law, Queen Mary, University of London, UK

Around the world, most states are faced with difficult issues arising out of cultural diversity in their territories. Within the legal field, such issues span across matters of private law through to public and constitutional law. At international level too there is now considerable jurisprudence regarding ethic, religious and cultural diversity. In addition, there are several layers of legal control – from communal and religious regulation to state and international regulation. This multiplicity of norm setting has been variously termed legal pluralism, inter-legality or inter-normativity and provides a fascinating lens for academic analysis that links up to cultural diversity in new and interesting ways. The umbrella of cultural diversity encompasses various population groups throughout the world ranging from national, ethnic, religious or indigenous groupings. This series particularly welcomes work that is of comparative interest, concerning various state jurisdictions as well as different population groups.

Legal Practice and Cultural Diversity

Edited by

RALPH GRILLO
University of Sussex, UK

ROGER BALLARD
University of Manchester, UK

ALESSANDRO FERRARI
University of Insubria (Come and Varese), Italy

ANDRÉ J. HOEKEMA
University of Amsterdam, The Netherlands

MARCEL MAUSSEN
University of Amsterdam, The Netherlands
and

PRAKASH SHAH
Queen Mary, University of London, UK

ROUTLEDGE
Routledge
Taylor & Francis Group
LONDON AND NEW YORK

First published 2009 by Ashgate Publishing

2 Park Square, Milton Park, Abingdon, Oxon OX14 4RN
711 Third Avenue, New York, NY 10017, USA

Routledge is an imprint of the Taylor & Francis Group, an informa business

First issued in paperback 2016

Copyright © 2009 Ralph Grillo, Roger Ballard, Alessandro Ferrari, André J. Hoekema, Marcel Maussen and Prakash Shah

Ralph Grillo, Roger Ballard, Alessandro Ferrari, André J. Hoekema, Marcel Maussen and Prakash Shah have asserted their right under the Copyright, Designs and Patents Act, 1988, to be identified as the editors of this work.

All rights reserved. No part of this book may be reprinted or reproduced or utilised in any form or by any electronic, mechanical, or other means, now known or hereafter invented, including photocopying and recording, or in any information storage or retrieval system, without permission in writing from the publishers.

Notice:
Product or corporate names may be trademarks or registered trademarks, and are used only for identification and explanation without intent to infringe.

British Library Cataloguing in Publication Data
Legal practice and cultural diversity. - (Cultural
diversity and law)
1. Sociological jurisprudence 2. Minorities - Legal status,
laws, etc.
I. Grillo, R. D.
340.1'15

Library of Congress Cataloging-in-Publication Data
Legal practice and cultural diversity / by Ralph Grillo ... [et al.].
p. cm.
Includes bibliographical references and index.
ISBN 978-0-7546-7547-1
1. Religious minorities--Legal status, laws, etc.--Congresses. 2. Legal polycentricity--Congresses. I. Grillo, R. D.

K3242.A6L44 2009
340'.115--dc22

2009003041

ISBN 13: 978-0-7546-7547-1 (hbk)
ISBN 13: 978-1-138-26783-1 (pbk)

Contents

Notes on Contributors

Veit Bader is Professor of Sociology and of Social and Political Philosophy in the University of Amsterdam. His research interests encompass theories of societies, social movements and collective action, modern capitalisms, ethics of migration and incorporation, and citizenship and associative democracy. Publications include: *Collective Action* (Leske + Budrich 1981); *Inequalities*, with Albert Benschop (Leske + Budrich 1989); *Racism, Ethnicity, Citizenship* (Westfälisches Dampfboot 1995); *Associative Democracy: The Real Third Way*, with Paul Hirst (Cass 2001); *Secularism or Democracy? Associational Governance of Religious Diversity* (Amsterdam University Press 2007).

Natasha Bakht is an assistant professor at the Faculty of Law, University of Ottawa, where she teaches a course entitled 'Multicultural rights in liberal democracies'. Her research interests are in the area of law, culture and minority rights and specifically in the intersecting area of religious freedom and women's equality. She has written extensively on the issue of religious arbitration in family law including 'Religious arbitration in Canada: protecting women by protecting them from religion' (*Canadian Journal of Women and the Law*, 2007, 19: 119–44).

Roger Ballard is Director of the Centre for Applied South Asian Studies. As an anthropologist he has had a long-standing interest in migration from South Asia to the UK, in the ethnic colonies and transnational networks created and maintained by settlers and their offspring, and the challenges for public policy to which their entrepreneurial initiatives have given rise. Editor of *Desh Pradesh: the South Asian Presence in Britain* (Hurst 1994) and the author of numerous papers, he has recently become active as a consultant anthropologist and prepared numerous expert reports for use in proceedings in the civil, criminal, family, administrative and asylum and immigration courts.

Martine Cohen is a sociologist of religion and secularism at the Groupe Sociétés, Religions, Laïcités (CNRS-EPHE, Paris). Her research concerns the historical sociology of the Jews in France and in Europe, comparisons between Jews' and Muslims' national integration, and recent transformations of secularism in France. She edited *Associations laïques et confessionnelles, identité et valeurs* (L'Harmattan 2006). Other publications include 'Les Juifs d'Europe sont-ils encore une minorité religieuse?', in *Minorités religieuses dans l'espace européen* (Bastian and Messner eds, PUF 2007); 'L'intégration de l'islam et des musulmans en France: modèles du passé et pratiques actuelles', in *La Laïcité, une valeur d'aujourd'hui?* (Baudoin and Portier eds, Presses Universitaires de Rennes 2001).

Alessandro Ferrari is Associate Professor in the Faculty of Law at Insubria University (Como-Varese). He studied at the University of Milan (PhD, 1999) and the University of Paris XI (PhD, 2003). His interests include the relationship between church and state; French laïcité; Islam in Italy and in Europe, and the comparative law of religions. He is associated with the Groupe Sociétés, Religions, Laïcités (CNRS-EPHE, Paris) and the Centre for Law and Religion of the Cardiff Law School, and member of the International Advisory Board of the *British Journal of Religious Education.*

Claire de Galembert is a sociologist at the National Centre for Scientific Research and the Vice-director of the *Institut des Sciences Sociales du Politique* (CNRS-École Normale Supérieure de Cachan-Paris X). Her research deals with Islam in France as object of public policy at the local and national levels, and in particular with the role of law in its public regulation. In 2008 she edited a thematic issue of *Droit et Société* about the headscarf (*Le voile en procès*, n° 68, 2008).

Jean-François Gaudreault-DesBiens is Professor of Law and Canada Research Chair in North American and Comparative Juridical and Cultural Identities and Associate Professor at the Université de Montréal. His interests are constitutional law (domestic and comparative), legal theory and epistemology, and the sociology of legal cultures. He has worked extensively on the law's apprehension of identity-related phenomena and published several books and articles in French, English and Spanish. Recent work focuses on the legal theory of federalism, the legal treatment of religious claims and the relations between the civil law and common law traditions in a globalized economy. He is a member of the Québec and Ontario Bars, and is the Canadian correspondent for the British journal *Public Law*.

Ralph Grillo is Emeritus Professor of Social Anthropology, University of Sussex. He is the author of *Ideologies and Institutions in Urban France: The Representation of Immigrants* (1985) and *Pluralism and the Politics of Difference: State, Culture, and Ethnicity in Comparative Perspective* (1998). He is co-editor (with Ben Soares) of *Journal of Ethnic and Migration Studies*, special issue, 30(5), 2004 on *Islam, Transnationalism and the Public Sphere in Western Europe*, and editor of *The Family in Question: Immigrant and Ethnic Minorities in Multicultural Europe* (Amsterdam University Press 2008).

André J. Hoekema holds a chair in legal pluralism at the Law Faculty, University of Amsterdam. His research has concerned the rights of indigenous peoples and the conditions under which local legal institutions and frames of interpretation are officially recognized, and processes of interlegality in Europe, studying cases brought before Dutch judges and other legal or semi-legal professionals by parties claiming allegiance to through adherence to a distinct religion or community different from the Dutch mainstream. Publications include 'A new beginning of law among indigenous peoples', in *The Law's Beginning*, edited by F.J.M. Feldbrugge

(Martinus Nijhoff 2003); *Multicultural Interlegality*, special issue of the *Journal of Legal Pluralism and Unofficial Law*, 2005; 'Un nuevo futuro codificado para la tenencia local de los recursos naturales?', in *Agua y Derecho* (Rutgerd Boelens et al eds, Instituto de Estudios Peruanos 2006).

Alison Dundes Renteln is Professor of Political Science and Anthropology at the University of Southern California where she teaches Law and Public Policy with an emphasis on international law and human rights. She was formerly Director of the Jesse Unruh Institute of Politics. Her publications include *The Cultural Defense* (Oxford University Press 2004), which received the 2006 USC Phi Kappa Phi Award for Creativity in Research, and *Multicultural Jurisprudence* (Hart 2009) co-edited with Marie-Claire Foblets. She worked with the United Nations on the Convention on the Rights of Persons with Disabilities, and has taught seminars on the rights of ethnic minorities for judges, lawyers, court interpreters and police officers. She has also served on several California civil rights commissions.

Samantha Knights is a barrister practising at Matrix Chambers, London, specializing in immigration and asylum law, public law and human rights. She is also a member of the executive committee of the Bar Human Rights Committee of England and Wales. Her publications include *Freedom of Religion, Minorities, and the Law* (Oxford University Press 2007).

Marcel Maussen studied political science and philosophy in Amsterdam and Paris, and is now Associate Professor at the Department of Political Science and researcher at the Institute for Migration and Ethnic Studies (IMES), University of Amsterdam. His doctoral thesis at the Amsterdam School for Social Science Research is entitled *Constructing Mosques. The Governance of Islam in France and the Netherlands* (2009). His current research focuses on issues of governance of religious and ethnic diversity in Europe. Recent publications include *Space for Islam? Urban Policies, Religious Facilities and Organizations* (in Dutch, 2006) and 'Islamic presence and mosque establishment in France. Colonialism, arrangements for guest workers and citizenship' (*Journal of Ethnic and Migration Studies* 2007).

Werner Menski is Professor of South Asian Laws in the School of Law at the School of Oriental and African Studies, University of London. He writes mainly on South Asian laws, both traditional and modern, comparative legal theory and ethnic minority legal issues. His recent publications include *Comparative Law in a Global Context: The Legal Systems of Asia and Africa* (second edition, Cambridge University Press 2006). He edits *South Asia Research* (New Delhi, Sage) and maintains an active teaching programme at undergraduate, postgraduate and PhD level that connects legal issues concerning pluralism and transnational reconstructions in a number of jurisdictions.

Mathias Rohe is Professor of Private Law, Private International Law and Comparative Law at the Department of Law, University of Erlangen-Nuremberg, and the founding director of the Erlangen Centre for Islam and the Law in Europe. He has studied law and Islamic sciences in Tuebingen and Damascus, and his interests include the legal state of Islam and its development in European contexts; Islamic law, especially its contemporary development; private international law; comparative law and banking; and securities law. Publications include *Muslims and the Law in Europe: Chances and Challenges* (Global Media Publications 2007), and *Das islamische Recht: Geschichte und Gegenwart* (Beck 2009).

Russell Sandberg is a lecturer in law at Cardiff University and an associate of the Centre for Law and Religion at Cardiff. He has written widely on the interactions between law and religion in England and Wales and has published in the *Law Quarterly Review*, *Cambridge Law Journal*, *Public Law*, *Modern Law Review* and the *Ecclesiastical Law Journal*. He is co-editor, with Professor Norman Doe, of *Law and Religion: New Horizons* (Peeters 2009).

Prakash Shah is a senior lecturer in the School of Law at Queen Mary, University of London. His research interests range across the legal questions arising in contexts of migration, diasporas, minorities, transnational communities and religion. His publications include *Legal Pluralism in Conflict: Coping with Cultural Diversity in Law* (GlassHouse 2005); *Migration, Diasporas and Legal Systems in Europe* (RoutledgeCavendish 2006, ed. with Werner F. Menski); *Law and Ethnic Plurality: Socio-legal Perspectives* (Martinus Nijhoff 2007, as editor).

Gordon R. Woodman is Emeritus Professor of Comparative Law at the University of Birmingham, UK. He has studied and written about customary laws and legal pluralism in many countries, and especially issues concerning the recognition of customary laws by the laws of various states. He is editor-in-chief of the *Journal of Legal Pluralism*. Publications include *African Law and Legal Theory* (Dartmouth Publishing Co. 1995, ed. with A.O. Obilade); *Local Land Law and Globalization: A Comparative Study of Peri-urban Areas in Benin, Ghana and Tanzania* (LIT Verlag 2004, with Ulrike Wanitzek and Harald Sippel); and *Law and Religion in Multicultural Societies* (DJØF Publishing 2008, ed. with Rubya Mehdi, Hanne Petersen and Erik Sand).

List of Cases

Chapter 1
Legal Practice and Cultural Diversity: Introduction

Roger Ballard, Alessandro Ferrari, Ralph Grillo, André J. Hoekema, Marcel Maussen and Prakash Shah

> We have to think a little harder about the role and rule of law in a plural society of overlapping identities
>
> (Dr Rowan Williams, Archbishop of Canterbury, 2008)

This collection brings together papers by anthropologists, political scientists and legal specialists who consider how contemporary cultural and religious diversity challenges legal practice, how legal practice responds to that challenge and how practice is changing in the encounter with the cultural diversity occasioned by large-scale, post-war immigration. Questions about cultural difference, and whether, or to what extent, such difference should be recognized by legal systems, have provoked much discussion among lawyers and others, and raise issues highly pertinent to current debates across the globe about integration, multiculturalism and the governance of diversity. They are also keenly contested. Well-documented controversies such as those over the demands of Sikhs to wear turbans or Muslim schoolgirls to wear the Islamic headscarf (*hijab*), over legislation to outlaw racial or religious hate-speech, or arranged and forced marriages, or about whether or not legal systems should acknowledge claims by Muslims to be able to live their lives according to shari'a principles, illustrate how contentious is the relationship between the law and diversity.

Building on these recent debates, the present book seeks to contribute to theoretical and comparative accounts of the interaction of legal practice and cultural diversity by observing actual practices and interpretations which occur in jurisprudence and in public discussion, and examining how the wider environment shapes legal processes and is in turn shaped by them. The chapters are based on papers presented to a conference held in London in July 2007, sponsored by IMISCOE (the EU-funded Network of Excellence for International Migration, Integration and Social Cohesion), and hosted by the Law School, Queen Mary,

University of London.[1] The idea for the conference emerged from an IMISCOE working group whose terms of reference included linguistic, cultural and religious diversity and related policies. Previous initiatives on the governance of Islam in Europe, and on immigrant/minority ethnic families as objects of reflection and sites of contestation among majority and minority populations in Europe, had raised important questions about how cultural diversification in Europe is being accommodated (or not) within various institutional systems, not least the law. This suggested the value of bringing together legal practitioners and academics from various disciplines to investigate how legal practice copes with the challenge of cultural difference.

In addressing such questions, those who contributed papers to the conference, and subsequently the present volume, have emphasized the value of working through case studies of events and situations, paying close attention to what actually happens in the application of the law, at the same time recognizing the need to locate particular cases in their widest context (for example, legal frameworks and their underlying historical philosophies) and to take into account international or transnational influences on the way in which actors, legal and other, respond. The issues are complex, and our aim is to document and explore that complexity and its implications from the perspective of the social sciences, rather than intervene on behalf of any particular normative stance. Nevertheless several contributors inevitably engage with the question whether, and if so under what conditions, legal systems might or should acknowledge cultural and religious difference.

Turning to the individual papers, although the book deals mainly with Western Europe, specifically Britain, France, Germany and the Netherlands, there are also accounts of experience in North America which provide a valuable comparative perspective. Indeed, it can be argued that we cannot ignore non-European models of governing diversity, including those in India and sub-Saharan Africa. The opening chapter by Werner Menski in fact places transatlantic debates in this wider context. South Asian experience is important partly because it may offer some lessons for Europe, but also because – through transnational migration – many individuals and families live multi-sited lives, and cross-national legal pluralism frames their everyday experience. Menski argues that India's long-standing multiculturalism has consistently cultivated a plurality-conscious legal culture. Respect for diversity and difference was reflected in pre-colonial legal structures, and deep-rooted awareness of internal plurality continues to assert itself in the contemporary context of 'social welfare', affirmative action or under headings such as 'secularism', which flourishes in its Indian manifestations. Despite uniformizing trends and globalizing pressures, Indian law maintains a plurality-conscious orientation with deep respect for cultural and religious diversity and thus for maintenance of a personal law system. Indian sensitivity for diversity and

1 We thank IMISCOE, the QMUL Law School and the British Academy who each provided generous financial support for the conference. For IMISCOE see< http://www.imiscoe.org/>.

specifically for the agency of the individual in a pluralistic setting offers a useful model for others.

The chapters which follow focus on Europe or North America, and deal with both the challenges presented to legal systems by populations of migrant origin with cultural and religious traditions different from those of the receiving societies, and with the question of accommodation. Veit Bader offers a wide-ranging and thought-provoking discussion of recent debates about how legal systems might approach the question of difference. Taking the controversy about shari'a in Europe and Canada as his starting point, he shows how that controversy is characterized by the interested construction and reproduction of highly aggregated stereotypes, myths, mutual misunderstandings and dramatized fears or panics, and it is important to define what is *not* at issue. Bader strives to transcend current thinking by seeking productive solutions in the tradition of institutional pluralism, legal pluralism in particular, and argues for a stance which avoids the imposition of a hegemonic moral order on the one hand, and moral and legal relativism, on the other. Bader tests his argument through an exploration of the debate in Ontario on the application of Muslim personal law in arbitrations sparked by a proposal to establish a Darul-Qada (Muslim Arbitration Tribunal).

As the chapter by Bader shows, what to do about shari'a has become a major concern of transatlantic legal systems. Nowhere was this more apparent than during the controversy which followed a speech by the Archbishop of Canterbury (Williams 2008), widely, if misleadingly, interpreted as calling for the introduction of shari'a in the UK. Prakash Shah seeks to place the debate on Muslims and the law in the UK within a wider frame of reference. He points out that directed as the speech was to the official legal system's need to adapt to changing social realities, many of the governing assumptions about the system of law came to the surface in response to it. He argues that from a socio-legal perspective the claim of a uniform, national system of law is not sustainable either in the UK or elsewhere, and comments that the widely articulated discomfort with the Archbishop's thoughts on shari'a, and the unwillingness to respond constructively to his suggestions, which build on Shachar's idea of 'transformative accommodation' (2001), reflect a continuing adherence to what Wimmer and Glick Schiller (2002) have called 'methodological nationalism'. Even though the Archbishop's remarks have not been totally rejected by lawyers and judges, Shah feels that unless legal pluralism and comparative methodology are introduced into law teaching, prospects for the acceptance of shari'a will not advance significantly.

Mathias Rohe, who has worked in Germany as both an academic specialist on the Middle East and a judge, points out that in Europe the application of shari'a rules has in fact become a daily practice, not only informally, but also with respect to the ruling official laws. These are laws granting far-reaching religious freedom or applying foreign legal rules within the limits of public policy. In some cases Islamic legal rules have been incorporated within the formal legal system. Reviewing these developments which are fuelling a lively discussion about the scope and the limits of religious and legal diversity and the necessary amount of unity in European states and their societies, Rohe argues that within the framework of the principles governing European legal orders, Muslims should be enabled to put their beliefs into practice their daily lives.

Against this wider background, Natasha Bakht focuses on one particular issue of recent concern, Muslim women's dress, not, in this instance, the headscarf (*hijab*), so controversial in France, but the *niqab* – a face veil – the use of which has provoked controversy in the UK and elsewhere in Europe, and in North America. Bakht deals specifically with opposition to the *niqab* in the courtroom context and asks whether there might be circumstances in which the removal of the *niqab* is necessary for justice to be done. In examining the arguments she scrutinizes judicial assessment of credibility based on demeanour evidence, and concludes by suggesting ways in which accommodation might be found for *niqab*-wearing women in circumstances when seeing the face is integral to the judicial task.

Although several contributors are concerned with the challenges to legal systems which come from the recent Muslim immigrant presence in Europe and North America, it is important to remember that not all immigrants and minority ethnic settlers of immigrant background are Muslim. Gordon Woodman, who has written extensively on legal pluralism, looks at another instance of the current ethnic 'superdiversity' in the UK (Vertovec 2007) by focusing on migrants from sub-Saharan Africa. African migrants in Britain are transnational, and remain active within their cultures of origin, including adaptation of their customary laws. At the same time, coming, as many do, from countries with strong colonial and post-colonial ties with the UK, whose structures were heavily influenced by British colonial policies and institutions, they often find much of English culture and laws quite familiar. Nevertheless, some customary laws they observe are quite different from English law, and demands for recognition of customary laws, for instance in the domestic sphere, present significant challenges to English law. He concludes that English law has generally been ready to recognize the customary laws of some of its minorities, and should therefore and where possible accommodate the customary laws of today's immigrant communities.

The issue of accommodation is central to many of the chapters. Jean-François Gaudreault-DesBiens' discusses the doctrine of 'reasonable accommodation', which Canadian courts have adopted since the mid-1980s and which, for example, allows claims for exemption from some rulings provided this does not impose an undue hardship upon the organization from which the accommodation is requested. Different types of claimants, but particularly religious claimants, have benefited from this doctrine. Until recently, the doctrine was widely accepted across Canada, and this remains the official position. In Québec, however, there have been serious misgivings and a lively political debate surrounding it, and the chapter looks closely at the socio-economic and political history of the province to determine why this is so. The Québec Provincial Government responded to the growing controversy by appointing a high-powered commission (the Bouchard-Taylor Commission) to report on the management of practices related to cultural diversity. Its report (Commission de consultation sur les pratiques d'accommodement reliées aux différences culturelles 2008) confirmed the doctrine of reasonable accommodation, and recommended public education about cultural diversity and transcultural reflection on Québec's particular cultural situation in Canada.

André Hoekema, who has wide experience of legal systems in Latin America and Europe, focuses on the renegotiation of norms and practices, and on sensitivity in the application of domestic law in the Netherlands. He examines judicial behaviour in multicultural cases and asks whether judges respond to the multicultural challenge or stick to standard (dominant) conceptions and perceptions only. In analysing the results of his survey of cases he asks whether the (admittedly weak) observed tendencies of accommodating distinct legal institutions or life patterns can be said to pluralize domestic (Dutch) law, or rather represent a step towards assimilating the distinct culture into the mainstream. He then goes on to explore whether or not the concept of 'interlegality' (Santos 2002) can serve to illuminate this accommodation and argues that many lawyers now accept that legal orders are relatively open structures and that pluralization is an empirical reality.

The legal system in the United States often seems more open to recognizing and accommodating cultural difference than does that of European countries such as France. Alison Renteln argues that in modern legal systems the arrival of immigrants from numerous countries has generated new controversies related to their worldviews. Most of the scholarship analysing culture conflicts has focused on criminal jurisprudence, which she herself has documented in her major study on the cultural defence (2004). Here she considers instead civil cases in which individuals make claims for larger damage awards based on their cultural backgrounds. The contention is that the plaintiffs experience greater trauma because the injury they suffer is considered more egregious in their cultures. This argument is advanced in cases involving issues ranging from unauthorized autopsies to illegal police searches. A comparative analysis of North American and European cases will afford insight into the difficulties associated with the adjudication of these claims.

In many ways the French experience offers a strong contrast with other countries, and two chapters examine that experience in the light of the challenges to the French legal system represented by a growing Muslim population, principally though not exclusively of North African origin. Martine Cohen provides an initial historical overview comparing the respective positions of Jews and Muslims in France before World War Two. More recently, she observes, after a period of openness to cultural diversity (in the 1970s and 1980s), a new debate on *laïcité* has emerged which oscillates between two extreme positions. On the one hand, there is a call for a return to private-discrete religious identities and, on the other, these identities are to be recognized as an assertive form of multiculturalism. The chapter analyses the national and international factors of this growing debate on *laïcité* and multiculturalism, and concludes by asking whether multiculturalism destabilizes 'old' national identities and secularization processes in a global world.

Claire de Galembert takes up one aspect of the *laïcité* debate in France by an analysis centring on the role of Article 9 of the European Convention on Human

Rights which provides a right to freedom of thought, conscience and religion, in the headscarves controversy. Examining the process through which the Islamic headscarf (*hijab*) has become and remained a public issue through the period 1989–2004, she shows how Article 9 came to be used as a *justification* for banning the wearing of the headscarf in schools in legislation passed in 2004. The claims of those belonging to different faiths is clearly central to contemporary debates about the law and diversity, and de Galembert's chapter is in fact the first of four dealing in various ways with the implications of human rights legislation and the impact of the European Court of Human Rights in Strasbourg for such claims.

Russell Sandberg continues this theme by discussing changes in the legal framework concerning religious minorities in England and Wales, which has been transformed in recent years: first by legislative developments (chiefly the Human Rights Act 1998, the Employment Equality (Religion or Belief) Regulations 2003 and the Equality Act 2006), and second by an emerging case law interpreting the effect of the new laws. Beginning with a brief historical overview, his chapter seeks to analyse how these changes have affected the legal position of religious minorities by a specific focus on the response of the judiciary to these legislative changes. Sandberg points to the importance of the House of Lords' judgment in *Begum*,[2] and how this has affected subsequent cases, thereby providing an assessment of how this emerging jurisprudence could impact upon the rights of religious minorities in the future.

Samantha Knights, a barrister, is also concerned with the implications of human rights legislation. There have been a number of cases reaching the High Court in England relating to the issue of freedom of religion and interference with that freedom in the context of education and employment. Like Sandberg, Knights points to the importance of the House of Lords decision in the *Begum* case, where a Muslim girl wished to wear her *jilbab* to school, that there was no interference with Article 9 ECHR because she was free to go to another school where she could wear the garment. This principle relating to freedom of choice has already been developed in case law relating to employment, and represents a distinct limitation on arguments relating to Article 9 in these situations. The chapter explores the underlying socio-political issues relating to freedom of religion in a democratic society, considers how freedom of religion has been interpreted by the UK in the area of civil law in light of Strasbourg decisions and concludes with concerns for future development of the law in this context.

Finally, Roger Ballard looks more generally at the development of human rights discourse in Europe and assesses its application to questions of cultural diversity in the legal sphere. He argues that a paradoxical weapon – human-rights based arguments – has appeared in the hands of those who maintain that the scale of the non-European presence in Europe, together with the determination to maintain alien ways, represents an unacceptable threat to the integrity of European

2 *R (on the application of Begum) v Head teacher and Governors of Denbigh High School* [2006] UKHL 15.

civilization. Arguing that family structures of non-Europeans in general, and Muslims in particular, support unacceptable practices which are contrary to human rights, those hostile to the new minority presence have legitimated their opposition on the grounds of protecting personal freedoms from corporate oppression. He concludes that the contemporary discourse of statutorily entrenched human rights must be regarded as double-edged.

References

Commission de consultation sur les pratiques d'accommodement reliées aux différences culturelles. 2008. *Fonder l'avenir. Le temps de la conciliation.* G. Bouchard and C. Taylor, co-chairs. Québec: Commission de consultation sur les pratiques d'accommodement reliées aux différences culturelles. Available at: <http://www.accommodements.qc.ca> [accessed 22 October 2008].

Renteln, A.D. 2004. *The Cultural Defense.* New York: Oxford University Press.

Santos, B.de S. 2002. *Towards a New Legal Common Sense: Law, Globalization and Emancipation* (2nd Edition). London: Butterworths.

Shachar, A. 2001. *Multicultural Jurisdictions: Cultural Differences and Women's Rights.* Cambridge, UK/New York: Cambridge University Press.

Vertovec, S. 2007. Superdiversity and its Implications. *Ethnic and Racial* Studies, 30(6), 1024–54.

Williams, R., The Rt. Rev. 2008. Civil and Religious Law in England: A Religious Perspective. Speech at the Royal Courts of Justice, 7 February 2008. Available at: <http//www.archbishopofcanterbury.org/1575> [accessed 22 October 2008].

Wimmer, A. and N. Glick Schiller. 2002. Methodological Nationalism and Beyond: Nation-State Building, Migration and the Social Sciences. *Global Networks* 2(4), 301–34.

Chapter 2
Cultural Diversity: Challenge and Accommodation

Roger Ballard, Alessandro Ferrari, Ralph Grillo, André J. Hoekema, Marcel Maussen and Prakash Shah

The Challenge of Cultural Diversity

There is growing interest across Europe, North America and elsewhere in the interaction between the emergent lifestyles of migrants and settled minority populations of migrant origin, and the law and legal processes. A major reason for the burgeoning of such concerns, in public debate and in the academy,[1] is the way globalization has intensified in recent years with improvements in the capacity of communications technology to ship goods, people, ideas and information cheaply around the globe. There has consequently been an upsurge in 'reverse colonization', as millions of villagers from the impoverished South have moved upwards and outwards to fill gaps in the labour markets of the prosperous North. In the current phase of globalization their passage abroad is a great deal speedier than those of their predecessors, and this has enabled them to keep in close contact with kinsfolk overseas. Thus many migrants, rather than orienting their lives exclusively to receiving countries, live transnationally, maintaining ongoing relations with places of origin and with international diasporas in the global ecumene, a term which the anthropologist Ulf Hannerz employed to refer to the 'interconnectedness of the world, by way of interactions, exchanges and related developments, affecting not least the organization of culture' (Hannerz 1996: 7).

Multi-sited living may of itself bring people and communities into the purview of, and sometimes conflict with, the law. Organizing families across borders, for example making caring arrangements for elderly parents or young children, frequently obliges migrants and their descendants to interact with legal systems and judicial processes in both receiving and sending countries around key life cycle events (birth, adolescence, marriage, death) as well as in their conduct of

1 See *inter alia* Bowen 2006; Ferrari et al. 2005, 2006; Foblets et al. (eds) 2009; Foblets and Renteln (eds) 2009; Foblets and Strijbosch (eds) 1999; Gaudreault-DesBiens 2004; Hoekema (ed.) 2005; Knights 2007; Mehdi et al. (eds) 2008; Pearl and Menski 1998; Renteln 2004; Shachar 2000; Shah 2005; Shah and Menski (eds) 2006, and contributions to the edited volumes.

everyday affairs (Baldassar et al. 2006). Moreover, instead of assimilating, many have, albeit to varying degrees, and often in a transformed fashion,[2] maintained cultural values and practices seemingly very different from those accepted as hegemonic and appropriate in contemporary receiving societies in Europe. The resulting ethnic plurality, and the values and practices which accompany it, have become the focus of debate about difference and its limits, the object of media comment, policy initiatives and legislation, and the daily preoccupation of social service practitioners, teachers and others (Grillo (ed.) 2008).

The way this cultural diversity in contemporary Europe and elsewhere tests dominant conceptions may become apparent in interaction with the law and thus poses a series of challenges to legal practice. These challenges are not just a matter of texts and lawyers but involve a wide range of social actors and stakeholders, inside and outside strictly legal processes:

- New issues are entering the legal arena requiring fresh interpretation or re-interpretation of existing law (e.g. in respect of marriage or divorce, or the custody of children).
- New arguments and justifications are proposed, such as 'cultural defence'.
- New demands by individuals or collectivities for special rights or treatment test the legitimacy of long-established principles such as 'equality before the law', which may no longer be seen as self-evident;[3] accepted values, e.g. concerning the relationship between the secular and the religious, may be contested.
- How the law is applied to particular minorities may become a matter of heated debate in political and religious circles within both minority and majority populations and may lead to strong public reaction, e.g. in the media.
- New types of inequality of power with respect to the law may become apparent. Minorities may not know how the law protects them, or how courts work.
- New or relatively new values, e.g. stemming from movements on behalf of human rights, or more specifically the rights of women and children, are being institutionalized and endowed with legislative authority, nationally and/or internationally, with implications for the daily lives of migrants

2 See *inter alia* Ballard (ed.) 1994, Menski 1993 or Werbner 2004 for processes of hybridity and cultural navigation in the British South Asian context.

3 We refer to ethnic, linguistic or religious minorities of migrant origin, though other kinds of collectivities (gays and lesbians, regional minorities) may make similar claims. Indeed these are an established feature of the socio-political scene in many countries. Claims for privileges based on membership of a distinct ethnic or religious community, e.g. within programmes of affirmative action, need not challenge the principle of equal treatment, indeed may serve to deepen and reaffirm it, though they may be viewed as unjustified demands for 'unequal' treatment.

and their descendants. Sometimes these developments benefit minority populations, sometimes they have a negative impact, limiting the extent to which cultural difference may be taken into account by courts.[4]

- National legal systems are increasingly affected by international legislation and decisions, as with the growing influence on judicial decisions of the European Court of Human Rights (ECtHR) and the interpretation of Article 9. This tests the adequacy of approaches to law grounded in 'methodological nationalism' (Shah, this volume).

When in Rome (or Paris)?

One consequence, then, of intensified migratory movements, transnationalism and the growing importance of communities living multi-sided lives is that there now exists a plethora of sometimes highly controversial cultural and religious norms, values, practices and institutions clamouring to be recognized and taken into account by the courts in criminal, civil and administrative cases. How far should societies and especially legal systems and legal actors go to accommodate the plurality which is an inescapable characteristic of contemporary societies?

A robust answer, gaining popularity amid growing scepticism about multiculturalism and increasing hostility to difference, is that far from coming to terms with minority cultural and religious diversity, receiving societies should insist on conformity with existing values and practices, and strive to maintain a minimum level of comprehensive national homogeneity. This would be consonant with the ideals of strongly republican states such as France, where historical commitment to a vision of homogeneity, currently articulated in terms of the principle of *laicité*, remains intense. It is argued on ideological grounds that the degree of commonality amongst its citizens is so profound as to render the public recognition of any kind categorical distinctions between them illegitimate (Cohen, this volume). 'According to the Republican way of thinking', says Bowen,

> living together in a society requires agreement on basic values … If the society has the right mechanisms to integrate people, to make them into citizens, then the state can be quite generous in welcoming immigrants, extending borders, even conceiving of a European Empire or a transoceanic one. But these mechanisms require immigrants to take on the values and the behaviors that signify that one has become French. (2006: 11–12)

Resistance to the recognition of the consequences of ethnic plurality is not, however, restricted to such republican contexts, and similar pleas for traditional assimilationism and cultural uniformity are now voiced widely across Europe.

4 See chapters by Ballard, de Galembert, Knights and Sandberg in this volume.

A second response to the challenges is to argue that although monoculturalism and agreement on basic values and behavioural norms may no longer be reachable in societies marked by migration and ethnic diversity, migrants should be obliged to adapt to the standards of the legal order of the receiving society and respect the laws of the country where they have settled. Societal cohesion and equality, it is argued, can only be maintained through a legal system which is the same for all without cultural or religious distinction. This is another modality of the 'When in Rome' argument that has grown in popularity in the current 'cultural-diversity skeptical turn' (Vertovec and Wessendorf 2006). Will Kymlicka, otherwise supportive of minority rights, argues that in societies of immigration it is reasonable to expect that newcomers give up some of the rights and entitlements grounded in the legal orders and value systems of their societies of origin. Migrants can legitimately be obliged to assimilate into the legal order of the receiving societies: 'the expectation of integration is not unjust … In deciding to uproot themselves, immigrants voluntarily relinquish some of the rights that go along with their original national membership' (1995: 96). More forcefully, Trevor Phillips, then chairman of the UK's Commission for Racial Equality, rejecting the availability of shari'a law for Muslim communities in the UK, affirmed:

> We have one set of laws. They are decided on by one group of people, members of Parliament, and that's the end of the story. Anybody who lives here has to accept that's the way we do it. If you want to have laws decided in another way, you have to live somewhere else.[5]

Although seemingly straightforward, this appeal to adapt to the prevailing legal order and take the laws of the country as they are is based on premises that are not entirely self-evident. First, the major reason to uphold a uniform legal system and one set of laws is that this allows for an equal and equitable treatment of all citizens, whatever their affiliations, values, needs and identities. In an address to the East London Muslim Centre, on 'Equality before the Law' – the title points to one of the key questions at issue – Lord Nicholas Phillips, then Lord Chief Justice, seemed to reflect his namesake's similar concern, and indeed he too asserted that 'those who come to live in this country must take its laws as they find them' (Phillips 2008). But he also emphasized that 'Muslim men and Muslim women are entitled to be treated in exactly the same way as all other men and women in this country', and spoke at length of the many Acts of Parliament legislating against racial and religious discrimination, reassuring his audience that 'the courts of this country offer the same justice to all who come before them, regardless of gender, race or creed'. Lord Phillips was, however, more accommodating than his namesake, and went on to show how legislation against discrimination could be interpreted so as to allow exemptions for certain minority cultural practices; he mentioned

5 'Muslims "must accept" free speech', BBC report, 26 February 2006, available at <http://news.bbc.co.uk/1/hi/uk/4752804.stm> [accessed 14 August 2008].

specifically Sikh headgear and shari'a-compliant financial instruments.[6] Equality before the law does not necessarily mean differences may not be recognized. In a contextualized view of equality, equal treatment sometimes requires that people are treated differently because their situations are different (Parekh 2000: 256).

Legislating against racial and religious discrimination provides what Isaiah Berlin called 'freedom from' (Berlin 2002: 178). But in Berlin's view there is another kind of freedom, 'freedom to', which he glosses as 'the freedom which consists in not being prevented from choosing as I do by other men' (ibid.). Gray extends the argument in favour of pluralism when he criticizes the pursuit of homogeneity:

> Liberal toleration is an ideal of rational consensus. As heirs to that project, we need an ideal based not on a rational consensus on the best way of life [but] on the truth that humans will always have reason to live differently. *Modus vivendi* is such an ideal. It embodies an older current of ... belief that there are many forms of life in which humans can thrive. ... People who belong to different ways of life need have no disagreement. They may simply be different. ... From a standpoint of *modus vivendi*, no kind of life can be the best for everyone. The human good is too diverse to be realized in any life. ... Different ways of life embody incompatible aspects of the human good. ... Yet no life can reconcile fully the rival values that the human good contains. The aim of *modus vivendi* cannot be to still the conflict of values. It is to reconcile individuals and ways of life honouring conflicting values to a life in common. We do not need common values in order to live together in peace. We need common institutions in which many forms of life can coexist ... A theory of *modus vivendi* is not the search for an ideal regime, liberal or otherwise. It has no truck with the notion of an ideal regime. It aims to find terms on which different ways of life can live well together. (Gray 2000: 5–6)

The principle of equality could be qualified by an insistence that its pursuit should never be allowed to undermine respect for, and hence a commitment to accommodate, ethnic and religious diversity.

Secondly, the proposition that 'we have one set of laws' is not self-evident. Observation of actual legal processes shows that practitioners (judges, lawyers, expert witnesses, etc.) are routinely compelled to take notice of claims based on other legal, religious or customary norms. In family matters, for example, deciding on parenthood, adoption, inheritance issues and child custody may well require practitioners to relate to, interpret and weigh claims based on non-indigenous legal values. The proposition also ignores the extent to which practices of (private) mediation and arbitration are regularly accommodated within current systems.

---

6 On shari'a banking in the UK, see <http://www.islamic-bank.com/islamicbanklive/VisionAndValues/1/Home/1/Home.jsp> [accessed 8 October 2007].

Instead of simply assuming that legal orders are singular, and migrants and their descendants should consequently 'adapt or leave', a more empirically oriented approach would build on practices which legal practitioners already employ.

After the Second World War, contemporary constitutionalism in many parts of continental Europe in fact formally recognized internal pluralism, with the consequent possibility of allowing different juridical systems in the same territory, with the central state taking the role of arbiter. However, it was as yet not possible to foresee the changes that would give juridical pluralism its present significance (Ost and van de Kerchove 2002). So, as against the 'When in Rome' perspective, should not the law make room for cultural values and practices which are different from those commonly regarded as standard, even 'normal', in the society in question?

Whether European legal systems should actively accommodate minority norms and practices, and if so how, are considered more fully below, but, first, why, in the light of the many material problems encountered by migrants and their descendants in Europe and North America, is culture so significant in relation to legal institutions and the practice of the law as to be accorded special consideration?

Diversity, Culture and the Law

There are actually two questions: why is culture significant? And what has the law to do with it? To some extent the answers to both were anticipated earlier: transnational migrants and their descendants have not abandoned their values in the way that some theorists or proponents of migrant assimilation have supposed; and the management of transnational migration itself brings them and their families within the purview of the law. But it goes deeper than this.

There are, of course, many ways in which law and diversity interact in the daily lives of migrants and their descendants, e.g. through discrimination in employment, housing, education, health care or relations with the police, and these forms of social exclusion would seem far more important than anything to do with 'culture'. Our concern, however, is not with such forms of discrimination as such. Undoubtedly racism and xenophobia are part of the environment in which issues about culture and cultural diversity enter into the law and the courtroom, not least in terms of the unspoken prejudices of legal actors; the relevance of the basic premises of current approaches to racism, to be found, for example in 'critical race theory' (Delgado and Stefancic 2000: xviii), is not questioned. Such studies have much to offer, but they sometimes overlook the significance of cultural alterity and its legal consequences – what happens within the legal process itself when the law comes up against cultural difference.

A focus on the 'different' cultural values associated with migrants and their offspring when these are of concern to the law, and on those aspects of legal practice which affect members of such groups, opens up a much broader vision of social exclusion. Certainly exclusion is frequently economic in character, and closely associated with jobs and education. But employment is by no means its beginning or end. Social exclusion is a wide-ranging phenomenon, and the exclusion which characterizes the way of life of migrants and their families, can by no means be reduced to matters of income or employment, no matter their importance. In this context, a concept of cultural exclusion needs to be deployed alongside that of social exclusion.

'Culture' here refers to way of life in general, and encompasses values, premises and practices in terms of which members of any given community order their interactions. It encode frames of meaning, moral orders and tacit understandings that guide social actors in the course of their daily lives. For many people it represents something profound about how they should order personal relationships, family and community, and may be no less important to them than job or salary. Culture in this sense is a universal phenomenon, playing as salient a role in the behaviour of members of hegemonic majorities as it does in that of excluded minorities. 'Cultural exclusion' arises when the provision of services in welfare, health, education, housing and so forth is ordered on the basis of institutional practices and conceptual frameworks in which no significant cognizance is taken of the preferred lifestyles of clients, patients, pupils and tenants in personal and domestic contexts. Such alternative and frequently counter-hegemonic frames of meaning, value and practice may contradict established expectations of assimilation or integration,[7] and are frequently underpinned, or believed to be underpinned, by religion. Consequently religious issues often come sharply to the fore in the course of debates about how far, and if so on what basis, the distinctive interests and concerns of minority communities should be accommodated within the established framework of law.[8]

Beyond this is the significance of the legal system itself. The law is a locus of power; 'to be there' means to be taken seriously. Formal judicial decisions are, of course, only part of the picture: there exist many forms of mediation which may or may not be facilitated by professional lawyers. But where sections of the population are leading 'parallel lives', at least in domestic contexts, the use of different premises in informal contexts may lead to many contradictions, and the imposition of formal premises may inhibit or prevent people ordering their lives in accordance with their religious beliefs. Moreover, because the legal sphere is intimately linked to the wider national symbolic and political order, for some people the very idea of acknowledging claims based on non-hegemonic values and practices, or recognizing values which stem from other legal norms or religious

---

7 'Assimilation' and 'integration' are sometimes used synonymously, but usually signal alternative approaches to insertion in receiving societies, with the latter allowing more room for difference. See Castles et al. 2003.

8 Although the importance, in this context, of religion, and the conflict with liberal and secular principles, cannot be denied, it is not the be-all and end-all of the relationship between culture and the law. See Woodman, this volume.

and customary systems, may be thought to undermine that order, not least when those claims are put forward by 'uninvited guests'.

This approach to exclusion may be contrasted with that which characterizes much scholarly work where 'race' and 'ethnicity' in the classic senses have been guiding themes. If there is a concern with culture, multiculture and threatened hegemonies it is largely in the context of identity politics ('culture wars, political correctness, and free speech', Abel 1998: 4). For many scholars in the United States, for example, the salient issue was and remains the 'American Dilemma' (Myrdal 1944), the historic social and political inequalities between racially defined groups, rather than religious and cultural diversity (see, however, Foley and Hoge 2007, Levitt 2007). The 'European dilemma' (Schierup 1996) manifestly shares this concern, but is more closely linked with the trajectory of immigrant minorities, many from former colonies, who often happen to espouse 'other' cultures and religions.[9]

Archbishops, Lord Chief Justices and Shari'a

Although we are not exclusively concerned with Islam – religious and cultural difference in Europe and North America takes many forms – nonetheless, Muslim beliefs and practices, for reasons obvious and not so obvious,[10] now seem especially problematic in many receiving countries. Across Europe there is what amounts to a 'great fear' of Islam, and Muslims believed to pose great difficulties for institutions such as reception centres, schools, hospitals, the social services, and so on, and provide an exemplary test for the law and legal practice. Worries that Muslims (and others) in Europe seek to lead 'parallel lives' and eschew inclusion has rightly or wrongly influenced debates about practices such as veiling and arranged marriages with implications for what courts decide. Moreover Islam is often represented not as a body of doctrine, but as the property of non-Western ethnic and cultural groups, and thus as an ethnic or 'racial' trait. That 'Muslim' has become in many eyes a racialized and demonized ethnic category, especially after 9/11, means that the situation of Muslim communities, especially where these consist of stabilized, or relatively stabilized, family groups, is of special significance for the study of social and cultural exclusion and the law.

One illustration of the way in which this broader (national and international) context impinges on the law is the debate about shari'a. To what extent can or should legal systems take into account shari'a principles and/or accord recognition

9 In the UK, minority ethnicity was in 1970s and 1980s characteristically viewed through a 'race' and 'class' perspective. While these remain important for many scholars and activists, from the 1990s onwards culture and religion grew in significance, both in the interpretative literature and in everyday life (Ballard 1992 among others).

10 One reason is that Islam is a juridical religion; the law is an integral component of the theology of Islam.

to Muslim organizations, formal and informal, which adjudicate on them? This issue, which informs several contributions to this volume,[11] provides an important case study in itself of the multiple voices engaged in these legal debates and the *rapports de force* they reveal.

In February 2008 there was, in the UK, a furore over a speech on 'Civil and Religious Law in England: a Religious Perspective' given by the Archbishop of Canterbury, Dr Rowan Williams (2008). The speech at the Royal Courts of Justice was the opening lecture for a series entitled 'Islam in English Law', part of the 400th anniversary celebrations of the foundation of the Temple, one of the most important institutions in the British legal establishment. It was a high-powered address to a high-powered legal audience, but the popular and media reaction to what he said, or was imagined to have said, led to calls for his resignation, if not impeachment for treason. Headlines such as 'Archbishop backs sharia law for British Muslims' (*Guardian*, 7 February), 'Archbishop of Canterbury warns sharia law in Britain is inevitable' (*Independent*, 8 February), were typical. 'What a burqha'[12] proclaimed the popular newspaper, the *Sun* (8 February).

It is salutary to note what the Archbishop said and did not say.[13] One issue concerned the complex question of what shari'a actually is. This exchange between the Archbishop and a BBC interviewer, Christopher Landau, on the afternoon preceding his lecture,[14] illustrates the confusion:

> [Christopher Landau] But I suppose Sharia does have this very clear image in peoples' minds whether it's stoning or what might happen to a woman who's been raped; these are big hurdles to overcome if you're trying to rehabilitate Sharia.
>
> [Archbishop] What a lot of Muslim scholars would say, I think, and I'm no expert on this, is that Sharia is a method rather than a code of law and that where it's codified in some of the ways that you've mentioned in very brutal and inhuman and unjust ways, that's one particular expression of it which is historically conditioned, not at all what people would want to see as part of the method of trying to make actual the will of God in certain circumstances. So there's a lot of internal debate within the Islamic community generally about the nature of Sharia and its extent; nobody in their right mind I think would want to see in this country a kind of inhumanity that sometimes appears to be associated

11 Bader, Bakht, Cohen, de Galembert, Gaudreault-Desbiens, Knights, Menski, Rohe, Sandberg and Shah, in this volume.

12 A play on words; in English slang 'berk' means 'fool'.

13 There is a growing exegetical literature. See Shah this volume, and *inter alia* Bano 2008.

14 From the transcript of an interview with Christopher Landau of the BBC *World at One* programme, 7 February 2008, available at <http://www.archbishopofcanterbury.org/1573> [accessed 13 August 2008].

> with the practice of the law in some Islamic states the extreme punishments, the attitudes to women as well.

While the Archbishop was trying to grapple with complex arguments about the nature of shari'a, the interviewer homed in on 'extreme punishments': 'I suppose more often than not, that is what Sharia is equated with, is it not?', and this interpretation was taken up by the press, notably the *Guardian* writer Andrew Brown (9 February): 'It is all very well for the archbishop to explain that he does not want the term "shari'a" to refer to criminal punishments, but for most people that's what the word means', the implication being that is what it actually is.

The Archbishop's speech was long, sophisticated, and not easy to summarize, but what he was advocating was the necessity of taking cognizance of the current condition of cultural, social and conceptual plurality, and its implications for the law. This became apparent in his reference to Ayelet Shachar's concept of 'transformative accommodation' (2001), which he glossed as 'a scheme in which individuals retain the liberty to choose the jurisdiction under which they will seek to resolve certain carefully specified matters'. In his address on 'Equality before the Law', Lord Nicholas Phillips sought to clarify the Archbishop's intention:

> It was, I believe, not clearly understood by all, and certainly not by sections of the media which represented the Archbishop as suggesting the possibility that Muslims in this country might be governed by their own system of Sharia law. That is certainly not what he was suggesting. On the contrary he made it plain that there could not be some subsidiary Sharia jurisdiction which, I quote, 'could have the power to deny access to rights granted to other citizens or to punish its members for claiming those rights' (Phillips 2008).

He emphasized that the Archbishop was arguing that it was 'possible for individuals voluntarily to conduct their lives in accordance with Sharia principles without this being in conflict with the rights guaranteed by our law', and he stressed that the Archbishop specified a limited number of domains (e.g. marital law) where this might occur. He concluded: 'It was not very radical to advocate embracing Sharia Law in the context of family disputes', adding 'our system already goes a long way towards accommodating the Archbishop's suggestion'.

By appearing to advocate the introduction of a stronger form of pluralism, and by suggesting that followers of the shari'a might be the most immediate beneficiaries, the Archbishop found himself mocked and harried from all sides. In fact, he was not pleading for group rights as a compulsory scheme for all Muslims, for example. He was calling for discussion of the need for the availability of voluntary tribunals covering a restricted range of issues under the same legal authority as other arbitration and mediation tribunals. This is not quite a system of personal laws of the kind which one sees in South Asia, for example. Rather, the paradigm which the Archbishop appeared to be advocating, in so far as he was suggesting state sanction and control of voluntary tribunals, already finds expression in the way Jews, in their Beth Din, have managed to reconcile the desire to manage their own affairs while operating under a system of state control. This model is not new and appears to be the way Jews have long managed to live within Christian-dominated environments and also reflects how Christian churches have acted as such agents under secular *concordats*. Such models do not finally resolve questions of equality (between men and women for example), in as much as it constitutes one of the core principles of Western legal orders, and suspicions remain about the extent to which the equality principle and other concerns such as true voluntariness of submission to them are guaranteed within informal dispute resolution fora, Christian, Jewish or Muslim. The recent Ontario experiment (Bader, this volume) represents one such live example which was temporarily resolved by provincial legislation demanding observance of official norms of equality and human rights. The British model seems as yet evolving.

Meanwhile, the Archbishop was not suggesting, as critics assumed, that the edifice of Euro-American jurisprudence be dismantled in the face of Muslim demands. Whilst action may be required, such iconoclasm is unnecessary; everyday legal decision-making in contexts of ethnic plurality has already begun to point in the direction suggested by the Archbishop.[15] What he was arguing was that once it is acknowledged that the concepts and values which underpin a jurisprudential edifice may conceal a hidden (or at least unacknowledged) dimension of ethnocentric parochialism, then the suggestion that its precepts are of universal validity, and/or are of equal applicability in the process of adjudging the significance of behaviour generated within all the many ethnic components of a *de facto* plural society, must be treated with scepticism.

Remarkable about this episode was not the opposition to the Archbishop's remarks, but the vehemence of the critics (including those in the liberal press) and the ignorance about shari'a. There are arguments for and against what the Archbishop suggested (see Bano 2007, 2008 on the work of shari'a councils from the perspective of women claimants), but in the light of the reaction rational discussion was barely possible. In the political climate, it became increasingly difficult to argue in favour of accommodation, especially where that involved Islam, with proponents seen as advocating a plurality of legal orders in contradiction to the idea of (singular) legal order. Nonetheless, the response to the Archbishop's

15 See Rohe this volume. There have been calls for the availability of Muslim family law in Britain since the 1970s (Poulter 1998, 201 ff.), though many Muslims oppose such measures. There already exists (among other such bodies) the Islamic Sharia Council, established 1982, through which UK Muslims can obtain advice on the application of shari'a principles, and have disputes settled (see <http://www.islamic-sharia.org/> [accessed 14 October 2008]); it deals mostly with family matters (guidance on appropriate practices around marriage, divorce, the custody of children, inheritance), and the religious propriety of issues ranging from in vitro fertilization to trading in shares and shari'a banking (Ansari 2004: 386–7, Bano 2007, 2008, Césari et al. 2004: 38–43, Keshavjee 2007, Poulter 1998: 234–5).

speech brought to the fore the debate about cultural plurality and the law, and illustrated that in some circles there was an awareness that equal treatment in a multi-ethnic society might require some change in legal practice and in legal arrangements. But what form of accommodation is possible or desirable?

Modes of Accommodation

By 'accommodation' we refer to practices through which the law, or social actors operating in its shadow, are sensitive to, take into account and make room for values and meanings which differ from their own. How far can or should such actors go to accommodate 'others' and 'otherness'? Is there anything special about religion? What are the limits, and how should these be set or negotiated?

Accommodation is a wide-ranging process operating at many levels and in many different sites, and does not only involve those engaged in legislation or in managing cases in the courtroom (judges, advocates, etc.). These are obviously important, but there are others directly or indirectly involved in the law such as the police, expert witnesses, juries, as well as social work practitioners, teachers and the like who may be drawn into the legal process. Accommodation encompasses, but is not confined to, changes in legislation to allow practices or institutions previously prohibited or discouraged, e.g. certain kinds of marriage, shari'a councils etc., or doctrines such as 'reasonable accommodation' (Gaudreault-DesBiens, this volume). It may be observed, for example, in the use of the discretion exercised by social workers who act or refrain from acting because they decide to take 'cultural factors' into account.

In Britain and elsewhere in Europe accommodation has often involved two complementary strands, both generally accepted, but neither uncontested. One strand is to allow specified exceptions, e.g. Sikh turbans, rather than according wholesale recognition, as in the Indian personal law system (Menski 2006). A second involves increasing the sensitivity of legal actors to diversity, principally through training. Wibo van Rossum, writing about such programmes in the Netherlands, proposes the concept of 'neo-modern' sensitivity or thinking which such training might cultivate:

> A modest belief in law's values, optimistic about its instrumental power to change society and to contain state powers, but realistic as regards law's ultimate capacities, effectiveness, and side-effects, and with awareness for and sufficient knowledge of other rule systems that from the point of view of its proponents are just as worthy as modern law is from ours. (van Rossum 2008)

A similar experience and approach can be found in Britain.

The Judicial Studies Board, which supervises the training of judges in the UK, publishes *The Equal Treatment Benchbook*, compiled by the Board's Equal

Treatment Advisory Committee, drawing on the advice of experts.[16] The current issue (Judicial Studies Board 2005–2008) replaced an earlier *Handbook on Ethnic Minority Issues*, published in 1994 and substantially revised and given the present title in 1999. It covers topics such as gender, sexuality, disability, and poverty and social exclusion as they relate to experience of the judicial system, and is a guide to the judiciary on best practice in the context of cases coming before the courts. In a speech at the launch of the 1999 revision, then Lord Chief Justice, Lord Bingham, emphasized that justice must be administered 'without prejudice and without partiality':

> it is possible for those free of any overt, conscious, card-carrying bias to be ignorant of or insensitive to the cultural traditions, habits, practices or mores of societies other than their own; to use language and make assumptions which betray ignorance and cause offence although not intended to do so; and perhaps even to accept unwarranted stereotypical generalizations and, as a result, to treat as equal things which should be treated as unequal or as unequal things which should be treated as equal.[17]

The purpose of the Benchbook was therefore to guide judges in this area. Lord Bingham's successor, Lord Woolf, commented in 2004: 'We live in a very diverse society and the justice system has got to be able to cope with that diverse society'.[18] This meant knowing about and being sensitive towards diversity, to ensure equal access for all within the judicial process. The Benchbook approvingly quotes the former Lord Chancellor, Lord Irvine of Lairg:

> A significant cause of perceived unfairness to ethnic minorities in the courts is a lack of judicial awareness of the mores of all those who come before them. Each of us comes from our particular section of the community, and has grown up with its customs, assumptions and traditions. A few have had the privilege of gaining insights into other cultures, whether through family or friendship. But I doubt that anyone here would affect real familiarity with each and every culture which together makes up our society. (Section 1.1.2)

'We all have prejudices', it added, 'they should not be allowed to influence our judicial decisions'.

---

16 The 1999 edition contained sections based on advice from Roger Ballard, Satvinder Juss and Werner Menski (among others); the 2004–2005 revision drew on Roger Hood, Emeritus Professor of Criminology at Oxford.

17 Text available at <http://www.judiciary.gov.uk/publications_media/speeches/pre_2004/28091999.htm> [accessed 11 November 2008].

18 Text available at <http://www.ejtn.net/www/en/html/nodes_main/4_1875_423/4_1949_443/5_1585_30/5_1070_1146.htm> [accessed 11 November 2008].

The Benchbook is about 'judgecraft', 'the ability to deal with all types of case and all types of litigant with fairness, humanity and courtesy in such a way that they leave the court feeling they have received justice' (Hall 2006). It provides information on various ethnic groups, and their (mainly) religious beliefs and practices, and advises judges to be aware of, and where possible sensitive to, those relevant to the conduct of a case. It emphasizes 'understanding the range of diversity within families [and] the many factors that lead to differences; being sensitive about not making assumptions' (Section 1.2.3). In the 2007 revision (updated March 2008) a subsection was inserted dealing with religious dress in the courtroom, notably what to do about witnesses who elect to wear the *niqab*, a matter of contemporary public and judicial concern (Bakht this volume).

While guiding judges in their knowledge and understanding of specific cultures and customs and their implications, the Benchbook does not tackle more fundamental questions, for example about marriage practices (Woodman, this volume). Nor is it a treatise on 'cultural defence' (Renteln, this volume), a point emphasized by Anne Phillips (2003: 514). The essence of the approach is conveyed in the judgement by Arden LJ, cited by Ballard (this volume, p. 319-20) in which she noted that in the context of a plural society the courts 'must pay appropriate regard' to different values and practices (*Khan v Khan* [2007] EWCA Civ 399). Her judgement did not, however, specify how this might be achieved, especially in cases where the underlying issues are knottier in conceptual terms than those at stake in *Khan v Khan*. Nonetheless, the most significant feature of Lady Arden's judgment is that she found a way of incorporating the outcome of an ethnically specific mode of dispute resolution, in this case a Punjabi 'family meeting', into the framework of English law, and did so without appearing to suggest that problems in this sphere might best be resolved by granting minority religious and/or ethnic legal systems (as opposed to informal processes of dispute resolution) a position of institutional parity with the established legal order.

Sensitization of judges and other legal actors is representative of approaches which puts the onus on the receiving society and its institutions to adapt and accommodate. There is, however, a perspective which challenges minorities themselves, not necessarily to adopt received norms, but to adapt to them. It is a form of integration which allows room for alternative values and practices, within limits, with minority populations adjusting their practices and negotiating a compromise in ways acceptable to both sides. In his speech the Archbishop of Canterbury frequently cited the Canadian theorist Ayelet Shachar and her influential book *Multicultural Jurisdictions* which is centrally concerned with the 'complex relations between cultural preservation, multicultural accommodation, and the in-group subordination of women' (Shachar 2001: 6), and the problem that multicultural accommodation may put women in an 'impossible bind', forced to choose between loyalty to their community and its values, and forgoing their rights. As we noted earlier, the Archbishop placed much emphasis on Shachar's concept of 'transformative accommodation', which, she argues, would allow society to 'identify and defend only those state accommodations which can be coherently combined with the improvement of the position of traditionally subordinated classes of individuals within minority group cultures' (Shachar 2001: 118). It is, she claims, in the group's own self-interest to accommodate, as transformative accommodation would 'create institutional conditions where the group recognizes that its own survival depends on its revoking certain discriminatory practices, in the interests of maintaining autonomy over sub-matters crucial to the group's distinct *nomos*'[19] (p. 125). What appealed to the Archbishop is that

> In such schemes, both jurisdictional stakeholders may need to examine the way they operate; a communal/religious nomos, to borrow Shachar's vocabulary, has to think through the risks of alienating its people by inflexible or over-restrictive applications of traditional law, and a universalist Enlightenment system has to weigh the possible consequences of ghettoising and effectively disenfranchising a minority, at real cost to overall social cohesion and creativity. Hence 'transformative accommodation': both jurisdictional parties may be changed by their encounter over time, and we avoid the sterility of mutually exclusive monopolies.

Thus at the core of the idea are intercultural dialogue and negotiation,[20] and she advocates 'making it worthwhile for those who care about the *nomos* (such as recognized spiritual leaders) to turn around the process of alienation from the group, by permitting internal change instead' (Shachar 2001: 160). Indeed, something of the sort already occurs, for instance in the debate in the UK about arranged marriages, and in the development of the Muslim Marriage Contract.[21]

At a more theoretical level, processes of transformative accommodation can be understood in terms of an encompassing concept such as 'interlegality' (Hoekema, this volume, and Santos 2002, Twining 2000).[22] Interlegality is the process through which new legal regimes emerge from the interaction between what are often, misleadingly, thought of as discrete legal systems or social entities. Although generally applied to the impact of dominant legal orders on 'local' (subordinate) systems, interlegality may also refer to the reverse situation. Interlegality of that kind may be observed in Europe (and elsewhere) at many different levels, and on a daily basis in the courts, though not necessarily to the same extent and in the same way in all circumstances. At the macro level one may thereby witness significant changes in the relationships between the historical juridical systems of states and

19 *Nomoi* communities 'refer primarily to religiously defined groups' with a comprehensive world view (Shachar 2001: 2).

20 Mitnick (2003) is sceptical about negotiation.

21 Published August 2008. Available at <http://www.musliminstitute.com/pdfs/Muslim_Marriage_Contract.pdf> [accessed 16 October 2008].

22 Transformative accommodation also bears a family resemblance to the process of ethnic reconstruction described by Nagel and Snipp (1993).

churches. States more used to recognizing the autonomy of the traditional churches have to extend the same recognition to new communities because of claims of individuals. On the other hand, the same individual claims push the states that are historically only used to considering individuals (e.g. France) to open their juridical systems to claims based on religious and communitarian laws.

The concept of interlegality is consistent with anti-essentialist accounts of culture predominant in post-modern anthropology where it is seen less as a body of lore (still less law), than as a set of frequently highly contested principles and practices: 'A thing of shreds and patches' (Hannerz 1992: 34). It is also consistent with accounts in various disciplines of cultural hybridity and *métissage*, of the idea of multiculturalism as a negotiated order, and of the transformation of the juridical world into a sort of market ('law shopping') where individual choice plays an essential role.

However, this leads to some difficult questions concerning culture and the 'distinct communities' (Hoekema) with which particular practices might be associated. When the law attempts to take into account difference, as in a 'cultural defence', what is the status of that which it is taking into account? How might legal practice avoid essentializing and stereotyping? Moreover, whose account of a culture is the court to accept? Culture constitutes, among other things, a moral order indicating sets of rights and duties, but it is a contested moral order. There is always a multiplicity of actors and of internal cultural debates. So who speaks authoritatively for whom?

This is a question which becomes significant if there are demands for recognition of alternative (informal, extra-legal) modes of arbitration and settlement, and has considerable pertinence to a proposal made by the Archbishop, concerning what he called 'supplementary jurisdictions', and the role of shari'a councils or institutions such as the Jewish Beth Din in respect of the courts. If Muslim, Jewish, Sikh or Hindu informal practice is to be accommodated more formally within judicial systems, how might this be done? Although there is an important distinction to be made between incorporation as a 'parallel' (i.e. relatively autonomous) or as a 'supplementary' (i.e. subordinate) system, which might allow the informal boards already in existence in several countries to receive greater legal recognition for the advice they provide on appropriate religious modes of conduct, this does not address the issue of how supplementary institutions are to be constituted.[23] Recent research by Samia Bano (2007, 2008), which examines how existing councils actually operate, and what (if anything) Muslims want from them, throws much light on the complex relationship of women to such councils. There is an important gender dimension here as elsewhere: 'accommodation' may mean conceding to patriarchal interests (Bano 2008, Shachar 2001).

23 In most jurisdictions, such councils would not be permitted to implement decisions which contravene national law and public policy. Some oversight would obviously be necessary.

Invariably there is restriction on what might be accommodated. Some practices and procedures are negotiable, some not; forced marriages or honour killings are clearly beyond the bounds, but different definitions of what constitutes a marriage might be accommodated. Many of the cases reviewed by contributors to this volume (e.g. the *Amselem* judgment in Gaudreault-DesBiens' chapter, *Begum* in the chapters by Knights and Sandberg, Bader's account of the proposal by the Canadian Islamic Institute of Civil Justice to establish a Darul-Qada, Muslim Arbitration Tribunal, in Ontario, de Galembert's analysis of the *hijab* issue in France) illustrate how frequently disputes are concerned with boundaries. There are obviously both maximalist and minimalist[24] approaches to accommodation and, although the maximalist view has very few proponents, identifying where the boundary might fall is both important and difficult.

Conclusion

This book demonstrates the multiple challenges thrown up by ethnic and cultural diversity, and the consequent problems of balancing rights and accommodating claims involving asymmetries of power. Resolving competing demands and entitlements grounded in a plurality of legal orders, themselves multiple, cross-cutting and internally complex, is never a straightforward task. In such circumstances it is tempting to fall back on the imposition of homogeneity of values and practices singularly enshrined in 'our' laws, implemented without regard to difference. We strongly doubt whether this is now realistic, if it ever was. New minorities have become an integral part of the established social order; their presence an irreversible social fact. If the society around us is inescapably plural, policies which seek to eliminate plurality in favour of comprehensive national homogeneity would seem misguided and counterproductive.

Plurality and equity are compatible provided that four propositions are taken seriously:

1. An equitable society demands the accommodation of the distinctive interests and concerns, as well as the values and priorities, of all sections of the population, regardless of how long ago their ancestors established themselves within the boundaries of the current social order.
2. This requires an even-handed sensitivity to difference, instead of a formal vision of equality which assumes that all citizens are intrinsically identical. If a legal system is to treat those over whom it exercises jurisdiction fairly,

24 Bader, this volume, proposes a libertarian perspective which calls for the law to be concerned only with 'minimal morality' and which rejects both the legal imposition of norms and practices advocated by assimilationists, and the idea of legal recognition or support for cultural specificities, or, for example, specific groups or collectivities (such as women).

it must take cognizance of who those people are, and how they choose to order their lives. The values they hold dear must be treated with respect, no matter how distinctive they may be.

3. Fairness does not mean that anything goes; cultural claims and priorities often contradict one another, but one cannot be allowed automatically to subsume another. What is required is the negotiation of a viable *modus vivendi* in which each is allocated an appropriate weight in the given circumstances, within the context of an overriding commitment to equal respect for all (Carens 1997: 818).
4. Accommodation of diversity means acknowledging that cultural and legal orders are both varied and cross-cutting, and that interlegality is a fact of life. There are no clearly bounded cultural or legal systems. The coexistence of diversity precipitates processes of hybridization; no system remains unaffected and static.

The trick is to find ways of respecting diversity and of balancing competing claims, whilst guaranteeing basic rights and entitlements to citizens and residents (nationals and non-nationals) and their families. Now that Europe is increasingly religiously and ethnically diverse there is something to learn from a country such as India with a long tradition of plurality, not least within its legal system. As Menski argues (this volume) Indian multiculturalism has 'consistently allowed cultivation of a plurality-conscious legal culture'. Despite the difficulties, discussed here, which should not be underestimated, it would seem that a similar plurality-consciousness must eventually permeate legal systems in Europe.

References

Abel, R.L. 1998. *Speaking Respect, Respecting Speech.* Chicago, IL: Chicago University Press.

Ansari, H. 2004. *The 'Infidel Within': Muslims in Britain Since 1800.* London: Hurst.

Baldassar, L., C. Baldock and R. Wilding. 2006. *Families Caring Across Borders: Aging, Migration and Transnational Caregiving.* London: Macmillan.

Ballard, R. 1992. New clothes for the emperor? The conceptual nakedness of the race relations industry in Britain. *New Community,* 18(3), 481–92.

— (ed.) 1994. *Desh Pardesh: The South Asian Presence in Britain.* London: Hurst.

Bano, S. 2007. Muslim Family Justice and Human Rights: The Experience of British Muslim Women. *Journal of Comparative Law,* 1(4), 1–29.

— 2008. In Pursuit of Religious and Legal Diversity: a Response to the Archbishop of Canterbury and the 'Sharia Debate' in Britain. *Ecclesiastical Law Journal,* 10(3), 283–309.

Berlin, I. 2002. *Liberty.* Oxford: Oxford University Press.

Bingham of Cornhill, Lord. 1999. Speech at the Launch of The Judicial Studies Board's Equal Treatment Benchbook, London, 28 September 1999. Available at <http://www.judiciary.gov.uk/publications_media/speeches/pre_2004/28091999.htm> [accessed: 13 August 2008].
Bowen, J.R. 2006. *Why the French Don't Like Headscarves: Islam, the State, and Public Space.* Princeton: Princeton University Press.
Carens, J.H. 1997. Two Conceptions of Fairness: a Response to Veit Bader. *Political Theory*, 25(6), 814–20.
Castles, S., M. Korac, E. Vasta and S. Vertovec. 2003. *Integration: Mapping the Field.* London: Home Office.
Césari, J., A. Caeiro and D. Hussain. 2004. *Islam and Fundamental Rights in Europe. Final Report.* Brussels: European Commission, Directorate-General Justice and Home Affairs.
Delgado, R. and J. Stefancic. 2000. *Critical Race Theory: An Introduction.* New York/London: New York University Press.
Ferrari, A., E. Dieni and V. Pacillo (eds) 2005. *Symbolon/Diabolon. Simboli, Religioni, diritti nell'Europa multiculturale.* Bologna: Mulino.
— (eds) 2006. *I simboli religiosi tra diritti e culture.* Milano: Giuffrè.
Foblets, M.-C., J.-F. Gaudreault-DesBiens and A.D. Renteln (eds) 2009. *The Response of State Law to the Expression of Cultural Diversity.* Brussels: De Boeck/Francqui Foundation.
Foblets, M.-C. and A.D. Renteln (eds) 2009. *Multicultural Jurisprudence: Comparative Perspectives on the Cultural Defense.* Oxford: Hart Publishing.
Foblets, M.-C. and F. Strijbosch (eds) 1999. *Relations familiales interculturelles/ Cross-cultural Family Relations.* Oñati: International Institute for the Sociology of Law.
Foley, M.W. and D. Hoge. 2007. *Religion and the New Immigrants: How Faith Communities Form our Newest Citizens.* Oxford/New York: Oxford University Press.
Gaudreault-DesBiens, J.-F. 2004. *From Bijuralism to Legal Pluralism.* Toronto: University of Toronto Faculty of Law.
Gray, J. 2000. *Two Faces of Liberalism.* London: Polity Press.
Grillo, R.D. (ed) 2008. *The Family in Question: Immigrant and Ethnic Minorities in Multicultural Europe.* Amsterdam: Amsterdam University Press.
Hall, J.V. 2006. Judgecraft and the Judicial Process. Paper Presented to the European Network for the Exchange of Information Between the Persons and Entities Responsible for the Training of Judges and Public Prosecutors, 8th Plenary Meeting, Strasbourg, 16–17 October 2006.
Hannerz, U. 1992. The Global Ecumene as a Network of Networks. In *Conceptualizing Society*, edited by A. Kuper. London: Routledge, 33–58.
— 1996. *Transnational Connections: Culture, People, Places.* London: Routledge.
Hoekema, A.J. (ed) 2005. *Multicultural Interlegality.* Special issue, *Journal of Legal Pluralism and Unfficial Law*, 51.

Judicial Studies Board. 2005–2008. *Equal Treatment Benchbook*. London: Judicial Studies Board.

Keshavjee, M. 2007. Alternative Dispute Resolution in a Diasporic Muslim Community. In *Law and Ethnic Plurality: Socio-Legal Perspectives*, edited by P. Shah. Leiden: Martinus Nijhoff, 145–75.

Knights, S. 2007. *Freedom of Religion, Minorities, and the Law*. Oxford: Oxford University Press.

Kymlicka, W. 1995. *Multicultural Citizenship: A Theory of Liberal Rights*. Oxford: Clarendon Press.

Levitt, P. 2007. *God Needs No Passport: Immigrants and the Changing American Religious Landscape*. New York: New Press.

Mehdi, R., H. Petersen and G.R. Woodman (eds) 2008. *Law and Religion in Multicultural Societies*. Copenhagen: DJØF Publishing.

Menski, W. 1993. Asians in Britain and the Question of Adaptation to a New Legal Order: Asian Laws in Britain? In *Ethnicity, Identity, Migration: The South Asian Context*, edited by M. Israel and N. Wagel. Toronto: Centre for South Asian Studies, 238–68.

— 2001. Muslim Law in Britain. *Journal of Asian and African Studies*. 62, 127-163.

— 2006. Rethinking Legal Theory in Light of North-South Migration. In *Migration, Diasporas and Legal Systems in Europe*, edited by P. Shah and W. Menski. London: Routledge-Cavendish, 13–28.

Mitnick, E.J. 2003. Individual vulnerability and cultural transformation. *Michigan Law Review*. 101(6), 1635–60.

Myrdal, G., R.M.E. Sterner and A.M. Rose. 1944. *An American Dilemma; The Negro Problem and Modern Democracy*. New York, London: Harper.

Nagel, J. and S.M. Snipp. 1993. American Indian Social, Economic, Political, and Cultural Strategies for Survival. *Ethnic and Racial Studies*, 16(2), 203–35.

Ost, F. and van de Kerchove. M. 2002. *De la pyramide au réseau? Pour une théorie dialectique du droit*. Bruxelles: Publications des Facultés Universitaires Saint-Louis.

Parekh, B. 2000. *Rethinking Multiculturalism: Cultural Diversity and Political Theory*. Basingstoke: Macmillan.

Pearl, D. and W. Menski. 1998. *Muslim Family Law*. London: Sweet & Maxwell.

Phillips, A. 2003. When Culture Means Gender: Issues of Cultural Defence in the English Courts. *Modern Law Review*, 66(4), 510–31.

Phillips, N. 2008. Equality before the Law. Speech by Lord Nicholas Phillips, Lord Chief Justice, East London Muslim Centre, 3 July 2008. Available at <http://innertemplelibrary.wordpress.com/2008/07/04/equality-before-the-law-speech-by-lord-phillips-of-worth-matravers/> [accessed: 13 August 2008].

Poulter, S. 1998. *Ethnicity, Law and Human Rights: The English Experience*. Oxford: Clarendon Press.

Renteln, A.D. 2004. *The Cultural Defense*. Oxford: Oxford University Press.

Santos, B. de S. 2002. *Towards a New Legal Common Sense: Law, Globalization and Emancipation* (2nd Edition). London: Butterworths.

Schierup, C.U. 1996. *A European Dilemma: Myrdal, The American Creed, and EU Europe.* Migration Papers 9, Danish Centre for Migration and Ethnic Studies. Esbjerg: South Jutland University Press.

Shachar, A. 2001. *Multicultural Jurisdictions: Cultural Differences and Women's Rights.* Cambridge, UK/New York: Cambridge University Press.

Shah, P. 2005. *Legal Pluralism in Conflict: Coping with Cultural Diversity in Law.* London: GlassHouse.

— (ed.) 2007. *Law and Ethnic Plurality: Socio-Legal Perspectives.* Leiden: Brill/Martinus Nijhoff.

Shah, P. and W.F. Menski (eds) 2006. *Migration, Diasporas and Legal Systems in Europe.* London: RoutledgeCavendish.

Twining, W.L. 2000. *Globalisation and Legal Theory.* London/Edinburgh: Butterworths.

van Rossum, W. 2008. Legal Professionals Working in the Shadow of Distinct Legal Cultures. Paper presented to the IMISCOE workshop on 'Legal and Normative Accommodation in Multicultural Europe', Brussels, 14–15 July 2008.

Vertovec, S. and S. Wessendorf. 2006. Cultural, Religious and Linguistic Diversity in Europe: an Overview of Issues and Trends. In *The Dynamics of International Migration and Settlement in Europe*, edited by R. Penninx, M. Berger and K. Kraal. Amsterdam: Amsterdam University Press, 171–200.

Werbner, P. 2004. Theorising Complex Diasporas: Purity and Hybridity in the South Asian Public Sphere in Britain. *Journal of Ethnic and Migration Studies*, 30(5), 895–911.

Williams, R. 2008. Archbishop's Lecture – Civil and Religious Law in England: A Religious Perspective. 7 February 2008. Available at <http://www.archbishopofcanterbury.org/1575> [accessed: 11 November 2008].

Chapter 3

Indian Secular Pluralism and its Relevance for Europe

Werner Menski

Summary

India's long-standing multiculturalism has consistently allowed the cultivation of a plurality-conscious legal culture and today underpins a well-tested unique approach to 'secularism' as equal treatment of all religions rather than as a division of 'church' and 'state'. Mainstream Eurocentric legal scholarship largely misunderstands and dismisses this approach, arguing simplistically that respect for 'group rights' infringes human rights, getting embroiled in narrow arguments over competing Christian and Muslim perspectives, forgetting the wider global dimension.

The chapter demonstrates that India's 'secularism', particularly recent advances in harmonizing personal laws rather than pushing for a Uniform Civil Code, can teach other jurisdictions how to fine-tune a nation's plural identity through culture-sensitive legal interventions without. Even in general law matters, Indian awareness of diversity and situation-specificity remains strong, with useful lessons for Europe. While countries of the North would not wish to re-introduce personal laws, current European strategies of making exceptions, in effect addressing only certain perceived 'problems', have now resulted in much-resented discriminatory rule systems that appear unsustainable.

Introduction

The increasingly strong realization that law remains everywhere linked to history and situation-specificity, intricately interwoven with culture and identity, throws up huge challenges for uniformizing, globalizing visions of law, let alone simplistic circular assumptions that 'law' is just 'law' because someone in power says so. While visions of 'world law' create terrifying thoughts of potential abuse, limitless diversity makes us wonder about the management of legal pluralism.

In postmodern, multicultural Britain, for instance, undeveloped formal processes of multicultural navigation appear to have run into deep trouble. The clumsy method of making exceptions for certain groups, scenarios or specific legal issues is now widely perceived as haphazard and discriminatory. While intended to facilitate justice, the legal recognition of cultural diversity is officially not admitted, remains misunderstood and is widely criticized as unjust differentiation. But the law cannot close its eyes to culture and values. The skilful use of equity, seen for example in recognizing the legal validity of an unregistered Sikh marriage in *Chief Adjudication Officer v Bath,* 2000 FLR 8, while a Muslim *nikah* contracted in Britain receives no such recognition, is not liked by mainstream lawyers, but also looks disturbingly discriminatory. Earlier legal recognition of an unregistered Coptic Christian marriage of only one year's duration in *Gereis v Yagoub* [1997] 1 FLR 854, because it resembled marriage under English law and was thus acceptable, indicates highly subjective assessment of cultural distances by state organs. British Muslims now vigorously complain about differential treatment, as Jews, Quakers, the Sikhs and other communities often seem to fare better in official responses to cultural and religious diversity. Islamophobia, real or alleged, lurks in many corners. Some Christian writing appreciates Muslim challenges to the division of law and religion (Newbegin et al. 1998), while still insisting that a Christian perspective alone can rescue the world.

History clearly remains relevant in that European nation states wish to stick to long-standing patterns of legal uniformity (at least fictions of such uniformity) which now need to be defended against the onslaughts of new minorities' claims to differential treatment. My central argument here is that the Indian legal system takes a historically grounded, sophisticated approach to such questions of uniformity and diversity, and does so much more readily than Britain or other European countries, in order to account for difference. But we do not understand why and how India manages this so successfully.

I first outline briefly what European legal systems assume they are doing when insisting on legal uniformity and 'one law for all' as a basic rule, as knee-jerk reactions to the Archbishop of Canterbury's speech of February 2008 so strongly confirmed (Williams 2008). I then consider some recent Indian legal developments, to explore several models of cultural co-existence that appear to be successfully cultivated in the mixed, personal law system of India.

European Visions of Legal Uniformity

In Europe and North America we are taught to believe that we have uniform legal systems with the same rules for everyone, that there are no exceptions and that everyone is happy with this. But these are just clever fictions. Deeper analysis of Northern legal systems uncovers much evidence of differential treatment, through making exceptions or targeting specific groups such as immigrants, certain ethnic minorities or a particular autochthonous group. English law has even made separate laws such as the Motorcycle Crash Helmet (Religious Exemptions) Act of 1976, which allows Sikhs to ride a motorcycle without a crash helmet. More recent examples indicate that our governments keep deliberately quiet about such sophisticated strategies of managing diversity.

Officially, European legal systems insist that they must retain uniform legal patterns, and that pluralizing reforms which would re-introduce personal law systems are particularly unacceptable. While I am not arguing for full-fledged personal law systems in Europe, it is indeed inevitable to recognize that such laws have today become, mostly in the unofficial realm (Chiba 1986), part of European legal systems. Simply ignoring existing patterns of unofficial legal pluralism and minorities' widespread refusal to adopt one-directional assimilation does not appear a realistic long-term perspective. Griffiths (1986: 4–5) rightly claimed that legal pluralism is a fact, while legal centralism is a myth. It follows that if official legal systems want to retain relevance and better control, they have to account for legal pluralism 'on the ground'. Recent attempts by the English Law Commission to think about bringing unregistered Muslim marriages within the formal law are indicative of such pressures, but there is no full discussion and clear answers are not forthcoming. Europeans seem afraid of legal pluralism.

We *assume*, as Northern people, to have developed superior methods of legal regulation which 'others' had better copy. Our uniformizing secular visions of lawmaking, transplanted worldwide through colonialism and cultural imperialism, remain supported by Eurocentric hubris and ambitions of civilizing missions. Unwilling to consider other ways of handling cultural and legal pluralism, we simply prefer our own 'modern' state-centric strategies.

Re-assertion of Diversity in English Law and Elsewhere

The histories of common law and other European legal systems and the resulting legal discourses appear to suggest that custom, in particular, is an element of the past. Accounting for cultural and ethnic difference today, let alone religion, is often seen as parochial and backward, supported by assertions that recognizing cultural plurality spells disaster for human rights protection. Legal uniformity is uncritically treated as desirable, conducive to good governance in modern nation states. However, notably in current southern African debates (Bennett 2004), in countries like South Africa and Namibia, and thus not only in India, customary laws remain enormously important as a living entity also in lawmaking processes.

Meanwhile social, cultural and religious pluralisms have also crept back onto the agenda in modern Europe, largely through 'ethnic implants' (Menski 2006b: 58–65). Various claims for recognition of specific diversities are perceived as undermining the basic structures of modern democracy, evident from obnoxious official statements by British public personalities like Tony Blair, Gordon Brown and Sir Trevor Philips that do not match socio-legal reality. The latter had this to say in 2006: 'We have only one set of laws and that's the end of the story. Anybody who lives here has to accept that. If you want to have laws decided in another way, you have to live somewhere else.'[1] Such digging-in of positivistic heels seems ridiculously out of tune with reality. Do we really only have one set of laws? And does this one set of laws treat everyone in the same way? Many legal experiences of ethnic minorities certainly do not match with such assertions of legal uniformity. Official statements about the nature of law and actual practices of handling diversity are two different things. Postgraduate student research now tells Prakash Shah and me that if English law is refusing to take Muslims and their legal needs seriously, then why should they even use English law? If it is true that more British Muslims are now consciously refusing to use English marriage law, and such re-assertions of religious and cultural plurality become statistically relevant as extremely significant reflections of 'inner migration', the boundaries between official and unofficial law become increasingly fuzzy.

A rather low-key, virtually silent counter-offensive by English law seems to ensure that some specific needs are officially taken into account. In post-2001 Britain we now have new statutes on Islamic finance, 'special guardianship' and divorce among Jews. But a marked reluctance to discuss such new legal developments openly (they are as yet unresearched) ruins whatever good intentions there may be. It reinforces impressions that the state only acts when there is sufficient pressure and when a reform fits the state's selfish agenda of seeking control, rather than acting in a positive spirit of inclusionary accommodation. The earlier fraught history in English law of accepting 'registered buildings' as a place in which ethnic minorities might register their culture-specific marriages under English law is a case in point. While the official law has long permitted such 'registered buildings', registration processes were made exceedingly difficult over decades, so that whole communities gave up on this route and re-organized their ways of getting married. While English law now proposes a more liberal regime for 'registered buildings', hardly any new applications are made. Meanwhile new 'ethnic' patterns of solemnizing and registering marriages have been developed and a growing number of British Muslims simply refuse to register their marriages under the British system altogether. Failed intercultural communication is obvious in such scenarios.

But the official law proudly asserts that it alone controls legal matters. One refuses to admit that much of official state law may not be state-made, but state-accepted. Such dubious assertions of legal centralism are evident from recent amendments to English divorce law, made only for Jews, but supposedly also available for Muslims – if they ask for this. However, Muslims no longer care to ask because meanwhile culture-specific internal mechanisms, often outside English formal legal structures, have been developed.

Official reluctance to take account of such legally relevant diversities in Britain and elsewhere is nurturing doubts among ethnic minorities whether official state laws are willing to listen and to account for diversity and value pluralism. Officious

1 Reported at <http://news.bbc.co.uk/1/hi/uk/4752804.stm> [accessed 10 November 2008].

preaching about inclusion and uniformity are not believed, since exclusion and differential treatment are practised at the same time. State-centric insistence on secular uniformity is now increasingly perceived as dishonest cultural imperialism, more or less silently resented. In many respects, state law has lost its moral claims to superiority, worryingly not only among minorities.

Unwillingness to Learn from Jurisdictions like India

It has long been known that millions of 'white' British people simply cohabit instead of marrying officially and thus demonstrate the limits of law (Allott 1980). But when minorities in the UK refuse to follow such secular state norms, allegations of human rights abuses fly fast, and always in one direction. Modernist Indian scholars, often from Western universities, also argue for more state involvement in family law, oblivious of Indian socio-cultural realities. Such 'secular' observers have developed a habit of blaming Hindu 'fundamentalism' and nationalism and allege all kinds of crises in Indian law and Indian secularism (Needham and Rajan 2007). A whole academic industry exists now in this arena, waiting eagerly for the next crisis to reinforce the message that the Indian state either does not know what it is doing or is discriminating systematically against non-majority members.

I am of course not saying that everything works properly in India. No legal system in the world operates perfectly, simply because legal 'perfection' cannot ever be a permanent equilibrium; it is always an ideal state that needs to be constantly re-negotiated. Law is never just a static given, it is inherently dynamic. Things can go wrong, at any moment, because so much depends on negotiation of conflicting inputs. Law and values, as Chiba (1986) highlighted, are always interconnected. Value-neutral secular lawmaking is simply a convenient myth.

My main argument here is that the systematic, so-called 'secular' recognition of the central importance of values is infinitely more plurality-conscious and better developed in Indian law than the simplistic secular insistence on supposedly value-neutral uniformity in English law. Indian law systematically and actively takes cultural values into account and thus empowers itself to balance conflicting claims in innovative ways. While we love to assume that the Indians should develop along 'our' lines, the Indians show us that navigating diversities, also within a harmonized personal law system, can lead to viable positive outcomes. But Europeans – and many Indians – appear simply incredulous.

The clearest example of this are still the obnoxious myths constructed around the so-called *Shah Bano* case of 1985 and its aftermath (*Mohd. Ahmed Khan V Shah Bano Begum & Ors* [1985] Rd-Sc 99 (23 April 1985), morphed by now into an aggressive system of post-divorce provisions for Indian ex-wives, making Indian men of all religions run for cover (Menski 2007, and see further below). European observers, and their Indian acolytes, are amazingly unwilling to 'see' what is going on in Indian law today when it comes to social welfare provisions for women, children and members of minorities. Muslim obfuscations do not help, of course, prominently the insistence that religious laws must not be changed by a modern state. The Indian Constitution, faced with hundreds of millions of citizens living below the official poverty line, and thus radically aware of systemic failures of even securing basic justice, is employed by a concerned elite of bureaucrats to implement radical social welfare measures that override such religious politics and protect the Indian state from claims by disadvantaged individuals. One only understands this if one is prepared to accept that India takes an activist realistic approach to handling diversities, rather than seeking to put everyone into a majoritarian box of legal uniformity. Indian claims about equality reflect an ideal, not a reality. The reality is equity.

Grounding Acceptance of Diversity in the Legal History of Personal Laws

This issue can be explained historically, demonstrating why Indian legal pluralism today is so activist and increasingly relevant for places like Britain. When India obtained independence in 1947, a clear commitment to democracy and equality was linked to an explicit acknowledgement of cultural, religious and ethnic pluralism and difference. India in 1947 could not become a Hindu state; it necessarily included minorities of all kinds, not only religious minorities. It included many desperately poor people. Such realizations deeply influenced the entire Indian legal system and India's model of secularism.

Pakistan, on the other hand, emphasized its identity as a state for Muslims, but soon had to realize that there also were lots of 'others', because not all Hindus, Christians and Parsis had left the new country. Even today, there is much reluctance to accept such pluralisms and no open debate about religious pluralism. The same scenario prevails in Bangladesh (earlier East Pakistan), even more so after independence from Pakistan in 1971. Bangladesh's new identity has remained a localized plural entity, with which even today at least one side of the bipolar political establishment in Bangladesh is not at ease. New 'fundamentalist' problems surfaced, with significant confusions about 'secularism' and dangerous self-destructive attempts to reject pluralism.

In India, however, deep commitment to ethnic and religious plurality, really a variety of pluralisms, is clearly expressed and reflected in the official legal structures. A symbolic example of historical continuity is Article 51-A(f) of the Constitution, which speaks of the fundamental duty of all citizens to 'value and preserve the rich heritage of our composite culture'. Such admonishments reinforce the guiding principle and policy of secularism in India, namely a deliberate policy of aiming for equidistance of the state from all religions.

The Preamble of the Constitution of 1950 described India as a Sovereign Democratic Republic. This set the scene for the modernist stage of Indian law from 1947 onwards. One can broadly divide Indian law into five overlapping stages, as follows:

Stage 1: 1947–c.1972: Period of democratic principles with undemocratic realities.
Stage 2: 1973–c.1978: Emergency period: admission of breakdown.
Stage 3: 1978–c.2000: Post-Emergency catharsis and activist restructuring.
Stage 4: c.2001–2002: Re-negotiation and perhaps global impact phase.
Stage 5: post- 2001: Various ongoing re-negotiations of postmodernities.

In the first stage, around 1947– c.1972, India firmly established democratic principles, but found herself defeated by undemocratic realities. These led to important law reforms in 1973 and the subsequent Emergency rule of Indira Gandhi. Significant elements in this period are the silent rejection of the British model of Parliamentary Sovereignty (the so-called Westminster Model) in favour of rule by the people, at least on paper. The Indian Constitution radically starts with 'We, the people of India', presenting a highly significant departure from colonial rule and dominant British models of governance, maybe not so radical from French or other continental perspectives. India, it appears, explicitly recognized the critical role of democratic pluralism with its complexity of norms and values, placing itself at the centre of the conceptual triangle that I have used to explain such developments (Menski 2006b).

At the same time it was and remains a fact that a rather small elite governs and lays down rules. Very soon India realized that this elite was exploiting lawmaking processes for its own benefit. The risks of majoritarian domination were becoming obvious, initially more in terms of class than religion. The defeat of the Hindu Code Bill of the early 1950s, an aborted project of comprehensive codification of all Hindu law, resulted in four separate Acts of Hindu law in 1955–6. This was not a totally uniformizing reform of Hindu law, but it turned modern Hindu law into a codified legal system. Less noticed initially were certain other positivistic principles of the Constitution which could also be easily abused. Two examples can be given:

1. The Parliamentary Sovereignty model of England suggests that Parliament can do what it wants and is supreme, but what about 'the people'? India's judges soon developed the so-called 'Basic Structure' doctrine of Fundamental Rights and held that the Constitution was a higher form of law that even a huge Parliamentary majority could not amend. Why this should have become a problem is rarely openly discussed: clearly, too much lawmaking by the elite for itself meant that gradually the Indian legal system failed to achieve basic justice – the poor were becoming poorer. Judges as an elite institution were assisting this process with much pro-Establishment and pro-property decision-making, so that the gap between rich and poor became ever larger. Eventually, this led to a crisis and the Emergency by Indira Gandhi, which must be seen not just as a means to retain power, but also a mechanism for taking more serious account of India's needs for social justice. To that extent, in particular, the Emergency

has been cathartic. A strong ruler taught the nation how easy it was to abuse the system.

2. More relevant for the present discussion, Article 44 of the Constitution, which appears to suggest that there should ultimately be a Uniform Civil Code for all Indians, indicated a typically positivistic modernist orientation. While this was eventually acknowledged as unsuitable for Indian conditions, this is not seen by most observers, and is thus not yet written about with sufficient clarity. Article 44 simply lays down that '[t]he state shall endeavour to secure for the citizens a uniform civil code throughout the territory of India'. What does this mean? It has been widely understood as a plan for a new civil law for all Indians, abolishing the traditional personal law system. Article 44 is a Directive Principle of State Policy (DPSP), part of a programme for future development, so it could wait, but it remains on the agenda. However, because it is a DPSP, and not a Fundamental Right, it cannot be claimed as a right in a court of law.

Article 44 thus suggests the *eventual* production of a uniform civil law for all Indians, following the supposedly uniform legal model of 'the West'. But significant misconceptions abound: we saw that, in English law, the general legal system makes certain exceptions for minorities and specific groups of people, mainly Jews and different types of Christians. More recently, as indicated, English law has permitted Sikhs to ride a motorcycle without a crash helmet, and to work on building sites without hard hats. This appears to give special privileges to certain 'friends of the state', while denying such favourable treatment to other communities, for example Rastafarians, who also brought hair-related legal issues to the English courts.

Clearly, the modernist vision was that India should have one law for all, as was assumed to exist in Western legal systems. While such assumptions about Western legal uniformity are not realistic, closer analysis demonstrates that the Indian Constitution is not actually one and the same law for all. Here, too, the law makes many exceptions, as Indian law is hypersensitive to difference. Prominent examples are:

- special provisions in Article 15(3), allowing the state to discriminate in favour of women and children;
- the first constitutional amendment in 1951 added Article 15(4) and other provisions about the protection for Scheduled Castes and Tribes. This strengthened the powerful policy of protective discrimination or affirmative action, which seeks a redressing of imbalances in society and continues to remain in place.

Basic concern about social and economic justice, rather than absolute equality, is strongly and most clearly reflected in Article 38 of the Constitution, also a DPSP, which provides:

38. State to secure a social order for the promotion of welfare of the people.

(1) The State shall strive to promote the welfare of the people by securing and protecting as effectively as it may a social order in which justice, social, economic and political, shall inform all the institutions of the national life.

(2) [added in 1979] The State shall, in particular, strive to minimise the inequalities in income, and endeavour to eliminate inequalities in status, facilities and opportunities, not only amongst individuals, but also amongst groups of people residing in different areas or engaged in different vocations.

Similar recognitions of diversity appear in Article 39, which further demands:

39. Certain principles of policy to be followed by the State:-

The State shall, in particular, direct its policy towards securing –

a. that the citizens, men and women equally, have the right to an adequate means of livelihood;
b. that the ownership and control of the material resources of the community are so distributed as best to subserve the common good;
c. that the operation of the economic system does not result in the concentration of wealth and means of production to the common detriment;

These are many idealist promises, while reality under the free play of democratic forces during the 1960s and 1970s worked in favour of 'big' men and propertied interests. This led to a huge crisis of values, a *dharma* dilemma, which brought Indira Gandhi onto the stage as a combination of an Indian ruler (*rājā*) wielding the punishing stick (*danda*) and the terrible goddess *Durgā Mātā*, leading to a process of renegotiation of power structures, a resetting of boundaries (*maryādā*), and thus a form of rather violent dispute renegotiation (*vyavahāra*).

Renegotiation of Legal Economics in Stage 2: 1973–c. 1978

The realization of differential developments and growing economic disparities led to extremely significant changes in the secular Criminal Procedure Code of 1973, replacing the colonial Criminal Procedure Code of 1898. In section 125 of the new Code, which in a patriarchal society puts a burden on men to support their children, wives and aged parents, most importantly, the definition of 'wife' was extended to include 'divorced wife'. This now meant that any Indian man who married a woman (whether monogamously or polygamously) would be responsible for her welfare until she died or remarried. It was not immediately realized how crucial this particular legal innovation would become, but within a patriarchal system, gender-sensitive re-balancing had begun.

This change in the criminal law affected all people, with special provisions for Muslims in S. 127 of the CrPC, in case they had already paid their customary dues to their ex-wives under the 'religious' shari'a law, which significantly continues to be valid in Indian law as a personal law. We see here an overrriding basic commitment to the redistribution of property through males, who are now held legally accountable for the welfare of the women they marry. At the same time in this turbulent period, important modern-looking family law reforms in Hindu law appear to suggest a strong belief in state control and state intervention in family life. Examples are:

- new and more grounds of formal divorce, such as cruelty and desertion;
- introduction of divorce by mutual consent (an increasing trend);
- relaxed nullity law, so that 'any material fact concerning the respondent' became a ground for nullity.

All of this seemed to abandon the sacramental *samskāra* principle of the eternal bond of traditional Hindu marriages, but basic sacramental notions were still upheld. Legal modernity did not replace Indic tradition, it supplemented it. But then, in 1976, followed hugely important changes to the Constitution in the 42nd Amendment. The main points are that the Preamble to the Constitution added 'Secular and Socialist', reflecting what was already known, so that India became now explicitly a Sovereign Socialist Secular Democratic Republic. Further, the fundamental right to property was abolished (Article 31). Instead Article 300-A now provides that '[n]o person shall be deprived of his property save by authority of law'. Significantly, a set of Fundamental Duties was introduced in Article 51-A. These read like a Hindu code of *dharma* to me, but of course if one does not know much about the underlying values of traditional Hindu law, one would not even notice this.

My argument is, however, not that this was Hinduization, or some form of creeping fundamentalization of the *hindutva* type. Rather, here is explicit recognition of the traditional focus on duties rather than rights, of secular commonsensical interlinkedness, of the fact that public interest is higher than private interest. This form of re-traditionalized accountability along gender lines thus introduced a fresh commitment to plurality-conscious secularism, not Hinduization, as some scholars have tried to suggest.

The Meaning and Implications of Secularism in Indian Law

Such secularism in the Indian context, as equitable recognition of cultural and religious diversities, has caused huge confusions in India and outside India. In America, secularism clearly means something like non-establishment, non-entrenchment of religion, and the Indian model seemed different. Indeed, in every European state, secularism means something different, from extreme forms of *laicité*, as in France, to different forms of division of religion and law. Generally speaking, there is supposed to be a separation of state and church, law and politics.

But this popular modernist image of the division of law and religion is Eurocentric and runs counter to the intrinsic link of law and values that Chiba (1986) illustrates through his concept of 'legal postulates', which in his model are always present, linked both to official and unofficial law. Similarly, the Indian model accepts not only that religion is always part of human life, but that there are many different religions to take account of, not just Christianity and Islam, as we appear to assume in today's British (and European) debates (Newbegin et al. 1998).

In India, as indicated, 'the people' are the supreme lawmaking entity, and there is deep awareness of many different religions, all interlinked with laws. Indian secularism thus seeks to guarantee equidistance from all religions; it provides an equal treatment guarantee to all religions, saying clearly enough that Indian law cannot be Hindu law alone, and should not be influenced only by Hindu law. It also means that India cannot be a Hindu state, which inevitably led to complaints from the Hindu majority, some of whom claim the democratic right to determine the rules of the state for everybody. Modernist scholarship has understood those forces rather one-sidedly as Hindu nationalism; in fact they concern more comprehensively values and 'culture' in all their diversity. Indian secularism, we learn, prevents value domination by the demographic majority in a way that Western anti-discrimination laws and assimilation expectations have manifestly failed to do.

For the Indian Uniform Civil Code (UCC) debate, this basic policy of secularism means that an Indian UCC would have to take account of all religions, rather than imposing Hindu law on all. Larson (2001) is by no means alone to notice a contradiction between Article 44 and the 'standard' policy of secularism. A truly secular uniform law could never be uniform, because all laws (in line with the legal triangle in Menski 2006b: 612, based on Chiba 1986) are linked intrinsically with a particular set of values and ethics. Unification would not result in uniformization, rather perhaps in harmonization.

Before coming specifically to Hindu law and the UCC debate, a little more focus on subsequent legal developments in India serves to indicate further lessons in diversity management for Europe. From about 1978 to 2000, the Indian Supreme Court, which most of the time clearly seems to know what it is doing, developed an explicit rejection of colonial models, a post-colonial re-orientation, in contrast to Britain, for one, which currently remains unwilling to re-adjust its lenses to the fact that we have become pluralized through South–North migration (Menski 2006c).

The claim that India can and needs to update itself, developing its own culture-specific jurisprudence, was made as early as 1976 by leading Supreme Court judges, in particular the legendary Krishna Iyer from Kerala. This made absolute sense in light of Chiba's (1986) plurality-conscious legal theory, and his powerful concept of law as a manifestation of 'identity postulates' (Chiba 1989). Thus, given many millions of Scheduled Caste and Scheduled Tribe persons, there was no let-up on India's policies of affirmative action, but because women remain structurally disadvantaged, there is also no realistic chance of introducing irretrievable breakdown of marriage as a major ground for divorce – it would empower men to throw women on the streets. Blind following of Western models is not advisable – Indian society is not US society, as Indian judges have been pointing out since at least the late 1980s. At the same time, the Indian courts and legislature have almost with one voice refused to accept that compulsory state registration of all marriages could be a realistic possibility. And, most significantly, and not because of often-alleged inefficiency, the Indian Supreme Court waited for 15 years to make a strategically important decision, clearly waiting for the right moment, as seen in the *Danial Latifi* case of 2001.[2] All of this indicates unspoken awareness of the central importance of negotiating conflicts, of *vyavahāra*, coupled with an acute awareness of judges' constitutional *dharma*.

But when it is appropriate, the Indian Supreme Court and even that sleepy colossus called Parliament are able to spring into action. This activism was manifest, amazingly a few weeks after 9/11, at a time when Indian Muslims would not dare go on the road for public protests. One may call this the 'global impact phase', reflecting a deliberate policy of renegotiation of important elements in the Indian legal system, covering the related issues of secularism and UCC debates, in a manner apparently not yet understood by Indian scholars. Thus Kumar (2003) still argued that Article 44 of the Indian Constitution expected a UCC, and should be implemented, not realizing that, by September 2001, the Indian Supreme Court and Parliament had in fact created a new form of UCC, a mirror image of the original concept (Menski 2006a).

The 2001 legal developments in India are also so badly understood because they have been overshadowed by the quite atrocious 2002 Gujarat anti-Muslim riots, which have given rise to new studies (Needham and Rajan 2007) that loudly proclaim the crisis of Indian secularism, relying also on the *Shah Bano* case as evidence for such analysis. However, such misguided writing constitutes scholarly politics rather than proper analysis of Indian laws. Personal politics and academic predilections on the part of certain prominent scholars have systematically prevented a fuller understanding of developments in Indian law today. As a result, important lessons from Indian law cannot be learnt, because we are constantly misinformed, and we do not even believe that certain things can happen in India!

The question remains, therefore, why we persistently fail to understand what is meant by Indian secularism, and what it implies. It does not help us that another phase may be detected, from about 2001–2003 onwards, certainly from 2005, marked by a new activism of legislative intervention, much influenced by

2 *Danial Latifi v Union of India* 2001(7) SCC 740.

international legal norms, human rights activism and activist pressures for changes to modernize Indian laws. These new laws, celebrated by some writers and activists as major achievements, are mostly broad-ranging types of legislation that are bound to remain symbolic laws. What this shows us, though, is that the Indian Parliament (like the British Parliament, in fact, at roughly the same time) has once again seized some initiative to intervene in legal developments. To that extent, this new phase may also be seen as a reaction to the growing 'juristocracy', and a sort of clawing back of parliamentary territory. It is clearly too early to sit in full judgment on such complex developments within the terrain of postmodernity.

Prominent examples of this kind of legal intervention would be, above all, the Hindu Succession (Amendment) Act of 2005, which directs that henceforth Hindu daughters shall be entitled to equal inheritance as their brothers in the Hindu joint family from birth. Preliminary research about the impact of such new laws points to abundant symbolism and little real legal effect. Similarly celebrated is the Protection of Women from Domestic Violence Act of 2005, a complex piece of legislation that sounds wonderful, but is bound to remain largely ineffective unless accompanied by much more activist implementation mechanisms. Other new Acts with direct financial impacts are notable, particularly the Maintenance and Welfare of Parents and Senior Citizens Act, 2007, which allows an old person to claim up to Rs 10.000/- per month from family members. Moral obligations are here skilfully turned into legal duties.

An important recent Act is the Prohibition of Child Marriage Act of 2006, which replaced the colonial Child Marriage Restraint Act of 1929 in India. Significantly, the new law only prohibits forced marriages and marital unions based on fraud. It otherwise does not nullify all child marriages, as activists had demanded, merely making them voidable. Most significantly, the Act leaves it to child spouses, mainly thus young women, to decide whether they are happy to remain legally married or not. Now, are these not lessons that we might learn in Europe about assessing sexual relationships of young people? At first sight this seems obnoxious, until we realize that under Indian law the minimum legal marriage ages are for 18 years for women and 21 years for men. So when is a child a child, and a marriage a child marriage? Whose values do we apply? Indian postmodern legal regulation displays remarkable courage and cultural wisdom in respecting a plurality of possible perspectives.[3]

Postmodern Indian law thus does not simply protect traditional Hindu law and local customary traditions for the sake of tradition, but is concerned to support individual agency and the timeless principle of individual agency (*ātmanastushti*) as a self-regulating principle of Indic laws, to be applied in preference to any form of state-imposed sanction. Thus, finding one's own path through largely informal

3 The new law also reflects the realization that simply nullifying child marriages would offer new weapons to devious men seeking to claim exemptions from maintenance payments and would be 'brutal', as one 1997 case significantly called it. See on this Menski 2003: 368–9.

and even purely mental processes of self-regulation is still a strong expectation also in light of the latest Indian legal developments of 2006. By comparison, state paternalism in Europe seems far too domineering to allow for such possibilities.

Cohabitation of Hindu and Muslim Law in India

A brief focus on how Hindu law in India cohabits with Muslim law displays more evidence of deep plurality-consciousness, realizing that massive Muslim presence is a fact in India and needs to be built into legal structures, in a way that Britain and other European countries still appear to resist. There is no doubt that Hindu law as the majority law shares the space of modern India with Muslim law and other legal systems. There is a long history of this pluralism, not directly relevant here, but with important consequences for India's secular set-up. First of all, because India is today not a Hindu state, we do not hear and read explicitly about Hindu law. But its concepts and principles are ever-present for those who know and continue to contribute significantly to India's current plural legal identity. So, contrary to the European historical experience, the personal law system for different communities is powerfully present and is there to stay in India, with Muslim law as an integral part of Indian legal identity. Question marks arise of course over the extent of this cohabitation, with deep reluctance to admit that Islamic law continues to influence the nature of India's plural legal system. Have we not just heard in London that, in such scenarios, Islamic law's influence is 'unavoidable'?

A brief examination of how India has recently reconstructed its uniform system of post-nuptial provision for all Indian ex-wives may help to illustrate the catalytic element of Muslim personal laws in modern secular, pluralist arrangements. First of all, the *Shah Bano* case of 1985 in India was not saying anything new when it granted the 70+ year old Shah Bano the right to be maintained by her ex-husband until death. The earlier case of *Bai Tahira* in 1979 had already established the obligation of a Muslim husband to pay for his ex-wife also beyond the traditional three months' *iddat* period.[4] The position today, under a special Act of 1986 for Muslims (which they rashly demanded of the Indian state) is that any Indian Muslim husband has to maintain his divorced wife during the *iddat* period and, in addition, he has during the *iddat* period to make a fair provision for her for the time after that period. This means that if the wife has not received what she is due by the end of this three-month period, she gains instant access to courts, and the courts are supposed to decide such a matter within 60 days (Menski 2007).

So how did India construct a UCC without knowing it, riding on the back of a Muslim legal tiger? After the *Shah Bano* case, there were instant riots by Muslims, claiming that their *shariat* law had been trampled upon by five Hindu judges of the Indian Supreme Court exercising neo-*ijtihad*. But these judges had produced an ingenious interpretation, finding that the Qur'an told divorcing Muslim men that

4 *Bai Tahira v Ali Hussain Fissali Chothia, AIR 1979 SC 362.*

they should be kind to the woman they divorced, which thus established a general moral obligation, though not quantified in terms of time and money. This surprising and almost unbelievable exegesis meant that there was actually no legal conflict between Section 125 of the secular CrPC and the relevant Quranic verses!

Faced with instant Muslim riots, Prime Minister Rajiv Gandhi, perhaps also concerned not to lose Muslim votes, skilfully created the impression that the new Act, the Muslim Women (Protection of Rights on Divorce) Act of 1986 (MWPRDA) shifted responsibility for the divorced woman's maintenance away from the husband and to her relatives or the Waqf Boards, religious trusts, which promptly protested that they had no money for such a social service. The ploy evidently worked, since nobody discussed s. 3 of the 1986 Act, which still holds the husband responsible as the first port of call; everybody stared at sections 4 and 5, which seemed to exonerate the ex-husband. Hence the academic myth was created that the 1986 Act nullified the good effects of the *Shah Bano* case and let down India's Muslim women. Additionally, since the 1986 Act was a special Act on Muslim law, a new personal law, it violated the secular principle of Article 44 of the Constitution with its claim that there should be a UCC. More confusion ensued amidst howls of dismay about India slipping into medieval laws.

Many cases were filed in 1986 to challenge the legal validity of the 1986 Act, but the Supreme Court, amazingly, stayed silent until 2000, by which time about 35 High Court cases had been decided, mostly holding that the 1986 Act had not overruled *Shah Bano* and was actually beneficial to Muslim women. Nobody wanted to believe this, and since hardly any scholar of international repute reads Indian High Court cases, the fake myth was perpetuated until September 2001, two weeks after 9/11, when the Indian Supreme Court held that (i) there was nothing legally wrong with having a separate Muslim Act and (ii) that the 1986 Act had not in fact nullified the effects of Shah Bano, but supported them. Thus, the post-divorce maintenance law for all Indians was restored to an equitable level. Only two days later, through amazingly swift action, India's Parliament removed the Rs 500/- upper limit for all other Indian ex-wives under s. 125 of the CrPC, and thus created an even higher level of legal uniformity. Only a few minutes later, Parliament proceeded to harmonize India's divorce laws further, introducing long-demanded additional grounds for Christian divorce, so that also Indian divorce laws are now virtually uniform across the board.

Even though the Muslim law of India remains uncodified, the picture is thus that all Indians marry according to their respective customary laws, with hardly any need to register (and even where this is demanded, strong presumptions of marriage apply). And since Muslim law knows many different grounds for divorce, India's internally plural divorce laws are now also virtually harmonized. Hence my claim that asking for the Uniform Civil Code in India was like asking for the moon (Menski 2006a).

So the majoritarian law in India today is certainly not just 'the law' for all Indians, but has become a closely interlinked internally pluralized legal phenomenon that has undergone many subtle reforms in family laws, mixing Hindu *masāla* with

Muslim, Parsi and Christian spice and identity elements into a plurality-conscious, harmonized legal system.

Concluding Comments

This sophisticated plurality-conscious reconstruction in a supposedly backward legal system is clearly marked by legal respect for cultural and religious diversity. The outcome cannot be superimposition of one particular type of dominant law, with reluctant pussyfooting over minority systems, but a newly navigated and negotiated legal construct that takes holistic account of the wider policy issues of the state as well as the needs of its different groups of people. The challenging and long process to construct such laws took India several decades to develop.

In Europe we can learn much from such processes. In the UK, we have only just begun to scratch the icy layer of resistance to pluralization that seems to cover the salad bowl of English law at the start of the twenty-first century. Unless we accept elements of the various ethnic minority laws as part of that 'salad', discrimination and unacceptably unfair treatment will prevail. Accounting for a higher form of public interest – in India the social welfare of women and children – a state can manage to counter otherwise potentially explosive oppositions to such pluralizing policies.

The modern British state will need to show that it can take notice of cultural diversity in law more fairly and equitably than has happened so far. Clearly, not to take account of such factors is not a sustainable solution. Refusing to learn from other multicultural legal models in the world looks like a recipe for disaster. Outright denial of the presence of ethnic minority laws and different sets of values, now part of the country's super-diverse living history, looks not only dishonest and but increasingly dangerous. It is also ignorantly unrealistic, because it refuses to accept the fact that law is everywhere more than state law.

References

Allott, Antony N. 1980. *The Limits of Law*. London: Butterworths.

Bennett, Thomas W. 2004. *Customary Law in South Africa*. Lansdowne: Juta & Company.

Chiba, Masaji (ed.) 1986. *Asian Indigenous Law in Interaction with Received Law*. London and New York: KPI.

— 1989. *Legal Pluralism: Towards a General Theory Through Japanese Legal Culture*. Tokyo: Tokai University Press.

Griffiths, John. 1986. What is Legal Pluralism?, *Journal of Legal Pluralism and Unofficial Law*, 24, 1-56.

Kumar, Virendra. 2003. Uniform Civil Code Revisited: a Juridical Analysis of John Vallamattom. *Journal of the Indian Law Institute*, 45(3–4), 315–34.

Larson, Gerald J. (ed.) 2001. *Religion and Personal Law in Secular India. A Call to judgment*. Bloomington: Indiana University Press.
Menski, Werner. 2003. *Hindu Law. Beyond Tradition and Modernity*. New Delhi: Oxford University Press.
— 2006a. Asking for the Moon: Legal Uniformity in India. *Kerala Law Times*, 2006(2), Journal Section, 52–78.
— 2006b. *Comparative Law in a Global Context. The Legal Systems of Asia and Africa*. 2nd rev. edn. Cambridge: Cambridge University Press.
— 2006c. Rethinking Legal Theory in Light of South-North Migration. In Prakash Shah and Werner Menski (eds) *Migration, Diasporas and Legal Systems in Europe*. London: Routledge Cavendish, 13–28.
— 2007. Double Benefits and Muslim Women's Postnuptial Rights. *Kerala Law Times*, 2007(2), 21–34.
Needham, Anuradha Dingwaney and Rajeswari Sunder Rajan (eds) 2007. *The Crisis of Secularism in India*. Durham and London: Duke University Press.
Newbegin, Leslie, Lamin Sanneh and Jenny Taylor. 1998. *Faith and Power. Christianity and Islam in 'Secular' Britain*. Eugene, OR: Wipf & Stock.
Williams, R., The Rt. Rev. 2008. Civil and Religious Law in England: A Religious Perspective. Speech at the Royal Courts of Justice. 7 February 2008. Available at: <http//www.archbishopofcanterbury.org/1575> [accessed 22 October 2008].

Chapter 4
Legal Pluralism and Differentiated Morality: Shari'a in Ontario?

Veit Bader

Introduction

Recently there have been heated debates concerning 'the shari'a' in Muslim-majority countries, as well as on 'shari'a in the West' where Muslims form a more or less significant religious minority. Like all debates on 'Islam' or 'Muslims' nowadays, these are characterized by the construction and reproduction of stereotypes, myths, mutual misunderstandings and dramatized fears or panics. In the context of securitization it seems nearly impossible to have a sober, problem- and solution-oriented discussion.

In section I of this chapter, I place these discussions in the framework of anthropological and sociological debates on legal pluralism and ethno-religious minorities and apply moral arguments for maximum accommodation within the constraints of minimal morality to debates on normative legal pluralism. I also claim that *institutional pluralism* or 'joint governance' approaches are superior to either *secularist absolutism* or *absolute accommodation*. In section II, I discuss what has been and what has not been at stake in the debates on private Islamic arbitration in Ontario, Canada, and claim that the outright rejection of all proposals and recommendations by the Ontario provincial government missed a golden opportunity to ameliorate the position of vulnerable minorities. In sections III and IV I discuss the main legal and social policy recommendations by Marion Boyd and others intended to ameliorate the position of vulnerable minorities. I conclude by summarizing my criticism of secularist rejections, and argue that 'transformational accommodation' (Shachar 2001) or my own proposals for 'associational governance' might better accomplish this than secularist 'zero accommodation' or 'absolutist deference'.

At the outset I briefly explain my general claim that liberal-democratic institutional pluralism or '*joint governance approaches*' provide more productive solutions to the inherent dilemmas of accommodation compared with two other prominent approaches. On the one hand, strictly individualist, secularist and context-insensitive universalism or *secularist absolutism* that proscribes all separate codes of religious law and even religious arbitration by insisting on a uniform civil code and civil courts only. It imposes an unfair choice for women between their 'rights and their culture' or 'religion' (Shachar 2001, Bakht 2006,

Williams 2007) neglecting cultural inequalities and requiring them to sacrifice their religion and community. But it also cannot guarantee their 'rights' because its preferred policies of state-imposed and stated-controlled liberal-democratic congruence plus external state-intervention cannot prevent the fact that women remain subject to informal and presumably misogynist 'shari'a practices'. On the other hand, 'free exercise', 'religious particularism' or unbounded, *absolute accommodationism*, defending complete deference to the *nomos* of religious groups, far-reaching autonomy and an absence of any state intervention or scrutiny, either in a libertarian variety (assuming free and informed consent by adults and free entry and exit) or in traditionalist, conservative communitarian or fundamentalist varieties. If the real issue is, as it should be, *how to ameliorate the position of vulnerable minorities within religious minorities (and within religious and secularist majorities!)*, we have to probe one or other variety of institutional, legal pluralism or joint governance that is compatible with minimal morality or with liberal-democratic morality, minimally understood.

I Legal Regimes and Vulnerable Minorities

Drawing on discussions on varieties of 'legal pluralism' in anthropology or sociology of law (e.g. Benda-Beckmann 2002, Hoekema 2004), I distinguish *four* analytically different but actually overlapping *legal orders or regimes, which are relevant for fair normative comparisons.*

> (a) *Informal practices of communal/religious 'law and jurisdiction'*: characterized by (i) oral transmission (either no written sources of law or nearly no use or reference to them); (ii) no organizational/institutional and/or role differentiation (rules are interpreted/changed and applied in decisions (case by case) by either communal assemblies and/or 'wise men'); (iii) no distinction between ethno-cultural and religious traditions, rules, customs, practices; and (iv) no distinction between different areas of law (criminal, procedural, civil).
>
> (b) *Formalized and institutionalized practices of communal/religious law and jurisdiction*: characterized by (i) written sources of law (codes and/ or case-law); (ii) organizational and institutional differentiation (courts); (iii) role differentiation (judges, kadi) and legal education and training; (iv) distinctions between religious law and ethno-communal customs/practices (e.g. female genital mutilation, 'honour killing') and between criminal, procedural and private law.
>
> (c) Communal/religious 'law and jurisdiction' in matters of marriage and divorce that explicitly ask for 'legal recognition' and support by state law. This regime has different varieties that should be clearly distinguished from

each other: separate religious codes and courts; international private law, and all varieties of existing or proposed officially recognized arbitration.

(d) Exclusive imposition of so-called 'secular' state-law and 'civil' jurisdiction.

These four regimes may be compared in terms of (i) (degrees of) visibility of practices, (ii) (degrees of) formalization and regulation, supervision, control from within the community of practitioners and from the outside, and (iii) overall consequences for the position of the most vulnerable minorities.

(i) *Degrees of visibility.* Informal practices of communal/religious 'law and jurisdiction' (regime (a)) are highly invisible even from the inside (insiders not directly involved are unaware of them) and often completely invisible to outsiders, whereas formalized and institutionalized practices of communal/religious law (regime (b)) are highly visible for (interested) insiders and much easier to access for (interested) outsiders, and this holds a fortiori for practices of regimes (c) and (d).

(ii) *Regulation, supervision and control from within communities* are obviously much easier under regime (b) than (a) because laws are written, 'rights and duties' are better known and decisions are written and can be appealed. The less developed procedural and substantive formalization is, the more vulnerable are vulnerable minorities: regime (a) provides most opportunities for unlearned and uncontrolled, self-declared 'sheiks' and (Internet-) 'Imams'. In other words, the '*nomos*' of communal groups is an important restraint on arbitrary power and violence (see Cover 1983), which should be used by state-law and courts instead of recklessly being overruled (see Gadirov 2006). Regime (a) is extremely difficult to regulate, supervise and control from the outside and 'from above' (e.g. through 'state' law, courts, and officials) compared with regime (b), which operates under communal law. All varieties of regime (c), private religious law/courts, private arbitration awards and civil courts applying IPL, are based on a clear differentiation of legal and jurisdictional areas: personal law only, no competence or jurisdiction in matters of criminal law or law affecting the legal status, etc. and on clear role differentiation: judges and arbitrators; legal education, training and experience. They directly and explicitly operate 'in the shadow of communal law' and of 'state law' under more or less strict procedural and substantive constraints: explicit legislation, regulation, supervision, monitoring and control of 'communal law/jurisdiction' from the outside and from above by 'modern' state law and courts.

(iii) If the actual practices of regime (a) are incompatible with minimal morality and law, if even the most basic interests and rights of *vulnerable*

> *minorities* (minors, women, dissenters) are violated, their position is clearly the most miserable compared with all other regimes. If communal law and jurisdiction (regime b) are 'decent' though not 'equal' (i.e. not based on modern concepts of equal respect) women and children have better chances that their basic interests/rights are internally guaranteed (internal mechanisms of control and sanction of violations in combination with easier and more effective control by community-external agencies, state-law and bureaucracies amongst them). The position of vulnerable minorities under regime (c) is considerably ameliorated, if and to the degree that 'modern' state-law and jurisdiction are actually based on equality between the sexes/gender and on protection of basic (or even best) interests of children, and if procedures and decisions are scrutinized, monitored and controlled. Then they are not forced to choose between their 'rights' and their 'culture/religion' (Shachar 2001). Here, community-internal and -external mechanisms to protect and guarantee their basic rights work together.

Regime (d) either ignores/neglects or tries to proscribe both informal and more formalized traditions and practices of 'communal/religious' law and jurisdiction and it is explicitly opposed to any official legal recognition of communal/religious law and jurisdiction in all varieties. Modern, 'secular' state law has to apply exclusively, equally and indiscriminately to all citizens and residents, and modern courts should exclusively decide all disputes. Strong legal pluralism is neglected and any form of normative legal pluralism is rejected. 'Modern secular' civil law is assumed to be culturally and religiously neutral (in two varieties, either culturally 'sensitive' or absolutely 'insensitive') and civil courts/judges are assumed to be fully competent experts in family and divorce issues and decide in a completely neutral and impartial way. What does this secularist-absolutist position actually do to ameliorate the situation of vulnerable minorities? First, it should be obvious that it is difficult or impossible to control more or less deeply ingrained communal/religious practices from the outside only. You cannot get rid of strong (empirical) legal pluralism by either ignoring, 'neglecting', its existence (particularly if outsiders, state-officials, judges don't know much about it) or trying to repress and prosecute it. Even a 'totalitarian' state wanting to see and to control all and everything, transforming societies into closed institutions or prisons, would not be fully able to do so. Second, it would most probably make existing communal practices even more invisible, particularly under conditions where the state is not perceived (for good or for bad reasons) to be 'friendly' to the communities in question (Bakht 2006). So it is most likely that it achieves exactly the opposite of the intended results to make practices more visible, stimulate community-internal public debate, etc. Third, it is most likely that it would contribute to fundamentalize existing practices. This is a consequence of reactive 'ethnicization' and 'religionization' of immigrant minorities (Shachar 2005) that perceive (again: for good of for bad reasons) receiving societies and states/policies as hostile. It would also most probably strengthen informal practices of dispute resolution (mediation) instead of more formalized and institutionalized forms which are easier to see, control and, if need be, to prosecute (in this regard, it would help to bring the worst, most fundamentalist, unlearned internet-imams and self-declared 'sheiks' to the top). It would most certainly not achieve intended processes of learning and adaptation of practices inside the respective cultural/religious communities.

In discussing the societal and legal relationship of these regimes, we can make use of four fairly *general insights from legal pluralism debates*.

First, 'strong' legal pluralism' (regimes (a) and (b)) cannot be effectively repressed. Modern states, laws, legislation and courts have, besides *ignoring/neglecting*, *two options of normative legal pluralism* in dealing with strong anthropological legal pluralism: they may *condone* practices, as in the case of condoning soft drugs, either for prudential reasons (unable to repress, better to control) or for ethical/moral reasons or they may *more or less directly and officially recognize* 'communal' legal regimes (all varieties of option (c) are versions of official legal pluralism).

Second, normative legal pluralism implies the *parallel existence or legal validity of two or more legal regimes*; it is an official recognition of 'inter-legality' or 'inter-sectionalism'. In a legal sense, these legal orders are or can be coordinated by two, connected, strategies: (i) a more or less *detailed division of competencies, jurisdictions or 'scope'* between either local, provincial/state, federal and supra-state legislations and courts (in the case of federal states or the EU) and/or between 'modern/civil' and communal courts (in the case of the co-existence of customary ethnic/tribal, religious and 'modern/secular' law and courts); (ii) a *hierarchical ordering ('supremacy')* containing 'conflict rules' in cases that rules and practices contradict each other or are incompatible with each other.[1]

1 See Hoekema this volume for normative conflict rules (IPL) and empirical conflict rules p. 177. For an excellent discussion of the problems of hierarchical ordering or 'supremacy' in the EU see Joerges 2005; Harlow and Rawlings 2006; Bader 2007b for alternatives to 'strict coupling'. Clearly 'parallel applicable religious rules and the parallel religious courts, cannot be all-inclusive and superior to the other legislation and jurisdiction, especially the constitution and its bill of rights' and have to be 'under review of the constitutional court'. So, constitutional 'courts turn out to be quintessential for safeguarding individual rights and gender equality' (Meerschaut and Gutwirth 2007: 5) for Malaysia where Islamic law is subject to the supremacy of the constitution and the federal law (Art. 4, Art. 75) but secular superior courts refuse to deal with apostasy and also in cases of states having 'penal provisions for lesbians, sodomy, premarital sex, *khlawat* ("close proximity"), pimps, incest and prostitution' in their criminal offences Acts, where constitutional law and courts would have to exercise their competences in order to protect basic rights of vulnerable minorities.

Third, normative inter-legality may be guided, steered or even imposed *from above*[2] *and/or may be campaigned for from below.* Inter-legality is always embedded in more or less serious structural power asymmetries between minorities and majorities/states. For any sober analysis it is crucial to keep these power asymmetries clearly in mind because usually the particularism of majority practices and 'modern' or 'secular' law is hidden from view by the famous strategies to universalize the particular and declare it as 'neutral': e.g. the Christian roots and remnants of 'modern', 'secular' family and divorce law and the normalization of 'romantic love', 'monogamous' marriage and 'nuclear family'.[3] If imposition from above, however, is (for good or for bad reasons) not accepted but more or less massively resisted, the gap between 'legal validity' of regimes and 'societal validity' is wide and this impacts on compliance and enforceability of 'supreme' state law and jurisdiction.

Fourth, and equally obviously, these power asymmetries do not enable but often block a minimally fair process of intercultural or inter-religious dialogue between legal traditions. Hence, learning often will not be mutual and fairly voluntary but one-sided: only minorities have to 'learn' and to be 'civilized'. A maximalist imposition of 'modern/civil' state law and jurisdiction makes legal pluralism void or 'pointless' (Moe 2005: 11, Meerschaut and Gutwirth 2007) and leaves no meaningful scope of legal and jurisdictional autonomy. Legal 'pluralism' is then used as a mask for hiding de facto assimilation policies. 'Learning from within' (Shachar 2005) or 'compatibilization' (Meerschaut and Gutwrith 2007) require meaningful accommodation and some degree of freedom in changing traditional practices.

Some 'Minimalist' Explications

Before turning to the Canadian case study, let me briefly summarize why we should accept a specific variety of normative legal pluralism, and how and in which way normative legal pluralism should be constrained by minimal morality.

My recent book (Bader 2007a) presents a new conception of minimal morality that can be combined with more demanding conceptions of liberal and democratic

2 As in most 'modern' Western states and in most law reforms in Muslim state-societies in the twentieth century (see Meerschaut and Gutwirth 2007 for Malaysia). Hoekema (this volume) rightly insists on bottom up or 'reverse interlegality'.

3 Conceptions of completely neutral 'secular law' and even 'secular society' are widespread amongst opponents (see Boyd 2004: 50, 94ff). Radical feminists should have second thoughts before defending the monogamy 'norm'. See my criticism of Parekh (Bader 2007a: 322) who himself had already explained that monogamy actually more often than not means serial polygamy and has miserable effects on children in cases of divorce. See Bowen (2001: 18) for polygamous *français de souche* families: legal equality in fiscal and other matters between 'legitimate wives' and 'concubines'.

moralities if this does not undermine the minimum (non-infringement proviso). Schematically, it reads as shown in Table 4.1 (2007a: 72).

Table 4.1 Differentiated morality

Minimal morality	**Liberal-democratic morality**	**More egalitarian morality**	**Comprehensive moral liberalism**
Basic rights to security and subsistence.	Equal civic and political rights.	Equal socio-economic and fair cultural rights and opportunities.	Specific way of a good life.
Rights to life, liberty, bodily integrity, protection against violence. Rights to basic subsistence, basic education, basic health-care; minimal due process rights; minimal respect; collective and individual toleration (freedom of conscience).	Equal legal rights. Free and equal active and passive voting rights. Freedoms of political communication. Modern (negative) non-discrimination rights (equal respect).	Policies of redistribution. Taking socio-economic and political equality of opportunity more serious. Affirmative action policies. Policies of cultural even-handedness.	Leading an autonomous, self-chosen and transparent life free of illusions.
Agency and legal autonomy	**Political autonomy**	**Substantive autonomy** Range of meaningful socio-economic and cultural options.	**Rational revisability**

Though the moral minimum is here phrased in the 'Western' language of 'basic rights' it is based in *basic needs*. It clearly distinguishes between 'basic interests' and 'best interests' and is designed to *prevent 'malfare' or 'evil'* instead of promoting 'welfare'.

My minimalism is more demanding than a strict minimum that is limited to protection against 'death or irreparable physical harm' (Renteln 2004: 419) or severe physical abuse or worse, a minimum which is near to moral or legal relativism. Yet it is *more restrictive* than the standards advocated by Parekh (2000) and Poulter (1998: 20ff). Like all general principles, even basic rights are *underdetermined* though this hard core of 'agreement' is as universal as one can get it. There are *tensions* even among these basic rights, most importantly between collective and individual toleration. Enforcing freedom of conscience which implies the right to exit (apostasy, conversion) may endanger collective toleration (Bader 2008).

The core of the distinction between minimal and minimally liberal-democratic morality is *equal respect* (equal rights, non-discrimination) *versus 'decent respect'* and some 'due process'. Instead of blurring this distinction it should be spelled out as clearly as possible[4] because here lies the basic dilemma of accommodation of non-liberal practices/minorities (basic tension within 'liberal' freedom between an extensive interpretation of associational freedoms and individual autonomy cum equal legal rights). Maximum accommodation of non-liberal and non-democratic but peaceful practices/minorities within the constraints of moral minimalism follows from an extensive interpretation of associational freedoms and is clearly opposed to 'liberal-democratic congruence' (Rosenblum 1998: 59) 'all the way down'.

My concept of differentiated morality favours the application of *more demanding standards* of minimal liberal-democratic morality, more egalitarian, more full-fledged liberal morality (autonomy) and pluralist morality under the *realist proviso* that they do not infringe on minimal morality. It is connected with a differentiated set of policy repertoires: use external legal intervention only to protect basic rights of vulnerable minorities; apply stricter but minimal liberal-democratic standards of public scrutiny and external control in cases where minority organizations ask for legal support and recognition, for subsidies and other privileges; most importantly: try to convince non-liberal/non-democratic minorities by means of persuasion and, particularly, by good examples/practices instead of enforcing demanding moralities by law and sanctions.

II 'Shari'a in Ontario'? What Was, and What Was Not at Stake

> I've come to the conclusion that the debate has gone on long enough. There will be no Shariah law [sic!] in Ontario. There will be no religious arbitration in Ontario [sic!]. There will be one law for all Ontarians.
>
> (Premier Dalton McGuinty, 11 September 2005)[5]

In 2004 a proposal by the Islamic Institute of Civil Justice to establish a Darul-Qada (Muslim Arbitration Tribunal) in Ontario led to a public debate about the application

4 The 'distinction between equity' (Boyd 2004: 49) or 'decency' (66, 97) and full equality is central for my differentiated theory of morality and its consequences for external state-intervention. The most important thing is: how to prevent 'evil' or 'malfare'?

5 <http://www.nosharia.com/McGuinty%20rejects%20Ontario's%20use%20of%20Sharia%20Law%20and%20all%20religious%20arbitration.htm> [accessed 18 November 2008].

of Muslim personal law in arbitrations. In 2004, the Ontario Attorney General and the Minister Responsible for Women's Issues asked Marion Boyd, a former Attorney General, to review 'the use of private arbitration to resolve family and inheritance cases, and the impact that the use of arbitration may have on people who may be vulnerable including women, persons with disabilities and elderly persons. The review will include consideration of religious based arbitrations' (Boyd 2004: 143). The rejection (quoted above) by Premier McGuinty at a stroke and without any good arguments dismissed the report's general recommendations that:

> 1. Arbitration should continue to be an alternative dispute resolution option that is available in family and inheritance law cases, subject to the further recommendations of this Review. 2. The *Arbitration Act* should continue to allow disputes to be arbitrated using religious law, if safeguards currently prescribed and recommended by this Review are observed. (Boyd 2004: 133).

This and the following sections examine some of the arguments deployed by various participants in this debate.

A mythical notion of 'shari'a law' is equally and indiscriminately used by *fundamentalists* (in some Muslim countries and in the 'West') as well as by radical secularist opponents of any legal accommodation (see, for criticism, Emon 2006). The Muslim Canadian Congress defends the legal character of shari'a, claims that 'a Muslim cannot be a Muslim without obeying Muslim law in its totality' (Syed Mumtaz Ali, quoted in Boyd 2004: 62) and that all 'good Muslims' in Canada have to settle their disputes before one and the same Islamic Institute of Civil Justice, registered as Darul-Qada. There is 'a clear choice for Muslim Canadians: Do you want to govern yourself by the personal laws of your religion, or do you prefer governance by secular Canadian family law?' (see Shachar 2005: 62). The *secularist opposition*, organized by the 'International Campaign against Sharia Court in Canada' takes these claims for granted and rejects any possibility that dispute resolution can be based on religious laws, particularly on Islamic personal law. This rejection is based on personal experiences of women with fundamentalist interpretations and applications of 'shari'a law' in Muslim countries such as Iran, Saudi Arabia, Yemen, Libya, Pakistan, Sudan, Mauritania and some northern states of Nigeria and on the theoretical claim that secularists family law (reform) is 'entirely contradictory with family law grounded in religious precepts' (LEAF, Women's Legal Aid and Action Fund, in Boyd 2004: 48). Fundamentalists and secularists consequently accuse each other of hidden agendas and dishonesty.

Both fundamentalists and secularist could and should have been aware of that they were employing a mythical notion of 'the shariah' or 'Muslim law'.[6] This is

6 See Bakht 2006: 70f. For a lucid criticism of the reproduction of this myth in the ruling of the European Court of Human Rights in the *Refah* case see Moe 2005: 27f ('the Court's particular construction of Islam'), Meerschaut and Gutwirth 2007: 3ff, 13, and Bayat 2007: 6. See Ferrari 2006 for an interesting comparison of the role of legislation, custom,

made quite clear by many Muslim voices and organizations opposing the 'denial of rights by those who claim to be acting in the name of Islam' (Canadian Council of Muslim Women, CCMW): the Qu'ran cannot be seen as a determinate law code, Muslim law depends on competing law schools and legal traditions (*fiqh*), Muslim laws are eclectic mixtures from various legal sources (customary cultural practices, mixes of Islamic legal traditions, *qunan,* modern state laws), so there is no such thing as a monolithic 'Muslim law' and also no monolithic 'Muslim personal law' or 'Muslim family law', as there is no such thing as 'Christian law', 'Asian law' or 'African law' (quoted from Boyd 2004: 41ff). 'There will never be a single, centralized Sharia Tribunal that all Muslims will accept'; the 'diversity of legal thought' is a 'mercy from your Lord'; Islam does not know 'a central Church or diocese of Islam to legislate such a thing' as one shari'a tribunal (evidence from Mubin Shaik of the Masjid El Noor in Toronto, cited in Boyd 2004: 43).

So, first, it is important to clarify what has *not been at stake* in these proposals:

> (i) The more or less encompassing or 'total' application or misapplication of fundamentalist interpretations of 'shari'a law' in criminal, procedural and private law in *Muslim majority countries.*[7] The focus is on 'Western' countries with 'liberal-democratic constitutions' and 'modern' criminal and civil codes; and not on the introduction or accommodation of contested varieties of 'Islamic criminal and procedural law'[8] but on private, personal law, family and divorce law in particular.

---

administrative acts and interpretation by learned scholars in the tradition of canon law, Jewish law and Islamic law: 'Hierarchical ordering' (authority of the religious legislator) in the tradition of canon law is linked to the centralized, pyramidal structure of church authority ('uniformity', 'always find one, and only one, legally correct answer' (61, 'ideology of juridical completeness'), whereas law as 'interpretation' in the Jewish and Islamic tradition is linked to 'a socio-religious structure designed as a network' (65; 'possibility that there are different solutions, all equally correct from the legal point of view, to the same problem'). See Emon 2006 vs the reduction of shari'a to an abstract body of doctrines disconnected from a historical or institutional context. This reduction is shared by both fundamentalist 'critics' of colonialism and Western modernity and radical secularist opponents of any legal accommodation).

7 Such as Iran, Saudi Arabia, Pakistan, Nigeria. Existing mixes of customary law, varieties of Islamic law and modern state law in countries such as Indonesia (Bowen 2001, 2003), Malaysia and some Arab countries (e.g. Morocco) are clearly more open and egalitarian.

8 This limitation to Islamic personal or private law is, obviously, crucial for the debate because all varieties of Islamic criminal law that are incompatible with minimal morality and law are excluded here: death penalty by stoning for adultery (and other cruel forms of physical punishment in *huduth law*), and apostasy: prohibition of proselytism; but also non-Islamic female genital mutilation, honour killing, marriage under duress; kidnapping of girls without their consent which is known from Turkish, not from Moroccan culture (*kaçirma* not *kaçisma)*, in short: the 'main areas of friction with modern criminal law' (Strijbosch 1993: 9ff).

(ii) The claim has not been for the official recognition of separate religious private law and courts for all or some religious majorities or minorities in 'liberal-democratic' states where Muslims form a more or less important religious minority, as in India, Mahajan 2005, Menski (this volume) or Israel (Shachar 2001), but state recognition of arbitral awards where the procedural and substantive 'autonomy' of arbitrators is, compared with fairly general constitutional and legal restraints in the countries mentioned above, much more restricted.

(iii) Not at stake are cases of marriage and divorce under *international private law* (IPL) where the relevant legal rules and sources may be very contested and where many points of conflicting rules exist between e.g. Dutch and international law, and Moroccan law until the *Muddawwana* was changed in 2003.[9]

So what has been at stake is not the establishment of some version of a 'shari'a court' but the establishment and legal recognition of one or more private arbitration tribunals or, more precisely, of arbitral awards in countries with liberal-democratic constitutions and modern criminal, procedural and private law codes such as Canada, where *Arbitration Acts* officially allow *private arbitration* for commercial disputes only (as in Québec and British Columbia) or for domestic conflicts which then may be used selectively also for religious family disputes (as has been done in Ontario by Jewish, Christian and Ismaili communities).[10] We have moved away now from the broad and dramatizing title 'shari'a in the West'

9 See Rutten 1998 and d'Oliveira 1995. Dutch judges regularly declared marriages as valid which would not be allowed in the Netherlands, declared polygamous marriages as legal, accepted unilateral divorces in cases that the wife explicitly or tacitly has agreed or at least appeased, etc. See Rohe (this volume) for Germany, Boyd (2004) for the UK, France and Germany. Moral limits to these versions of legal pluralism should be: no marriage under duress; limits to enforcement of pre-arranged marriages if girls explicitly resist; no wife- or child-beating; no gross inequalities between the sexes in cases of divorce or custody regulations (see Strijbosch 1993: 16, very similar to my own moral minimalism). See also Meerschaut and Gutwirth for 'points of collision' (2007: 13), Moe 2005: 14, Bowen 2001, 4.

10 This is clearly different from cases in which the direct official recognition of Muslim family and divorce law are claimed. The public utterance of the former Dutch Minister of Justice, Donner, in 2007, that if a two-third majority would vote for 'the shari'a in the Netherlands' democracy would require to change the Dutch constitution and laws accordingly only demonstrates Dutch madness: no Muslim organization in the Netherlands ever raised such a claim; it is absolutely incompatible with any defensible notion of constitutional changes of liberal-democratic constitutions; it has nothing to do with the debates on private arbitration in Ontario. Space prevents a comparison with the 'anti-Shari'a storm' in the UK in response to the Archbishop of Canterbury's lecture (see this volume chapters 2 and 5. For a defence see Feldman 2008).

towards the much less contentious issues of limited, procedurally and substantively regulated recognition of arbitration in family and divorce disputes.

In the perspective of elaborating more productive procedural and substantive solutions to inherent problems of legal accommodation of the *nomos* of religious groups, particularly to tensions between associational religious freedoms and equality/non-discrimination, the debate in Ontario is an excellent test case.[11]

As we know, the proposal to establish a Darul-Qada tribunal was rejected. This astonishing victory of unreconstructed secularist liberals, republicans and feminists has been hailed around the globe. Like other proponents of democratic institutional pluralism (Shachar) or liberal multicultural accommodation (Williams), I intend to show that this was a missed opportunity. It did nothing to ameliorate the situation of Muslim women, particularly the most vulnerable women. It brushed aside the important changes of the original proposal by the Islamic Institute of Civil Justice as a result of these debates and completely failed to learn from the broad and intense debate in civil society (see Emon 2006; Williams 2007).

III The Main Legal Recommendations to Ameliorate the Position of Vulnerable Minorities: What Law Can and Should Do

The main legal and social policy recommendations to ameliorate the position of vulnerable minorities presented during this debate have been guided by such an intent. In a brief article it is impossible to compare mediation and arbitration practices prior to 1992, and from 1992 until 2004, and the different recommendations in Boyd's report. I have to confine myself to a cursory discussion of Boyd's most important legislative and regulatory recommendations and her recommendations on independent legal advice, supplemented by Shachar's recommendations and my own proposals (in this section). In section IV I briefly discuss the main social policy recommendations.[12]

11 Will Kymlicka (2005) has convincingly argued that this is a misleading or poor test-case for 'liberal multiculturalism' but he has bracketed the discussion of procedural and substantive criteria that would allow us to find forms of alternative dispute resolution that are affordable, accessible and non-adversarial, yet still provide adequate safeguard for equality rights.

12 My discussion of the case is severely limited in many regards: I do not discuss the history and recent changes of family law and arbitration law in Ontario (or comparatively in Québec); I do not discuss the contested issue whether arbitration should be allowed in family and divorce matters at all (or, as Gaudreault-DesBiens 2005 argues, should be forbidden); I analyse neither the societal and political debate of the proposal and the many detailed alternatives nor the astonishing victory of the opponents (Simmons 2008). For reasons of space, my defence is also fairly general and does not even pretend to present clear-cut answers to the many controversial issues such as the defence of minimal morality and its relation with more demanding liberal and democratic moralities (particularly: basic vs. best interests; equity vs. equality); what to do in cases of 'mixed marriages'? How to deal with

Consultation during the Process of Debating and Establishing an Islamic Arbitration Tribunal

In the initial process of proposing a Darul-Qada there has been little or no dialogue within the internally differentiated and divided Muslim community, particularly no consultation with the Canadian Council of Muslim Women, and also no deliberation and negotiation with various levels of provincial government. Eventually, as a result of significant mobilization against the proposal from Muslim women and other Muslim organizations, from women's organizations and human rights organizations (see <www.nosharia.com>) and heated local-to-global public debate and mass media coverage, the Ontario government initiated a consultation process open to all interested and affected parties as stakeholders to examine religious arbitration in the family law context (Boyd 2004). Two issues are particularly difficult to resolve:

1. Who speaks for Muslims or Islam(s) in Canada in this process: representative organizations and leadership under conditions of diversity and conflict ('intra-group politics of representation')? My preferred 'associationalist' solution favours a wide use of associational freedoms and a spontaneous process of self-organization from below building on self-definition and mobilization of diverse categories of Muslims instead of state crafting from outside and above (Bader 2007a, Chapter 8; see Kymlicka 2005 from the perspective of liberal multiculturalism).
2. What role can and should law and institutional design play in this regard to empower women without neglecting associational autonomy and intervening into the 'internal autonomy' of groups and their decision-making procedures? My general argument is: if minorities ask for public money and or public/legal recognition then the state has a right and a duty to see that all relevant groups/organizations or internal 'voices' are represented at the negotiation table(s), protecting their right to speak and to be listened to (see Bader 2005: 335f, Kymlicka 2005). The proposed recognition of one or many arbitration tribunals or of arbitrators or arbitral awards clearly rely on Ontario and Canadian law in order to legitimize their operation and will ultimately depend on the civil court system to ensure the enforceability of the decisions (see Reitman 2005 for Jewish family law in the UK).

---

the numerous conflicts? Which standards and procedures of certification of arbitrators? If one opts in favour of individual arbitrators instead of tribunals or 'courts': aren't they the least controllable and democratic? Etc. etc. All these limitations have been lucidly and critically raised during the presentation of this paper at the University of Toronto, Centre of Ethics in May 2008.

Legislative Changes to the Arbitration Act and the Family Law Act

Boyd's main recommendations in this regard were: add mediation agreements and arbitration agreements to the definition of 'domestic contracts' (Section 51 of the Family Law Act) to bring these agreements into the general protections of Part IV: 'in writing, signed, and witnessed' (Rec. 3). Earlier arbitration agreements are 'not binding unless reconfirmed in writing at the time of the dispute and before the arbitration occurs' (Rec. 5). Courts should be permitted 'to set aside an arbitral award' if: '(a) the award does not reflect the best interest of any children affected by it; (b) a party to it did not have or waive independent legal advise; (c) the parties do not have a copy of the arbitration agreement, and a written decision including reasons; or (d) a party did not receive a statement of principles of faith-based arbitration. The parties should not be able to waive this provision.' (Rec. 8). Most of these recommendations have been included in The Family Statute Law Amendment Act (see Bakht 2006: 80).

Which Legal Traditions/Practices and Arbitrators?

There seems to be broad agreement that 'if no changes are introduced to existing legislation, the Darul-Qada will be free to apply, when both parties are consenting, the *fiqh* on any Islamic school in any interpretation to resolve divorce disputes in lieu of the application of secular Canadian law' (see Rec. 12; see Shachar 2005, Emon 2006, and also Ali and Whitehouse 1991). Two problems, however, are not dealt with properly:

1. One should not exclusively focus on *fiqh* (law-schools or 'lawyer's/judges law'), let alone on 'codified shari'a' (see Emon 2006). Muslim legal traditions and practices are actually more complex: which combination of customary law (*adat* or *urf* [Masud 2001: 11]), *fiqh* and *quanun* (state law) and modern state law (see above).
2. What and who should be recognized? Here we have two options. First, if a *tribunal* or a 'court': why only *one* Islamic Arbitration Tribunal instead of more (*as many as would actually be campaigned for and eventually recognized*). The latter option would clearly be preferable because the choice of law would be already in the name of the tribunal and nobody could assume that there would be One Islamic Family and Divorce Law (as if there would be One Christian Ecclesiastical Law, see above with Mubin Shaik). It is clearly not a task of the state to back monopolistic claims by particular organizations, leaders or traditions to 'speak for Islam or Islamic law'.[13] More important is the second option: the state need not and should

13 Emon (2006) rightly stresses the task of the state to 'protect against monopolistic control' (see 353f in favour of doctrinal and institutional pluralism versus a monopoly for MUIS in Singapore). Yet the proposed social service organizations by and for Muslims

not recognize 'tribunals' or 'courts' but *individual arbitrators* and *arbitral awards*. Within the arbitration framework, it is not tribunals but individual arbitrators (who have the option of organizing themselves as tribunals) that receive recognition (Melissa Williams, personal communication). More precisely: state *recognition* (by courts) should be restricted to *arbitral awards*, individual arbitrators as well as arbitration tribunals should be certified, undergo training and be supervised/monitored.

Procedural Safeguards

1. Before entering the arbitration process there should be: (a) *mandatory and independent legal advice* (Rec. 8a, 13 and 21–24); see Shachar: 'for each party regarding the *choice of forum*, the *choice of law* under the tribunal (if religious law: which school, which interpretation, etc.)'; Rec.16: 'statement of principles of faith-based arbitration that explains the parties' rights and obligations and available processes under the particular form of religious law', 'to be distributed to all prospective clients' (Rec. 17); (b) *limits on waivers* (Boyd 2004: 8a, 12, 13); (c) arbitrators have to '*screen* the parties separately about issues of *power imbalance and domestic violence*, prior to entering into an arbitration agreement, using a standardized screening process' (Rec. 18 and 19); (d) *information*-materials translated into all relevant languages and also made broadly available within 'communities' (Rec. 25–30 on Public Legal Education, see below).
2. During arbitration: (a) ensure *legal representation for both parties*; (b) *permit non-governmental organizations to act as amicus curiae* to assist women, (c) *register consent*; (d) file a *written affidavit* confirming the consultation session and the choices made by each party with a civil registration authority or local court (to remedy the defect that Ontario Arbitration Act permits oral agreement which impairs the ability to monitor decisions (Shachar 2005: 76), see Rec. 20 and 37–39 for required records); (e) permit parties to turn to civil courts. Turning to civil court on appeal, however, is daunting (financial resources, threats of ostracization). Then 'choice' or 'free will' may be robbed of any substance.
3. Judicial review: (i) How to address the fear of social ostracism (Bader 2007a, 212ff, Reitman (2005) or of being branded a 'traitor' to the faith or the community? Shachar 2005 proposes a *structural reversal point:* the introduction of a mandatory review of all family law arbitration settlements or awards prior to their finalization that would not have to be initiated by the vulnerable party but would be a required part of the process. Assessment

(Emon 2006: 354) still suggest '*tribunals*' instead of individual arbitrators 'providing mediation or adjudication services'. Boyd and Shachar also seem to think of tribunals instead of the recognition of arbitral awards and of appropriate measures of training, scrutiny and control of both individual arbitrators and possible tribunals.

requires agreed standards of an orderly or equitable settlement of e.g. property matters. If standards are violated then civic authorities should have the power to overrule this aspect of arbitration settlement. Boyd (2004) recommends (no. 46) an 'analysis of the legality and desirability of providing a higher level of court oversight to settlements of family and inheritance cases based on religious principles than is available to non-religiously based settlements under Part IV of the Family Law Act in addition to the several additional grounds set out in these recommendations under which arbitral awards may be challenged';[14] (ii) Under present law judicial review is too narrowly defined and limited to procedural defects in the arbitration process (Shachar 2005; see Boyd below for a more substantive reading of 'fair and equal treatment'); (iii) In addition: monitoring and control (see Rec. 36–42 for Oversight and Evaluation of Arbitrations).

Substantive Constraints

Space prevents any detailed discussion so I have to confine myself to very brief, critical remarks and recommendations:

First, some of these proposals, appeal at any time; mandatory review of all and every arbitration settlement; some of Boyd's recommendations for oversight and evaluation, require much time and personnel and may not be *not feasible.* Some issues of practicability, however, may be remedied, e.g. by a highly selective application: the 'threat' of review and oversight then doing much of the expected beneficial work.

Second, one should be very careful *not to require from arbitration more than is actually required in Civil Court procedures* as may be the case in a strict application of Boyd's screening requirements and the standardized procedure. Rules, standards and actual comparisons of arbitration with civil procedures should be fair.

Third, one also should take care *not to make legal pluralism pointless*, e.g. by making judicial review fairly maximalist and extensive. At least one Ontario court 'has interpreted the obligation to treat the parties equally and fairly as not limited to procedural fairness but even-handed in substance' (*Hercus v Hercus* [2001] quoted in Boyd 2004: 16, see also Rec. 15). A substantive reading of 'fair and equal treatment' for instance should allow for *even-handedness different from strict equality* even in matters of 'property', etc. Otherwise maximalist interpretations of

---

14 Under the existing Arbitration Act, 'arbitration must be conducted fairly and the parties must be treated equally. The parties cannot opt out of this obligation … parties must both be given proper notice of the arbitration; time limits prescribed in the Act can be extended by the Court; courts may set aside an award that was obtained by fraud or if the arbitrator is or reasonably appears to be biased; appeals to the court on questions of law or on questions of fact' (Boyd 2004: 15). Obviously 'the court may refuse any order that it would not have had jurisdiction to make itself or would not have granted' (16).

Canadian family and divorce law are smuggled in via the back door.[15] In this regard, I propose to distinguish more clearly between *'basic interests' and 'best interests' of children.* In my view, one should restrict the role of arbitrators and judges to act as guardians of their basic interests instead of stipulating that they would be able to act as guarantors of their 'best interests' (Bader 2007a, 211f. quoting Judge La Forest in *B (R) v Children's Aid Society of Metropolitan Toronto; 112f*). This proposal is clearly more contested than my recommendation to restrict the role of courts and judges to act as guarantors of the basic interests and rights of women because any anti-paternalist understanding of modern law and democracy should conceive of *mature women as the guardians of their own best interests.* Boyd clearly recognizes the tension inherent in this discussion 'between protection of the vulnerable and a degree of paternalism that involves controversial assumptions about vulnerability' (2004: 11). Radical feminists, like radical Marxists earlier, seem not to understand or tend to easily override this crucial principle of modern liberal democracy and law. They should learn to oppose the familiar caricature of the 'imperilled Muslim women', as a 'content housewife' with 'adapted preferences' and no choice or agency, who needs to be rescued from the 'dangerous Muslim man' (Razack 200: 131, Bakht 2006).

Fourth, the restriction of the role of appeal to what I call moral and legal minimalism, instead of imposing maximalist interpretations of 'modern', 'secular' or civic law, is essential. It is hard enough for courts and state administration to protect and guarantee the basic interests of vulnerable minorities, particularly of children. This they should do in all situations regardless whether minorities or majorities are concerned or whether minorities ask for legal recognition or not. Standards can and should be more demanding but still minimal if minorities ask for legal recognition of arbitral awards. If they are minimalist, there are excellent reasons for strong judicial activism by courts of appeal that should operate as protectors of basic rights under regimes of legal pluralism (see above). If they are maximalist, they lose legitimacy in the eyes of those for whom these arbitration procedures are designed and meant to serve.

Last, it seems quite obvious that any such recommendations for changing the Arbitration Act and the Rules and Regulations would have considerably ameliorated the legal position of Muslim women compared with the initial proposal for one Darul-Qada in Ontario. The recommendations would also have increased the range of choice of women between informal mediation, regulated arbitration and civic courts considerably (choice of law and choice of 'courts') and by this would

15 Shachar's principle of 'division of authority' (2005): dissolve marriage in accordance with religious requirements (here too some re-interpretation may be required) and apply Canadian family and divorce law in property, alimony, inheritance, etc. matters (application of her 'principle of sub-matter allocation of authority') is indeterminate: it may require 'strict substantive equality' or allow for 'evenhandedness'.

have contributed to increase their actual freedoms.[16] They would have allowed the building of coalitions with different groups within the Muslim community to fight against the worst forms of violence, particularly in order to prevent violence instead of sanctions ex post but clearly also in order to achieve effective enforcement and compliance with the minimal moral and legal core. Furthermore, they would have permitted the discussion of 'decent' but inegalitarian customs and drawing on more egalitarian sources within the global *umma* in order to criticize gender inequality from the inside.[17]

Even the initial proposal would have ameliorated their position compared with informal practices of mediation and arbitration. It also seems quite obvious that the outright rejection of regulated and controlled religious arbitration does near to nothing to ameliorate their legal or actual position making them worse off even compared with the initial proposal because:

> there are too many unqualified, ignorant imams making back-alley pronouncements on the lives of women, men, and children. The practice will continue, without any regulation, oversight or accountability … Nothing has really changed, except the fact that we have missed a golden opportunity to shine light on abuses masquerading as faith, and to ensure that rulings don't contradict our Charter of Rights and Freedoms. (Sheema Khan, quoted from Emon 2006).

IV Policy Options to Ameliorate the Position of Vulnerable Minorities: What Law Can't Do

Law is not all-powerful in changing socio-economic situations of vulnerable minorities. Muslim women may be in a position of 'subjugation and powerlessness', and this is the generalized assumption of opponents: Muslim women are subject to *domestic violence* (Boyd 2004: 32f, 51 and Section 6.5); they are subject to 'economic', 'social', emotional' or 'psychological' pressure or '*coercion*', all based in 'culture and/or religion' (50), particularly to (threat and fear of) '*social exclusion*' or social ostracism: their *economic lives* (also jobs and social security) depend on a close association with their faith-based community or cultural groups, so that, in addition to the cultural and identity costs of ostracism ('apostate', 'alone, shunned in their communities or even houses of worship', they also have

16 For court shopping in the *millet* system see Adanir 2000, for cases of native communities see Hoekema 2004. From an actor-oriented approach 'individuals are not the prisoners of their own supposedly integrated and homogeneous culture, but shop forums, choose among legal orders, pressure their own leaders and authorities to take other legal elements into consideration and also, the other way round, challenge national authorities to take local legal sensibilities into consideration' (Hoekema 2004: 14).

17 See Walinda Valiante for the Canadian Islamic Congress (quoted in Boyd 2004: 98f.) and many famous Muslim feminists such as Leila Ahmed or Fatima Mernissi.

to face economic deprivation and impoverishment (102–104); their *legal status as resident immigrants* is threatened (51f. sponsoring); they lack crucial *information* (51), are unaware of their rights in Canada (52) and 'have no way to know what Canadian law is'; they lack *educational* resources (51) and *language* skills (52). All this is a serious concern to the *degree* in which these statements are actually true (particularly in a *comparative* perspective with other religions/denominations and so-called 'secular' families). Opponents assume that they apply to all Muslim women regardless whether they belong to Sunnite, Shiite, Alevite, Ismaili, etc. traditions; to divergent law schools and traditions; come from South-East Asian countries, from India or Pakistan, from Arab countries, Turkey, Iran, from East- or West-African countries; are of peasant or working-class or 'upper-class' descent; have no or high education and professional skills, etc.

Hence the Boyd report mentions, in addition to its legal recommendations, various policy initiatives in the areas of *public legal education* 'aimed at creating awareness of the legal system, alternative dispute resolution options, and family law provisions' (Rec. 25–30) to be developed in collaboration with community organizations and experts; of *training and education for professionals* in collaboration with professional associations (education about arbitration and independent legal advice, training on power imbalances, screening protocols for domestic violence, professional duty to report children in need of protection) (Rec. 31–35); *community development* (encourage and fund community organizations who run arbitration services to develop information materials and to work with experienced public legal education providers) and to encourage *professional self-regulation* and *guidelines for conduct and competency* (Rec. 45). All these initiatives are completely in line with recommendations from an associational governance perspective (Bader 2007c).

Clearly, the success of all these socio-legal recommendations depends on a broader set of economic, social, educational policies to ameliorate the position of vulnerable minorities. The measures to reduce (the threat of) *domestic violence* against women and children mentioned above work best if backed by community-internal allies. (Actual threat of) social *ostracism* is reduced if women are not forced to choose between their rights and their culture. Yet not much can be done to soften identity costs and the loss of social relations in cases when women still are expelled from their 'communities'. Importantly though, the high material costs of ostracism can be considerably reduced by socio-economic policies that guarantee a sufficient, work-independent individual minimum income to all residents (preferably by an individualized basic income scheme as proposed by associative democrats) and that offer minority-women fair chances for (qualification for) work and employment (preferably by prudent affirmative action policies) (Engelen 2004) that make use of 'suspect classifications' (Bader 1998), the reason why they are so often rejected by defenders of 'one law for all only' who also reject any legal accommodation in family and divorce law. If effective, policies like these would *increase the actual exit options* for women instead of only, rightly, stressing their exit rights (Bader 2007a, 212ff).

Economic impoverishment may not only follow from ostracism but quite often as a consequence of seriously unequal property division in divorce decisions. Readings of Canadian and Ontario family and divorce law in property, alimony and inheritance matters may differ: see above on substantive 'fair and equal treatment' in the sense of strict equality versus 'even-handedness' (insistence on adequate, sufficient means instead of equal means). For a minimalist reading, the protections by Canadian and Ontario law in cases of domestic violence would be much stronger than against poverty in divorce law. A maximalist reading and law enforcement also in cases of Islamic arbitration would help to address this concern.

Lack of or seriously insufficient *information* may be addressed by adequate information policies (making use of information rights and duties). Lack of or insufficient *education* requires adequate, cost-free language courses for minorities and, much more demanding, policies of fair access and fair financing of educational opportunities. Obviously, such socio-economic and education policies are very hard to implement effectively even under conditions of fairly well-established welfare-states. To the degree that they succeed they would clearly be the most important measures in realizing higher degrees of informed consent and of voluntarism for those (not all!) Muslim women who are actually in a position of serious subjugation or powerlessness. But even here, we should not forget that the 'powerless', contrary to 'victimization' talk in 'feminist and human-rights paternalism', command the 'weapons of the weak' and do not lack significant degrees of agency (Scott 1985, 1990, Bader 2007d).

Concluding Remarks

We have to insist that comparisons between different legal regimes are fair, that is compare actual options in the 'real world' instead of opposing the idealized model of 'secular law' with the muddle of actual options and recommendations of recognized private arbitration or with dramatized myths of 'shari'a law'. Fair comparisons require as much context-specific information as is available on actual legal practices of different Muslim 'communities' and on the actual 'ethnic', socio-economic and educational background and position of Muslim women in Ontario instead of dramatized stories of completely subjugated Muslim women lacking any significant degree of agency and choice. Such a comparative, sober perspective is, understandably, completely absent from the stories of all opponents of any form of legal accommodation but also amongst some defenders of alternatives. If it is true that patriarchal practices 'are usually hidden from secular society' (Boyd 2004: 49) one would immediately have to qualify statements like: 'the danger is that once these tribunals are set up people from Muslim origin will be pressured to use them' (49). One would have to ask whether the pressure would be greater compared with the pressure to follow informal procedures (regime (a) as discussed at the beginning of this chapter) or more formalized but unregulated procedures of mediation and arbitration (regime (b)) and with 'secular/civic' courts only (regime (d)). The real issue is how to most effectively prevent the violation of the most basic rights of vulnerable minorities. If it is true that religious communal leaders are 'primarily male, and primarily traditionalists who hold tightly to outdated beliefs and outdated laws' (51) it is by no means clear that 'women will fare better in courts than in private arbitration' (53) because the imposition of 'secular' law and courts may contribute to fundamentalize communities and this may prevent women to make use of 'secular courts'. If one compares the first two legal regimes even with the original, unmodified proposal for an Arbitration Tribunal by Mumtaz Ali, his arguments for 'a more formal establishment of Muslim arbitration' are to the point: 'arbitration cannot apply those provisions of Muslim laws and Shari'a which do not agree with Canadian laws or the Canadian value system' (61).[18] If the issue is how to effectively prevent domestic violence (96f, 99f) an approach that trusts exclusively on what state law and courts can do, is manifestly insufficient. If the issue is to prevent women's choice or appeal from causing communal 'shame to them or to their spouses', prescribing 'secular courts' only 'because the law requires to take that route' is clearly not the best option. If the issue is to actually increase choice between legal options, regime (c) fares much better than all other regimes.

Space prevents discussion of the recommendations made during the debate in Ontario in any detail and time and also competence prevent me from gathering all necessary contextual anthropological and sociological information. We have seen that many recommendations in the Boyd report are clearly in line with a more general institutional model of associational governance of religious diversity (Bader 2007a, Part IV) that cannot be compared here with alternative varieties of liberal accommodationism such as moderate civil libertarianism (Rosenblum 2000), liberal pluralism (Galston 2002, Kymlicka 1995, Selznik 1992), structural accommodation (Glendon 1991, McConnell 1992), joint governance, 'transformative accommodation' (Shachar 2001) all opposing 'zero accommodation' and 'absolute deference' but productively disagreeing in many important respects. The controversy over private Islamic arbitration in Ontario would be an ideal case to compare these varieties in more detail, but this would be another story.

References

Adanir, Fikret 2000. Religious Communities and Ethnic Groups under Imperial Sway. ENCS conference paper. Bremen, 18–21 May 2000.

18 Mumtaz Ali (even in 1991) is clearly a modest traditional Muslim compared with Salim Ibn who rejects German legal rules and judgments as 'rules of infidelity', advocates flogging or stoning to death for adultery, and believes the social security system is 'evil' because it stimulates disobedience to husbands (see Rohe this volume).

Ali, Syed Mumtaz and Anab Whitehouse. 1991. Oh! Canada. Whose Land, Whose Dream? Available at: <http: //muslim-canada.org/ocanada.pdf> [accessed 22 September 2008].

Bader, Veit 1998. Egalitarian Multiculturalism. In *Blurred Boundaries*, edited by R. Bauböck and J. Rundell. Aldershot: Ashgate, 185–222.

— 2005. Associative Democracy and Minorities within Minorities. In *Minorities within Minorities. Equality, Rights and Diversity*, edited by Avigail Eisenberg and Jeff Spinner-Halev. Cambridge: Cambridge University Press, 319–39.

— 2007a. *Secularism or Democracy?* Amsterdam: Amsterdam University Press.

— 2007b. Komplexe Bürgerschaft. Einige Probleme politischer, sozialer und Minderheiten-Bürgerschaft in politischen Mehrebenensystemen am Beispiel der EU. In *Bürgerschaft und Migration. Einwanderung und Einbürgerung aus ethisch-politischer Perspektiv*, edited by Simone Zurbuchen. Münster: LIT Verlag, 53–90. (Short English version: Complex Citizenship and Legitimacy in Compound Polities. MLPs and MLG: The EU as Example. Eurosphere, Online Working Paper 05, 2008. Available at <http: //eurosphere.uib.no/knowledgebase/wpsdocs/Eurosphere_Working_Paper_5_Bader.pdf> [accessed 23 September 2008].)

— 2007c. Regimes of Governance of Religious Diversity in Europe. The Perils of Modelling. *Journal of Ethnic and Migration Studies*, 33(6), 871–87.

— 2007d. Misrecognition, Power, and Democracy. In *Recognition and Power. Axel Honneth and the Tradition of Critical Social Theory*, edited by B. van Brink and D. Owen. New York: Cambridge University Press, 238–69.

— 2008. Religions, Toleration, and Democracy. Moral Minimalism and Doctrinal, Attitudinal and Institutional Learning. Paper presented at ECPR workshops in Pisa, August 2007, and Keele University, 12 June 2008.

Bakht, Natasha 2006. Were Muslim Barbarians Really Knocking on the Gates of Ontario? The Religious Arbitration Controversy, Another Perspective. *Ottawa Law Review* 40th Anniversary Volume, 67–82.

Bayat, Asad. 2007. *Islam and Democracy. What is the Real Question?* International Institute for the Study of Islam in the Modern World (ISIM) Paper No. 8. Amsterdam: Amsterdam University Press.

Benda-Beckmann, F. v 2002. Who's Afraid of Legal Pluralism? *Journal of Legal Pluralism*, 47, 37–82.

Bowen, John R. 2001. *Shari'a, State and Social Norms in France and Indonesia.* International Institute for the Study of Islam in the Modern World (ISIM) Paper No. 3. Amsterdam: Amsterdam University Press.

— 2003. *Islam, Law and Equality in Indonesia.* Cambridge: Cambridge University Press.

Boyd, Marion. 2004. *Dispute Resolution in Family Law: Protecting Choice, Promoting Inclusion.* Report of Review of Arbitration of Family Law and Inheritance Matters to Sandra Pupatello (Minister Responsible for Women's Issues), Ontario: Minister. and Michael Bryant, Attorney General.

Cover, Robert. 1983. Nomos and Narrative. *Harvard Law Review*, 97, 4–68.

Engelen, Ewald 2004. The Economic Incorporation of Immigrants: the Netherlands. In *Employment Strategies for Immigrants in the EU*, edited by J. Blaschke and B. Vollmer. Berlin: Edition Parabolis, 445–96.

Emon, A.E. 2006. Conceiving Islamic Law in a Pluralist Society. *Singapore Journal of Legal Studies*, 331–55.

Feldman, Noah. 2008. Why Shariah? *New York Times Magazine*, 16 March 2008.

Ferrari, Silvio. 2006. Adapting Divine Law to Change. *Cardozo Law Review*, 28(1), 53–65.

Galston, W. 2002. *Liberal Pluralism*. Cambridge: Cambridge University Press.

Gadirov, Javid. 2006. *Plurality of Legal Systems and Religious Freedom*. Available at <http://www.strasbourgconference.org/papers/Plurality%20of%20Legal%20Systems%20and%20Religious%20Freedom.pdf> [accessed 22 October 2008].

Gaudreault-DesBiens, J.F. 2005. The Limits of Private Justice? The Problems of the State Recognition of Arbitral Awards in Family and Personal Status Disputes in Ontario. *World Arbitration and Mediation Report*, 16(1), 18–32.

Glendon, M.A. and R.F. Yanes. 1991. Structural Free Exercise. In *Michigan Law Review* 90(3), 477–550.

Harlow, Carol and Richard Rawlings. 2006. Promoting Accountability in Multi-Level Governance: A Network Approach. *European Governance Papers* (EUROGOV), Number WP-C-06-02.

Hoekema, André. 2004. *Rechtspluralisme en interlegaliteit*. Amsterdam: Vossiuspers, Uva.

Joerges, Christian. 2005. *Rethinking European Law's Supremacy*. EUI Working Paper LAW 2005/12. Florence: European University Institute.

Kymlicka, Will. 1995. *Multicultural Citizenship*. Oxford: Oxford University Press.

— 2005. Testing the Bounds of Liberal Multiculturalism? In *Muslim Women's Equality Rights in the Justice System: Gender, Religion and Pluralism*. Toronto: Canadian Council of Muslim Women, 51–68. [French translation: Tester les limites du multiculturalisme libéral? Le cas des tribunaux religieux en droit familial, in *Éthique Publique*, 9(1), 27–39.]

Mahajan, Gurpreet. 2005. Can Intra-group Equality Co-exist with Cultural Diversity? In *Minorities within Minorities. Equality, Rights and Diversity*, edited by Avigail Eisenberg and Jeff Spinner-Halev. Cambridge: Cambridge University Press, 90–112.

Masud, Muhammad Khalid. 2001. *Muslim Jurists' Quest for the Normative Basis of Shari'a*. Inaugural lecture. Leiden: International Institute for the Study of Islam in the Modern World (ISIM).

McConnell, Michael 1992. Accommodation of Religion. *George Washington Law Review* 60(3), 685–742.

Meerschaut, Karen. 2006. Diversiteit en Recht. PhD thesis, VU Brussel.

Meerschaut, Karen and Serge Gutwirth. 2007. Secularism, Legal Pluralism, Islam and Human Rights in Europe and Malaysia. Unpublished paper for conference on 'Secularism and Beyond'. Copenhagen, 29 May–1 June 2007.

Moe, Christian. 2005. Refah Revisited: Strasbourg's Construction of Islam. Available at <http: //www.strasbourgconference.org/papers/Plurality%20of%20Legal%20Systems%20and%20Religious%20Freedom.pdf> [accessed 22 October 2008].

Oliveira, H.U. Jessurun d'. 1995. Le droit international privé Nérlandais et les relations Maroc-Pays Bas. *Cahiers des Droits Maghrébins*, 1, 137–66.

Parekh, Bhikhu 2000. *Rethinking Multiculturalism*. Basingstoke: Macmillan.

Poulter, S. 1998. *Ethnicity, Law, and Human Rights*. Oxford: Clarendon Press.

Razack, S. 2004. Imperilled Muslim Women, Dangerous Muslim Men and Civilized Europeans. *Feminist Legal Studies*, 12(2), 129–74.

Reitman, Oonagh. 2005. On Exit. In *Minorities within Minorities. Equality, Rights and Diversity*, edited by Avigail Eisenberg and Jeff Spinner-Halev. Cambridge: Cambridge University Press, 189–208.

Renteln, Alison. D. 2004. *The Cultural Defense*. Oxford: Oxford University Press.

Rosenblum, Nancy 1998. *Membership and Morals*. Princeton NJ: Princeton University Press.

— 2000. Introduction: Pluralism, Integralism, and Political Theories of Religious Accommodation. In N. Rosenblum (ed.), *Obligations of Citizenship and Demands of Faith*. Princeton NJ: Princeton University Press, 3–31.

Rutten, S. 1988. *Moslims in de Nederlandse rechtsprakk*. Kampen: Kok.

Scott, J. 1985. *Weapons of the Weak*. Yale: Yale University Press.

— 1990. *Domination and the Arts of Resistance*. Yale: Yale University Press.

Selznick, Philip 1992. *The Moral Commonwealth*. University of California Press.

Shachar, Ayelet. 2001. *Multicultural Jurisdictions*. Cambridge: Cambridge University Press.

— 2005. Religion, State and the Problem of Gender: New Modes of Citizenship and Governance of Diverse Societies. *McGill Law Journal*, 49, 49–88.

Simmons, H. 2008. The Curious Case of the Disappearing Islamic Tribunals in Ontario, Now you See Them, Now you Don't. Unpublished ms.

Strijbosch, F. 1993. *Aan de grenzen van het Rechtspluralisme*. Nijmegen: Reeks Recht en Samenleving.

Williams, Melissa 2007. The Politics of Fear and the Decline of Multiculturalism. Unpublished paper, University of Toronto.

Chapter 5
Transforming to Accommodate? Reflections on the Shari'a Debate in Britain

Prakash Shah

Introduction

This chapter is a response to the widely reported speech by the chief cleric of the Church of England, the Archbishop of Canterbury, Dr Rowan Williams, at the Royal Courts of Justice in London on 7 February 2008.[1] It is an attempt to place the current debate on Muslims and the law in the UK within a wider jurisprudential frame of reference. The response to Dr Williams' suggestions was already predetermined by certain constraints, subsequently characterized by Tariq Ramadan (2008) as 'psychological', rather than 'historical' or 'normative'. Ramadan sees the constraints as primarily to do with the mental images provoked by references to the shari'a in the West. While there is certainly a psychological element of fear present in the responses to Dr Williams' lecture, it is possible to include both historical and normative limits to explain the constraints a legal system faces in its attempt to 'integrate' non-national 'others', in this case Muslims and shari'a, within its frame of reference. These limits can be seen to operate in various interrelated fields, and are typified by the contemporary scope of legal comparativism, the limited historical perspective through which law is conceived, the educational and jurisprudential orthodoxies that dominate the scene, and a judicial system that seems too tied to positivism to be responsive enough to the socio-legal field.

Indeed, the contemporary 'discourse of nationalism' (Özkırımlı 2000) internal and external to official British legal systems helps to ground better an analysis of the resistance to the acceptance of Muslims and the shari'a, currently cast as the 'constitutive outside' within that discourse. Even though its influence has been particularly pervasive in law, I do not wish to give the impression that legal thought is irretrievably trapped within the confines of 'methodological nationalism' (Wimmer and Glick Schiller 2002). Scholarship from a variety of subfields,

1 The speech can be found at <http//www.archbishopofcanterbury.org/1575> and is linked to a fairly long question-and-answer session which followed it (<http//www.archbishopofcanterbury.org/1594>). An interview was recorded earlier the same day for the BBCs *World at One*, available at <http//www.archbishopofcanterbury.org/1573>. [All accessed 18 November 2008.] The Archbishop's speech was the first in a series of discussions to be held on Islam and English law.

including comparative law, legal pluralism and legal sociology, has been making significant in-roads, mitigating the effects of methodological nationalism, while concepts such as 'transnationalism', 'globalization' and 'glocalization' have added to the arsenal of vocabulary now aiding the analyst to overcome the nationalist paradigm. Nor do I wish to imply that the state has now reached the end of its legal relevance. Far from it; the state precedes modern nationalism, it continues to be a critical feature in the legal equation, and will forseeably remain so. My task here is specifically to highlight, with reference to the debate on the encounter of Muslim and British laws, the ways in which non-national influences are also integral features of plural legal orders which cannot simply be legislated away or ignored on the basis of the modernist assumption that the object of state made law is a unitary national community. Thus, as Cotterrell (2008a: 11) notes, under conditions of cultural pluralism, 'perspectives on law and its bases of authority tend to become increasingly diverse and relativistic, dependent on standpoint'.[2]

Legal Plurality and States, Standard or Exceptional?

The UK is not the only ethnically or religiously diverse country. This is a general condition of the world. From a socio-legal perspective the claim of a uniform, national system of law is not sustainable either in the UK or elsewhere. In Asia and Africa, state legal systems have accommodated plurality by institutionally recognizing a multiplicity of personal laws, running concurrent to a general law which applies to all of a country's citizens (Hooker 1975). There are also cases in Latin America of accommodation by state legal systems of the legal orders of different population groups. States in Europe therefore appear to be running counter to globally preferred models of state–society relations.

When we examine the imperial period, we find that the co-existence of different laws was readily conceded. As leaders of an empire, like other empires, the British rulers had to recognize their domains as inherently legally plural. India is often cited, particularly by informed observers (Griffiths 1986: 6), and not least by informed Muslims, as a country where the colonial authorities recognized Muslim law. Such reminders appear to be necessary particularly given the state of post-imperial nationalistic amnesia in which British legal systems appear to be currently languishing. Before European colonizers arrived, there was already the prevailing norm of local laws existing side by side with the state law. In pre-British India, and in other parts of the Muslim world, this latter law was the sultan's *kanoon* (state-

2 The concept of 'standpoints', which Cotterrell applies to the manner of viewing legal phenomena, is potentially very useful for legal pluralist theory and parallels the Jain teaching of *anekāntvāda* (doctrine of multifacetedness of reality and non-absolutism) and its linked concept of *syādvāda* (theory of relativity of propositions or judgements).

made law). This co-existence and interaction of laws of different provenance is now fascinatingly expressed in the recent Hindi film *Jodha Akbar*.[3]

The vast Ottoman Empire, actually building upon Roman and Byzantine principles, had a similar system. The concept of *millet*, generally applicable to the empire's non-Muslim communities, who were recognized as having considerable powers of self-regulation, is not the only method by which such semi-autonomous status was recognized. Muslim communities, while having access to *qadi* courts which applied both the shari'a and *kanoon*, were also recognized as having considerable self-regulatory freedom. Although post-imperial, modern Turkey has chosen to homogenize top-down along French lines, one can see the continuing influence of the earlier modelling on many existing West Asian/Middle Eastern legal systems (Dupret et al. 1999, Mallat 2007), including that of Israel, which also recognizes a Muslim personal law and *qadi* courts to apply it (Edelman 1994).

Although the construction of 'Europe' has relied significantly on an opposition to its Muslim and Jewish 'others' (Ballard 1996), in practice, the boundaries between these constructions had of necessity to be porous, and mutual legal recognition, however grudging or limited, was unavoidable. One Orientalist adventurer, Sir Richard Burton, wrote in the introduction to his 1885 translation of *Alf Laylah wa Laylah* (better known as the *Thousand and One Nights*) that 'England is ever forgetting that she is at present the greatest Mohammedan empire in the world' (Burton 1894: xxiii). He further counselled:

> Now Moslems are not to be ruled by raw youths who should be at school and college instead of holding positions of trust and emolument. He who would deal with them successfully must be, firstly, honest and truthful and, secondly, familiar with and favourably inclined to their manners and customs if not to their law and religion.

And British policy indeed rested on the recognition of Muslim law in most parts of the empire as a personal law. Nowadays, the Austro-Hungarian Empire is recalled as the easternmost bulwark of the civilization formerly known as Christendom against the Muslim world in particular.[4] This idea can be seen even in recent works introducing the Austrian legal system (Hausmaninger 2000: 1), and that historical baggage also partially accounts for the refusal of Austria to countenance the accession of Turkey to the EU.[5] However, the Austro-Hungarian

3 Interestingly the film has proved controversial and faced a ban in some Indian states, eventually lifted by the Indian Supreme Court – <http//in.reuters.com/article/topNews/idINIndia-32293320080304> [accessed 25 April 2008].

4 The term 'Christendom' persisted until recently in the usage of British courts, see e.g. *Cheni v Cheni* [1963] 2 W.L.R. 17, *Qureshi v Qureshi* [1972] Fam. 173 at 182 (used by counsel in argument). As a consequence of citation and quoting of earlier cases, it can be found up to the present day.

5 Hungary, on the other hand, has announced that it favours Turkey's accession.

Empire was itself plural in terms of its population, as well as its legal structures. It was Eugen Ehrlich, who hailed from and subsequently worked as a professor of law in the empire's pluralistic, eastern frontier province of Bukovina (Likhovski 2003: 639–42, Hertogh 2004: 474), who bequeathed the idea of studying the 'living law' of the people, as opposed to the formal lawyers' law that was already being overemphasized in his day. After its takeover of Bosnia-Herzegovina in 1878, the Austro-Hungarian Empire recognized the continued operation of shari'a courts as inherited from the Ottomans (Pinson 1993), a system which continued until the establishment of the Yugoslav Republic (Friedman 1996: 72). Interestingly, the legal remains of those earlier days have been found by the Austrians, not more than two decades ago, to be useful in according official legal status to Muslims living there (Schmied and Wieshaider 2004: 202–204). In Greece, as a consequence of the Treaty of Lausanne (1923), shari'a is still recognized with respect to the Muslims of Western (or Greek) Thrace (Tsitselkis 2004: 102–105).

After the colonial experience many countries retained their systems somewhat along the lines of what the Archbishop termed 'supplementary jurisdictions', or personal laws. So, nowadays, the vast majority of the world's legal systems are not disintegrating because they fail to operate a uniform legal system applicable to all of their population. Indeed, the opposite may be the case; countries which came under the influence of European-style nationalist theories may find themselves experiencing ethnic conflict or secessionist pressure because of the non-recognition of constituent group identities. Elites from these states, among them many lawyers reared in models of Euro-focused, methodologically nationalist legality, nevertheless tend to downplay the extent to which 'their' legal systems make, or should make, concessions to diversity (Griffiths 1986: 7–8).

Even in Euro-American legal systems, particularly the European settler colonial states, there are instances of concessions to local socio-legal realities. The Canadian accommodations to First Nations people are one example; Australians are experimenting with alternative dispute resolution mechanisms drawing on indigenous Australian legal precepts. Under current constitutional arrangements in the UK different state laws operate in England, Wales, Scotland and Northern Ireland. This could be regarded as a British model of 'asymmetrical federalism' although that term is not generally used. It is arguable that the currently fervid promotion of a post-imperial and rather sclerotic notion of 'Britishness' (a form of British nationalism) by government ministers and their appointed quangos is meant to mask the increasing legal divergence among the UK's national components. The effects of European law are another example of legal pluralism in British law, and here we see a series of backlashes against too much Euro-interference. This may partly be put down to the fact that EU law asserts a supremacy over British law, as the reception of 'European law' in the British Isles is otherwise centuries old. The EU's neo-imperial legal order has thus constantly to be sensitive to carefully reconciling its inherent legal plurality, however much this too is infected by methodological nationalism.

The Williams Affair

The Rushdie Affair (1989) which erupted in response to the publication of the novel the *Satanic Verses* was one of the first occasions where Muslim concern came onto the public scene in post-war Britain.[6] The Archbishop of Canterbury's speech of 7 February 2008 came after a series of events which have kept the Muslim presence in the public frame since the Rushdie Affair. Dr Williams set out some of his thoughts regarding 'what might be entailed in crafting a just and constructive relationship between Islamic law and the statutory law of the United Kingdom', although he was careful to say that the relevance of his argument was not restricted to Muslims, but more generally to people with a religious conviction. However, he also noted, 'Among the manifold anxieties that haunt the discussion of the place of Muslims in British society, one of the strongest, reinforced from time to time by the sensational reporting of opinion polls, is that Muslim communities in this country seek the freedom to live under sharia law.' Concerns among Muslims were therefore at the heart of Dr Williams' speech.

Responding to this felt desire he suggested that there were two possible levels at which a new relationship could be recast. At one level he asked whether there should be (and clearly he thinks that there should be) a 'higher level of attention to religious identity and communal rights in the practice of law'. At another level he foresaw 'something like a delegation of certain legal functions to the religious courts of a community'. Dr Williams envisaged a 'much enhanced and quite sophisticated version' of the Islamic Shari'a Council, with 'increased resource and a high degree of community recognition'. For Dr Williams this system of 'supplementary jurisdiction' would include the fields of marital law, financial transactions and authorized structures of mediation and conflict resolution. He drew upon the concept of 'transformative accommodation' proposed by the Canadian Jewish scholar, Ayelet Shachar (2001), as the core academic basis for his own thoughts on the interaction between religious and state dispute resolution mechanisms.

Shachar's is a very compelling discussion of the problem of multicultural societies in which religious groups, which she refers to as *nomoi* or 'identity' groups, share a comprehensive world view which extends to creating a law for the community which differs from that encoded in state law. Although her discussion is mainly restricted to religious groups, the *nomoi* group could be any identity group organized along ethnic, racial, tribal or national-origin lines. Identifying a lack of discussion in the literature on multicultural societies on the 'rougher business' of the institutional allocation of power and structural design, she proposes a concept

6 On the response by the official courts to the claim by some Muslims that the blasphemy law be applied in this case see *R v Chief Metropolitan Stipendiary Magistrate, ex p. Choudhury* [1991] 1 All ER 306 eventually leading to a challenge at Strasbourg, *Choudhury v UK*, Appl. no. 17439/90 (1991) *Human Rights Law Journal* 172, Eur. Comm. H.R.

of 'multicultural jurisdictions'. Crucial to this is the allocation of sub-matters (for example, immigration, family, criminal) to the jurisdiction of *nomoi* groups, with the proviso that neither the *nomoi* group nor the state would enjoy a monopoly of decision-making over the allocated matters. Instead, she foresees cooperation and competition among state and community decision-makers so that both have to work harder to win the support of their constituents. Although an allocation of power between the two realms of law would have to be decided beforehand to prevent opt outs at the slightest opportunity, she also advocates the possibility of selective exit by individuals where remedies are not being provided to them. A primary advantage Shachar foresees in her proposals is that identity groups would not thereby have to retreat into a 'reactive culturalism' because of the threat of assimilation into the dominant culture, while those made vulnerable by the impact of the decisions of the groups' leaders could also be protected.

Drawing closely on Shachar's argument, Dr Williams advocated that litigants be offered a choice of forum as between communal or state legal mechanisms. In the process both agencies would be transformed into recognizing their own limits since the former jurisdiction would have to take into account 'the risks of alienating its own people by inflexible and over-restrictive applications of traditional law', while the latter would need to 'weigh the possible consequences of ghettoizing and effectively disenfranchizing a minority, at real cost to overall social cohesion and creativity'. As in the case of shared responsibility in education,[7] such competition for loyalty could ensure that groups with 'serious and profound conviction are not systematically faced with the stark alternatives of cultural loyalty or state loyalty'.

In order to achieve this, Dr Williams argued, there was a need to rethink the rule and role of law according to which citizenship is premised on a monopolistic abstract legal universality in which individuals live under a rights-based culture 'irrespective of the custom and conscience of those groups which concretely compose a plural modern society'. Rather, in his view, the Enlightenment achievement needs to be recast in a negative way, as a guarantee of equal accountability and access, whereby any human participant is protected against the loss of certain elementary liberties of self-determination and guaranteed the freedom to demand reasons from others for actions and policies which infringe that self-determination. This way of reconceptualizing the rule of law would honour 'what in the human constitution is not captured by any one form of corporate belonging or any particular history, even though the human constitution never exists without those other determinations'.

Besides addressing the perceived dilution of Enlightenment achievements, Dr Williams dealt with two other possible objections to his proposal. The first

7 English education law recognizes denominational schools which can operate under different structures reflecting different levels of state support and intervention. Around a third of all schools within the state maintained sector in England have a religious character (Department for Children Schools and Families 2007: 3).

involves the question of vexatious appeal to religious scruple, to which his response is to have a method of separating those claims where the 'potential conflict is real, legally and religiously serious' from those which are 'grounded in either nuisance or ignorance'. The second possible problem with the recognition of 'supplementary jurisdiction' could be the reinforcing in minority communities of repressive and retrograde elements, 'with particularly serious consequences for the role and liberties of women'. He gave the examples of inheritance for widows and apostasy in Islamic law. In such cases he felt that a legal system could not allow the taking away of rights and liberties that individuals were allowed to enjoy or claim as citizens, and so religious courts could not be given a final say. There were, in other words, to be 'no blank cheques'.

Perhaps predictably, the reaction against this speech was immediate and forceful among different sections of society and exposed a range of ideological positions held by those who fear a threat to the clasp by which Christianity is held in place in the constitutional system ('Britain is a Christian country'); those who fear that religion is rearing its ugly head in a time when secular beliefs are making rapid advances within society at large, and within the official legal framework; and those who suspected ulterior motives behind the speech. Among some other minority communities there is a palpable sense that, once again, Muslims are dominating the public agenda while some Muslims also feel that the Archbishop's position did not reflect theirs. Directed as the speech was to the official legal system's need to adapt to changing social realities, many of the governing assumptions about the system of law came to the surface in response to it. There was vociferous defence of the prevailing order (whether properly regarded as secular or Christian). The 'fact' that only one law could and should govern Britain's population was expressed most loudly in the aftermath of Dr Williams' speech. Meanwhile, a number of moderate voices also expressed themselves as not entirely dismissing Dr Williams' suggestions, and this was particularly notable among the published views of legal professionals to whom the speech had, after all, been addressed (Ballantyne 2008, Botsford 2008, Dyke 2008, Smith 2008, Turner 2008).

The Williams Affair was not the first occasion during which the operation of shari'a had been discussed. For the better part of the post-war period which has seen significant Muslim settlement in Britain, campaigns for recognition of rules of shari'a in family matters have taken a rather low profile, although they have not disappeared from the agenda altogether. Consistent rejection by state officials of the prospect of shari'a being recognized has not excluded, but has probably reinforced, the quietistic reconstruction of *angrezi shariat* as a socio-religious legal phenomenon (Pearl and Menski 1998). The existence of officially unregulated so-called 'shari'a councils' had been coming under scrutiny in the months preceding the Archbishop's intervention (Shah 2007).[8] Such councils are frequently referred

8 Lively debates among Muslims have been taking place in various fora, a sampling of which can be seen on the Channel 4 series *Sharia TV*.

to as 'Muslim courts' but, although official courts and tribunals have been aware of their operation, their decisions are not given official sanction.

Once Dr Williams had taken the proverbial bull by the horns, writers who had not yet traversed the territory of shari'a to any significant extent began to take notice of the need to enter the arena. For instance, the leading sociologist Tariq Modood (2005) has been discussing the struggles for recognition by Muslims within the context of official British multiculturalism, inter alia, under the anti-discrimination law, the racial hatred laws, more visible recognition within the census figures and state recognition of Muslim denominational schools. However, Modood had rarely addressed the shari'a issue, giving the impression that it was of negligible concern among Muslims, but has since also responded to Dr Williams' speech and incorporated it within his concept of 'multicultural citizenship' (Modood 2008). Perhaps more significantly, the Lord Chief Justice of England and Wales, Lord Phillips, having chaired the Archbishop's speech, entered the discussion himself, taking a position sympathetic to the Archbishop's in a lecture at the East London Muslim Centre on 3 July 2008. While there is some space which separates Dr Williams' position and Lord Phillips', the fact that a senior judge, soon to take the position of the President of the UK's newly created Supreme Court, came out in support of recognizing a supplementary jurisdiction for Muslims, was probably unparalleled among the European judiciary.

Excess *Mirchi* in the *Masala* of Law?

The legal adaptation of European societies to the reality of the encounter between North and South occasioned by large-scale and continuing immigration from outside Europe is an ongoing process, with the shari'a debate only the latest in a long list of struggles for what Modood (2005) describes as 'multicultural citizenship'. Ostensibly superficial interpretations of the creolization of British society appear to stop at admiration for the diversification of food culture, markedly celebrated in the elevation of chicken tikka masala to a 'national' dish. The food metaphor can usefully be kept in view here since the kind of creolization of law we are dealing with may well turn out to be too spicy or be thought to have too much *mirchi* (chilli) added to it. What was sometimes called the 'saris, steel bands and samosas' approach to multiculturalism, while representing a minimalist concession to ethnic plurality, did not expect or demand equitable treatment on the part of the ethnic majority. Although even this limited concept is now in question under the new banner of promoting a cohesive concept of Britishness, a number of counter-trends already set in motion must be reckoned with.

British laws have for some time made minor concessions to minority communities. Since the mid-1970s a statutory exemption has been made to Sikhs who wish to be exempt from wearing crash helmets while riding motorcycles and several other individual examples can be mentioned, including some specific concessions applicable to Muslims in legislation and case law (Menski 2008). This methodology of responding to the individual facts and circumstances of cases and the need for exemptions in general laws seems to have worked up to a point, and is a further indication that a total prescription of legal uniformity is never desirable in a plural society. Shachar (2001) speaks of a specific manifestation of this model as 'temporal accommodation' whereby time bound (related to life cycle events) and issue specific measures are accepted officially as being governed by a group's traditions. Shachar's (2001: 101) criticism of such a model of accommodation is that the costs and efforts of establishing a claim for validity falls 'upon the vulnerable group members who must negotiate their rights on a case-to-case basis, and often against ingrained prejudices and suspicions regarding their *nomoi* groups' traditions'. In the British case, too, such accommodation appears to have operated largely unsystematically and without a more comprehensive constitutional commitment to build in the legal requirements of different communities and individuals in an ethnically plural society.

Sooner or later, the larger question about a paradigmatically different approach appears to present itself. Rather than insisting on the historically fairly recent model of legal equality within which some exceptions are made, often through a happenstance combination of circumstances, should we instead be talking of a generalized right to be different? There is no such right in any international human rights instrument although, as Ballard (see Chapter 16) argues, that may well reflect the constrained nature of human rights lawmaking. But this issue of a right to be different and to have that difference respected in law appears to be the critical issue here and is underlined by the Archbishop's references to plurality and pluralism. It goes far beyond the question of principles and rules of shari'a being recognized in British law. The issue is relevant not only for Muslims but for everyone, since everyone is different from the 'other'. Viewed in this light, the Archbishop provokes us into thinking more deeply about the general implications of living in a plural society from a legal perspective. And it is not that there are no existing models on which to draw and learn from.

In my view the Archbishop rightly views shari'a – literally the path or way to the source of water – as a methodology of arriving at a just answer to legal problems, and not simply a set of rules that can be applied mechanically. As he states:

> Thus, in contrast to what is sometimes assumed, we do not simply have a standoff between two rival legal systems when we discuss Islamic and British law. On the one hand, sharia depends for its legitimacy not on any human decision, not on votes or preferences, but on the conviction that it represents the mind of God; on the other, it is to some extent unfinished business so far as codified and precise provisions are concerned. To recognise sharia is to recognise a method of jurisprudence governed by revealed texts rather than a single system.

The content of the shari'a is thus widely contested and internally plural albeit with many historical and contemporary trends. Some of those contemporary trends indicate a worrying reliance on extremist interpretations, thus giving rise to some troubling scenes occasionally represented in the media. But there is rarely one single right answer to any situation.

Typecasting Muslim judicial decision-making as '*kadijustiz*', to repeat the phrase used by Max Weber (1954: 351),[9] later adapted by Anglo-American judges to stereotype it as a rather arbitrary, irrational system of dispute processing under trees,[10] is to ignore the complex hybridity that enters into Muslim decision-making. Studies on contemporary decision-making by judges in Muslim contexts by scholars such as Lawrence Rosen (1989, 2000 on Morocco), Karim Wazir Jahan (1992, on Malaysia), Lynn Welchman (2000, on Palestine) and Susan Hirsch (1994, in Kenya, where Muslims are a minority), as well as a number of historical studies (Peirce 2003, Hasan 2004), reveal a number of important facets of this kind of judging activity.

First, judges are required to be as alive to the socio-legal reality of the disputants as to the Islamic doctrines in which they have been schooled. Second, this involves their taking into account not just the *fiqh* jurisprudence as developed by scholars over time but also the socio-cultural norms by which disputants live. As Welchman (2000: 6) remarks in her book on the West Bank, 'Customary rules frequently constitute a stronger force than "law", particularly over matters involving women and the family.' Of course Muslim dispute resolvers will have their own assessment about what is right and wrong, as do judges in official British legal systems, and judges everywhere. Third, it is notable that the customer base of Muslim courts, including shari'a councils in Britain (Shah-Kazemi 2001; Bano 2007; Keshavjee 2007), substantially consists of women, while judges are of course men. No doubt this introduces its own gender-laden dynamic. But it is difficult to conceive of any courts, Muslim or otherwise, changing social structures by themselves; the best that they can achieve is to help make the life conditions of people who come before them more tolerable.

Maleiha Malik, whose work was cited by the Archbishop, has written about the Discrimination Law Review exercise initiated by the government (Malik 2007). One of the stated aims of the review is to 'tackle disadvantage' of the structural sort but, having studied the details of the proposals, Malik finds that it is unlikely to be able to tackle systematic disadvantage and she argues that perhaps it is, after all, unrealistic for official law to be able to do so. This is a good illustration of how the liberating potential of law is often exaggerated, but also reminds us how such unrealism can be projected onto others when they fail to live up to our already bloated claims of what law can achieve. Therefore, Muslim courts, or our home-grown version, the 'shari'a councils', are probably as ill placed fully to live up to the concerns expressed in relation to their ability to tackle patriarchal social

9 The term may not be Max Weber's however, but may have been coined by R. Schmidt in 1908 – see Manzoor (2000).

10 *Metropolitan Properties Co Ltd v Purdy* [1940] 1 All ER 188, per Lord Goddard CJ; *Terminiello v Chicago* 337 U.S. 1, 11 (1949), per Frankfurter J dissenting.

structures. The best we may realistically expect of them is that they alleviate their worst effects and then throw the rest back on to the socio-legal sphere to right its own wrongs. This is not to argue against judicial activism, which I favour, but to acknowledge that any such activism is restrained by socio-legal realism.

Shari'a as a Part of English law?

Dr Williams does not restrict his proposals to a shari'a council being officially recognized, but also envisages that official fora accommodate Muslim legal requirements. At least that is what appears to be subsumed under his plea for 'a higher level of attention to religious identity and communal rights in the practice of the law'. How could the official courts consider and incorporate issues of Muslim law? As may be expected, the present picture is considerably mixed. In some cases Islam is seen and treated as the foreign 'other', or as Glenn (2003: 99) would say, a source of 'distant law'. Indeed, in one case involving a Muslim *nikah* celebrated in London, the High Court judge referred to it as a marriage according to a *foreign religion*, thus highlighting that some judges still do not see Islam as being part of the British way of life.[11] However, while steadfastly refusing to treat the London *nikah* as legally valid for English law purposes, the judge went on to apply the 'presumption of marriage' principle to validate this quite long-standing union, also thereby paving the way to awarding remedies to the divorcee woman. Interestingly, English judges have recently seen the utility of using the presumption of marriage in a series of ethnic minority cases, deriving the principle from Scottish law. However, the Scottish Parliament, without much debate, has now, through Section 3 of the Family Law (Scotland) Act 2006, disallowed courts from using the principle, and it is to be speculated what the Westminster Parliament's move will be.[12] It has not gone unnoticed that Muslim and other ethnic minority marriages are recognized much more easily in circumstances which entail penalties. Thus for the purposes of the Forced Marriage (Civil Protection) Act 2007 a marriage is defined as 'any religious or civil ceremony of marriage (whether or not legally binding)' (Section 16). This is reflective of an underlying tendency to view Muslims and other minority family arrangements negatively, and this approach will need to be recalibrated in a much more balanced manner.

11 *A.M. v A.M.* [2001] 2 FLR 6.

12 Werner Menski recently acted as an expert witness in a case involving a transnational telephone marriage of a man with severe impairment of intellectual functioning and autism. Although it was valid under Muslim law and under Bangladeshi law, as attested by Menski's report, the Court of Appeal judges argued on various grounds that English law principles dictated that the marriage should be held not valid. The man was even prevented from going abroad to continue his married life, see *City of Westminster Social & Community Services Department v IC (a protected party, by his litigation friend the Official Solicitor) and another* [2008] EWCA Civ 198.

Another paradigmatic illustration of what is now being widely felt to be the courts' seeming reluctance to enter into the religious sphere is found in a bank loan dispute decided by the English Court of Appeal. In this case, *Shamil Bank*, the choice of court in the loan contract was an English court, but the clause stipulating the law to govern the contract referred to the 'glorious shari'a'.[13] Despite the submission of expert evidence on both sides explaining the Islamic rules on banking and the taking of interest, the Court of Appeal decided the matter solely on the basis of English law. Among the reasons given were that Islamic rules were really only religious principles and far too imprecise to be applied, while the international rules applicable to contracts envisaged only the law of a particular state legal system. This view of shari'a as being couched in general principles is not unknown among experts of Islamic law (Vikør 2005: 1–2), and was also reflected in the Archbishop's remarks about shari'a being an 'unfinished business', particularly when the principles of Muslim law are contended to apply to situations, like bank loans, which call for fresh answers to problems arising in contemporary circumstances. We are therefore bound to find much 'unfinished business' in such contexts, but is this open texture a ground for saying that we ought simply to apply the better-known principles and rules of English law? It remains to be seen how the British courts get actively involved in deciding about their own approach to particular questions of shari'a, rather than standing back and fudging issues in the manner demonstrated in *Shamil Bank*, or effectively applying shari'a rules without saying as much, as the *nikah* case above demonstrates.

One particular and more obvious way in which the courts will face continued pressure for so doing is when arguments are made under Article 9 of the ECHR. In the much cited *Shabina Begum* case,[14] the English courts were faced with the dilemma of not only deciding the correctness of a school's refusal to allow the wearing of a *jilbab* by the applicant schoolgirl, but also indirectly to decide whether such dress was required by Islam. It may be relevant, although the Court of Appeal was subsequently overturned by the Lords in the outcome of the case, that two judges (Brooke and Scott Baker LJJ) said that, unlike Turkey, the United Kingdom is not a secular state.[15] This appears to be a subtle indication that there is some judicial willingness not to distance questions of religion from judicial oversight although, at present, that might be too sanguine a view of judicial (non-)activism.[16]

13 *Shamil Bank of Bahrain EC v Beximco Pharmaceuticals* Ltd (No.1) [2004] 1 WLR 1784.

14 *R (on the application of Begum (Shabina) v Denbigh High School Governors* [2005] 2 All ER 396, HL. See the chapters by Sandberg and Knights in this volume for more on this case.

15 *R. (on the application of Begum (Shabina)) v Denbigh High School Governors* [2005] 1 WLR 3372, CA, at paras. 73 and 94 respectively.

16 See the chapters by Sandberg and Knights in this volume for critiques of judicial distancing from religious questions.

It is possible to argue that there is wisdom in the Archbishop's position because allowing courts greater oversight of shari'a councils in particular could provide the state legal system with a control mechanism over their activities. This was done in Ontario after it was realized that Muslim bodies too would be using the existing arbitration mechanisms to allow official legal force to be given to their awards; Jews and Catholics had been doing so for some time already. New legislation demanding procedural and human rights guarantees was passed and Muslim bodies not achieving compliance with this legislation would simply not be recognized in official terms (Bakht 2006, see also Bader, this volume). But such attempts at control of Muslim arbitrations or to apply Muslim law rules in official courts will not necessarily be trouble free. In the UK, the Arbitration Act of 1996 offers a perfectly operable system and the Jewish Beth Din have been using this mechanism for decades, but no reported case of a Muslim arbitration can be found as having been settled under its auspices although certain Muslim bodies are gearing up to use this legislation effectively, while Lord Phillips, in his speech of July 2008, certainly seemed to favour this option.

In India, some *ulema* have for decades been irritated at interventions by official lawmakers and courts in questions of Muslim law, and may even prefer them to stay out of decision-making in Muslim matters altogether. Maintenance of this position purportedly to protect a group's authentic interest, termed by Shachar as a form of 'reactive culturalism', is hardly realistic since states would, and arguably should, want to ensure that certain controls and checks are applied. Such control may also be useful in other senses. In the British case, it could lift *angrezi shariat* out of its confinement to the unofficial sphere and quicken its development by allowing British courts to also have a say in its shaping. In other words, it could make *shariat* more *angrezi*, partly by stimulating the kind of 'transformative accommodation' to which Shachar and Dr Williams refer. This might also act as a signal to other European countries, assuming they do not consider the concessions to Muslims in Britain to have gone far enough already. Expert European legal commentators have not welcomed the possibility of some type of personal law system being implemented (Ferrari 2000: 5, Rohe 2006: 61).

It is not clear whom the Archbishop consulted prior to making his views public; no Muslim organization appears to have made a well-argued case for official recognition. There have been general demands for the recognition of shari'a particularly in family matters previously and such demands have resurfaced from time to time or appear in survey evidence. But this is far from making a good argument for why shari'a should be recognized officially and what the mechanisms of any such recognition should be. It may well be that some Muslim organizations and clerics, as in India, do not want to see shari'a rules and bodies being controlled by the state too closely. They may see the British state as being far too hostile and untrustworthy in this respect anyway, particularly in the tense post-9/11 climate. The relative public silence may also reflect the narrowness of their own training and outlook, engendered though the barrenness of the contemporary curricula in madrassas. Olivier Roy (2008) has recently suggested that, with the extension of the secular educational sphere in South Asian Muslim countries (even though drastically undernourished in Pakistan), madrassas have adopted very narrowly *fiqh*-focused curricula whereas in times past they would have a much more holistic approach to education (see also Dalrymple 2005). The question of education is, however, of far wider significance.

Educational Priorities

Beyond the practical question of dispute solving and integrating shari'a within the framework of officially sanctioned legal practice there are some conceptual hurdles which would first need to be overcome. Without addressing this backdrop the ground upon which the re-adaptation of legal practices is to take place would remain unprepared. The concept of legal pluralism is particularly helpful in attenuating the ideological blockages of methodological nationalism. The Archbishop did not actually use the phrase 'legal pluralism' but he clearly referred to several senses of the word 'pluralism' and certainly I would classify him as a legal pluralist. At one level, legal pluralism can be seen as the presence of more than one legal order in a social field (Moore 1978, Griffiths 1986). But it has received more complex definitions including a compelling one by Menski (2006) who asks us to think about law as an inherently plural and dynamic phenomenon, not susceptible to exhaustive definition by any one of the positivist, natural law, or sociological methods, but really needing a combination of all approaches to be able to 'see' how it works. This methodological pluralism would also help us to remain critical of the official legal mechanisms as well as the shari'a councils' engagement with Muslim communities.

Legal pluralism brings out some of the most troubling and crucial challenges which face legal systems today, but which lie buried beneath a hubristic glorification of unification through law and the prioritization of nation-state laws (for example, Britain), national-state laws (for example, Scotland), or indeed inter-state laws, at the expense of allegedly lesser forms of social organization. We still shy away from teaching legal pluralism in jurisprudence courses in British universities because, possibly, we have acquired our own 'legal socialization' (Kourilsky-Augeven 2007), in types of jurisprudential thought which assume a homogenous national social whole as the only relevant form of social organization with any legal power.

It is not therefore enough for us to recognize ourselves simply as sexist or classist legal ideologues, but also as representing a particular nationalist perspective. We are increasingly therefore called upon to stand back, recognize and analyse the nation as a particularistic 'imagined community' (Anderson 1983) and thereby recognize that it cannot represent itself, nor should it be represented as, offering a universalistic claim to truth or justice, often now hiding behind liberal discourse which elevates individual autonomy and treats all other bonds as if they were stapled on by rational choice. According to this view, the bonds of kinship and religion would not be chosen by rational thinking individuals as if the worship of individual autonomy can liberate us from the oppression of kinship and religion. Dr Williams' criticism of such positions is quite compelling.[17]

Jurisprudence, the home of legal theory in British law schools, however, appears to have so far failed to lift the veil of nationalism and incorporate legal pluralism that would account for 'other' laws, or the laws of the non-national other. But this is changing slowly as postmodernist writing increasingly looks back at the historical role of nationalist thinking in law. Roger Cotterrell (2008a) has argued that the currently revered fathers of jurisprudence assume a homogenous, undifferentiated body of citizens, and so disregard or fail to account for the presence of the other in our midst. Implicitly, they assume also that this is a body of equal nationals within a nation with legal autonomy. As Moore (1978) tells us, it is more advisable to conceive of state law as a 'semi-autonomous social field', whose 'limited degree of control and predictability is daily inflated in the folk models of lawyers and politicians all over the world' (Moore 1978: 2).

Recently, Cotterrell has been writing about notions of community as intermediate entities between nations and individuals, and indeed now writes about transnational communities and the law (Cotterrell 2008b) whose legal role we are ill placed to analyse because of our methodologically nationalist legal inheritance. The Archbishop's concern also rightly focuses on how we can account for those *nomoi* groups who have little legitimation in the legal theoreticians' pages or in the law of the nation. Historically such groups have been subdued by the nation, and it continues to fight them now with discourses of social inclusion and community cohesion, which arise a priori, imagined and bound to be resisted by various means. Besides such discourses there is the actual practice of extremely hostile immigration and other controls.

Silvio Ferrari (2000: 6) has argued in a book on Islam and European legal systems that we ought to be teaching about the laws of religions in universities. While this was an allusion to the increasing secularity in legal education nowadays, with religion at best a marginal add-on, Ferrari's point was also that increasing knowledge about religious laws would have made us more receptive to the recently felt legal needs of Muslims of immigrant origin living in Europe. It is perhaps no coincidence therefore that the author of the speech under discussion here is a scholarly priest, already highly sensitized to the needs of the religious conscience in humans.

Besides the teaching of religion and law the question of Islamic law teaching might also have to be considered. We do not teach Islamic law in British universities to any appreciable degree, particularly within law curricula. SOAS and Warwick University (after an initiative by Prof. Shaheen Ali) are among the only places where Islamic law is offered as part of an undergraduate curriculum within a law department. Much more energy is spent discussing *hijabs*, *niqabs* and *jilbabs* and

---

17 Ballard also critiques this methodological individualism in his chapter in this volume.

whether Muslim women should or should not be allowed to wear them, but there does not yet appear to be appropriate respect for the fact that Islamic law is a well-established field, older than the common law (which arguably draws upon some of the methodology of Muslim law, Glenn 2007: 227–9), with its own global claims. If the common law's claim to respectability rests on its pragmatism, Muslim law offers the ideal of *adil* or *insaaf* (justice) as a core value (Darling 2008).

It is not that the demand for studying Islamic law is not there. I have (predominantly Muslim) students appearing every year who want to research some topic connected to it within the space allowed to them in the curriculum through dissertations or theses. However, not having had any grounding in Muslim legal history, the principles of Muslim law or indeed exposure to any non-Euro-centred comparative law, few such students are well placed to write on this kind of subject matter. While one may concede that there is some intensity of discussion on Islamic banking that may be explained by its obvious economic attractions, and does not extend to detailed coverage of other areas. Meanwhile, as teachers, we tend to find it easier to communicate the misogynistic elements of Muslim law, to be inevitably out-trumped by the superior claims of modern, secular, individualistic and methodologically nationalist, human rights perspectives.

Conclusion

Currently, we appear to be in a strange and largely unexplored landscape, with senior religious figures and other state officers, as well as a number of academics and legal practitioners, discussing the legal implications of the large-scale Muslim presence in Britain. There is deep unease about the matters being raised, let alone about what directions official legal systems should be taking to constructively respond to the question of shari'a. It is probable that Dr Williams' foray into the shari'a debate will have lasting implications, and it may possibly be regarded as part of a longer-term strategy of reorienting the inter-relationship of Islamic law and British legal systems. It can only be a long-term strategy since contemporary conditions appear to coalesce around the problem of legal nationalism and these will not be easily shaken off, even though it may be easy enough to argue academically for seeing things from different viewpoints. However, the future looks interesting.

References

Anderson, B. 1983. *Imagined Communities, Reflections on the Origin and Spread of Nationalism*. London: Verso.

Bakht, N. 2006. Were Muslim Barbarians Really Knocking on the Gates of Ontario? The Religious Arbitration Controversy – Another Perspective. *Ottawa Law Review 40th Anniversary Volume*, 67–82.

Ballantyne, W. 2008. Sharia, Setting Straight. *Counsel*, April, 6.

Ballard, Roger. 1996. Islam and the Construction of Europe. In *Muslims in the Margin*, edited by W.A.R. Shahid and P.S. Koningveld. Kampen: Kok Pharos, 15–51.

Bano, S. 2007. Muslim Family Justice and Human Rights: The Experience of British Muslim Women. *Journal of Comparative Law*, 1(4), 1–29.

Botsford, P. 2008. Religious Courts, Sharia Unveiled. *Law Society Gazette*, 28 February 2008.

Burton, Sir Richard F. 1894. *The Book of the Thousand and One Nights*. London: Nichols & Co.

Cotterrell, R. 2008a. The Struggle for Law, Some Dilemmas of Cultural Legality. Paper delivered at the Second International Journal of Law in Context Annual Lecture, Georgetown University, Washington, DC, 17 January 2008.

— 2008b. Transnational Communities and the Concept of Law. *Ratio Juris*, 21(1), 1–18.

Dalrymple, W. 2005. Inside the Madrasas. *New York Review of Books*, 1 December 2005, 16–20.

Darling, L. 2008. Islamic Empires, the Ottoman Empire and the Circle of Justice. In *Constitutional Politics in the Middle East with Special Reference to Turkey, Iraq, Iran and Afghanistan*, edited by Saïd Amir Arjomand. Oxford and Portland, OR: Hart, 11–32.

Department for Children Schools and Families. 2007. *Faith in the System: The Role of Schools with a Religious Character in English Education and Society*. Nottingham: DCSF Publications.

Dupret, Baudouin, Maurtis Berger and Laila al-Zwaini (eds). 1999. *Legal Pluralism in the Arab World*. The Hague: Kluwer Law International.

Dyke, T. 2008. Sense on Sharia. *Prospect Magazine*, 143, February <http://www.prospect-magazine.co.uk/article_details.php?id=10038>.

Edelman, M. 1994. *Courts, Politics, and Culture in Israel*. Charlottesville and London, University Press of Virginia.

Ferrari, S. 2000. Introduction. In *Islam and European Legal Systems*, edited by S. Ferrari and A. Bradney. Aldershot: Ashgate, 1–9.

Friedman, F. 1996. *The Bosnian Muslims*. Boulder, CO: Westview Press.

Glenn, H.P. 2003. The Nationalist Heritage. In *Comparative Legal Studies: Traditions and Transitions*, edited by Pierre Legrand and Roderick Munday. Cambridge: Cambridge University Press, 76–99.

— 2007. *Legal Traditions of the World*. 3rd edition. Oxford: Oxford University Press.

Griffiths, J. 1986. What is Legal Pluralism? *Journal of Legal Pluralism and Unofficial Law*, 24, 1–56.

Hasan, F. 2004. *State and Locality in Mughal India: Power Relations in Western India, 1572–1730*. Cambridge: Cambridge University Press.

Hausmaninger, H. 2000. *The Austrian Legal System*. 2nd edition. Vienna/Manz/ The Hague: Kluwer Law International.

Hertogh, M. 2004. A 'European' Conception of Legal Consciousness: Rediscovering Eugen Ehrlich. *Journal of Law and Society*, 31(4), 457–81.

Hirsch, S.F. 1994. *Kadhi's Courts as Complex Sites of Resistance: The State, Islam and Gender in Postcolonial Kenya*. London: Routledge.

Hooker, M.B. 1975. *Legal Pluralism: An Introduction to Colonial and Neo-colonial Laws*. Oxford: Clarendon Press.

Keshavjee, M. 2007. Alternative Dispute Resolution in a Diasporic Muslim Community. In *Law and Ethnic Plurality: Socio-legal Perspectives*, edited by P. Shah. Leiden: Martinus Nijhoff, 145–75.

Kourilsky-Augeven, C. 2007. Legal Socialisation: From Compliance to Familiarisation through Permeation. *European Journal of Legal Studies*, 1(1). Available at: <http://www.ejls.eu/index.php?mode=presentanddisplayissue=2007-04> [accessed 22 October 2008].

Likhovski, A. 2003. Czernowitz, Lincoln, Jerusalem, and the Comparative History of American Jurisprudence. *Theoretical Inquiries in Law*, 4, 621–57.

Malik, M. 2007. 'Modernising Discrimination Law': Proposals for a Single Equality Act for Great Britain. *International Journal of Discrimination and the Law*, 9, 73–94.

Mallat, C. 2007. *Introduction to Middle Eastern Law*. Oxford: Oxford University Press.

Manzoor, S.P. 2000. Legal Rationality vs. Arbitrary Judgement: Re-examining the Tradition of Islamic Law. *Muslim World Book Review*, 21(1), 3–12.

Menski, W. 2006. *Comparative Law in a Global Context. The Legal Systems of Asia and Africa*. 2nd edition. Cambridge: Cambridge University Press.

— 2008. Law, Religion and Culture in Multicultural Britain. In *Religion and Law in Multicultural Societies*, edited by Rubya Mehdi et al. Copenhagen: DJØF Publishing, 37–51.

Modood, T. 2005. *Multicultural Politics: Racism, Ethnicity and Muslims in Britain*. Edinburgh: Edinburgh University Press.

— 2008. Multicultural Citizenship and the Anti-sharia Storm. *Open Democracy*. Available at <http://www.opendemocracy.net/article/faith_ideas/europe_islam/anti_sharia_storm> [accessed 23 October 2008].

Moore, S.F. 1978. *Law as Process*. London: Routledge and Keegan Paul.

Özkırımlı, U. 2000. Theories of Nationalism: A Critical Introduction. Basingstoke: Macmillan.

Pearl, David and Werner F. Menski. 1998. *Muslim Family Law*. London: Sweet and Maxwell.

Peirce, L. 2003. *Morality Tales: Law and Gender in the Ottoman Court of Aintab*. Berkeley: University of California Press.

Pinson, M. 1993. The Muslims of Bosnia-Herzegovina under Austro-Hungarian Rule, 1878–1918. In *The Muslims of Bosnia-Herzegovina*, edited by Mark Pinson. Cambridge, MA: Centre for Middle Eastern Studies/Harvard University Press, 84–128.

Ramadan, T. 2008. Discussion on 'Can Moral or Religious Obligation ever Justify the Use of Force Inadmissible under Secular Law?' Temple Church, London, 19 May 2008.

Rohe, M. 2006. The Migration and Settlement of Muslims: the Challenges for European Legal Systems. In *Migration, Diasporas and Legal Systems in Europe*, edited by Prakash Shah and Werner F. Menski. London: Routledge-Cavendish, 57–72.

Rosen, L. 1989. *The Anthropology of Justice: Law as Culture in Islamic Society*. Cambridge: Cambridge University Press.

— 2000. *The Justice of Islam*. Oxford: Oxford University Press.

Roy, O. 2008. Secularization and Fundamentalism: Two Faces of the Same Coin? Lecture at City University, London, 16 January 2008.

Schmied, M. and Wieshaider, W. 2004. Islam and the European Union: the Austrian way. In *Islam and the European Union*, edited by R. Potz and W. Wieshaider. Leuven: Peeters, 199–217.

Shachar, Ayelet. 2001. *Multicultural Jurisdictions: Cultural Differences and Women's Rights*. Cambridge, UK, New York: Cambridge University Press.

Shah, P. 2007. Between God and the Sultana? Legal Pluralism in the British Muslim Diaspora. Paper for conference on Sharia as Discourse, University of Copenhagen, 20–22 March 2007.

Shah-Kazemi, S.N. 2001. *Untying the Knot: Muslim Women, Divorce and the Shariah*. London: Nuffield Foundation.

Smith, R. 2008. Caesar's Palace, not Lambeth's. *New Law Journal*, 158(7308), 229.

Tsitselkis, K. 2004. Muslims in Greece. In *Islam and the European Union*, edited by R. Potz and W. Wieshaider. Leuven: Peeters, 79–107.

Turner, A. 2008. Has the Archbishop Lost the Plot? *Justice of the Peace*, 172, 92.

Vikør, K S. 2005. *Between God and the Sultan: A History of Islamic Law*. London: Hurst and Co.

Wazir Jahan, K. 1992. *Women and Culture, Between Malay Adat and Islam*. Boulder, CO: Westview.

Weber, M. 1954. *Max Weber on Law, Economy and Society*. New York: Simon and Schuster.

Welchman, L. 2000. *Beyond the Code, Muslim Family Law and the Shari'a Judiciary in the Palestinian West Bank*. The Hague/Boston: Kluwer Law International.

Williams, R., The Rt. Rev. 2008. Civil and Religious Law in England: A Religious Perspective. Speech at the Royal Courts of Justice, 7 February 2008. Available at: <http//www.archbishopofcanterbury.org/1575> [accessed 22 October 2008].

Wimmer, A. and N. Glick Schiller. 2002. Methodological Nationalism and Beyond: Nation-state Building, Migration and the Social Sciences. *Global Networks*, 2(4), 301–34.

Chapter 6
Shari'a in a European Context

Mathias Rohe

Introduction

Shari'a has entered European parliaments, administrations and courts. In several European states legislation on Islamic norms concerning clothing, slaughtering and family law practices has recently been passed or is on the way. Administrations have to deal with the religious or political convictions of Muslims applying for citizenship, and courts are every day applying foreign law in civil law matters according to the provisions of private international law. In a hopefully singular case in 2007, a judge in Frankfurt/Germany refused to grant legal aid for a wife of Moroccan origin who wanted to obtain an immediate divorce because she was severely beaten by her Moroccan husband (according to the legal hardship clause). The judge in her reasoning said that, according to the provision in Qur'an Sūrah 4: 34, beating wives was common in the culture of origin of the parties, and therefore denied a case of hardship. This decision contains several severe mistakes, ignoring Moroccan law, which does not permit domestic violence (see art. 98 sect. 2, 99 of the Family Law Code), as well as German law of conflicts, which would refuse the application of a foreign provision 'allowing' domestic violence on the grounds of German public policy. Besides that, she ignored new interpretations of the Qur'anic provision mentioned, saying that the term *daraba* has to be interpreted as 'to separate' instead of 'to beat' (Zentrum für Islamische Frauenforschung und Frauenförderung 2005). This decision, which was reversed shortly after being made public, caused a heated debate in Germany on an alleged 'Islamization' of the German judiciary.

This case was certainly exceptional for various reasons, one of them being the fact that no Muslim whosoever demanded the application of such an alleged 'shari'a norm'.[1] Some anti-Muslim fanatics confused the Frankfurt decision with the legitimate exercise of religious rights according to European and German constitutional provisions granting freedom of religion, obviously ignoring the very constitutional order they pretend to defend.[2] These days, the establishment of

1 The same was true earlier in 2006 when a Berlin opera decided to cancel the performance of Mozart's opera *Idomeneo* for obscure security reasons, where the beheading of gods and prophets including Muhammad was added by the 'artistic' leader.

2 Some time earlier a certain Hans-Peter Raddatz went so far as to publicly declare that 'a Christian using violence abuses his religion; a Muslim not using violence abuses

mosques including minarets has become a key issue in continental debates on the scope and limits of religious freedom. In Switzerland a right-wing party has launched a campaign against any further mosques on Swiss soil. In Austria, legislation aimed at preventing Muslims from building mosques has been promoted.[3] In Germany, the plans of DITIB, one of the major Turkish-Muslim organizations, to build a mosque with 55m-tall minarets in Cologne, triggered protests by extreme right-wing nationalists, which is no surprise, but also by otherwise celebrated personalities who have so far not been known for extremist views. Their reasoning was directed against the 'visible claim of power' symbolized by such mosques, and manifested obvious distrust as regards the initiators. It should be mentioned here that a very broad political majority in Cologne supports the plans, arguing that Muslims being a part of German society are right to demand visibility in this way. German law would certainly support this view, provided that the construction and environmental regulations applicable to all kinds of construction projects for religious purposes[4] are met. Interestingly, the establishment of synagogues in German city centres happened in the later nineteenth century, when German Jews were granted equal rights for the first time in German history.

Thus, the democratic secular legal order granting human rights including the freedom of religion and conscience equally for all religions and beliefs has came under fire from Muslim extremists like Hizb al-Tahrir, Murabitun, Khilavet Devleti and others, who reject that order as incompatible with their interpretation of Islam, and at the same time by self-appointed defenders of the enlightened West/the Christian occident. Even scientific research does not remain untouched by these developments, according to my personal experience with extremists. Having published books and articles on the issues I am dealing with here, I read on websites and in emails that I was an enemy of Islam, and worse than the commentator on Nazi racial laws, Hans Globke, because I dared to mention legal conflicts regarding problematic rules e.g. in the traditional Islamic law of personal status concerning women and non-Muslims applied in several parts of the world. On the other hand, having given interviews on the application of 'foreign' legal and religious rules

his religion, too' ('vereinfacht laesst sich sagen, ein Christ missbraucht seine Religion, wenn er Gewalt anwendet, und ein Muslim missbraucht seine Religion ebenso, wenn er nicht Gewalt anwendet'), cited in weltwoche.ch Ausgabe 16/04, Weltwoche-Gespraech (Thomas Widmer), <www.weltwoche.ch/artikel/print.asp?AssetID=7478&CategoryID=62 > [accessed 14 March 2007]. For critical voices with regard to this 'expert' see Troll (2002), Hoebsch (2005).

3 See 'Kärnten beschließt ein Gesetz gegen Moscheen', *Die Presse* 11 February 2008. Available at: <http://www.diepresse.com/home/politik/innenpolitik/362068/print.do> [accessed 26 November 2008]; 'Kritik an Kärntner "Moscheen-Verhinderungsgesetz"'. Available at: <http://religion.orf.at/projekt03/news/0802/ne080212_kaernten.htm> [accessed 26 November 2008]. For current anti-minaret legislation in the state of Vorarlberg see 'Vorarlberg verhindert Minarette per Gesetz', *Der Standard* 9 April 2008. Available at: <http://derstandard.at/druck/?id=3296706> [accessed 26 November 2008].

4 These are privileged under German law (Rohe 2007: 83).

including Islamic ones according to the provisions of European legal orders (!), some bloggers (anonymously) declared they had enough ammunition left for people of my kind, and a German Islamophobic activist, Alice Schwarzer, repeatedly tried to defame me by taking my publications and interviews on the existing legal order as an attempt to replace the German legal order by shari'a rules.

Obviously the existing, well-balanced constitutional orders opening up a broad space to religious life and convictions within the indispensable frame of democratic secular states under the rule of law are threatened from several sides. There is urgent need to clarify the facts and intentions as regards the scope and limits for the application of shari'a rules in a European context between the journalistic Guantánamo of an Alice Schwarzer on the one side and the ignorance of existing conflicts between European legal orders and several traditionalist or extremist interpretations of shari'a rules among some Muslims on the other side.

My discussion has to be limited to legal aspects of shari'a in a European context. But one should not forget that religious rules can be applied and followed on an informal basis in daily life without any restriction in most cases. As it comes to the formal application or recognition of 'foreign' norms, we have to differentiate between religious and legal issues. The former are regulated by the European and national constitutional provisions. It is mainly in the sphere of religious rules – concerning the relations between God and human beings (*'ibādāt*) and the non-legal aspects of the relations between human beings (*mu'āmalāt*) – where a European shari'a is possibly developing.[5] With respect to the application of legal rules, the conflict between possibly contradictory rules of the law of the land and the law of religious/cultural origin has to be solved.

The Application of Islamic Legal Norms

In the field of law, most of the existing legal orders have a territorial basis; everyone within the territory of a specific state has to abide by the same laws. Only the state can decide whether and to what extent 'foreign' law can be applied and enforced on its territory. Thus the legal system is not 'multicultural' as far as the decisive exercise of legal power is concerned. Therefore, the application of foreign legal provisions – including Islamic ones – is exceptional. However, this does not mean that foreign legal principles and cultural influences are kept out. Nevertheless, the constitutional principles of the inviolability of human dignity, democracy, the rule of law with the binding force of all state power, separation of powers, majority rule and minority protection, as well as the essential elements of constitutional civil rights, such as the equality of the sexes, freedom of opinion, religious freedom and protection of marriage and family etc., are among the basic principles which cannot be dispensed with. Within this framework, foreign legal provisions can

5 See Rohe (2004b: 161), Shadid and van Koningsveld (2003), Waardenburg (2003) for excellent studies of present developments.

be formally applied on three different legal levels. Besides that, the state has no control on informal ways of application as long as its bodies are not called upon by one of the parties involved.

Private International Law Rules

Private international law rules are the rules regulating the conflict of laws in matters concerning civil[6] law, and form a possible level for the direct application of Islamic legal rules. In the area of civil law, the welfare of autonomously acting private persons is of prime importance. If someone has organized his/her life in accordance with a certain legal system, this deserves protection when the person crosses the border. However, it is also within the interest of the legal community that in certain matters the same law should be applicable to everyone resident in a particular country. This would be especially the case in matters touching the roots of legal and societal common sense, like the legal relations between the sexes or between adherents of different religions. The question as to whether foreign or national substantive law should be applied must therefore be determined, and this is done by private international law provisions (conflict of laws), which weigh up the relevant interests.

In family law and the law of succession, the application of legal norms in European countries is often determined on the basis of the nationality of the persons involved rather than by their domicile (for further details see Rohe 2003c: 46). Unlike in Canada or in the US (Foblets and Overbeeke 2004, Rude-Antoine 2001), European courts are therefore often obliged to apply Islamic legal rules. In this respect it may generally be stated that Islamic law has a strong position especially within these areas. This can be explained by the fact that Islamic law in this area has a multiplicity of regulations derived from authoritative sources (Qur'an and *sunna*). Furthermore, a powerful lobby obviously tries to preserve this area as a stronghold due to religious convictions as well as for reasons of income and the exercise of power (which was very similar in Europe in former times). The Tunisian lawyer Ali Mezghani states that '[i]n Islamic countries, it is difficult to deny that family law is the site of conservation' (2003: 721–2). This is true despite the fact that in several Islamic countries reforms have taken place and still are in progress.[7] In others, there is even a remarkable reversion to traditional standards.

However, the application of such provisions must comply with the rules of public policy. If the application of legislation influenced by Islamic law would lead

6 In the sphere of public law and especially penal law, foreign law is not applicable. Public law regulates the activities of the sovereign himself; and penal law has to define rules which are necessary to grant a minimum consensus of common behaviour in the relevant society.

7 See Rohe (2001: 53, 112); for recent developments in the Maghreb see Nelle (2004).

to a result that is obviously incompatible with, for example, the main principles of German law, including constitutional civil rights, the provisions in question cannot be applied. The main conflicts between 'Islamic' and European legal thinking in family law concern the constitutional (and human) rights such as equality of the sexes and of religious beliefs and the freedom of religion including the right not to believe. Conflicts mainly arise from provisions reflecting classical Islamic law, which preserve a strict separation between the sexes with respect to their social roles and tasks as well as the far-reaching legal segregation of religions under the supremacy of Islam. In such cases, public policy will prevent the application of these norms, if the result of their application would substantially contradict the fundamental rules of the law of the land. This is a mechanism accepted and used in private international law all over the world (for details see Rohe 2004c).

Optional Civil Laws

A further area of – indirect – application opens up within the framework of the so-called 'optional' civil law. Private autonomy is the core value of the liberal European civil law orders. Thus, in matters exclusively concerning the private interests of the parties involved, these parties are entitled to create and to arrange their legal relations according to their preferences. Legal rules regulating such matters are 'optional' within a certain framework.

As an example we may note the fact that various methods of investment are offered which do not violate the Islamic prohibition of usury ('*riba*', which according to traditional views means the general prohibition of accepting and paying interest; see Saeed 1996). Concerning project finance, Islamic legal institutions like the *murabaha* or the *ijara* can be used (Klarmann 2003, Bälz 2004). These are certain forms of partnerships intending to attract capital owners to participate instead of merely giving credit, the latter bearing the risk of contradicting the *riba* rules. Commerce and trade have already responded to the economic/legal needs of traditional Muslims in several European countries. In the UK a special concept of 'Islamic mortgages' was developed, which allows Muslims willing to purchase chattel to avoid conflicts with provisions concerning *riba* (when paying interest on 'normal' mortgages; Asaria 2003). The 'Islamic' mortgage consists of two separate transactions aiming at one single result. Until recently each transaction was subject to taxation, but a key reform abolished the double 'stamp duty', which was an economic barrier to Muslims engaging successfully in property buying. Even the German state of Sachsen-Anhalt has recently placed an Islamic bond ('*sukuk*',[8] €100 million to begin with), based on a Dutch foundation.[9] For traditionally orientated Muslims, the offer of such forms of investment in Europe

8 It is based on a combination of leasing contracts concerning the state's real property, see 'Finanzmarkt: Islam-Anleihe aus Magdeburg', *Die Bank* 1 January 2004.

9 See 'Sachsen-Anhalt bereitet erste islamische Anleihe vor', *FAZ* 6 November 2003; 'Anlegen mit Allahs Segen', *Handelsblatt* 14 July 2004.

is of considerable importance. According to my knowledge many of them have lost huge sums of money in the past to doubtful organizations from the Islamic world or based in Europe and wearing a 'religious' veil.[10]

On the other hand, contractual regulations, especially those discriminating against women, could be void according to laws on the protection of good morals.[11] There are no court decisions on such issues so far published or known. However, to my knowledge some German notaries refuse to assist in formulating wills[12] containing the classical Islamic regulation on half-shares for female heirs. In this field new perceptions and interpretations of shari'a rules could be possibly found (see, for example, Ucar 2005, Rohe 2001). Muslims following this approach hold the view that the goals of Islamic norms can be fulfilled by due application of the respective Western laws. For example, within the Canadian context (as well as according to the respective European laws) Islamic law prescribes distributing property acquired during marriage pursuant to Canadian law. In inheritance cases, equal shares for males and females would meet Islamic standards as well. Where women had legally and often also factually to contribute to the family upkeep in the same way as men, the argument for a global preferential treatment of men in the calculation of the shares of an inheritance was unfounded. Therefore, Muslims should abstain from dividing their estate in wills according to the traditional model, giving females only half shares.[13] Representatives of this approach would see no structural problems or even differences in the application of Western substantive law to Muslims – these laws, too, were bound to find and to implement just solutions.

Specific Provisions Concerning Islamic Law

In addition to general rules of private international law and optional civil law, a few European states introduced Islamic legal provisions concerning family and succession matters to be applied to the Muslim population. In Britain Muslim institutions may apply to register marriages. Furthermore, according to the Divorce (Religious Marriages) Act 2002, courts are enabled to require the dissolution of a religious marriage before granting a civil divorce (Ahmad 2005, Khaliq 2004).

10 See the recent reports on doubtful investments in Turkey supported by certain organizations in 'Neuer Markt auf Türkisch', *Spiegel Online* 29 January 2004, available at: <http://www.spiegel.de/0,1518,283591,00.html> [accessed 29 January 2004].

11 § 138 sect. 1 of the German Civil Code states: 'A legal transaction which offends public morals is void' (see Rohe 2003c).

12 The validity of wills does not depend on such assistance according to German law of succession.

13 Information given by barrister Faisal Kutty (Member of Board Canadian Council on American Islamic Relations CAIR-CAN and the Islamic Social Services Association of North America, General Counsel of the Canadian-Muslim Civil Liberties Association) in Toronto, 28 June 2006.

The Adoption and Children Act 2002 amended the Children Act 1989 with provisions (Sect. 14 A ss.) introducing a 'special guardianship' as a legal means of parental responsibility in addition to adoption, which is forbidden by Islamic law.[14] In Spain, since 1992 Islamic rules regulating the contracting of marriages can be applied to Muslims (Mantecón 2004). In order to ensure the necessary legal security there are compulsory provisions for the registration of these marriages.[15] This kind of legal segregation is very much limited, concerning mere formal regulations without any relevant material quality. Interestingly, and also in Spain, the legislator has amended Art. 107 Código Civil regulating the right to divorce. The amendment enables women resident in Spain to get divorced even if the law of origin or of their matrimonial home prevents them from doing so. The legislator has stated expressly that this amendment was intended specifically to address the situation of Muslim women.[16]

Within the European Union only in Greece are Muslims (of Turkish origin) still living under traditional shari'a rules for historical reasons (Tsitselikis 2004), while the Turkish Republic has continuously reformed its civil laws and since 2002 introduced the legal equality of sexes in family law. This can hardly serve as a model for Europe. Despite widespread tendencies in the Islamic world to improve women's rights, many legal orders in this region are still far from the legal standard of equality of sexes achieved in Europe. It would simply be unacceptable to implement such rules into the existing systems.

Nevertheless, in Britain the Union of Muslim Organizations of UK and Eire has formulated a resolution demanding the establishment of a separate Muslim family and inheritance law automatically applicable to all Muslims in Britain (Poulter 1993). The underlying idea might be found in the legal situation on the Indian subcontinent – being the prevailing region of origin of Muslims in Britain – which was and still is ruled by a system of religious separation in matters of family law.[17] The same is true for most of the Islamic states in past and present. But introducing religiously or ethnically orientated multiple legal systems into Europe does not represent a realistic or even desirable option (Rohe 2003b). Such systems may be helpful and historically even exemplary in the past, if they granted rights and freedoms for minorities which would otherwise be lost. However, this will always result in problems in the form of an inter-religious conflict over laws, as can be

---

14 Qur'an surah 33: 4. s; art. 'tabanni', in wizārat al-awqāf, al-mawsū'at al-fiqhīya vol. 10, Kuwayt 1987. For present legal orders in the Islamic world see Pearl and Menski (1998).

15 See Article 59 Código Civil in conjunction with the administrative provision of the general directorate of the Civil Registry and the Notary from 10 February 1993.

16 BOE 30-09-2003, Ley Orgánica 11/2003, de 29 de septiembre, de medidas concretas en materia de seguridad ciudadana, violencia doméstica e integración social de los extranjeros, 4.

17 See Levy (2000); Poulter (1993: 148); and Ahmad (2003: 74) referring to the demands of the UMO and the Muslim Council of Britain.

seen outside Europe. The most powerful religious group will almost inevitably enforce the ultimate right of its legal system to adjudicate. This would subdue the minority to the rules of the majority's religion in inter-religious relations. It would be impossible to establish such an ultimate right to adjudicate within the framework of European constitutional law.

Besides that, freedom of religion contains the freedom to change one's religion or not to belong to any religion. This freedom would be unduly constrained by forcing people into a legal regime defined by religion.

Taking religious affiliation as the basis for civil legal relations would raise serious questions besides that. Clearly, several aspects of Islamic law – in its various existing forms – would not be acceptable within the European legal-political context, examples being the ongoing inequality with respect to the legal position of non-Muslims in several Islamic countries, e.g. in matters of marriage, damages or succession (e.g. Art. 881 Sect. 2 of the Iranian civil code, Mehrpour 2004, Valavioun 2004). The German Supreme Court[18] has clearly stated that there is no room for the presumption of Turkish wives living in a 'typical Muslim marriage' to be deprived of autonomous decision-making in daily life. On the other hand problems, often caused by cultural motivation, are obvious and openly discussed among Muslims themselves. The Commissioner for Women's Affairs of the Central Council of Muslims in Germany has stated in an interview:[19] 'Islam is not in need of a commissioner for women's affairs. It is not Islam who suppresses women, but men. And therefore Muslim women are indeed in need of a commissioner for women's affairs.' It is remarkable in this context that the Central Council of Muslims in Germany declared in its charter on Muslim life in German society on 20 February 2002 that Muslims are content with the harmonic system of secularity and religious freedom provided by the Constitution.[20] According to Art. 13 of the charter, 'The command of Islamic law to observe the local legal order includes the acceptance of the German statutes governing marriage and inheritance, and civil as well as criminal procedure.'

Thus, in my opinion the solution has to be found in formulating common laws under the constitution as a result of debates in parliament and society. Common convictions are changing with respect to important parts of the legal order; European family law in force at present is fundamentally different from the respective rules thirty or fifty years ago. One of the most striking examples might be found concerning homosexual life. Whereas forty years ago homosexual activities were punishable under German penal law even among adults, homosexual persons now may enter into a registered partnership granting them rights not far from marriage. Considering this fact, it is upon society as a whole to (often controversially) discuss these issues, thus enabling the legislator to legally define the fields where unity in

18 BGH NJW 1999: 135.

19 'Verschleiert, aber selbstbewußt', FAZ 27 February 2001, 14.

20 English version available at: <http://www.islam.de/?site=sonstiges/events/charta&di=en> [accessed 30 January 2004].

standards and behaviour is necessary and others, where diversity may take place and might be even desirable. The characteristics of the European legal system of managing diversity may be described firstly by granting diversity under the rule or a uniform law. This task cannot be fulfilled in a uniform abstract way covering all fields of possible regulation equally. Instead of that, the legal and social functions of different spheres of regulation necessarily lead to different levels of possible diversity. Where common rules are an inevitable basis for granting peace in society, which is the main function of penal law, legal diversity has to be reduced to marginal cases (see further below). However, in private international law and in private substantive law the leading idea of private autonomy requires a broad space of self-determination and thus possible diversity.

In addition to that, the focus of self-determination lies in granting individual rights. In the field of legal norms, there is no option for claiming competing collective rights. The main reason for that is to be found in the European perception of the law itself. There is no sphere of law being restricted to group interests which could then be regulated autonomously by these groups. The law governing private aspects of family life may serve as an example. Certainly family life primarily is a matter concerning the persons involved. Nevertheless, the legal framing of family life is intrinsically linked to social cohesion.[21] The centralization of power in the hands of the democratic legislator under the rule of law has replaced former weak political unities which had to rely on far-reaching communitarian structures. The latter would open space for exercising collective rights at the expense of conflicting individual rights of the weaker members of the community, which would simply be unacceptable under a constitution demanding the efficient protection of human rights.

Besides that, such a model would ignore the vast pluralism of Muslim minds and creeds, forcing them into a homogeneous regime of internally disputed norms. But there is no uniform Islamic legal system of substantive rules to be identified. The Turkish Republic, being the state of origin of the Muslim majority in many parts of Europe, completely abolished the shari'a rules, and the vast majority among Turks would reject the re-introduction of such rules in European countries. The same would be true for the considerable number of Iranian refugees, for example. The European model therefore is that every individual and every group may participate in political life to make the legislative bodies aware of their needs and convictions, enjoying religious freedom in this way within the constitutional limits.

One of the few extremist voices publicly demanding the introduction of Islamic law and Muslim arbitration in Germany is the founder of an Islamic centre in Berlin (Rohe 2005). In a book on *The Rules of Personal Status of Muslims in the*

21 Lebanese and Indian experience shows that separate systems of family law, rather than unified systems granting a certain range of options, can contribute to social tensions and lead to the emergence of exclusive self-definitions partly directed against other groups in society.

West,[22] he constantly declares non-Muslims to be infidels and rejects German legal rules and judgments as 'rules of infidelity'.[23] Consequently, he urges Muslims in Germany to maintain the rules of traditional Islamic family law. He even argues that the traditional punishment for adultery – flogging or stoning to death – should be applied to Muslim women in Germany (!) who are married to a non-Muslim, even if they are unaware of the 'applicability' of these rules in their cases.[24] He then denounces the German system of social security to be an evil, because it grants wives independence from their husband's maintenance payments and thus enables them to 'disobey' their husbands.[25] A book edited and translated by British Muslim authors tried to justify the practice of female genital mutilation (Abu Bakr Abdu'r-Razzaq 1998). The danger of empowering such persons by opening ways for them to participate in legal life is obvious. On the other hand, it is an important task for the state and its bodies to convince all parts of society again and again of the advantages of a secular, neutral legal order protecting human rights. This includes the necessity to strengthen cultural sensitivity in administrations and courts.

Some aspects of the distrust or wrong perception of the ruling legal order may result from a widespread lack of understanding with respect to loyalties within an extended family or to the living conditions of newly immigrated people in a 'foreign' environment. Therefore, broader information about such facts and the improvement of cultural sensitivity are urgent needs for socio-legal education and training on the job. I myself was involved as a judge at the Court of Appeals of Nuremberg in a case concerning an appellant of Mauritanian origin suing a municipality for allegedly having caused damages by breach of a sales contract. Obviously, the representatives of the municipality had not treated him in the way one should expect during the negotiations preceding the court procedures. Interestingly, at a time in the hearing of the case the appellant described his position as 'having lost his honour over all these quarrels'. This was a formula unknown to the bench, since the average German appellant would rather complain about the 'fools in our administrations paid by our taxes and now even working against us', perhaps expressed slightly more politely, but in any case without raising the question of honour. Therefore we realized that the appellant's true concern was much more the 'restoration of his honour' than the payment of damages. Given the fact that his claim was weak for reasons of causation, we proposed to state officially in the records of the proceedings that the court shared the opinion of the appellant concerning the behaviour of the respondent's representatives, and suggested he abstain from further proceedings. Indeed the appellant agreed to this solution and seemed to be rather content with it. I am convinced that in daily court

22 Sālim Ibn ʿAbd al-Çanī al-Rāfiʿī, ahkām al-ahwāl al-šakhsīya li-l-muslimīn fī-l-gharb, Riyadh 2001.

23 Op. cit., n. 22, 618.

24 Op. cit., n.22, 394.

25 Op. cit., n. 22, 79.

practice there is broad space for this manner of resolving the true conflicts behind the nominal conflicts brought into court.

Religious Freedom and the Application of Islamic Religious Norms

Applying religious norms is fundamentally different to applying legal ones. Religious norms may be applied within the framework of the territorial legal order, thus there is no possible conflict concerning the hierarchy of norms. Besides that, in most European states religious freedom is far reaching – the application of foreign legal norms may be described as an exceptional case, whereas in the field of religious norms their application is the rule on the legal basis of equality of religions. European constitutions, like Art. 9 of the European Convention on Human Rights, guarantee that people will not be deprived of the basic requirements for complying with the demands of their religion. No Muslim will be prevented by the state from adhering to the 'five pillars' of Islam, for example.

Religious freedom in this sense includes all kinds of religions, not only those of the majority of the population or the established ones. Furthermore, according to these provisions religion is not restricted to the private sphere; its manifestation in the public sphere is protected as well. To take an example, the Administrative Court of Appeal of Koblenz decided in a case concerning the erection of a minaret in a rural area of Germany that there is no kind of 'protection of the cultural status quo' according to the law.[26] Times are changing, and as Muslims now are an important part of the community: society as a whole has to accept this fact.

Nevertheless, there are some differences in the application of religious freedom between European countries. This is due to different views of the distance between the state's activities and religion should be. France or Switzerland for example have chosen a strict separation between state and religion. Therefore officers or even pupils in France, according to the new legislation, are not allowed to show ostensible religious symbols during their working times e.g. in schools, whereas in Britain teachers or lawyers in court may wear an 'ordinary' veil leaving the face visible. Recently the President of the Danish Supreme Court Melchior has stressed that according to his conviction Muslim female judges or lawyers wearing the headscarf in court could contribute to integration; a similar view was expressed by Prime Minister Rasmussen.[27] I am sure that the headscarf issue will continue to occupy broad space in parliamentarian and public discussions in Europe, mostly by male discussants on all sides.

---

26 *OVG Koblenz* 20 November 2000, *Neue Zeitschrift für Verwaltungsrecht* (NVwZ) 2001.

27 'Rasmussen, rest çekti: Başörtülüleri rahat biraktın', *Zaman Denmark* 7 June 2007 (Hasan Cücük).

In Germany, the most important provision to regulate religious affairs is Art. 4 Sections 1 and 2 of the German Constitution.[28] This article – as well as Art. 9 of the ECHR, which is less far reaching in granting rights – is not limited to private religious conviction. It also grants the public manifestation of belief and the state is obliged to ensure that this right is not unduly limited. Of course there are legal limits for rights including religious ones. Nobody would be allowed to threaten others on religious grounds, to take an example. Nevertheless, the German legal system provides a far-reaching freedom of religion. This freedom is, according to the unanimous opinion among legal experts and the German government and administration, not restricted to established religions like Christianity and Judaism, but also applies to Islam. Furthermore, Art. 3 Sect. 3 of the German Constitution prescribes that no-one may be discriminated against, or given preferential treatment, for reasons of their religious belief.[29]

In sum, the secular legal orders in Europe do not refuse religion; they are not at all anti-religious (‘*lā-dīnī*’) as it is sometimes wrongly understood.[30] On the contrary they open a broad space for religious belief and life, including the establishment of religious organizations, places of worship or private schools, not to mention religious instruction in public schools according to the German educational system, social security payments for religious burials and other rites for those in need.[31] It is only that the state itself has to be neutral and is prevented from interference in religious affairs. The most important result of this legal secularism is the equivalence of religions including the freedom not to adhere to a religion or the freedom to change it.[32] According to a unanimous understanding in Europe this neutrality is a prerequisite of true religious freedom, which cannot be dispensed with. A prominent French Muslim accordingly calls this system to be of ‘positive neutrality’ (i.e. towards religions: Bencheikh 1998: 57).

The constitutional protection of the freedom of religion even affects private legal relations e.g. in the sphere of employment law. In a number of cases concerning Muslim women wearing a headscarf, German employers forbade them to wear the headscarf at work especially when they had functions in dealing with the public (e.g. in warehouses, offices etc.). In a case in the state of Hesse, a Muslim clerk working in a warehouse in the countryside was given notice to terminate the contract due to her refusal to work unveiled. There was a generally accepted rule within the company that everybody had to wear ‘decent’ clothes which would not give offence to customers. The employer stated that he himself

28 The wording is as follows: Art. 4 [Freedom of faith, conscience and creed] ‘Freedom of faith and conscience, and freedom to profess a religious or philosophical creed, shall be inviolable. The undisturbed practice of religion shall be guaranteed.’

29 For practical examples see Rohe (2007: 82).

30 See Bielefeldt (2003: 60) for critical Muslim voices.

31 For details concerning several European states see Aluffi and Zincone (eds.) (2004).

32 For the intrinsic connection between full religious freedom and secularism see Bielefeldt (2003: 15).

did not care about the headscarf, but that there was some evidence that the mainly conservative customers would not accept to be served by a veiled clerk and would certainly change to competing warehouses. The appeal of the employee against the notice was dismissed by the Labour Court of Appeal of Hesse on the same grounds.[33]

There was considerable and in part understandable irritation among Muslims concerning this decision. But it has to be taken into consideration that in such cases the state alone has to grant religious freedom according to the Constitution. In the field of private law, however, the constitutional rights exert a so-called 'indirect' influence on the rules of law. This means that they have to be taken into consideration without being enforced in a similarly direct and far-reaching manner as it is the case in conflicts between individuals and the state. In these private cases there are two constitutional rights in conflict: the freedom of religion in favour of the employee and the freedom of personality which implies the right to create and to terminate contractual relations according to personal interest. Nevertheless, the Federal Labour Court finally accepted the appellant's claim.[34] It stressed the great importance of religious freedom which cannot be ruled out by mere suppositions of possible economic disadvantages to the detriment of the employer. Even in case of proven disadvantages the employer would first have to consider whether the employee could be occupied in a less sensitive space before being entitled to terminate the contract. The new European anti-discrimination provisions[35] concerning employment law grant even broader protection in this field.[36]

The last field to be mentioned here is penal law. The function of penal law consists in granting a minimum of regulations which are indispensable for a peaceful life in society, and to defend these rules by punishing the offenders by all the harshest means available under the rule of law within the limits of human rights, up to lifetime sentences. Therefore uniform standards have to be applied to everybody present on the respective territory; there is no space for cultural defences in cases like 'honour killings' whatsoever. Nevertheless, religious needs are recognized even in penal law in singular cases. The most important topic for Muslims (as well as for Jews) is the legal treatment of male circumcision. Although inflicting bodily harm, it is justified and therefore exempt from punishment if performed by state of the art methods, because there is an obvious religious need to carry out this procedure which at the same time is of minor impairment to the boy concerned (Troendle and Fischer 2007: § 223 n. 6 b, Gropp 2005: § 6 n. 231). The opposite is true, of course, for female genital mutilation, which is not a

33 LAG Hessen NJW 2001, 3650.

34 BAG NJW 2003: 1685.

35 Directive 2000/43/EG (29.06.2000), see Rohe (2004a).

36 See e.g. ArbG Hamburg 04.12.2007 (20 Ca 105/07, BeckRS 2008 52272), where even the churches and their bodies, legally privileged like all religious communities, were held liable for damages for preventing a highly skilled Muslim social worker from being employed in a task outside the narrower space of religious teaching or preaching.

genuine Islamic practice, but which is found in several regions of the Islamic world, namely in parts of West and East Africa and in Egypt,[37] and which regrettably is also practised secretly in Europe among certain immigrants. It has to be severely punished, but unlike in France[38] no case has been dealt with in a German court so far, supposedly due to a 'wall of silence' among the persons involved.

Can Shari'a Rules Fit into the European Legal Context?

'Islam' means 'subjection to God'. This subjection is understood comprehensively: it concerns the inner religious conviction as well as the religious practice and the way of life. It is concerned with both this world and the one beyond. The widespread misunderstanding according to which Islam does not distinguish between religion on the one hand and the state, law and politics on the other is founded upon this. However, the claim to provide binding norms for believers regulating various fields of life does not distinguish Islam from Christianity and other religions. The existence of religious and legal rules within a set of norms does not mean that it is impossible to distinguish between them (Johansen 1999: 265, Arkoun 1999: 43).

Shari'a in a wider sense is the general term for both areas, 'the path which has been prepared; the divinely appointed path'. The term 'Islamic law' is an extremely short translation. It is even wrong if the normal term of 'law' is applied without specification. The 'law' mainly lives on its peace-keeping function; in order to apply efficiently it uses compulsion by state bodies if necessary. Thus the enforcement of rules in this world is the characteristic feature. This concerns the relationship of legal subjects among each other and their relationship with those responsible for the legal system – today that is mainly the state and its subdivisions.

The main feature of religious provisions is that they cannot be enforced legally, but only through social pressure. If they are not followed the consequences lie in the next world, unless the state provides for sanctions in this world for public order reasons. Thus, the crucial difference is not to be found in the claim to be binding – both religious as well as legal provisions want themselves to be binding. The system of sanctions is rather the place to look for the difference. This kind of distinguishing according to the type of sanction can also be found in shari'a. Shari'a contains both evaluations concerning this world such as 'ordered' (*wāğib*), 'allowed' (*mubāh*) and 'prohibited' (*harām*) and evaluations concerning the next world such as 'recommended' (*mandūb, mustahabb*) and 'disapproved' (*makrūh*).[39]

37 See Muslim Women's League (1999) and Shamiri (2000–2001: 344).

38 See 'Urteil mit symbolischer Wirkung', *Frankfurter Allgemeine Zeitung* 18 February 1999.

39 See El Baradie (1983: 62); al-KhuÃarī (1988: 30).

Furthermore religious and legal provisions are often linked to different connecting factors. Today the law is almost always applicable territorially, thus independent from the person staying within the territory of the legislative power. With regard to religion, however, reference can only be made to the person as such: the connecting point is the religious conviction and practice of the individual. Even a state religion cannot change this, as a state cannot have a religious conviction, a state cannot 'believe in something'.

Finally, religious and legal provisions can also be distinguished as regards the method of their transformation, even if the believer and the legal subject feel bound by both. Legal provisions are comparably precise as regards their prerequisites and consequences. The transformation of religious provisions outside rigid rites is a lot more complex. A politician, for instance, can hardly, while doing his job, be led by the order to hold his left cheek out if he is struck on his right one.[40]

According to this understanding the largest part of the shari'a and the Qur'an, in particular, concern the law to a comparably little extent. Out of the thousands of verses in the Qur'an only a few dozen are of a legal character.[41] Already the classic shari'a literature from the eighth century onwards clearly distinguishes between religious and legal provisions. Usually these writings are split into two large parts. The first part deals with crucial questions concerning the religious rites (particularly concerning the prayer rules, the giving of alms, the fasting during Ramadan and the Pilgrimage to Mecca). These are described as '*Ýibādāt*', which is a complex term, in which 'the divine services; the acts of worship' can be discerned. The second part then deals with legal issues such as consummating a marriage and divorce, particular criminal actions, contract law, company law, tort law, procedural law and the law of succession. This matter is called '*muÝāmalāt*', elements of 'human interaction'.[42] Law in this sense has only regulated a fragment of all legal areas in the untouchable, although often requiring interpretation, legal sources of the Qur'an and the transmissions of the words and deeds of Muhammad (*sunna*) (see Hallaq 1997, Kamali 1997, Coulson 1997).

Besides that, a large part of classic Islamic law, from both the Sunni and Shi'i schools, is founded upon secondary legal finding such as interpretation and conclusions on the base of human reasoning. It may be cautiously said that there is not a single binding provision in Islamic law which can be applied without such interpretation and interpretations can change as human beings and their living conditions do (Seddik 1998). The plurality of opinions within Islamic law is evidence for this. The statement that only God himself can be the legislator is thus very restricted in practice. From the earliest days of Islam human beings

---

40 See Matthew 5: 39 in the Bible.

41 For example MuÎammad SaÝīd al-Ašmāwī, al-šarīÝat al-islāmīya wa l-qānūn al-miÒrī, Cairo 1996: 7, refers to this.

42 It is assumed, with regard to particular criminal offences such as the prohibition of alcohol consumption, that they also protect rights of God, depending how they will be interpreted; also see El-Baradie (1983: 44).

interpreted the divine statutes and developed the norms for application. For over one hundred years there have been far-reaching efforts to create a large area of application for independent legal reasoning (*iğtihād*); see Ramadan (1999: 82, 93). By doing this a certain amount of flexibility which is necessary for legal practice is held ready so that it is possible to react adequately to the situation of the Muslims in the Diaspora. I would like to quote a European Muslim here:

> we had very vital, very alive, very evolving jurisprudential activities up to the fourth century of Islam. Then suddenly the community was declared to go braindead. No longer are we allowed to develop our ideas. For it became doctrine that everyone must follow one of the present current schools. I believe that our crisis starts from this point. (Badawi 1995: 43)

As it comes to the self-definition of Muslims adherent to Islamic norms in Europe, there are two main aspects to be kept in mind. Firstly, shari'a is no fixed body of legal or religious rules, laid down in laws or canons of religious obligations, but rather a system of identifying rules and then applying them to certain cases and situations. Secondly, Islamic norms are not necessarily considered to be valid and binding at every time and place, but are subject to interpretation whether and to which extent they have to be applied in time and space. Some, for example, only applied to the wives of the prophet of Islam, Muhammad; others were aimed at the non-Muslim population of the Arabian Peninsula in the first century AH.[43] Only a relatively small number of rules are taken to be binding at any time and at any place. These rules are mostly concerning the individual relation between God and man, the core of belief itself – the so-called five pillars of Islam. But even in this field, Muslims have found and developed interpretations which are allowing them to arrange their living conditions in a society which is predominantly non-Muslim (e.g. in the field of delaying or contracting the obligatory prayers). Furthermore, these rules are not enforceable in this world and therefore restricted to rule the relations between God and man.

Concerning Muslim presence outside the 'Islamic world', in the past many Muslim lawyers advised against long stays abroad, fearing that Muslims could be prevented from fulfilling their religious duties.[44] This fear is obviously due to historical events and experiences during the Reconquista (Dressendörfer 1971), the crusades and later hostile encounters between Christian European and Islamic powers. The central point always seems to be the fear that the Islamic world might be weakened by migration. Complementary to this the Spanish Christian sovereigns at times prohibited their Muslim subjects from emigrating,[45] thus preventing them

43 That is, in the first century after the year 622 CE.

44 See Ibn Rušd, al-muqaddimat al-mumahhida, Cairo 1325/1907 Vol. 2, p. 286; Khoury (1985: 128); also Miller (2000: 258).

45 Miller (2000: 256, 260 with n.17); but also see van Koningsveld and Wiegers (1996: 9, 44).

from transferring their goods 'to the enemy', and personally strengthening their camp.

The background is that of two camps in principle adversely opposing each other. The important medieval lawyer al-Qayrawānī[46] found a clear formula for the Muslim side when interpreting prayer rules; there cannot be a permanent stay outside the Islamic territory. It is not by accident that the concept of the fundamental distinction between two opposite houses (*dar al-Islam*, house of Islam, and *dar al-Air*, house of war) was mainly elaborated in these times. Similar points of view can still be found today among very traditional, sometimes extremely anti-Western lawyers.[47] However, this obviously does not correspond with our present reality: according to a new survey one third of all Muslims live outside Islamic states, many of them by their own choice (Kettani 1986: 18, Abedin 1990: 1).

Nevertheless, it has been broadly accepted since the Middle Ages that the legal rules of Islam cannot be applied outside 'Islamic' territory and that Muslims are obliged to either respect the law of the land or to leave the country and to return to countries ruled by Muslims. This view is based on the third category between *dar al-Islam* and *dar al-Air*, the so-called '*dar al-Yard*' (house of a (peace) treaty).[48] A historical reference for this was found in the emigration of a group of Muslims from the then pre-Islamic Mecca to Christian Ethiopia during Muhammad's lifetime. This is supposed to be a model for staying in a non-Islamic, but just environment.[49] The foreign power is qualified as being useful and therefore deserves respect. From the Muslim point of view it was and is important that the imperative provisions of Islam can be complied with. This concept may serve as a basis for peaceful co-existence in a diaspora situation. It obliges Muslims to keep the law of the land in return for being granted personal security and protection by the state of residence. Still this concept is based on the fundamental distinction between opposite camps. Thus, it is doubtful whether the self-definition of a 'diaspora' and the development of a separate order for a more or less homogenous Muslim minority ('*fiqh al-aqallīyāt*') would be very helpful for actively being part of and contributing to society as a whole. Therefore, other Muslim thinkers are seeking new approaches to defining Islamic life as a part of the given legal and societal conditions of life in Europe. They reject the former division between *dār al-Islām* and *dār al-Îarb*, saying that in our days earth is simply 'one house' for mankind

46 Al-Qayrawānī kitāb al-ğihād min kitāb al-nawādir wa l-ziyāda (ed. v Bredow), Stuttgart 1994: 373: 'dār al-Îarb laysat bi-dār iqāmat'.

47 See Ibn Baz and Uthaymeen (1998, especially 71); The Fiqh Council of the Muslim World League on its 16th session in Mecca, reported in 'A message from Muslim scholars to Muslim Minorities in the West', *Daawah* No. 4 1422 A.H./Feb. 2002: 8, 11.

48 See article 'dār al-Ýahd', in Wizārat al-awqāf wa al-šuÞūn al-islāmīya (ed.), al-mawsūÝat al-fiqhīya Vol. 20, 2nd ed. Kuwait 1990; Khālid ÝAbd al-Qādir, fiqh al-aqallīyāt al-muslima, Óarābulus 1419/1998: 59 as well as the references in *Encyclopaedia of Islam II*, Leiden 1991 under *dar al-sulh* (Macdonald).

49 Ibid at p. 27.

as a whole, and that every Muslim is entitled to live in any part of the world and is responsible for the society he/she is living in as an equal member. They stress that that there is no support for the classical view, neither in the Qur'an nor in the *sunna*, and that it is no more than an invention of the classical lawyers.[50] Instead of that, intense international cooperation and common legal rules and values are creating completely different conditions that do not allow a concept of general hostility, as developed in the past in Europe and in the Islamic world alike to be maintained. According to them, the entire world nowadays constitutes one single camp ('*dār wāÎida*'), one all-embracing '*dār al-Ýahd*'.[51] This new approach opens a broad space for the harmonization of Islamic life in Europe with the European legal framework. There is an urgent need to use this space, since among many Muslims as well as in European societies as a whole there is widespread fear of a shari'a which would undermine basic European values such as democracy and the rule of law including the protection of human rights. Some provisions and traditional interpretations of shari'a rules clearly contradict this consensus, e.g. in the fields of state organization, penal law, the law of personal status and rules governing non-Muslims. Therefore it is more than desirable to find and to promote interpretations in harmony with the European legal orders. Muslim scholars are working on this already, but such attempts are still in their very beginning and so far nearly unknown to a broader public.

In conclusion it can be said that there is a 'de-territorialization' regarding the non-legal parts of shari'a. The legal provisions, being enforceable by a state's sanction system alone, remain territorially connected to the exercising of 'Islamic' state power. The religious provisions are principally universal and are therefore also open for application and further development within the regional environment. This would include active participation in societal life. Concerning the consecration of public buildings for example, which is a widespread practice in Germany, it makes a difference whether only representatives of Christian churches are invited to participate, or whether imams, rabbis and others are invited and ready to participate, too.

---

50 For example Zakaria (1989: 54); Oubrou (2003: 193, 197); 'Graz Declaration' of a conference of leaders of Islamic centers and Imams in Europe in Graz/Austria, June 13-15, 2003: 'The medieval distinction between opposite "dar al-Islam" and "dar al-harb" has to be objected. It is based neither in the Qur'an nor in the sunna, and has no relevance whatsoever nowadays, being a historical phenomenon which is outdated since a very long time' (translated from German by the author). The declaration was published on the homepage of the Central Council of Muslims in Germany (<http://www.islam.de/?site=articles&archive=euro-islam&article_number=1651>); also see the references in Shadid and van Koningsveld (1995: 3.2).

51 At the ISESCO-conference in Frankfurt am Main/Germany on 29–30 September 2003 on 'Dialogue among Civilizations: Diversity within Complementarity' the Muslim participants from all over the Islamic world and Europe unanimously agreed on this concept.

The crucial task will be to find the optimal balance in maintaining and enforcing the necessary amount of uniformity in defining rights and duties in order to stabilize the state and its society on the long run on one hand and in granting individual rights and thus diversity to a degree which meets the human rights standard of the freedom of religion on the other hand. In Europe, the basic order, which is the democratic secular state under the rule of law, cannot be part of those negotiations, but has to be the starting point of further reflections. My thesis is that it is only the secular state under the rule of law which enables true freedom of more than one (i.e. the predominant) religion. But it has to prove this principle in daily practice. Equal treatment in legal and religious matters is a core prerequisite for that. Whereas majorities tend to protect themselves in daily life, minorities usually need the help of institutions which are bound to implement equal rights (and duties) according to the law, not according to changing preferences of the public.

References

al-KhuÃarī. 1988. *Dar al-Fikr*. Beirut: Al Fikr.

Abedin, S.Z. 1990. Muslim Minority Communities in the World Today. *Islamochristiana*, 16, 1–14.

Abu Bakr Abdu'r-Razzaq. 1998. *Circumcision in Islam*. London: Waley.

Ahmad, Lord Nazir. 2005. Notes on the Judicial Situation of Muslims in the United Kingdom. In *Muslime im Rechtsstaat*, edited by T.G. Schneiders and L. Kaddor. Münster: Veröffentlichungen des Centrum für Religiöse Studien, 71–8.

Aluffi, B-P, and G. Zincone (eds) 2004. *The Legal Treatment of Islamic Minorities in Europe*. Leuven: Peeters.

Arkoun, M. 1999. *Der Islam*. Heidelberg: Palmyra.

Asaria, I. 2003. Islamic Home Finance arrives on UK's High Streets. *Muslim News* 171, 25 July 2003, 6.

Badawi, Zaki. 1995. Muslim Justice in a Secular State. In *God's Law versus State Law. The Construction of an Islamic Identity in Western Europe*, edited by M. King. London: Grey Seal, 73–80.

Bälz, K. 2004. A Murbaha Transaction in an English Court. *Islamic Law and* Society, 11(1), 117–34.

Bencheikh, Soheib. 1998. *Marianne et le Prophète – L'Islam dans la France laïque*. Paris: Bernard Grasset.

Bielefeldt, Heiner. 2003. *Muslime im säkularen Rechtsstaat*. Bielefeld: Transcript Verlag.

Coulson, N.J. 1997. *A History of Islamic Law*. Edinburgh: Edinburgh University Press.

Dressendörfer, P. 1971. Islam *unter der Inquisition. Die Morisco-Prozesse in Toledo 1575–1610*. Wiesbaden: Franz Steiner Verlag.

El Baradie, Adel. 1983. *Gottes-Recht und Menschen-Recht*. Baden-Baden: Nomos.

Encyclopaedia of Islam II. 1991. Brill: Leiden.

Foblets, M-C, and A. Overbeeke. 2004. Islam in Belgium. In *Islam and the European Union*, edited by R. Potz and W. Wieshaider. Leuven: Peeters, 1–39.

Gropp, W. 2005. *Strafrecht Allgemeiner Teil*. 3rd edition. Berlin: Springer.

Hallaq, W.B. 1997. *A History of Islamic Legal Theories*. Cambridge: Cambridge University Press.

Hoebsch, Werner. 2005. Diffamierter Dialog. Hans-Peter Raddatz und das christlich-islamische Gespraech. *Die neue Ordnung* 6/2005. Available at: <http://www.die-neue-ordnung.de/Nr62005/WH.html> [accessed 17 March 2006].

Ibn Baz, Sheikh and Sheikh Uthaymeen. 1998. *Muslim Minorities, Fatwa Regarding Muslims Living as Minorities*. London and Hounslow: Message of Islam.

Iqbal, M. and D.T. Llewellyn. 2002. *Islamic Banking and Finance*. Cheltenham: Edward Elgar.

Johansen, B. 1999. *Contingency in a Sacred Law*. Leiden: Brill.

Kamali, M.H. 1997. *Principles of Islamic Jurisprudence*. Cambridge: Islamic Texts Society.

Kettani, M. Ali. 1986. *Muslim Minorities in the World Today*. London: Mansell/ Institute of Muslim Minority Affairs.

Khaliq, U. 2004. Islam and the European Union: Report on the United Kingdom. In *Islam and the European Union*, edited by R. Potz and W. Wieshaider. Leuven: Peeters, 219–62.

Khoury, A.T. 1985. *Islamische Minderheiten in der Diaspora*. Mainz: Kaiser.

Klarmann, R. 2003. *Islamic Project Finance*. Zurich/Bâle/Genève: Schulthess.

Levy, J.T. 2000. *The Multiculturalism of Fear*. Oxford: Oxford University Press.

Mantecón, S. 2004. L'Islam en Espagne. In *Islam and the European Union*, edited by R. Potz and W. Wieshaider. Leuven: Peeters, 109–42.

Mehrpour, H. 2004. An Overview of Inheritance in the Legal System of Iran. In *Iranian Family and Succession Laws and their Application in German* Court, edited by J. Basedow and N. Yassari. Tübingen: Mohr Siebeck, 103–110.

Mezghani, Ali. 2003. Le juge français et les institutions du droit musulman. *Journal du droit international*, 130(3), 721–65.

Miller, K.A. 2000. Muslim Minorities and the Obligation to Emigrate to Islamic Territory. *Islamic Law and Society*, 7(2), 256–88.

Muslim Women's League. 1999. *An Islamic Perspective on Sexuality*, available at <http://www.mwlusa.org/topics/sexuality/sexuality_pos.html> [accessed 26 November 2008].

Nelle, D. 2004. Neue familienrechtliche Entwicklungen im Maghreb. *StAZ Das Standesamt*, 9, 253–69.

Oubrou, T. 2003. Die 'Minderheits-Scharia' in Frankreich: Reflexionen zu einer rechtlichen Integration des Islam. In *Der Islam in Europa. Der Umgang mit dem Islam in Frankreich und Deutschland*, edited by A. Escudier. Göttingen: Wakkstein Verlag, 193–214.

Pearl, D. and W. Menski. 1998. *Muslim Family Law*. London: Sweet and Maxwell.

Poulter, S. 1993. The Claim to a Separate Islamic System of Personal Law for British Muslims. In *Islamic Family Law*, edited by C. Mallat and J. Connors. London: Graham and Trotman, 147–66.

Ramadan, T. 1999. *To Be a European Muslim*. Leicester: Islamic Foundation.

Rohe, M. 2001. *Der Islam – Alltagskonflikte und Lösungen. Rechtliche Perspektiven*. 2nd edition. Freiburg: Herder.

— 2003a. Islam und deutsches Zivilrecht. In *Beiträge zum Islamischen Recht II*, edited by H-G. Ebert and T. Hanstein. Frankfurt am Main: Peter Lang, 35–51.

— 2003b. Religiös gespaltenes Zivilrecht in Deutschland und Europa? In *Festschrift für Christoph Link*, edited by H. de Wall and M. Germann. Tübingen: Mohr Siebeck, 409–29.

— 2003c. Islamic Law in German Courts. *Hawwa*, 1, 46–59.

— 2004a. Schutz vor Diskriminierung aus religiösen Gründen im Europäischen Arbeitsrecht – Segen oder Fluch? In *Gedaechtnisschrift fuer Wolfgang* Blomeye, edited by R. Krause, W. Veelken and K. Vieweg. Berlin: Beiträge zum Europäischen Wirtschaftsrecht, 217–44.

— 2004b. The Formation of a European Shari'a. In *Muslims in Europe*, edited by J. Malik. Münster: Lit-Verlag, 161–84.

— 2004c. The Application of Islamic Family Law in German Courts and its Compatibility with German Public Policy. In *Iranian Family and Succession Laws and their Application in German Courts*, edited by Jürgen Basedow and Nadjma Yassari. Tübingen: Mohr Siebeck, 19–32.

— 2005. Islamisten und Schari'a. In *Islamismus*. Berlin: Senatsverwaltung fuer Inneres, Abteilung Verfassungsschutz, 98–115.

— 2007. *Muslim Minorities and the Law in Europe*. New Delhi: Global Media.

Rude-Antoine, E. 2001. La coexistence des systèmes juridiques différents en France: l'exemple du droit familial. In *L'étranger et le droit de la famille*, edited by P. Kahn. Paris: La Documentation française, 147–79.

Saeed, A. 1996. *Islamic Banking and Interest. A Study of the Prohibition of Riba and its Contemporary Interpretation*. Leiden/New York/Köln: Brill.

Seddik, Youssef. 1998. Avon-nous jamais lu le Coran? *Esprit*, 239(1), 99–108.

Shadid, W.A.R. and P.S. van Koningsveld. 1995. *Religious Freedom and the Position of Islam in Western Europe*. Kampen, The Netherlands: Kok Pharos.

— 2003. Religious authorities of Muslims in the West. In *Intercultural Relations and Religious Authorities: Muslims in the European Union*, edited by W.A.R. Shadid and P.S. van Koningsveld. Leuven: Peeter, 149–70.

Shamiri, N. 2000–2001. Ban on Women's Circumcision. In *Yearbook of Islamic and Middle Eastern Law*, Volume 7, edited by E. Cotran. Leiden: Brill, 307–26.

Troendle, H. and T. Fischer. 2007. *Strafgesetzbuch*. 54th edition. Muenchen: Beck.

Troll, C.W. 2002. Islamdialog: Ausverkauf des Christlichen? Anmerkungen zum Buch von Hans Peter Raddatz. *Stimmen der Zeit*, 2002(2), 1–7.

Tsitselikis, K. 2004. The Legal Status of Islam in Greece. *Die Welt des Islams*, 44(3), 402–31.

Ucar, B. 2005. *Recht als Mittel zur Reform von Religion und Gesellschaft. Die türkische Debatte um die Scharia und die Rechtsschulen im 20. Jahrhundert*. Würzburg: Ergon Verlag.

Valavioun, R. 2004. Succession Laws of Religious Minorities. In *Iranian Family and Succession Laws and their Application in German* Court, edited by J. Basedow and N. Yassari. Tübingen: Mohr Siebeck, 111–22.

van Koningsveld, P.S. and G.A. Wiegers. 1996. The Islamic Statute of the Mudejars in the Light of a New Source, al-Qantara. *Revista de Estudios Árabes*, 17, 19–44.

Waardenburg, J. 2003. *Muslims and Others*. Berlin/New York: Walter de Gruyter.

Zakaria, Rafiq. 1989. *Is Islam Secular?* Aligarh: Sir Syed Academy, Aligarh Muslim University.

Zentrum für Islamische Frauenforschung und Frauenförderung. 2005. *Ein einziges Wort und seine grosse Wirkung. Eine hermeneutische Betrachtungsweise zum Qur'an, Sure 4 Vers 43, mit Blick auf das Geschlechterverhältnis im Islam*. Köln: Zentrum für Islamische Frauenforschung und Frauenförderung.

Chapter 7

Objection, Your Honour! Accommodating *Niqab*-Wearing Women in Courtrooms[1]

Natasha Bakht

Introduction

In 2006, a lawyer named Shabnam Mughal represented a client at the Asylum and Immigration Tribunal in England. Ms Mughal is a Muslim and wore a *niqab* or full-face veil in public places. During her submissions, she was told by Judge George Glossop to remove her *niqab* because he could not hear her. Perhaps a more appropriate response to the legitimate concern of not being able to hear an advocate as she made her submissions would have been, 'please speak up'. However, because such a request was not made, and because the lawyer refused to remove her veil,[2] the case was adjourned and Mughal was replaced by a male lawyer from her firm.[3]

This chapter is an attempt to analyse opposition to the *niqab* in courtroom settings. It is argued that permitting women to wear the *niqab* in courtrooms does not impede justice. Opposition to the *niqab* is usually a knee-jerk response to difference that is typically not grounded in any rational understanding of the actual circumstances at issue. The question that arises when such unfounded and unexamined objections to the *niqab* are raised is whether the restriction on attire is actually a subterfuge for discrimination (Renteln 2004: 140). Part I of this chapter

---

1 I am grateful for the outstanding research assistance provided to me by Jennifer Dick and Andrea Skinner. Funding for research assistance has been provided generously by the Law Foundation of Ontario and the Social Sciences and Humanities Research Council. I also thank Prof. Vanessa Gruben, Dr Sheema Khan, Dr Carmela Murdocca and Dr Baidar Bakht for their helpful comments.

2 My use of the term 'veil' refers to any of the head coverings used by Muslim women. I am always cautious of the use of broad non-specific terminology because emphasis on particularity tends to coincide with accuracy and nuance which is critical in debates such as that at hand. However, while I recognize that there are multiple ways in which women may cover portions of their faces/heads/bodies, at times I use this generic term 'veil' because it pervades the literature in this area and opponents of the 'veil' tend to conflate the different types of head coverings making it difficult to assess the specific nature of their objections.

3 Nick Britten 'Lawyer in a Veil is taken off Case', *The Telegraph* (15 November 2006). Available at: <http://www.telegraph.co.uk/news/uknews/1534084/Lawyer-in-a-veil-is-taken-off-case.html> [accessed 5 November 2008].

scrutinizes judicial assessment of credibility based on demeanour evidence, suggesting that demeanour is an inherently unreliable tool by which to judge truthfulness. Based on this scrutiny, this section of the chapter considers whether there might be instances in which the removal of the *niqab* may be necessary for justice to be done. Part II of the chapter suggests accommodation measures for *niqab*-wearing women in the few instances in which seeing their faces is necessary for the judicial task at hand. The illustrations in this chapter are drawn primarily from cases in Canada with some examples from Britain, the United States and New Zealand.

This chapter does not set out to explain why women might choose to cover their faces. Despite little qualitative research done to date on this question, some of the excellent research that has been done on women who wear the *hijab*[4] suggests that there are several possible reasons why some Muslim women cover their faces. Because cultural symbols are socially constructed and contested, and are also the result of intersecting phenomena, the meanings attributed to the *hijab* or *niqab* are not endemic to the veil itself; rather they are produced through cultural discourses and social practices – they operate through vast networks of social relationships. The studies of women from several countries indicate that the veil is not a one-dimensional symbol. The veil means different things to different people within Muslim societies and different things again to Westerners than to Middle Easterners (Read and Bartkowski 2000: 396–7). This may well mean that the cultural significance of this symbol will have overlapping and opposing characteristics.

Whether it is in resisting racism (Hoodfar 1983: 18), expressing cultural difference (Atasoy 2006: 211; see also Read and Bartkowksi 2000: 404), making a fashion statement (*Middle East Times* cited in Eum 2000: 112), articulating a religious identity (Wiles 2007: 720), helping as a device in the competition for husbands (Mule and Barthel 1992: 329) or some combination of the above, the veil cannot be understood as a symbol with singular meaning. Rather than conceptualizing the veil as a frozen embodiment of a particular culture or its subversion, most women actively engage with the symbols that the veil represents (Atasoy 2006: 218–19).

For the purposes of this chapter one is better served by acknowledging that regardless of the reasons why some Muslim women wear the veil, no matter the kind of veil it may be, and even if one believes that their choice is the result of false consciousness (Mackinnon 1983, cited in Wiles 2007: 719), for these women the veil is a critical factor of their being. To deny them access to a fundamental

4 The *hijab* literally means both 'modesty' and the 'veil' in Arabic. There are a variety of different forms of *hijab* or veils ranging from the headscarf (*hijab*) to the face veil (sometimes called the *hijab* or the *niqab*) to the *burqa* which covers the entire face and body. This chapter will refer to the headscarf as the *hijab* and the face-veil as the *niqab*, unless otherwise indicated.

legal institution on the basis of their identity is to deny them their dignity: as the Judicial Studies Board (JSB)[5] in Britain noted:

> To force a choice between that identity … and the woman's involvement in the criminal, civil justice, or tribunal system (as a witness, party, member of court staff or legal office-holder) may well have a significant impact on that woman's sense of dignity and would likely serve to exclude and marginalise further women with limited visibility in courts and tribunals. This is of particular concern for a system of justice that must be, and must be seen to be, inclusive and representative of the whole community. While there may be a diversity of opinions and debates between Muslims about the nature of dress required, for the judicial system the starting point should be respect for the choice made, and for each woman to decide on the extent and nature of the dress she adopts. (JSB 2005–2008: 3-18/2)

In her study of colonial images of Muslim women, Hoodfar argued that the visibility of Muslim women's bodies became a battlefield in a struggle between modernist and conservative forces (Hoodfar 1993: 12). We cannot allow the hyper-*in*visibility of the bodies of *niqab*-wearing women to become the battlefield in a vague cultural conflict.

Part I: Opposition to the *Niqab* in the Courtroom

Alison Dundes Renteln (2004: 149–50) has argued that justifications for particular dress codes in courtrooms ordinarily include the need for the judge to maintain dignity, decorum and order, and the need to ensure the proper administration of justice, including the need to avoid jury bias and prejudice to guarantee a fair trial. While arguments against women who wear the full-face veil in courtrooms are sometimes articulated with more sophistication than is opposition to the *niqab* heard more generally, many of the justifications for this opposition are equally indefensible.

Immediately following the Shabnam Mughal event, the President of the UK's Asylum and Immigration Tribunal (AIT), Mr Justice Hodge, provided interim

5 The Judicial Studies Board (JSB) is directly responsible for training full- and part-time judges in England and Wales, and for overseeing the training of lay magistrates, chairs and members of tribunals. See <http://www.jsboard.co.uk/index.htm> [accessed 5 November 2008]. The JSB also produces publications that provide tools and guidance on topics of relevance to judges including an *Equal Treatment Benchbook*. Chapter 3.3 ('Religious dress') specifically provides guidance to judges on the wearing of the full veil or *niqab* in court: available at <http://www.jsboard.co.uk/downloads/ettb_veil.pdf> [accessed 5 November 2008].

advice for judges in his jurisdiction on the wearing of *niqab*s by representatives of parties in cases before the AIT. He stated:

> Immigration judges must exercise discretion on a case-by-case basis where a representative wishes to wear a veil. The representative in the recent case has appeared veiled previously at the AIT hearings without difficulties. It is important to be sensitive in such cases. The presumption is that if a representative before an AIT tribunal wishes to wear a veil, has the agreement of his or her client and can be heard reasonably clearly by all parties to the proceedings, then the representative should be allowed to do so.[6]

In February 2007, the JSB published a chapter addressing religious dress in their *Equal Treatment Benchbook*. This chapter deals in greater detail with the issue of women wearing the *niqab* in the courtroom context. Importantly, the chapter reiterates Justice Hodge's pronouncement following the Shabnam Mughal incident that 'it should not automatically be assumed that any difficulty is created by a woman in court, in whatever capacity, who chooses to wear a *niqab*'(JSB 2005–2008: 3-18/3).

Niqab-wearing women hold multiple roles in the courtroom context. This section of the chapter canvasses the many roles that *niqab*-wearing women do or could play in the courtroom. Opposition to the *niqab* in this context must be able to definitively respond to the question 'What is the significance of seeing this woman's face to the judicial/legal task at hand?' I suggest that the instances in which seeing a woman's face is critical for the legal task are, in fact, quite limited.

The Perils of Relying on Demeanour Evidence

Before beginning an examination of each courtroom function, this section will address the most commonly held reason for why judges need to be able to see the faces of the people who come before them.

Often trial judges bear the responsibility of being triers of fact. As such, judges are permitted in law to assess the credibility of witnesses and the accused based on demeanour evidence. That is, judges are permitted to evaluate the trustworthiness of a person in court based on their appearance, attitude and/or disposition. Juries, who are also triers of fact, are expected to assess the sincerity of a witness's testimony as well. In Canada, as early as 1947, Justice Estey of the Supreme Court of Canada held in *R. v White* that

---

6 Judicial Communications Office, press release, 29/06, 'Guidance on the wearing of veils by representatives in courts and tribunals' (9 November 2006). Available at: <www.judiciary.gov.uk/publications_media/media_releases/2006/2906.htm> [accessed 5 November 2008].

> The general integrity and intelligence of the witness, his powers to observe, his capacity to remember and his accuracy in statement are important. It is also important to determine whether he is honestly endeavouring to tell the truth, whether he is sincere or frank or whether he is biased, reticent and evasive. All these questions and others must be answered from the observation of the witness' general conduct and demeanour in determining the question of credibility.[7]

Justice O'Halloran noted in the 1952 case of *Faryna v Chorny* that '[t]he law does not clothe the trial judge with a divine insight into the hearts and minds of witnesses'.[8] Yet case after case makes reference to the special position of trial judges, as triers of fact. In *R. v Francois*, Justice Carthy of the Court of Appeal for Ontario stated: 'I cannot see the complainant, hear that voice as it offers explanations, or observe the body language that we all use to separate truth from fiction in face-to-face encounters.'[9] The advantage of seeing and hearing the testimony of witnesses is often made reference to by appellate courts. In *Laurentide Motels v Beauport (City)*, Madam Justice L'Heureux-Dubé remarked:

> [A]n appellate court which has neither seen nor heard the witnesses and as such is unable to assess their movements, glances, hesitations, trembling, blushing, surprise or bravado, is not in a position to substitute its opinion for that of the trial judge, who has the difficult task of separating the wheat from the chaff and looking into the hearts and minds of witnesses in an attempt to discover the truth.[10]

Similarly, in *R. v Jabiaranha*, the Supreme Court of Canada approved of the trial judge's reasons where she did not believe the defence witness in part because his demeanour demonstrated signs of untruthfulness:

> [The accused and the defence witness] exhibited classic signs of discomfort when challenged on points and then would elaborate the details. Each was evasive at times or his eyes shifted around. Thus in certain points … each by the story and his demeanour, displayed signs of untruthfulness.[11]

Subjective factors clearly play a decisive role in the evaluation of credibility and the demeanour of a witness may lead to the rejection of that person's evidence. A witness may present a 'positive' demeanour, including a good tone of voice and appropriate body language that succeeds in overcoming any concerns the trier of

7 *R. v White,* [1947] S.C.R. 268.

8 *Faryna v Chorny*, [1952] 2 D.L.R. 354 at 357 (B.C.C.A.) [*Faryna*].

9 *R. v Francois* (1993), 14 O.R. (3d) 191 at 202 (C.A.), Carthy J.A., dissenting [*Francois*].

10 *Laurentide Motels v Beauport (City),* [1989] 1 S.C.R. 705 at 799.

11 *R. v Jabarianha*, [2001] 3 S.C.R. 430 at para. 29.

fact may have with respect to the content of the testimony.[12] By contrast, there may be something about a person's demeanour in the witness box which may lead to the rejection of that person's evidence.

It may be that the juror is unable to point to the precise aspect of the witness's demeanour which was found to be suspicious, and as a result cannot articulate either to himself or others exactly why the witness should not be believed. A juror should not be made to feel that the overall, perhaps intangible, effect of the witness's demeanour cannot be taken into consideration in the assessment of credibility.[13]

Judges and juries are permitted in law to assess credibility based on demeanour and given what little we know about human beings, it may in fact, be our tendency to depend to some extent on indications of demeanour. Indeed several scholars have pointed out rather convincingly that evidence is less what is produced at trial and more the interaction of what is produced with the background and experience of the fact-finder (Seniuk 2000: 5).

But if the judge is not given divine insight into the hearts and minds of witnesses appearing before her/him, what are the telltale signs that reveal dishonesty? What are the badges of sincerity? How much importance should be assigned to subjective factors such as the tone of voice, the presence of an ironic smile or a nervous twitch of the face? How does one ascertain, relying on Justice Estey's words, whether a witness is sincere or frank or whether he is biased, reticent or evasive? Is not the acceptance or rejection of testimony on such grounds fraught with danger?[14] Paul Ekman in his study of lying found that with rare exception, 'no one can do better than chance at spotting liars simply by their demeanour' (Ekman 1992: 285).

> It is amazing to many people when they learn that all of the other professional groups concerned with lying – judges, trial attorneys, police, polygraphers who work for the CIA, FBI or NSA (National Security Agency), the military services, and psychiatrists who do forensic work – did no better than chance. Equally astonishing, most of them didn't know they could not detect deceit from demeanour. (Seniuk 2000: 4)

Demeanour may, of course, indicate truthfulness but it can also be misleading. Judging demeanour in the courtroom context is particularly challenging because judges and juries do not know the people who testify before them and thus have no sense of how they might react to stress. They do not have the opportunity to observe a person for a very long period of time or in an environment more natural to the witness. In *R. v Nelles*, the prosecution sought an inference of guilt from a

12 *Francois*, *supra* note 10.

13 *R. v Lifchus*, [1997] 3 S.C.R. 320 at para. 29.

14 Gilles Renaud 'Credibility and Demeanour: An Examination based on the World of Literature' (2001) Ontario Court of Justice, available at <http://www.trussel.com/maig/credibil.htm> [accessed 5 November 2008].

doctor's observation that the accused, a nurse charged with the murder of babies at the Hospital for Sick Children in Toronto, had 'a very strange expression on her face' and showed 'no sign at all of grief' when one of the babies died.[15] In discharging Ms Nelles at the conclusion of the preliminary inquiry, Judge Vanek said:

> Dr Fowler barely knew Susan Nelles, if at all; he knew nothing about her emotional range, her reaction to stress, or her manner of expressing grief. I am unable to find any evidence of guilt from what a doctor thought from a passing glance was 'a very strange expression' on the face of a young woman he barely knew [and] who had suffered a most harrowing experience.[16]

Judges are subject to the same cognitive biases as everyone else. Not surprisingly then, there is much case law that cautions against the use of demeanour evidence in determining credibility. In the often-cited case *Faryna v Chorny*, the British Columbia Court of Appeal stated that if 'a trial judge's finding of credibility is to depend solely on which person he thinks made the better appearance of sincerity in the witness box, we are left with a purely arbitrary finding and justice would then depend upon the best actors in the witness box.'[17] The evaluation of demeanour may be far less reliable a gauge for the veracity of testimony than is the examination of the logic and coherence of an account. It would be a shame for a witness to be disbelieved simply because she made a poor impression due to her clothes, her mannerisms or her attitude, and yet the testimony was logical, coherent and consistent. By the same token, a witness may be able to look at counsel straight in the eye, be calm, cool and confident and yet advance a fact that is quite simply impossible to accept.[18]

Some of the dangers of relying on demeanour outside the judicial context have been documented in the context of policing. Prof. David Tanovich has written that in racial profiling cases, perfectly innocuous behaviour is often interpreted as suspicious simply because the observation was occurring through stereotypical lenses.[19] As Justice Rosenberg has noted '[p]erceptions of guilt based on demeanour are likely to depend on highly subjective impressions.'[20]

The cross-cultural context is but one example of a common erroneous interpretation of body language and behaviour. Possibly the best known concern

15 Mark J. Sandler 'Lessons for Trial Courts from the Morin Inquiry' (2005) at 38 [unpublished, on file with author].

16 *R. v Nelles*, [1982] O.J. No. 3654 (Prov. Ct. Crim. Div.) (QL) at para. 62.

17 *Faryna, supra* note 9 at 356. See also *R. v Pressley* (1948), 7 C.R. 342 (B.C.C.A.) at 347.

18 Renaud, *supra* note 14.

19 David M. Tanovich, 'The Further Erasure of Race in *Charter* Cases' (2006) 38 C.R. 84 at 10.

20 *R. v Levert* (2001), 159 C.C.C. (3d) 71 (Ont. C.A.) at 81.

in this respect surrounds the demeanour of First Nations witnesses whose testimony may have been discounted by resort to the apparent badge of sincerity associated with looking someone in the eyes. Some researchers have documented that Aboriginals who adhere to the unspoken rules about avoiding eye contact for courtesy reasons 'may appear to be shifty and evasive' (Shusta et al. 1995: 251).[21]

In *R. v Norman*, the Ontario Court of Appeal noted that the appearance of honesty and integrity on the part of witnesses may provide little assistance in assessing the reliability of their testimony because witnesses may well believe in what they are saying, regardless of whether it is accurate or not. Justice Finlayson stated:

> I do not think that an assessment of credibility based on demeanour alone is good enough in a case where there are so many significant inconsistencies. The issue is not merely whether the complainant sincerely believes her evidence to be true; it is also whether this evidence is reliable. Accordingly, her demeanour and credibility are not the only issues. The reliability of the evidence is paramount.[22]

Thus, in determining credibility, judges and juries are on firmer ground if they go beyond demeanour and seek support for their findings of credibility from the entire trial record (Sangmuah 1994: 4). A finding of credibility ought to depend not solely upon the impression made by the personal demeanour of a witness but also upon an examination of all of the elements and probabilities existing in the case. The appearance of telling the truth is but one of the elements that enters into the credibility of the evidence of a witness. 'Opportunities for knowledge, powers of observation, judgment and memory, ability to describe clearly what he has seen and heard, as well as other factors, combine to produce what is called credibility.'[23] In cases of conflict of evidence, the test of the story of a witness as it relates to credibility must be 'its harmony with the preponderance of the probabilities which a practical and informed person would readily recognize as reasonable in that place and in those conditions'.[24] In other words, the testimony of each witness must be regarded in light of all of the circumstances, including what other persons have said. Judges must subject the witness' story to an examination of its *consistency* with the probabilities that surround the existing conditions. Finally, the search for credibility ought to be grounded in more objective criteria such as prior inconsistent statements, contradictory assertions in examination-in-chief

21 This reference is not cited to suggest that all First Nations peoples react in such a fashion, merely that some do, as do many members of other groups for a variety of reasons.

22 *R. v Norman* (1993), 26 C.R. (4th) 256 (Ont. C.A.) at para. 47.

23 *Faryna, supra* note 8 at 356–57.

24 *Ibid.* at 357.

and during cross-examination and illogical propositions in the circumstances of the specific case at hand. Trial judges must be asked to go further and say that the evidence of the witness one believes is in accordance with the preponderance of probabilities in the case and, importantly, if their views are to command confidence, judges must also state their reasons for that conclusion.[25]

Given the unreliability of depending solely on demeanour evidence, women whose faces are covered by the *niqab* should not then pose an insurmountable problem to the dispensation of justice in a courtroom setting. Though demeanour as a tool for assessing credibility is available to trial judges as a matter of law, using demeanour as the sole criterion upon which to base credibility is highly suspect because of the inherent dangers associated with accurately assessing the meaning of say a gesture or a look. Because a court of appeal must be satisfied that the trial judge's finding of credibility is based not on one element to the exclusion of others, but rather on all of the elements by which it can be tested in the particular case, judges who are unable to see a witness' face are not at such a great disadvantage.

Courtroom Roles: Examining the Impact of the Niqab

Women who wear the *niqab* have been in the courtroom context in several different capacities. This section of the chapter examines the impact of the *niqab* on these differing roles to determine whether the *niqab* poses an obstacle to justice.

As an Advocate Women who wear the *niqab* have acted as advocates in a courtroom. Lawyers are not examined for the truthfulness of what they say, thus evidence as to their demeanour and identity are irrelevant. The only real issue that could arise where an advocate or representative appears in a *niqab* would be concerns that the woman could not be heard, rather than seen. 'Just as in any case where a judge might have difficulty in hearing any party, witness or advocate, sensitively enquiring whether they can speak any louder or providing other means of amplification should suffice and such measures should be considered with the advocate before asking her to remove her veil' (JSB 2005–2008: 3-18/6).

Because judges retain a great degree of discretion in how their courtrooms are run, women wearing the *niqab* may find, as Shabnam Mughal did, that they are prohibited from representing their clients as a result of this discretion. In Pakistan, there appear to be signs of keeping veiled women from pleading in court. In November of 2006, Chief Justice Tariq Pervaiz Khan of the Peshawar High Court banned lawyer Raees Anjum from wearing the *hijab*[26] in his courtroom. He is quoted as saying, 'You are professionals and should be dressed as required of lawyers … We [judges] cannot identify veiled woman lawyers and suspect

25 *Ibid.*

26 Although the word *hijab* is used in the article by Olden, cited below, reference is made to a full-face veil.

that veiled lawyers appear to seek adjournment of proceedings in other lawyers' cases.'[27] That veiled advocates are suspected of misrepresenting themselves when lawyers have codes of conduct that they are required to abide by, indicates that even those most educated in justice do injustice by resorting to biased beliefs about a marginalized group of women. The JSB's Equal Treatment Advisory Committee in Britain has suggested that the starting point for a *niqab*-wearing woman in the courtroom must be that she is entitled to appear as an advocate wearing it (JSB 2005–2008: 3-18/6). They nonetheless state that judges retain the discretion to permit or forbid the *niqab* on a case-by-case basis. This general policy, as the JSB acknowledges, puts women who wear the *niqab* and their clients at a disadvantage because they would never know in advance of a hearing whether a judge would allow them to appear in their *niqab*s.

Judges should not be permitted to use vague or biased discretionary means to prohibit *niqab*-wearing lawyers from arguing in court. Logical lines of reasoning must be established and only where measures of accommodation have been exhausted should a refusal to permit an advocate to wear a *niqab* be acceptable.

As a Judge There are not many known instances of judges wearing the *niqab*. Apparently, some women judges in Peshawar's North West Frontier wear the *hijab* during hearings.[28] Some have suggested that lawyers must be able to read a judge's expressions. It might be argued that the inability to see a judge's face could compromise an accused's right to a fair trial. Although there is no 'right' to see a judge's face, some may argue that because judges are the 'face' of justice, questions around the transparency of the judicial process may be made.

In their report to the Québec provincial government on practices related to accommodation, Gérard Bouchard and Charles Taylor recommended that those employees of the state 'who occupy positions that embody at the highest level the necessary neutrality of the State, such as judges … impose on themselves a form of circumspection concerning the expression of their religious convictions' (Bouchard and Taylor 2008: 151). Although the report goes to great lengths to articulate that the appearance of neutrality does not warrant a general rule that would prohibit agents of the state from wearing religious signs, little explanation is given as to why such a rule is necessitous for judges or police officers.[29] In

27 Ryan Olden, 'Pakistan Judge forbids Muslim Veils in Courtroom' *Jurist* (4 November 2006). Available online: <http://jurist.law.pitt.edu/paperchase/2006/11/pakistan-judge-forbids-muslim-veils-in.php> [accessed 25 November 2008].

28 It is unclear from this news report whether these judges wore the *hijab* or the *niqab*. What is known is that 'the local government in Pakistan is divided on the issue of veiled professionals'. *Ibid.*

29 Indeed this recommendation is entirely antithetical to a Federal Court of Appeal decision in Canada wherein it was held that accommodating Sikh men such that they could wear the turban as part of the official uniform for the Royal Canadian Mounted Police was

focusing on the importance of the appearance of neutrality, the report asks the rhetorical question: 'Could a Muslim respondent assume the impartiality of a Jewish judge wearing a kippah or a Hindu judge displaying a tilak?' (Bouchard and Taylor 2008: 151). The insinuation from such a question is that neutrality and impartiality would be impossible in this situation. But judges already have an explicit duty to maintain impartiality. Should they be unable to preside over a case impartially, they are required to recuse themselves. Moreover, if neutrality were based entirely on appearance rather than conduct, one would be left in a situation where members of the same ethnicity or gender would not be capable of judging others. As Madam Justice L'Heureux Dubé and McLachlin noted in their concurrence in *R. v R.D.S.*:[30]

> [J]udges in a bilingual, multiracial and multicultural society will undoubtedly approach the task of judging from their varied perspectives. They will certainly have been shaped by, and have gained insight from, their different experiences, and cannot be expected to divorce themselves from these experiences on the occasion of their appointment to the bench. In fact, such a transformation would deny society the benefit of the valuable knowledge gained by the judiciary while they were members of the Bar. As well, it would preclude the achievement of a diversity of backgrounds in the judiciary. The reasonable person does not expect that judges will function as neutral ciphers; however, the reasonable person does demand that judges achieve impartiality in their judging.

Rather than concentrating on the appearance of neutrality, where judges may never be successful in the sense of being purely objective, they must rather strive for impartiality. The genuine concern for transparency would be fulfilled by the judge's rendering of precise reasons which could be appealed if necessary.

As Courtroom Staff The least contentious positions for women who wear the niqab are likely their roles as courtroom staff. Because courtroom staff, similar to advocates, are not being evaluated for the truthfulness of their comments, indeed some staff may say nothing at all during a hearing, issues surrounding the need to see their faces or hear their voices should not arise.

As a Witness or Defendant Arguably, niqab-wearing in court is likely to be most contentious when the woman wearing the niqab is testifying before the court. Generally speaking, courts seem to be satisfied of a witness's identity if the witness swears or affirms her/his identity prior to giving any testimony. It would only be

---

consistent with the *Canadian Charter of Rights and Freedoms*. *Grant et al. v Attorney General (Canada)*, [1995] 1 F.C. 158 (F.C.A.). Leave to appeal to the Supreme Court of Canada was dismissed without reasons and with costs. 130 D.L.R. (4th) vii (S.C.C. Feb 15, 1996).

30 *R. v R.D.S.*, [1997] 3 S.C.R. 484 at para. 38.

just that the word of a veiled woman should also be considered sufficient to prove her identity.

In the absence of clear rules to the contrary, judges have a great deal of discretion over the demands they can make of witnesses. On certain occasions judges have even dismissed cases outright where a woman has refused to remove her *niqab*. In *Muhammad v Enterprise Rent-A-Car*, Ginnah Muhammad tried to bring a suit in Michigan over the nearly $3000 that a car rental company charged her for damage done when thieves broke into her rental car.[31] Judge Paul Paruk dismissed the case when Muhammad refused to remove her *niqab* explaining that it was part of her religious way of life. Judge Paruk explained that he needed to see Muhammad's face in order to determine if she was telling the truth. He then went on to tell her that wearing the face veil was 'not a religious thing … [but] a custom thing.'[32] It is unclear that Judge Paruk actually needed to see Ginnah Muhammad's face in this case. There were likely no identification arguments to be made in this garden-variety small claims dispute. While judging her credibility may well have been an important aspect of the case, as previously noted, even this could likely have been done without resort to unreliable demeanour evidence.[33] Furthermore, it is unclear why Muhammad's evidence could not have even been admissible. Had the judge truly felt constrained in his ability to evaluate her evidence, he could simply have considered this when weighing her testimony.

Consideration should also be given to the fact that a *niqab*-wearing woman may be in a court not of her own choice. She may be a reluctant witness or a fearful victim/complainant who has been subject to abuse. In such instances the very act of removing the veil combined with the added pressure of appearing in a court could be traumatic enough to have an adverse impact on the quality of evidence given. Judges will be unlikely to distinguish these various strains on a woman's testimony. In ensuring a fair hearing, judges should ask, 'What is required to enable a woman wearing a *niqab* to participate in the legal process, to facilitate her ability to give her best evidence and to ensure, so far as practicable, a fair hearing for both sides?' (JSB 2005–2008: 3-18/3). Forcing a woman to choose between giving evidence to secure a conviction and wearing the *niqab* seems contrary to a just and impartial process.

While it may be difficult in some cases to assess the evidence of a woman wearing a *niqab*, the experiences of other judges demonstrates that it is possible to do so (JSB 2005–2008: 3-18/4). Judges must use their discretion carefully by considering whether the veil represents a true obstacle to the evaluation of the

---

31 *Muhammad v Enterprise Rent-a-Car*, No. 06-41896-GC (Mich. 31st Dist. Ct. Oct. 11, 2006) [*Muhammad*].

32 Transcript of Record at 4–5, *Muhammad, ibid.*

33 As one author has noted, Judge Paruk may have benefited by recalling that 'Themis, the goddess of justice wears a blindfold for a reason'. Steven Lubet, 'When does a Muslim Veil become a Poker Face? A Judge who Insisted a Woman remove her *Niqab* was Wrong', *The Chicago Sun Times* (11 March 2007) B2.

evidence. The exclusion of women who wear the *niqab* from courtrooms should not be justified with resort to the amorphous phrase: in the 'interests of justice'. Judges must be able to state categorically the judicial reason for needing to see a woman's face.

Perhaps of greater concern for the witness or defendant who is permitted to wear the *niqab* in a courtroom is the implications that the veil could have on perceptions of her credibility or right to receive a fair trial. 'If a woman wears a full veil in court, then I'm very concerned that negative implications will be subconsciously drawn and will work to the detriment of an advocate, a defendant or a witness. There is also a higher likelihood of alienation.'[34] Because most people have little contact with fully veiled women and because many preconceptions against veiled women confirm their status as 'other', juries are likely to draw adverse inferences from their testimony or mere presence. As Judge Gloria Epstein noted, 'The reality is that people tend to be more comfortable with, and therefore believe, their own kind' (Epstein 2002: 11). While judicial education on the unreliability of demeanour evidence is having the result that some judges 'strenuously resist allowing demeanour to factor into an assessment of credibility' (Epstein 2002: 12), the same cannot be said of juries. It is probable that juries will perceive, even if subconsciously, *niqab*-wearing women as being less credible. Just as bell hooks has argued (1981) that black women are not seen as trustworthy because they do not conform to our socially held images of figures of authority, *niqab*-wearing women are likely to be perceived as untrustworthy because they do not 'look' honest or deserving of respect. In addition to keeping their own prejudices in check, judges must then play the very important role of instructing juries, who may be susceptible to subconsciously devaluing the testimony of a veiled witness, to remain impartial.

In Canada, the Supreme Court has held that it is appropriate to question potential jurors as to their racial bias during the jury selection process.[35] Bias may affect a trial in different ways; for example, by inclining a juror to reject or put less weight on the evidence of the accused. Bias may also 'predispose the juror to the Crown, perceived as representative of the "white" majority against the minority-member accused … to resolve doubts about aspects of the Crown's case more readily'.[36] Many of the biases which people hold against African and Aboriginal Canadians relate to notions of higher criminality associated within these groups. Given the multiple and often irrational objections that people have to the *niqab*, it would not

34 Interview of Homa Wilson by Tilly Rubens (6 February 2007) in 'Should the Veil be Worn in Court?' *Times Online*, <http://business.timesonline.co.uk/tol/business/law/article1331659.ece> [accessed 25 November 2008]. Judge Moore in *Razamjoo, infra* note 42 at para. 71 also expressed concern that 'evidence given from beneath a burqa would, consciously or unconsciously, be accorded less weight than the same evidence given by that witness when her face was visible.'

35 *R. v Williams*, [1998] 1 S.C.R. 1128 [*Williams*].

36 *Ibid.* at para. 11.

be difficult to make an argument that jurors could see a veiled accused as more likely to commit crime, particularly certain kinds of offences or that they may hold a negative view of her and her faith which could impact upon their partiality.[37]

As a Juror Women who wear the niqab may also be summoned for jury duty. While lawyers have peremptory challenges and challenges for cause available to them in order to exclude a woman wearing the full-face veil as a member of a jury, these challenges cannot be based on bias. Rather, they can only be used to avert the possibility that a niqab-wearing woman is incapable of treating the accused person impartially. Judges must ensure that there is a genuine and legitimate basis for such a challenge and not improper predispositions of the kind that stereotype women who wear the niqab.

Part II: Accommodating *Niqab*-wearing Women in the Courtroom

'The justice system should encourage practices which will enable as many people as possible to participate and engage with judicial processes' (JSB 2005–2008: 3-18/2). To force a choice between religious identity and participation in the justice system is to put women with already limited visibility in courts in an untenable situation.[38] Indeed the impact of being excluded from the justice system is not insubstantial. Ginnah Muhammad, whose case was dismissed after Judge Paul Paruk refused to let her testify with the *niqab*, said: 'When I walked out, I just really felt empty, like the courts didn't care about me.'[39] After being told by the Chief Justice to remove her face veil if she wished to act as an advocate, Raees Anjum commented: 'I was embarrassed when the chief justice asked me not to wear veil in courtrooms [*sic*]. I feel more confident in my hijab … [It] reflects a

37 *Ibid.* at para. 28. 'Evidence of widespread racial prejudice may, depending on the nature of the evidence and the circumstances of the case, lead to the conclusion that there is a realistic potential for partiality. The potential for partiality is irrefutable where the prejudice can be linked to specific aspects of the trial, like a widespread belief that people of the accused's race are more likely to commit the crime charged. But it may be made out in the absence of such links.' *Ibid.* at para. 27.

38 Importantly, marginalized communities feel deeply the efforts made by institutions such as courts to include them in their processes. The Islamic Human Rights Commission welcomed the JSB guidelines. Chairman Massoud Shadjareh said: 'In the climate of Islamophobia that we live in, it is heartening to see the courts base their guidelines on the merits rather than on intolerance and prejudice.' 'Muslim Veil Allowed in Courts', *BBC News* (24 April 2007). Available online: <http://newsvote.bbc.co.uk/mpapps/pagetools/print/news.bbc.co.uk/1/hi/england/staffordshire/6588157.stm> [accessed 25 November 2008].

39 Paul Egan, 'Muslim Woman told to Remove Veil in Court Files Lawsuit', *The Detroit News*, 28 March 2007. Available at: <http://www.muslimnews.co.uk/news/news.php?article=12521> [accessed 5 November 2008].

woman's modesty.'[40] And finally, in a New Zealand case that considered whether two witnesses could give their testimony in a criminal trial while wearing the *burqa*, one witness said that she would rather kill herself than reveal her face while giving evidence (Ahdar 2006: 654).

These reactions to the removal of the *niqab* in the courtroom must be taken seriously as the removal of the veil can be profoundly disorienting and can lead to serious vulnerability. As the JSB in Britain has noted, there are many alternatives available to judges wishing to accommodate women who wear the *niqab*. Judges can typically rely on the inherent powers of the court to regulate the conduct of its procedures.[41] Just as courts can prevent abuse of its procedures, judges can also depart from normal trial processes when this might assist in the participation of otherwise marginalized groups. As a New Zealand court in *Police v Razamjoo* noted, 'The court has those inherent powers so that justice might the better be done.'[42]

An often cited reason for prohibiting the *niqab* in the courtroom is the inability of the judge or jury to hear the woman because her words are not being clearly transmitted through her veil. Measures can easily be taken to rectify such a problem including politely asking the woman to project her voice or arranging to have the woman use a microphone.

In situations where the identity of the *niqab*-wearing woman must be verified, women court staff can simply validate a woman's identity by asking her to remove the veil for the purposes of comparing a piece of photo identification with her face. As Homa Wilson, has noted, 'Muslim women don't object to removing their face veils in the presence of other women.'[43]

While claims about the necessity of seeing a woman's face in a courtroom context will undoubtedly be repeated, it should not be forgotten that there are circumstances where judges will take evidence without being able to see the witness's face: for example, where evidence is taken over the telephone[44] or where

---

40 Olden, *supra* note 27.

41 In Canada see *MacMillan Bloedel Ltd. v Simpson*, [1995] 4 S.C.R. 725 at paras. 15 and 33 and H. Jacob, 'The Inherent Jurisdiction of the Court' (1970) 23 Current Legal Problems 23 at 27. In the United Kingdom see: *The Civil Procedure Rules 1998* (U.K.), S.I. 1998/3132, L.17, rr. 32.1(1)(c), 32.3, 39.2(3)(g). US federal courts possess an inherent authority to impose sanctions for the conduct of litigants in counsel regardless of whether the behaviour at issue would be covered specifically under a rule or statute. *O'Brien v Ed Donnelly Ents., Inc*., 2006 WL 2583327, at 2 (S.D. Ohio Sept. 5, 2006).

42 *Police v Razamjoo,* [2005] D.C.R. 408 (D.C.N.Z.) at para. 99 [*Razamjoo*].

43 In Rubens, *supra* note 35.

44 Section 714.3 of the *Criminal Code of Canada* permits the reception of evidence in certain circumstances by telephone. To invoke the provision, the court must be of the opinion that it would be appropriate in all of the circumstances. In *R. v Chapdelaine,* 2004 CarswellAlta 48 (Q.B.) (WLeC) an application to bring evidence pursuant to s. 714.3 of the *Criminal Code* to have two witnesses provide evidence by telephone was granted.

the judge is visually impaired.[45] Clearly, if testimony can be given without resort to visual cues in some situations the requirement to see a witness's face is contrary to logic. Moreover, any prejudice associated with not being able to see the witness's face can be dealt with at the stage of weighing the evidence rather than prohibiting its admissibility.

The JSB has stated that any request to remove a veil should be accompanied with an explanation by the judge of his/her concern that 'where there are crucial issues of credit, the woman might be at a disadvantage if the judge or jury is not able to assess her demeanour or facial expression when responding to questions' (JSB 2005–2008: 3-18/4). It has also been suggested that the woman be given the opportunity to consult with her legal representative or witness-support worker. The importance of judicial sensitivity in this matter cannot be overstated. Some judges have used their cultural sensitivity to come up with creative solutions to such issues.

In New Zealand, Judge Lindsay Moore devised what has been described as an 'elegant compromise' (Ahdar 2006: 205) in *Police v Razamjoo*, a criminal case involving false statements made to the police as part of an insurance fraud.[46] In this case, the issue was whether the two Muslim witnesses for the Crown could wear *burqas* while giving their testimony. Defence counsel argued that the inability to observe the demeanour of the witnesses would impair the accused's right to a fair trial. Judge Moore acknowledged that what was at stake in the case were the rights of the witnesses to manifest their religious belief, the defendant's right to a fair trial[47] and the public's right to an open and public criminal justice system.[48] Judge Moore concluded that the two witnesses would be allowed to give their evidence from behind screens so that only the judge, counsel and female court staff would be able to see the witnesses' faces.[49] He also provided that so long as the witnesses' faces were visible, the witnesses could wear a hat or scarf to cover their hair. The trial proceeded according to these guidelines and the defendant was convicted.

---

45 JSB 2005–2008: 3-18/5. In the United Kingdom, there are a number of blind justices who sit regularly. Their blindness is only an obstacle in a small number of cases where there were exhibits requiring visual scrutiny. *Razamjoo, supra* note 42 at para. 48.

46 *Ibid.*

47 Importantly, what constitutes a fair trial is a balance between the rights of the accused and the public interest in the effective prosecution of criminal charges through criminal processes that are sensitive to the needs of victims and witnesses. For a Canadian case that balanced the accused's right to a fair trial with the complainant's privacy rights see: *R. v Mills* [1999] 3 S.C.R. 668.

48 *Razamjoo, supra* note 42 at para. 107.

49 The courtroom staff in this case were women. While the two counsel and judge were men, Judge Moore relied on the evidence of one of the witnesses', Mrs Salim's, beliefs regarding some relaxation in relation to being unveiled in the presence of relatively aged male authority figures as opposed to males generally. *Razamjoo, supra* note 42 at para. 111.

Judge Moore's intermediate solution between the two stark alternatives of taking off the veil or not giving testimony was thoughtful in its attempt to accommodate these Muslim women. He realized that exposing one's self to an entire courtroom of people would be upsetting to these women: 'to require her to remove her burqa in public (dire emergencies or other very compelling reasons excepted) would be to shame and disgrace her both in her own eyes and in those of the community of like believers whose customs and beliefs she is proud to uphold.'[50]

Interestingly, in order to create the compromise that he did, Judge Moore agreed to hear the testimony of Mrs Salim in her *burqa*. Although Judge Moore found receiving evidence from a *burqa*-wearing witness difficult, it was not impossible. 'A sense of the witness's character emerged, though much more slowly than is usual when a witness can be seen ... Courts (and people) adjust over time to the new or strange. Written statement or tape recorded evidence is even more impersonal than listening to a person whose physical appearance and reaction one cannot see.'[51] Judge Moore went so far as to say that 'the Court is reluctantly forced to the conclusion that there could be a fair trial even if Mrs. Salim and other witnesses of like belief gave evidence wearing their burqas'.[52] Judge Moore ultimately decided upon the compromise rather than permit evidence from being given wearing a *burqa* because he was concerned that adopting procedures so out of keeping with the expectations of the community would seriously call into question the confidence in the justice system.[53]

Importantly, in the aftermath of *Razamjoo*, policy-makers responded to the issues that arose in this case by proposing a statutory means of accommodation. Section 103 of New Zealand's *Evidence Act 2006* provides that a judge may permit a witness to give evidence 'in an alternate way' on the grounds of 'the linguistic or cultural background or religious beliefs of the witness'.[54]

Conclusions

This chapter has examined a variety of objections to the wearing of the *niqab* in courtroom settings. Most of the objections articulated have no basis in critique or can be managed with minor accommodations that would permit *niqab*-wearing women to participate fully in public life. The most contentious objection to *niqab*-wearing women appears to be the inability of the judge to adequately make determinations of credibility. However, given the growing case law and academic research that points to the unreliability of demeanour evidence, judges must seriously question reliance on this antiquated method of assessing behaviour.

50 *Ibid.* at para. 67.
51 *Ibid.* at para. 69.
52 *Ibid.* at para. 106.
53 *Ibid.* at para. 95.
54 *Evidence Act 2006* (N.Z.), 2006/69, s. 103.

When opposition to Muslim women's attire is irrational, one must ask what is really going on.

Women who wear the *niqab* seem to challenge people's core convictions about how one should pursue the good life. Rather than reacting with suspicion, we might be better served to question our own cultural assumptions. In the courtroom context, there are very few instances that would make it necessitous to see a woman's face. Thus, judges should not have unfettered discretion to exclude *niqab*-wearing women from courtrooms absent the inability to complete their judicial duty without seeing the woman's face. Even in such situations, judges must be sensitive to the impact that removing the veil can have in such a public space and be creative in their measures of accommodation.

References

Ahdar, R.J. 2006. Reflections on the Path of Religion-state Relations in New Zealand. *Brigham Young University Law Review*, 619–60.

Atasoy, Yilkdiz. 2006. Governing Women's Morality: a Study of Islamic Veiling in Canada. *European Journal of Cultural Studies*, 9(2), 203–21.

Bouchard, G. and C. Taylor. 2008. *Building the Future: A Time for Reconciliation. Commission de consultation sur les pratiques d'accommodement reliées aux différences culturelles*. Quebec: Gouvernement de Québec.

Ekman, Paul. 1992. *Telling Lies*. New York: W.W. Norton.

Epstein, Gloria. 2002. What Factors affect the Credibility of a Witness? *Advocates Soc. Journal*, 21, 10–16.

Eum, Ikran. 2000. Discourses on (un)veiling in Egypt. *Asian Journal of Women's Studies*, 6(4), 102–13.

Hoodfar, Homa. 1993. The Veil in their Minds and on our Heads: the Persistence of Colonial Images of Muslim women. *Resources for Feminist Research*, 22(3/4), 5–18.

hooks, bell. 1981. *Ain't I A Woman: Black Women and Feminism*. Boston: South End Press.

JSB. 2005–2008. *Equal Treatment Benchbook*. London: Judicial Studies Board.

MacKinnon, Catherine. 1983. Feminism, Marxism, Method and the State: Towards Feminist Jurisprudence. *Signs*, 8, 635–58.

Mule, Pat and Diane Bartel. 1992. The Return to the Veil: Individual Autonomy vs. Social Esteem. *Sociological Forum*, 7(2), 323–32.

Read, Jen'nan Ghazal and John P. Bartkowski. 2000. To Veil or not to Veil? A Case Study of Identity Negotiation among Muslim Women in Austin, Texas. *Gender and Society*, 14(3), 395–417.

Renteln, A.D. 2004. *The Cultural Defense*. Oxford: Oxford University Press.

Sangmuah, Egya N. 1994. After B. (R.H): Continuing Need to give Adequate Reasons for Findings of Credibility. *Criminal Reports 4th Series*, 135–42.

Seniuk, Gerald T.G. 2000. Liars, Scoundrels, and the Search for Truth. *Criminal Reports 5th Series*, 30, 244–54.

Shusta, R.M., D.R. Levine, P.R. Harris, and H.Z. Wong. 1995. *Multicultural Law Enforcement. Strategies for Peacekeeping in a Diverse Society*. Englewood Cliffs: Prentice Hall.

Wiles, Ellen. 2007. Headscarves, Human Rights and Harmonious Multicultural Society: Implications of the French Ban for Interpretations of Equality. *Law and Society Review*, 41(3), 699–736.

Chapter 8
The Challenge of African Customary Laws to English Legal Culture

Gordon R. Woodman

African Customary Laws in England

Around half a million people, or about one per cent of the population of England and Wales, were identified as black African in the 2001 population census (ONS 2003a: 230, Rees and Butt 2004, Grillo and Mazzucato 2008: 193 n.5). To what extent and in what circumstances does English law allow the various customary laws of these residents to take effect in England, or enforce them through its own institutions and procedures?[1]

The people concerned are mostly immigrants or the descendants of immigrants who have arrived in Britain during the past half-century from territories which were British colonies for about the first sixty years of the twentieth century.[2] Before the 1970s Africans came primarily for educational purposes (Goody and Groothues 1977), and they generally stayed less than ten years. More recent immigrants are motivated more by the prospect of advancing economically through paid work, and they often stay for several decades. There are concentrations in some districts of large cities, but many are quite widely dispersed (ONS 2003b: 65–78).

Most remain effective members of their communities of origin. Modern technology enables them to communicate frequently with relatives in Africa. They can easily transfer funds to assist relatives or to be used for projects such as house-building. They can travel back for visits. Nearly all would state that they have the intention eventually to return home, at the latest when they retire from gainful employment, and many former immigrants have done so. However, they may see themselves less as temporary migrants in a foreign land than as individuals who have acquired a second, additional place of residence and nationality, in fact,

1 The social characteristics of this group of immigrants, including their customary laws, have not been much studied. For this chapter I have drawn on the small volume of literature reporting research on the group, on my own impressions gained from contact with members and work as an expert witness in court cases involving them, and on studies of customary laws in African state legal systems. I do not consider here Islamic law, which does not form a significant element in most sub-Saharan African states' laws.

2 The main exceptions are immigrants from Somalia and immigrants who are asylum seekers, whether from Somalia or from other countries not formerly British colonies.

if not in law.[3] Today there are increasing numbers of people around the world who are 'transnationals' (Grillo and Mazzucato 2008), that is, who belong to more than one place and community, or have 'double engagement' (Grillo and Mazzucato 2008; see also: Baumann 1996, Modood 1997, Vertovec and Cohen 1999, Vertovec 1999, 2006: 22–24, Akyeampong 2000, Kabki et al. 2004, Black and King 2004, Mazzucato 2008. This and other claims in this chapter find support also in Appiah 2006). The group with which this chapter is concerned consists largely of first-generation immigrants who came to the UK as adults. Where they have had children in Britain, if they have not been sent back to Africa for parts of their childhood, there is a question as to the degree to which these children will continue their parents' connections with their African families.

The first-generation migrants have much contact with fellow immigrants. There are many organizations for immigrants from particular countries, ethnic groups, towns, schools and other institutions (Killingray 1994). Whether it is more accurate to say that there is a community of Africans, or that there are communities of various African nationalities in Britain, is debatable, but it is clear that African immigrants come together because of their strong, continuing links to their home communities in Africa.

We are concerned here with that portion of 'cultural diversity' in England which arises from this particular instance of immigration, and its relationship to 'legal practice'. Without investigating here the much-debated issue of the meaning of 'culture', it is sufficient to note that culture is or includes the normative order which is partly constitutive of a community. This type of normative order, like the law of a state, consists not only of rules in a narrow sense, but also of accepted principles (Dworkin 1977: Chaps. 2–4). Rules and principles (together 'norms') state imperative requirements as to subjects' conduct, such as those prohibiting certain acts ('primary norms'), or stipulate conduct and events which produce changes in members' relationships, such as those defining the processes which create a marriage ('secondary norms') (Hart 1994). Such a normative order may appropriately be called a law. Where the law of a community arises from social interactions within the community, not from the lawmaking activity of state or quasi-state institutions, it is customary law (Griffiths 1986, Woodman 1998). The term 'customary' is not used here to indicate that the origin of the law is necessarily ancient. In all African customary laws there have been important developments in

3 The laws of most African countries exclude dual nationality, so that if a national acquires British nationality (as many do to avoid bureaucratic obstacles to life and work in Europe), they lose their nationality of origin. However, this may be changing. Ghana, realizing the benefit obtained from its nationals resident abroad, has amended its law to permit dual nationality: Constitution of the Republic of Ghana (Amendment) Act, 1996 (Act 527); Citizenship Act, 2000 (Act 591). Ghana also recently changed its electoral law to give voting rights to citizens resident abroad: Representation of the People (Amendment) Act, 2006 (Act 699).

recent years, such as the adoption of documentary transactions and the recognition of greater individual autonomy.

African immigrants come from societies which belong to states that were created by British colonizers, the independent states of modern Africa being lineal descendants of the colonial states. The legal and administrative state systems established during the colonial period were modelled on the British systems (Woodman 2008a). The common law of England, with modifications, was introduced into the colonies of West, East and Central Africa, and is still applied today concurrently with African customary laws. In the colonies of southern Africa the received law was Roman–Dutch law, but it also was applied through legal procedures of an English type. African immigrants to England are thus familiar with the main features of English law, and accustomed to mixed legal systems in which English common law co-exists with customary laws. It is sometimes said that received law, being imposed by the colonial state, has not penetrated into indigenous African society, but this claim can be overstated. Especially in urban areas and among the economically advantaged sections of society, exposed to governmental powers and global economic and cultural influences, the received laws have significant effect; and immigrants tend not to come from the most isolated, disadvantaged sectors of society in the countries of origin.

Thus this aspect of the cultural diversity of England[4] today arises from persons who remain active within their cultures of origin, continuing to observe their customary laws, but who find much of the English cultures and laws not unfamiliar. Some of their customary laws are different in fundamental respects from English law, and this fact presents challenges to English law.

English Legal Practice and Legal Culture: Principles of Recognition

Many lawyers and legal theorists see the concept of law as concerning state law alone. In this chapter the references to customary law have already implicitly departed from this usage. If law is viewed as a social phenomenon many non-state normative orders do not differ in significant characteristics from state law. On this view any population with a diversity of cultures, such as England, observes a variety of legal orders – that is, legal pluralism prevails (Griffiths 1986, Woodman 1998). The present chapter considers a portion of English legal pluralism, namely, the 'legal practice' of English state law and its norms and practices regarding African customary laws.

That legal practice is conducted in a limited area of society, by officials and other specialists such as judges, police, barristers and solicitors. It has developed a culture which is closely associated with the English common law. This culture cannot be properly understood if seen simply as a body of norms. It is rather a system of thought with its own methods of reasoning, assumptions, preferences,

4 For the present purpose 'England' means England and Wales.

habits, attitudes and policies (Llewellyn 1960 on 'reckonability', Simpson 1970, Friedman 1975: 223, Nelken 1997). The question here is: how does this culture of the English common law respond to the observance of African customary laws by a portion of the population of England for some aspects of their lives? Part of the answer may be contained in the norms of English state law expressed in legislation and other authoritative pronouncements, but also significant are less clearly explicit aspects of English legal culture.

The proposed answer to the question uses the notion of *recognition* of a law or laws (in this case African customary laws) by another law (in this case English state law). Forms of recognition are complex and varied, but a distinction between normative and institutional recognition may assist analysis (further developed in Woodman 2008b: 33–4). *Normative recognition* is given when the norms of the recognized law are treated as valid norms of the recognizing law. This occurs, for example, in many African states when claims under customary laws are enforced as legal rights by state court judges and other state officials. This normative recognition follows from the requirement in many African state laws that the customary laws of the indigenous ethnic groups be observed by state institutions as parts of the state law. *Institutional recognition* occurs when institutions of the other law are treated by the recognizing law as producing binding legal effects. In a common instance in Africa decisions of customary dispute resolution institutions such as chiefs' tribunals are treated by the state as valid judicial decisions. Here the tribunals are treated as courts of the state judicial system.

The question thus becomes, to what extent does English law grant either normative or institutional recognition to the various African customary laws observed by immigrants? The issue has arisen in English courts and other state institutions in recent years because of the transnational situation of African migrants. Resident in England, they are necessarily involved with English state institutions. For example, they become parties to divorce and other matrimonial proceedings, especially when claims to houses and other property in England are in issue. But these proceedings may turn on events, such as the alleged formation of a marriage, in which immigrants have followed their customary laws. Two sets of principles opening possibilities of recognition need consideration.

(a) Recognition through Private International Law

The law of every state contains a body of private international law, or conflict of laws. This regulates the modes of determining legal issues in which there is some foreign element. In England, as elsewhere, it is divisible into two main branches, concerning respectively the questions whether English courts have jurisdiction over the issue, and whether English law or some other state law is to be applied to it.[5] It is not unusual for private international law to determine that an English court has jurisdiction over an issue, but that a foreign law is applicable.

Private international law is concerned in principle with the state laws of other countries, not their non-state customary laws. However, since the laws of African states give normative recognition to parts of the customary laws of ethnic groups within their populations, private international law may require normative recognition of African customary laws. As present no question of institutional recognition of African customary laws arises.[6]

It is arguable that private international law is an inadequate basis for the recognition of the laws of immigrant minorities. Its effect is that the customary law of persons who are or should be considered part of the population of England is recognized on the ground that it is a foreign law which has to be applied because of foreign elements in a case. Private international law sees the laws of the world as a number of distinct and separate state laws. It does not allow for the possibility of hybrid laws. When it accords a status to persons it assumes that every individual belongs at any moment to one state, usually that of their domicile, residence or nationality, although it is recognized that an individual's state membership may sometimes change. Immigrants are thus seen as either temporary, short-term residents who are not part of English society, or as fully settled English to whom African customary laws should be inapplicable. The peoples under discussion fall into a third category, or transnationals (above), having homes in both continents. It would seem appropriate that issues concerning their status should be regulated sometimes by English law and sometimes by the laws of the African states to which they also belong. However, at present all issues of the legal status of any person must by private international law be determined by a single 'personal law'. Other issues are open to choice of law.

Anglophone African state laws give recognition to customary laws primarily in the fields of domestic relations (family law), and of private property. The recognized customary laws are applied in state courts concurrently with transplanted English laws and local statutory replacements of these.[7] That portion of customary property law which regulates land and buildings does not need examination, because by

5 Another branch of private international law, concerning the question whether a decision of a foreign court is to be accepted as determinative by English courts, does not arise in the present discussion: see the next note.

6 Institutional recognition would arise if English courts were required to accept decisions of an African customary legal institution which had received institutional recognition in the law of the African state. There appear to be no instances of this. As mentioned below, divorce in customary law is not granted through court (or any other) 'proceedings'.

7 Customary laws of chieftaincy are also recognized in many state laws, but these have no parallel in the received laws. The term 'family law' is ambiguous in the present context. In African customary laws 'family' generally refers to the lineage or descent group. This group has a corporate personality and can hold property. The law relating to the family in customary law thus includes domestic relations, but also much more.

private international law immovable property is subject to the law of the place where it is situated and to the exclusive jurisdiction of the courts of that place (Collins 2006: Chapter 23). Thus English courts apply English law to immovables in England, and do not accept cases concerning land elsewhere.

Several categories of questions concerning domestic relations may result in the recognition of African customary laws by English state law. First, the question sometimes arises whether a marriage has been validly contracted under a customary law. The answer can be decisive if one of the parties has subsequently attempted to contract another marriage. If the customary law marriage was valid (and had not been terminated), the subsequent marriage is normally void for bigamy. The validity of a customary law marriage can also be an essential condition in English law of claims under immigration and naturalization law, entitlement to social welfare benefits, matrimonial proceedings (which frequently involve applications for financial and property orders), and succession on death. Private international law holds that the law determining the formalities of marriage is the law of the place of celebration (Collins 2006: 789, Rule 66), while the capacity of the parties to marry is determined by the law of the prior domicile of each as their personal law (Collins 2006: 810, Rule 67).

These rules of private international law give rise to recognition in England of African customary laws on the validity of marriages. Some immigrants have sought to contract customary law marriages before migrating to England, and some after migrating visit their African countries to contract customary law marriages.[8] If there is later a dispute in England as to whether the ceremony was sufficient to create a marriage, this must be decided in accordance with the state law of the place of celebration. That state law is likely for this purpose to recognize customary law, which will therefore be recognized in English law.

This does not amount to the recognition of more norms of customary law than those which determine the mode of formation of marriage. Questions of the capacity of the parties to marry do not seem to arise. Furthermore, when a customary marriage ceremony is recognized, the applicable regime of marriage law, governing the legal obligations of the spouses and the modes of termination of the marriage, is, for all cases brought in the English courts, the single body of English law on the subject (subject to the issue considered in the following two paragraphs). This result diverges markedly from that in African state laws, in which there is a plurality not only of forms of marriage ceremonies but also of regimes of marriage law.

The second instance of recognition of customary law in domestic relations is in African customary laws of divorce. The validity of a customary law divorce may become an issue in English law through a dispute as to the validity of a subsequent marriage of one of the parties. If a previous marriage, validly contracted, has not been terminated by a valid divorce at the time of a subsequent marriage, the

8 This has been done in a number of cases in which I have been engaged to provide evidence on the relevant customary law.

latter is void. The question also arises if a party to a marriage brings matrimonial proceedings, typically for divorce with an ancillary application for financial relief, and the respondent applies for the case to be dismissed on the ground that the marriage has already been terminated under customary law.

The rules on the recognition of foreign divorces are contained in statute. The Family Law Act 1986, s. 46, refers to divorces 'obtained otherwise than by means of proceedings' in other countries. Divorces under African customary laws fall into this category, since they are not granted by courts through 'proceedings', but are negotiated between the lineages of the spouses or are dependent on acceptance within the community. Such a divorce is to be recognized by English courts if it is effective under the law of the country in which it is obtained, if both parties are domiciled there or one there and the other in a country under the law of which the divorce is recognized, and if neither has been habitually resident in the UK throughout the year preceding the obtaining of the divorce (Collins 2006: 906). The effect of these conditions is that normally only a customary divorce obtained before immigration to England can be considered for recognition. Even in this case it will be a valid divorce under the law of the African state, and therefore recognizable in English law, only if the marriage which it terminated was a customary law marriage. The pluralism in African states' marriage laws does not enable the mixing together of different regimes of law in relation to one marriage, so that generally a customary law divorce can terminate only a customary law marriage.

Also on questions of parentage, guardianship, legitimacy and adoption English courts may recognize foreign laws in certain circumstances. The establishment of a legal parent–child relationship can be essential for the purposes of immigration regulations. There can be difficult issues when a biological and legally recognized parent has died. Not infrequently in systems of customary law some other relative is then regarded as assuming the position of the deceased parent. There is considerable difficulty in bringing customary law norms in such circumstances into the categories to which English law is accustomed. English law normally holds that, unless this other relative has completed a formal adoption under an adoption statute (which is unusual in Africa, notwithstanding that many states have enacted adoption statutes), they cannot in law be a parent. A related category of cases, concerning the custody of children present in England, are usually decided on the basis of the best interests of the child. This may require a decision which takes account of social relationships in African societies but it does not entail the application of customary or other legal norms.

It is also arguable that, when private international law in cases on contract or tort, and possibly other fields, causes the law of an African state to be applied by an English court, this could result in recourse to a customary law of contract, tort or other field. However, in practice the state courts of anglophone African states rarely find it appropriate to apply customary laws in these areas in cases involving issues of much economic value. Since English courts are most unlikely to be called on to recognize or enforce decisions of foreign courts on matters of small value, it is unlikely that private international law will result in the application of African customary law here.

(b) Normative Recognition through English Legal Doctrine: The General Question

The question arises whether there are doctrines of English law that provide for the recognition of norms of African customary law not on the ground that they are foreign state laws, but on the ground that they are customary laws of a type which English law recognizes as such. This subsection considers whether there is a general doctrine of English law requiring recognition of customary laws. The following subsection considers whether there are doctrines in specific branches of English law which cause customary laws to be recognized in these branches.

The scope and status of these English legal doctrines are controversial, and there is little evidence that any such doctrines, if they exist, are yet producing significant recognition of African customary laws. Much of the discussion here must be about the policy of English common law culture towards such developments.

Some observers take the view that English law is unreceptive to any such development (e.g. Menski 2006: 13, cf. Shah 2005: 11–17). It will be argued here to the contrary that the culture has given rise to doctrines which require such recognition, and that these will be followed unless the legal profession rejects a substantial portion of its heritage. (See further: Greer 1893; Woodman 1987, 1989, 2006, 2008c.)

At the dawn of the English common law, in the century after the Norman Conquest of 1066, the function of the royal courts was seen as the application of the customary laws of the peoples of the realm. Debate and legal learning were concerned largely with questions of the jurisdiction and procedures of the courts. It was assumed that the substantive law was to be found in social practice. 'Customary law ruled supreme' (van Caenegem 1988: 12). Furthermore, it was accepted that a plurality of local customary laws was to be recognized by the central courts. However, there was also a political drive towards the consolidation of central state power and the suppression of local centres of authority, and the royal justices were primary agents of the Crown in its accumulation of central power. Consequently normative recognition of local customary laws was common during this period, but there was a decline in institutional recognition as the royal courts superseded local courts.

By the seventeenth century a general English common law had been established, but its doctrines included a principle that local customs were to be recognized and enforced, subject to conditions. A rule claimed to be a custom must be shown to have existed 'since time immemorial', not be contrary to reason and be sufficiently certain for there to be no serious doubt about whether or not it was applicable in a given case (Baker 1998: 153; see also Allen 1964: 129–60, 614–32). However, the legal culture also displayed a contrary, centralizing tendency in some instances. Thus it was held in a leading case that most Irish customary law failed to meet the conditions for recognition, and ethnocentric comments were made by the judges as to its uncivilized nature (*Le Case de Tanistry* (1608) 10 ER 516, discussed Allen 1964: 144–5, 619).

In the seventeenth to nineteenth centuries the common law showed a readiness to recognize other customary laws. With the growth of commerce and international trade the common law courts were ready to discover and apply the customary laws known as the 'law merchant' or *lex mercatoria*, especially under Lord Mansfield, Chief Justice of the Court of King's Bench (1754–83) (Holdsworth 1938: 525–9, Fifoot 1936: Chap. IV, Heward 1979: Chap. 8). The courts also showed a willingness to take account of the customs (sometimes referred to as 'usages') of particular trades and professions when interpreting contracts between their members (Baker 1998: 203–207, 238–42).

Also, and most significantly, during this period of colonial expansion the British state showed itself willing to recognize the existing laws of colonized peoples, repeatedly providing that the colonial courts were to observe and enforce 'native laws and customs'. English legal culture here held to the view, dating from medieval and Roman times, that all persons had a 'personal law', acquired at birth, rarely changed during their lives and accompanying them wherever they travelled (Blackstone 1765, 106–7).

These were all mainly instances of normative recognition. But institutional recognition was developed in the case of commercial customary law, where arbitral and other tribunals functioned, and in overseas territories, where recognition was accorded to indigenous governmental institutions, including judicial institutions. In African colonies local institutions of chieftaincy were recognized, and then in the first half of the twentieth century an explicit policy of 'indirect rule' was based on this recognition. However, that policy was eventually abandoned everywhere, and institutional recognition was weakened by the centralizing, nation-building forces of the independent states in the latter half of the century.

Through these centuries there were also instances of immigrant groups in England who were permitted to govern themselves according to their own laws, including most notably the Huguenots in the seventeenth and eighteenth centuries, until they became assimilated (Gwynn 1985), the merchants of Hansa who settled in London in the eighteenth century (Kiernan 1978), gypsies/Roma, who had been in England since the fifteenth century (Kiernan 1978), and Jewish communities after their re-admission around 1660 (Hyamson 1908, Roth 1941, Freedman 1955, Gartner 1973, Henriques 1980). The legal culture was manifested in a tacit policy of non-interference rather than an explicit institutional recognition based on an acceptance of diversity. Nevertheless it entailed the self-limitation of jurisdictional claims which is inherent in all institutional recognition.

On the other hand this period also saw a development of theory which questioned the legal credentials of customary, non-state law. Reflecting the rise of legislative sovereignty of parliament, and building on the theories of sovereignty emanating from Bodin, Hobbes and other political philosophers, a theory of positive law was propounded. The clearest and most notable version was that of John Austin in the first half of the nineteenth century. This declared the general commands of the sovereign to be the sole 'law properly so called'. Austin relegated customary law to the sphere of 'positive morality' (Austin 1954: 30–2). This is the basis in England of today's 'legal centralism' (Griffiths 1986) which denies the possibility of legal pluralism in the sense of the co-existence of state law with other laws. This view has gained many adherents, but it has not attracted unanimous support. At the same time that in the nineteenth century Austinian views were being propounded in some parts of the state apparatus, the Colonial and Indian Offices were drafting those statutes already mentioned which enabled customary laws to be recognized and enforced in the state laws of the colonies.

In the past century these opposing tendencies have continued. Some forces have encouraged the positivist view. The state has increasingly come to exercise control over new areas of life through its law expressed in vast numbers of detailed regulations, so that the fields in which state law may be expected to tolerate the operation of customary laws have declined in extent. On the other hand a recognition, and even a celebration, of increasing cultural diversity, demonstrated by the development of anti-discrimination law, may be leading to greater receptivity to the idea of not only tolerating but also endorsing and supporting the observance of the customary laws of minority groups. Furthermore, the elaboration of human rights law has given added force to arguments that communities as well as individuals should be left free to develop their own ways of life through their own customary laws. Thus to its long history of receptiveness to the recognition of customary laws within England, there are added new grounds for English law to pursue this policy today. It is suggested that modern English legal culture, although equivocal, is on balance stronger in favour of recognition (cf. Ballard no date(a)).

(c) Normative Recognition through English Legal Doctrine: Instances in Specific Legal Fields

English law may already require normative recognition of customary laws for particular purposes in certain fields.

The availability in various criminal laws of a culture defence has been discussed in recent years (Renteln 2004, Renteln and Foblets 2009). This operates where an accused has committed a criminal act because the norms of their culture permitted, encouraged or required them to do it. There is no culture defence as such in English law. Aspects of an accused person's culture are sometimes held to be relevant facts in establishing guilt or innocence (Ballard 2006, no date(b), Shah 2005: 70–87), but this is not recognition of a customary law.

There is a stronger possibility that the cultural norms of a convicted person may be taken into account in the determination of sentence. Penalties have been less than they would otherwise have been on the ground that the accused had followed their own customary legal norm in committing the offence, thereby giving it a limited form of recognition (e.g. *R. v. Singh and Singh* [1967] Crim. L.R. 247; *R. v. Adesanya*, noted Poulter 1975). However, courts have often stressed that the accused were recent immigrants, who had not 'settled down' in England, or had not been aware of rules of English criminal law (e.g. *R. v. Adesanya*), showing that this possibility is excluded for long-term immigrants.

The state law governing contracts and unilateral dispositions such as wills generally leave parties free to make their own terms, so that they may provide that an African customary law is to govern a transaction or disposition. There is no evidence that this possibility is being used by African immigrants. It would be difficult although not impossible to give effect in England to customary law rules on the administration and distribution of estates or the communal holding of property.

The formalities required to celebrate a marriage in England are provided for in the Marriage Acts. These generally do not allow a marriage to be validly concluded through a customary law process. However, the Marriage Act 1994 has made it easier to arrange for non-Christian religious ceremonies of marriage to meet the requirements of the Marriage Acts by broadening the categories of premises in which marriages may be celebrated. Some adaptability by both lawmakers and law-appliers might enable customary and state ceremonies to be combined into one.

The Challenges Arising in Recognition

The principal challenge posed by African customary laws to English legal culture lies in the claim for normative recognition. Whenever it is given, further, more specific challenges may arise. They concern the difficulties for governmental institutions such as courts to incorporate in their own bodies of law norms which have been developed in a different culture and for application to different processes from those of a modern state.

There are relatively few such difficulties in the first category of cases, arising from private international law. This requires the application of foreign state laws. An English court required to apply a foreign law takes evidence from expert witnesses of the provisions of that law. When a court hears evidence of an African customary law as a foreign law, it seeks not the norms observed in practice within the African society, but the norms applied by the state courts in the African state. The problematic process of converting 'people's customary law' into state or 'lawyers' customary law' has already been conducted in the African state legal system. Far greater difficulties will arise in the second and third categories of recognition, if they are developed.

First, a problem of understanding arises. The institutions of the recognizing state law need to take expert evidence to provide them with knowledge of the norms which are to be recognized. But the laws which need to be communicated are fundamentally different from that which the English officials are accustomed to apply. Moreover, judges and other officials do not have the facilities or time to conduct social scientific research, or even to receive the fullest possible reports from all those who have (see further: Ballard 2006, Woodman 1969). Furthermore, normative recognition over time will require the recognising state institutions to grapple with the constant processes of adaptation and development of African customary laws, so that a norm proven and applied in one case will not necessarily be applicable in another a few years later.

Secondly, it is in most cases impossible to give recognition to a customary law without changing it. For example, an English court, required to determine the validity of a customary law marriage, will frequently need to decide whether the requisite ceremony was completed in a particular place on a certain date. Anthropological evidence shows that in some societies a marriage is created and its existence established over a period of time (Woodman 1977). Private international law has accepted that the spouses need not be physically present at the celebration if the relevant customary law permits the formalities to be performed in their absence (*McCabe v. McCabe* [1993] 1 F.L.R. 410, noted Woodman 1993). However, generally customary law practices have to be fitted into the doctrinal structure of English law for recognition. This has happened in Africa whenever state courts have recognized customary law (Woodman 1988). The rules of recognized customary laws must be such as to enable a court to give judgment in favour of one of the parties, and to issue one or more of the permitted remedies such as damages, injunctions and orders for accounts.

Third, a series of other issues will arise regarding the scope of recognition. Just as private international law has developed rules stating when a foreign law is to be applied, so where there are other grounds for recognition it will be necessary to develop a new body of choice of law rules to determine when recognized customary law, rather than general English law, is to be applied. This will need to take account of the practices of the persons involved, who are themselves accustomed to moving between African customary laws and English common law.

Finally, another set of issues will become more numerous and acute. Portions of a customary law may conflict with overriding principles of human rights, public order or public policy. Claims for the recognition of these portions will be rejected, and this again will alter the main body of customary law of which they are parts. However great the concern to avoid ethnocentrism, the acceptance of cultural diversity and normative relativism will be subject to limits.

Conclusion

This chapter concerns one issue in the debates about legal responses to cultural diversity, namely, the possible recognition by English law of the customary laws of African communities. It has been suggested that English legal culture is equipped with the techniques and has an inclination to recognize the customary laws of today's immigrant communities. It appears that any recognition is likely to be normative, not institutional recognition. The chapter has not advocated recognition, but has sought to suggest that the possibilities and difficulties of recognition may be better understood in the light of legal experience in England and Africa.[9]

References

Akyeampong, E. 2000. Africans in the Diaspora: the Diaspora and Africa. *African Affairs*, 99, 183–215.

Allen, C.K. 1964. *Law in the Making*. 7th edition. Oxford: Clarendon Press.

Appiah, K.A. 2006. *Cosmopolitanism: Ethics in a World of Strangers*. Harmondsworth: Penguin Books.

Austin, J. 1954. *The Province of Jurisprudence Determined*. London: Weidenfeld and Nicolson.

Baker, J.H. 1998. Custom and Usage. In *Halsbury's Laws of England*. London: Butterworths, 4th edition reissue, 12(1), 153–259.

Ballard, R. 2006. Ethnic Diversity and the Delivery of Justice: the Challenge of Plurality. In *Migration, Diasporas and Legal Systems in Europe*, edited by P. Shah and W. Menski. London and New York: Routledge–Cavendish, 29–56.

— no date(a). *Polyethnic Britain: A Comparative and Historical Perspective*. Manchester: Centre for Applied South Asian Studies Online Papers. Available at: <http://www.arts.manchester.ac.uk/casas/papers/pdfpapers/britain.pdf> [accessed 22 October 2008].

— no date(b). *Common Law and Uncommon Sense: The Assessment of 'Reasonable Behaviour' in a Plural Society*. Manchester: Centre for Applied South Asian Studies Online Papers. Available at: <http://www.arts.manchester.ac.uk/casas/papers/pdfpapers/commonsense.pdf> [accessed 22 October 2008].

Baumann, G. 1996. *Discourses of Identity in Multi-Ethnic London*. Cambridge: Cambridge University Press.

Black, R. and R. King. 2004. Editorial Introduction: Immigration, Return and Development in West Africa. *Population, Space and Place*, 10(2), 75–83.

9 The value of such studies is illustrated by the unsatisfactory nature of the controversy over a recent public lecture by the Archbishop of Canterbury suggesting that there should be discussion of the possibility of some normative and institutional recognition of religious law, especially shari'a (Williams 2008). Critics argued vehemently that Britain should not depart from the principle that one law applied to everyone, overlooking the extent to which today, as always in the past, British law already provides for different rules to apply to certain groups. Some critics assumed that, if shari'a were recognized as law by the state, all branches, including criminal law, would be recognized, whereas the experience of recognition of laws shows that it is common for a part only of a body of customary or religious law to be recognized by a state law. On the other hand, the critics made no mention of the practical difficulties in a policy of recognition.

Blackstone, W. 1765. *Commentaries on the Laws of England.* Vol I. Oxford: Clarendon Press. Reproduced in facsimile, Chicago and London: University of Chicago Press, 1979.

Caenegem, R.C. van. 1988. *The Birth of the English Common Law.* 2nd edition. Cambridge: Cambridge University Press.

Collins, L. ed. 2006. *Dicey, Morris and Collins on The Conflict of Laws.* 14th edition. London: Sweet and Maxwell.

Dworkin, R. 1977. *Taking Rights Seriously.* Cambridge, MA: Harvard University Press.

Eberhard, C. and G. Vernicos eds 2006. *La quête anthropologique du droit: Autour de la démarche d'Étienne Le Roy.* Paris: Éditions Karthala.

Fifoot, C.H.S. 1936. *Lord Mansfield.* Oxford: Clarendon Press.

Freedman, M. ed. 1955. *A Minority in Britain: Social Studies of the Anglo-Jewish Community.* London: Vallentine, Mitchell and Co.

Friedman, L.M. 1975. *The Legal System: A Social Science Perspective.* New York: Russell Sage Foundation.

Gartner, L.P. 1973. *The Jewish Immigrant in England 1870–1914.* 2nd edition. London: Simon Publications.

Goody, E.N. and C.M. Groothues. 1977. The West Africans: the Quest for Education. In *Between Two Cultures*, edited by J.L. Watson. Oxford: Blackwells, 151–80.

Greer, F.A. 1893. Custom in the Common Law. *Law Quarterly Review*, 9: 153–70.

Griffiths, J. 1986. What is Legal Pluralism? *Journal of Legal Pluralism*, 24, 1–55.

Grillo, R. and V. Mazzucato. 2008. Africa< >Europe: a Double Engagement. *Journal of Ethnic and Migration Studies*, 34(2), 175–98.

Gwynn, R.D. 1985. *Huguenot Heritage: The History and Contribution of the Huguenots in Britain.* London: Routledge and Kegan Paul.

Hart, H.L.A. 1994. *The Concept of Law.* 2nd edition. Oxford: Clarendon Press.

Henriques, H. 1980. *The Jews and the English Law.* Oxford: Horace Hart at the University Press.

Heward, E. 1979. *Lord Mansfield.* Chichester and London: Barry Rose.

Holdsworth, W.S. 1938. *A History of English Law.* Vol XII. London: Methuen and Co.

Holmes, C. ed. 1978. *Immigrants and Minorities in British Society.* London: George Allen and Unwin.

Hyamson, A.M. 1908. *A History of the Jews in England.* London: Chatto and Windus.

Kabki, M., V. Mazzucato and E. Appiah. 2004. 'Wo benane a eye bebree': the Economic Impact of Remittances of Netherlands-based Ghanaian Migrants on rural Ashanti. *Population, Space and Place,* 10(2), 85–97.

Kiernan, V.G. 1978. Britons Old and New. In *Immigrants and Minorities in British Society*, edited by C. Holmes. London: George Allen and Unwin, 23–59.

Killingray, D. 1994. Africans in the United Kingdom: An Introduction. In *Africans in Britain*, edited by D. Killingray. London: Cass, 2–27.

Llewellyn, K. 1960. *The Common Law Tradition: Deciding Appeals.* Boston: Little, Brown and Co.

Mazzucato, V. 2008. The Double Engagement: Transnationalism and Integration. Ghanaian Migrants' lives between Ghana and the Netherlands. *Journal of Ethnic and Migration Studies*, 34(2), 199–216.

Menski, Werner 2006. Rethinking Legal Theory in Light of South–North Migration. In *Migration, Diasporas and Legal Systems in Europe*, edited by Prakash Shah and Werner Menski. London: Routledge Cavendish, 13–28.

Modood, T.1997. Culture and Identity. In *Ethnic Minorities in Britain: Diversity and Disadvantage, Fourth National Survey of Ethnic Minorities*, edited by Tariq Modood, Richard Berthoud et al. London: PSI, 290–338.

Nelken, D. ed. 1997. *Comparing Legal Cultures*. Aldershot: Dartmouth.

ONS. Office for National Statistics. 2003a. *Census 2001 National Report for England and Wales*. London: ONS.

— 2003b. *Census 2001 Key Statistics for Local Authorities in England and Wales*. London: ONS.

Poulter, S. 1975. Foreign Customs and the English Criminal Law. *International and Comparative Law Quarterly*, 24(1), 136–40.

Rees, P. and Butt, F. 2004. Ethnic Change and Diversity in England, 1981–2001. *Area*, 36(2), 174–86.

Renteln, A.D. 2004. *The Cultural Defense*. New York: Oxford University Press.

Renteln, A.D. and M.-C. Foblets. eds. 2009. *Multicultural Jurisprudence: Comparative Perspectives on the Cultural Defense*. Oxford: Hart Publications.

Roth, C. 1941. *A History of the Jews in England*. Oxford: Clarendon Press.

Shah, P. 2005. *Legal Pluralism in Conflict: Coping with Cultural Diversity in Law*. London, Sydney, Portland Oregon: Glass House Press.

Simpson, A.W.B. 1970. The Common Law and Legal Theory. In *Oxford Essays in Jurisprudence*. 2nd edition, edited by A.W.B. Simpson. Oxford: Clarendon Press, 77–99.

Vertovec, S. 1999. Conceiving and Researching Transnationalism. *Ethnic and Racial Studies*, 22(2), 447–62.

— 2006. *The Emergence of Super-diversity in Britain*. Centre on Migration, Policy and Society Working Paper 25. COMPAS: University of Oxford.

Vertovec, S. and R. Cohen. eds. 1999. *Migration, Diasporas and Transnationalism*. Cheltenham, UK/Northampton MA, USA: Edward Elgar.

Williams, R., The Rt. Rev. 2008. Civil and Religious Law in England: A Religious Perspective. Speech at the Royal Courts of Justice. 7 February 2008. Available at: <http//www.archbishopofcanterbury.org/1575> [accessed 22 October 2008].

Woodman, G.R. 1969. Some Realism about Customary Law – the West African Experience. *Wisconsin Law Review*, 1: 128–52.

— 1977. Judicial Development of Customary Law: the Case of Marriage Law in Ghana and Nigeria. *University of Ghana Law Journal*, 14: 115–36.

— 1987. Studying the Laws: Respecting Customary Laws in the Curriculum. *Melanesian Law Journal*, 15, 118.

— 1988. How State Courts create Customary Law in Ghana and Nigeria. In *Indigenous Law and the State*, edited by B.W. Morse and G.R. Woodman. Dordrecht: Foris, 181–220.
— 1989. The Peculiar Policy of Recognition of Indigenous Laws in British Colonial Africa. A Preliminary Discussion. *Verfassung und Recht in Übersee*, 22(3), 273–84.
— 1993. Essentials of an Akan Customary Marriage. *McCabe* v. *McCabe*. *Journal of African Law*, 37(2), 199–205.
— 1998. Ideological Combat and Social Observation: Recent Debate about Legal Pluralism. *Journal of Legal Pluralism*, 42: 21–59.
— 2006. The Involvement of English Common Law with Other Laws. In *La quête anthropologique du droit: Autour de la démarche d'Étienne Le Roy*, edited by C. Eberhard and G. Vernicos. Paris: Éditions Karthala, 477–500.
— 2008a. From Alien Intruder to Nation's Monarch to International Agent: the Changing Roles of the African State in the Realm of Law. In *Globalisierung und Entstaatlichung des Rechts – Teilband 2: Nichtstaatliches Privatrecht: Geltung und Genese*, edited by R. Zimmermann. Tübingen: Mohr Siebeck, 187–204.
— 2008b. The Possibilities of Co-existence of Religious Laws with Other Laws. In *Law and Religion in Multicultural Societies*, edited by R. Mehdi, H. Petersen and G.R. Woodman. Copenhagen: DJØF Publishing, 7–22.
— 2008c. The Limits of Individualisation in the Risk Society: Social Security in the Customary Laws of Immigrant Communities. In *Risk and the Law*, edited by G.R. Woodman and D. Klippel. Abingdon: Routledge–Cavendish, 184–200.

Chapter 9
Religious Challenges to the Secularized Identity of an Insecure Polity: A Tentative Sociology of Québec's 'Reasonable Accommodation' Debate

Jean-François Gaudreault-DesBiens

Introduction

Norms (or practices or circumstances) which are not per se discriminatory may sometimes entail prejudicial effects for certain individuals on the basis of a prohibited ground of discrimination. Although these norms may have been adopted in view of fulfilling a legitimate objective and the means by which they seek to achieve it are proportionate to that objective, they may still unduly affect some individuals in the exercise of a right or of a freedom recognized by law. Imagine, for example, the case of non-Christian employees who would be financially penalized as a result of their decision to take a day off to celebrate some religious holiday in the context of a working calendar that is loosely based on the Christian calendar.[1] In this example, the mere adoption of such a calendar, which also happens to be the calendar adopted by other similar employers in a society where the majority has historically been Christian, is not per se discriminatory.[2] Indeed, in every society, norms often reflect the social habits or the deeply entrenched cultural preconceptions of the majority, and the fact that the penultimate origin of these norms, when adopted for a secular purpose, can be found in a religious tradition, is not immediately tantamount to discrimination, unless the intent of the author of the norm is to coerce individuals to follow a particular creed.[3] Thus, such norms, which can be characterized as reasonably neutral, would, in Canada, normally withstand a judicial challenge based on their alleged unconstitutionality.

But even if the objective of the norm is legitimate, and even if that norm is neutral in its application to a majority of individuals, some may still be unduly affected by it on the basis of a prohibited ground of discrimination. To tackle this type of problem, Canadian courts have adopted, since the mid-1980s, the doctrine of reasonable accommodation.[4] This doctrine essentially allows an individual who

1 *Commission scolaire régionale de Chambly v Bergevin*, [1994] 2 S.C.R. 525.

2 *R. v Edwards Books and Art Ltd.*, [1986] 2 S.C.R. 713.

3 Big M Drug Mart Ltd., [1985] 1 S.C.R. 295.

4 Ontario Human Rights Commission v Simpsons-Sears, [1985] 2 S.C.R. 536.

is detrimentally affected by an otherwise neutral norm the possibility to require, as a matter of law, to be accommodated. This accommodation, which essentially consists in the bending of an existing norm or in the creation of a particularized regime for the claimant (whether through an exemption or through a specific permission to do something), can only be refused if it imposes an undue hardship upon the organization from which the accommodation is requested.

The origins of that doctrine can be traced to a series of American labour statutes and cases of the 1970s.[5] Any claim to the effect that accepting the accommodation requested would actually constitute an undue hardship must be buttressed by tangible evidence; mere conjectures are not enough. In other words, it is up to the organization to prove the contextual unreasonableness of the demand. In practice, considerations such as the cost of accommodation, the morale of the personnel, the size of the organization from which the accommodation is requested, the adaptability of human resources, and safety risks may be, and have been, invoked by organizations in view of demonstrating that acquiescing to the accommodation would impose an undue hardship upon them.[6] This list, however, is not exhaustive and must be adapted to the contexts in which accommodation requests are made.

Since the adoption of the doctrine of reasonable accommodation by the Supreme Court of Canada, several cases, from different levels of courts, have contributed to circumscribing its reach. Different types of claimants, but particularly religious claimants and claimants suffering from physical disabilities, have benefited from its adoption. However, the highly contextual and casuistic nature of the inquiry pursued by courts adjudicating upon disputes concerning the application of the doctrine has inevitably left some questions unanswered; the doctrine is a never-ending work in progress.

Until recently, the doctrine seemed widely accepted, and virtually no one radically questioned its soundness. This remains the case in most Canadian provinces, except Québec. Even there, its application is raising questions only in respect of religious claims, but the questions that have been raised lately are serious indeed.

This chapter circumscribes the main parameters of the Québec debate over the reasonable accommodation of religious claims, and then suggests a tentative explanation of the emergence of this debate in Québec and not elsewhere in Canada. While the framing of this debate is inevitably influenced by events and discussions taking place at the global level, the very peculiar evolution of Québec society and its particular ideological-cultural situation in Canada and in North America also significantly contribute to the distinct turn that it has taken there.

A caveat is warranted. This chapter does not seek to analyse the substantive (and often legally grounded) claims made in support or against the accommodation of religious practices by the different participants. Instead it proposes a macroscopic

5 *Trans World Airlines Inc. v Hardison*, 432 U.S. 63 (1977).

6 *Central Alberta Dairy Pool v Alberta* (Human Rights Commission), [1990] *2 S.C.R. 489; Central Okanagan School District No. 23 v Renaud,* [1992] 2 S.C.R. 970.

explanation of the emergence of that debate in Québec. That explanation constitutes, in essence, a 'tentative sociology' for two reasons. Firstly, given the complexity of the stakes involved, monocausal explanations or systematically empirically verifiable explanations are out of reach. Secondly, the debate is not over yet. Without the benefit of time, any sociological explanation can only be 'tentative' or 'provisional'. The objective of this interpretive essay is thus to present as complex a picture as possible of some societal features that may explain how the debate was framed, and to draw some conclusions on the basis of the available historical and sociological data.

What Provoked the Debate?

It is only recently that the accommodation of religious claims has become a topic of debate in Québec, and certain practices of accommodation the target of vigorous criticism. Arguably, it is the proliferation of borderline cases of legally mandated accommodation, the intensification and radicalization of demands of religious accommodation and a series, over a short period of time, of non-legally compelled forms of accommodation, that have provided the backdrop for this debate. Uneven media coverage and sometimes opportunistic political appropriations of the topic of reasonable accommodation have only added fuel to it.

The first case that attracted substantial media and public attention was decided in the mid-1990s, but the political debate had begun long before. In the *Grant* case,[7] the Federal Court of Canada held that the Commissioner of the Royal Canadian Mounted Police could validly allow Sikh officers to wear a turban while wearing the well-known red costume of this police force, instead of the hat that usually accompanies it. What was challenged here was an accommodation measure *already* accepted by the Royal Canadian Mounted Police, firstly, on the basis of the organization's understanding of the religious rights of its employees and, secondly, in view of diversifying its workforce in an increasingly multicultural society. The court challenge of this accommodation policy had been brought by a coalition of citizens, including veterans of the police force, who essentially opposed what they saw as a dilution of a national symbol.

While the legal debate itself mostly revolved around the evaluation of the reasonableness of the constraints, real or symbolic, that the wearing of the turban would impose upon the Royal Canadian Mounted Police *qua* employer and upon members of the public interacting with turban-wearing police officers, the non-legal debate predictably took a much broader turn. Indeed, as evinced by the political (as opposed to the legal) argument underlying the court challenge, the red attire of Royal Canadian Mounted Police's members is an important identity marker for many Canadians, particularly in the Western provinces where this police force has played an important historical role in the pacification of the 'Canadian frontier'.

7 *Grant v Canada* (A.G.), [1995] 1 F.C. 158.

Well-known internationally, this attire is even a component of the traditional, clichéd brand image of Canada, alongside the Indian, the Great White North and the Rocky Mountains. It is thus no surprise at the outcry when the *Grant* case came to the public's attention. Inevitably, questions were raised about the compatibility of the Sikh turban with a quintessentially, albeit essentialized, Canadian symbol. Because of its connection with such a symbol, this case was among the earliest to provoke reflection on the actual, and not merely virtual, expansion of the meaning of 'Canadian'. Ironically, the Royal Canadian Mounted Police's accommodation policy highlighted the integrative potential of Canada's multicultural model.

The debate provoked by the *Grant* case was pan-Canadian, but possibly more vigorous in English-speaking Canada because of the stronger role that the 'Mountie' plays in this community's identity reference,[8] as opposed to that of French-speaking Québec. Further cases would reveal an opposite tendency.

The next debate involving the reasonable accommodation of religion was triggered by a young girl who in 1994 was expelled from her state school for wearing a *hijab*, on the basis of a rule prohibiting the wearing of head covers at school. The same year, a Muslim private school imposed upon all of its female teachers, including non-Muslims, the obligation to wear the *hijab*. Thus, just a few years after the first '*hijab* debate' in France, this head cover stirred a controversy in Quebec. By and large, the arguments invoked against or in favour of the *hijab* were more or less the same as in France. They even included, somehow surprisingly as we shall see later, references to the principle of *laïcité*. However, these cases were not litigated, since settlements occurred prior to the formal lodging of complaints. Nevertheless, the public reaction that they provoked prompted the Québec Human Rights Commission to issue, in the ensuing months, a major policy document on religious pluralism and its socio-legal implications in Québec.

In it, the commission offered an advisory opinion on the legal framework governing both of the situations that gave rise to the debate. It first found that the law precluded state schools from expressly prohibiting the *hijab* and imposed upon them the duty to accommodate *hijab*-wearers if they otherwise 'neutrally' prohibited head covers. It also stated that while private religious schools may validly require, as a condition of employment, that their employees share the declared creed of these schools and follow religious prescriptions believed to be compulsory by the schools' management, such schools could not, if they hired employees holding different religious convictions, impose upon them to follow the schools' 'official' creed (Commission des droits de la personne et des droits de la jeunesse 1995). In addition to clarifying the legal framework, the Human Rights Commission aptly characterized the reflection on the management of religious pluralism as posing an important challenge in terms of social ethics.

---

8 'Identity reference' designates the set of shared representations, ideologies and memories that provide the intellectual, affective, epistemic and thus cultural foundation of a particular community (Dumont 1993).

Prior to, and after, this mid-1990s '*hijab* debate', the Québec Human Rights Commission published several other documents (formal advisory opinions, decisions, informal analyses) on topics related to the accommodation of religious practices, ranging from the religious diet of Jewish prison inmates to the prayer needs of Muslim students in a university.[9] In these documents, it adopts what could be characterized as the standard Canadian legal approach to the question of religious accommodation, which reflects the logic exposed above. However, it avoids adopting a Pollyanna-like approach to religious phenomena and multiculturalism, sometimes found in Canadian courts (Gaudreault-DesBiens 2007), recognizing that while religion does raise important questions pertaining to fundamental rights, it may also be a locus of oppression. Indeed, culture sometimes becomes an alibi for the majority (or the most powerful) group within a minority to impose its rule on a more vulnerable segment of that same group (Abou 1992). This is what Ayelet Shachar has appropriately called the 'paradox of multicultural vulnerability' (Shachar 2001). This *hijab* debate proved to be the start of a broader debate about the place of religion in the so-called 'public sphere' which crystallized around two court cases .

In the *Amselem* case,[10] Orthodox Jews who had bought apartments in a luxurious Montréal building had been asked by the management of the building to remove a temporary *succah* that they had erected on the balconies of their respective apartments. A *succah* is a small enclosed temporary construction, a kind of hut, built by observant Jews for the festival of Souccoth which commemorates the period during which, according to biblical texts, the Children of Israel lived in temporary shelters while wandering in the desert. This construction is used by Orthodox Jews as their primary residence during the festival.

The declaration of co-ownership, which all owners of apartments in the building had signed, generally prohibited any construction or decoration on the building's balconies, for aesthetic and safety reasons. However, this prohibition did not deter the Orthodox Jewish residents from constructing, or at least wanting to construct, their own *succah*s. This request was rejected, but, as an alternative, the co-ownership's management proposed they set up a communal *succah* in the gardens. While some accepted this offer, Mr Amselem rejected it, arguing that his subjective understanding of Jewish law obliged him to erect an individual *succah* on his own balcony. Evidence was also given that although he had signed the declaration of co-ownership, he had not read it. In any event, he argued that the prohibition it contained infringed his freedom of religion protected by Québec's *Charter of Human Rights and Freedoms*.

The trial court initially found that, on the basis of contradictory evidence about the nature of the religious obligation to erect a *succah*, there was no objective obligation in Jewish law to erect an individual *succah*, and that, as such, the

9 These issues are discussed extensively in various reports of the Commission des droits de la personne et des droits de la jeunesse, e.g. 1999, 2006, 2007.

10 *Syndicat Northcrest v Amselem*, [2004] 2 S.C.R. 551.

declaration of co-ownership did not infringe on Amselem's freedom of religion. The court went on to say that even if it had found that freedom of religion had been infringed by the declaration of co-ownership, the accommodation proposed by the management, i.e. the erection of a communal *succah*, would have been reasonable. In appeal, two judges found that by signing the declaration of co-ownership, the Orthodox Jewish residents had waived their freedom of religion to erect individual *succah*s, and that the impugned provisions of that declaration did not discriminate these residents since the provisions in question did not establish any distinction based on religion. Even if they had found such a distinction, the judges held that the Orthodox Jewish residents' freedom of religion was not impaired since they were not objectively religiously obligated to erect an individual *succah*. In a concurring opinion, another judge argued that while the declaration of co-ownership did indirectly infringe the Jewish residents' freedom of religion, the management of the building had satisfied its duty to accommodate these residents and should not suffer consequences from Mr Amselem's 'intransigence'.

In a five-to-four opinion, a bitterly divided Supreme Court of Canada allowed Mr Amselem's appeal. The majority judgment adopted a subjective understanding of religion and, on that basis, held that Mr Amselem's freedom of religion had to prevail over the declaration of co-ownership. Most importantly, the majority rejected the view that the subjective understanding of a believer, i.e. that an individual *succah* was an absolute necessity, could be second-guessed in light of evidence establishing that what the believer deems to be a religious obligation is objectively not compulsory in his or her particular religious tradition. The majority judgment also refused to allow the aesthetic preoccupations of other non-religious co-owners to trump the believer's religious freedom. In the case at bar, it finally concluded that Mr Amselem's religious freedoms should trump the fact that he had signed, without reading it, the declaration of co-ownership which contained a provision expressly prohibiting the erection of dwellings, even temporary ones, on balconies. Being a contract of adhesion, that declaration had not really been negotiated, and the provision at stake was too ambiguous to be characterized as a waiver of Amselem's religious freedoms.[11]

Three minority justices rejected the majority's subjective approach to religion and argued that some minimally objective test was appropriate instead. Another justice expressed a dissenting view, arguing that Mr Amselem's signature to a contractual instrument that clearly prohibited the erection of structures on balconies should not be so easily disregarded. Although the *Amselem* case did not raise public ire, several commentators expressed their surprise at seeing the Supreme Court legitimizing the religious claims of an educated individual who had wilfully signed a contract containing a prohibition that could easily be read as encompassing *succah*s and who had refused, contrary to other Orthodox Jews

11 According to article 1379 of Civil Code of Québec, '[a] contract of adhesion is a contract in which the essential stipulations were imposed or drawn up by one of the parties, on his behalf or upon his instructions, and were not negotiable'.

living in the same building, to accept the communal *succah* proposed by the administration of the building.

Two years later a case decided by the Supreme Court of Canada really ignited public debate. In *Multani*,[12] the Supreme Court held in favour of a Sikh high school student who wanted to wear a ritual knife (*kirpan*) at school in spite of the school's zero tolerance policy against any type of weapon. Since the *kirpan* could also be used as a weapon, it was deemed to contravene the policy. The Supreme Court pointed out that although safety concerns can provide a legitimate reason for refusing an accommodation, these concerns have to be more than mere speculations. At trial level, the Québec Superior Court had confirmed the claimant's freedom to wear the *kirpan* but had attached conditions to it, i.e. that the *kirpan* be placed in a box around which a piece of cloth would be sewed. The Court of Appeal overturned that decision on the basis of the reasonableness of both the zero tolerance policy and the decision that a *kirpan* could create a safety risk.

Polls conducted after the Supreme Court's ruling showed that while a coast-to-coast majority of Canadians opposed the decision to allow the *kirpan* in schools, the opposition was much stronger in Québec. This shared opposition to the *kirpan* was probably the only identifiable commonality between the attitudes of Quebeckers, on the one hand, and Canadians living outside Québec, on the other, as the former expressed strong opposition to other religious signs as well (for example, *hijab*s or turbans) while the latter's opposition to such signs was negligible (Gagnon and Gruda 2006). One thing is clear: following this *Multani* decision, the doctrine of reasonable accommodation for religious reasons became highly contentious in Québec.[13]

Negative attitudes towards that doctrine were reinforced by a series of events that were perceived as instances where some organizations had 'caved in' to minority religious groups.[14] The first of these was a resolution of the Québec Human Rights Commission enjoining an engineering school to give Muslim students access to a prayer room (Commission des droits de la personne et des droits de la jeunesse 2006). Other events, which resulted from administrative decisions in no way related to reasonable accommodation, were nevertheless associated with it by the media. Since some of these decisions were highly debatable, the doctrine of

12 Multani c. Commission scolaire Marguerite-Bourgeoys, [2006] 1 S.C.R. 256.

13 Technically, the principal opinion in *Multani* approaches the *kirpan* case from a constitutional standpoint, which essentially means that it evaluates, under the Canadian Charter of Rights and Freedoms, the proportionality of the zero tolerance policy as it was applied to *Multani*. Thus, it is not strictly speaking a 'reasonable accommodation' case. However, the judges who co-signed that opinion expressly mention that the underlying logic of their constitutional analysis is the same as the quasi-constitutional logic inspiring the doctrine of reasonable accommodation proper.

14 For a complete list of the 'incidents' that led to the debate, see: Commission de consultation sur les pratiques d'accommodement reliées aux différences culturelles (2008).

reasonable accommodation somehow became 'tainted' by them, for example, the decision of a YMCA in a neighbourhood with a significant Hassidim community to change the windows of the training room for shaded ones in order to prevent pupils from an adjacent yeshiva from looking at women exercising (Seljak et al. 2008). A yeshiva is a school where Orthodox Jewish boys study the Talmud and the Torah. In general, the very existence of a yeshiva presupposes a separation of males and females, which explains the discomfort felt by the heads of the yeshiva at the idea that their young male pupils would have a privileged view of women exercising in sport attire. The decision to change the YMCA's windows, at the request and at the expense of the yeshiva, was not legally obligatory and did not constitute, strictly speaking, a reasonable accommodation.

Another instance was a recommendation in a document used by the Montréal police force to have incidents involving Hassidic Jews dealt with by male police officers only, for fear of offending the sensitivities of Hassidic males. This recommendation, which had not been requested by the Hassidic community, was construed in the public debate as a formal 'directive'. At the same time, news spread that municipal parking by-laws were systematically not applied during Jewish religious holidays in that particular neighbourhood. It was soon clarified that this tolerance for illegal parking equally applied to the religious celebrations of other communities (*L'Express d'Outremont* 2007).

During the 2007 election, a major controversy arose as a result of a directive issued by the chief electoral officer, which stated that women wearing *burqa*s, *niqab*s or functional equivalents would not have to remove their face-covering veils to be admitted to vote. Under public and political pressures, the chief electoral officer modified his decision and required that such veils be removed for the purpose of voting. A few months later, his federal counterpart was embroiled in a similar controversy during by-elections. However, he opted for maintaining the possibility to vote while being veiled in spite of a pan-Canadian political uproar. Several Muslim women, including some wearing *niqab*s or *burka*s, were equally outraged by this 'accommodation' that they had not requested (CBC News 2007).[15]

The world of sports was not spared, nor were age-old customs. *Hijab*-wearing Muslim girls were indeed expelled from soccer and taekwondo competitions, either for safety reasons or as a result of the enforcement of 'neutral' rules prohibiting the wearing or headgear while playing (Karim and Hirji 2008: 110). On the customary front, decisions by sugar shack owners to adapt the meals served to accommodate the diet of Muslim clients, or to ask the local fiddler to stop playing for a few minutes to allow Muslim clients to pray on the shack's dance floor, thereby expelling non-Muslims from the dance floor, were received rather

15 The debate about allowing *niqab*-wearing or *burka*-wearing women to vote at provincial and federal elections was overblown; only a few dozen potential voters wear such attire in Québec, and, as far as identity checks are concerned, voting by mail is allowed without any such checks being performed.

negatively (LCN 2007). Some took offence at the idea that the traditional sugar shack menu, heavy on pork, would be altered because of the religious sensitivities of some clients.

In any event, the accumulation of 'incidents' such as these provided the backdrop for what was arguably the most spectacular moment of the reasonable accommodation debate in Québec. Indeed, in January 2007, the municipal council of the village of Hérouxville adopted a non-prescriptive 'life code' informing immigrants of the mores of the inhabitants of the village, notably that they eat pork, drink alcohol, do not stone adulterous women, etc. (Hérouxville 2007). Ironically, this village, located in the Québec hinterland, does not have any immigrant population. Thus, the threat to its traditional way of life was rather remote at the time its 'life code' was released.

Predictably, the 'semi-serious' (Stevenson 2008: 54) and certainly caricatural aspect of the code, which relied heavily on ethno-religious stereotypes, was denounced in most circles. However, it showed the existence of a certain divide between urban, multicultural, Québec, especially Montréal, and a more homogenous rural Québec. The village's initiative also led to a string of events, some anecdotal, others of significant political importance. On the anecdotal front, a delegation of Muslim women from Montréal travelled to Hérouxville to launch a conversation with the villagers, an initiative that was well received and that turned into a kind of love-in. On the political front, the question of the management of ethno-religious diversity became a hot topic in the provincial election, and the *Action démocratique du Québec*, the right-of-centre party that advocated a strong affirmation of 'Québec values', particularly equality between men and women and respect for the Catholic heritage of the province, became the official opposition.

Prior to the election, the Liberal government, which was eventually re-elected with a minority of seats, had reacted to the growing controversy surrounding the 'reasonable accommodation' of religious claims – many of the instances in fact did not constitute legal cases of reasonable accommodation – by creating an inquiry commission on the management of practices related to cultural diversity. This commission was headed by two prominent Québec intellectuals, sociologist and historian Gérard Bouchard and philosopher Charles Taylor.

The commission triggered a lot of interest. It received close to 1000 briefs from individual citizens, non-governmental organisations and public institutions, heard hundreds of personal testimonies, held four national (i.e. Québec-wide) forums on specific issues and conducted 22 regional public hearings between September and December 2007. More than 3000 citizens participated in those hearings, which were broadcast on the two French-language all-news channels existing in Québec.

It is impossible to summarize what was said in these briefs and during the hearings. Heinrich and Dufour (2008: 180) provide an accurate, albeit impressionistic, narrative of their tone:

> C'est ainsi que nous avons eu droit, pêle-mêle, à des aveux touchants, à des opinions tranchées, à des commentaires posés, à des propos haineux, à des appels à la tolérance, à des doléances, à des incohérences de la part de centaines de citoyens tout ce qu'il y a de plus ordinaires qui, après avoir soigneusement rédigé leur mémoire dans leur sous-sol ou dans leur cuisine, sont venus défendre leur opinion sous les projecteurs. Ce pot-pourri populaire était d'ailleurs souvent beaucoup plus intéressant que les interventions des divers groupes de pression, des organismes communautaires, des élites locales et des intellectuels experts de telle ou telle question pointue.[16]

It would not be entirely incorrect to say that Québec society underwent a catharsis during the hearings of the Bouchard-Taylor commission.[17] The commission gave a forum to all sorts of groups and individuals whose views are rarely heard in mainstream media, such as rural Quebeckers of French origin and recent immigrants. Predictably, some of these views clashed brutally, but, in spite of its weaknesses, this democratic exercise could prove fruitful in the long term, as the malaise affecting diverse segments of the society has at least been *named*. That being said, it remains to be seen whether or to what extent the proposals contained in the Bouchard-Taylor report will facilitate the healing or reconciliation of the opponents.

Now, what does the report say?[18] First, it finds that the 'reasonable accommodation debate' largely amounted to a 'crisis of perceptions' rather than a real crisis. The report does not hesitate to question the role that media have played in manufacturing, at least in part, the said crisis. Yet, it acknowledges the cultural insecurity of the French-speaking majority in Québec, which, as I will later point out, is a minority within both Canada and North America. Given the particular challenges that this fragile majority faces, notably in defending its language in an English-speaking sea, the report advocates the formal adoption and promotion by Québec of a policy of 'interculturalism'. In brief, this policy seeks to reconcile, on the one hand, the legitimate need of the historical French-speaking majority

16 'We have been able to hear, higgledy-piggledy, touching admissions, sharp opinions, moderate comments, hate speech, calls for tolerance, grievances and inconsistencies on the part of the hundreds of ordinary citizens who, after having carefully drafted their briefs in their basement or kitchen, defended their position under the limelight. This popular medley was often much more interesting than the interventions of lobbies, community groups, local elites and intellectuals with an expertise on pointed questions' [my translation].

17 'Catharsis' presupposes some form of societal malaise. Interestingly, a group of psychoanalysts published after the hearings a collection of texts on Québec's malaise, as evinced by the reasonable accommodation debate (Clément and Wolf 2008).

18 See Commission de consultation sur les pratiques d'accommodement reliées aux différences culturelles 2008. The complete version of the report is only available in French, but an abridged version in English is on the Bouchard-Taylor Commission's website. The background studies by sociologists, political scientists, anthropologists, jurists, etc. are also available on the website.

to perpetuate itself by integrating immigrants with, on the other hand, respect for cultural diversity. Contrary to the Canadian policy of multiculturalism, which the authors find inapplicable to a small nation such as Québec, interculturalism affirms the existence of a host culture in which newcomers must integrate (but not necessarily assimilate). However, the recognition of the particular needs of that host culture is balanced by the duty of that culture to open itself to cultural diversity. Thus, interculturalism refers to a process of reciprocal acculturation through contact and communication involving both the majority and the various minorities. Lastly, as far as the *law* of reasonable accommodation is concerned, the Bouchard-Taylor report is by and large a defence and an illustration of the legal status quo. As regards the position of the state toward religions, the report advocates a form of 'open *laïcité*', which emphasizes the equality of all, believers and non-believers alike, freedom of religion and conscience, state neutrality in respect of religion, and the separation of state and religion. However, that separation is not envisaged as a justification for relegating religious expression to the so-called 'private sphere'. The only recommendation that derogates from this stance consists in a proposal that judges, crown attorneys, prison guards, as well as the president and vice-president of Québec's legislature (the National Assembly), be prohibited from wearing religious signs, because of the coercive powers that they exercise on behalf of the state and of their 'duty of reserve'. All other state officials or civil servants would be allowed to wear religious signs, which is a freedom they already enjoy.

Resort to formal legal means to affect religious behaviours is therefore not an option that is really contemplated in the Bouchard-Taylor report. The general approach advocated is rather one that privileges public education about cultural diversity, ethno-religious stereotypes, as well as a shared and transcultural reflection on Québec's peculiar cultural destiny in Canada and North America. Favouring ethics over law, it offers an interesting road map for ethically, but never naïvely, posing questions about the management of cultural diversity.

Why These Debates in Québec?

The management of cultural and religious diversity is difficult for any society. However, as far as the management of religious diversity is concerned, it seems that Québec is, as is often the case, quite distinct from the rest of Canada and of North America. Debates about religion take a turn in this province that they simply do not take elsewhere in Canada. This is not to say that religion does not trigger debates in the other provinces. For instance, in the past five years, the neighbouring province of Ontario has gone through heated debates about the formal legal recognition of shari'a courts awards rendered in the field of family law (see *inter alia* Gaudreault-DesBiens 2005–2006, Khan 2007, and Bader's chapter in this volume) and about the state funding of religious schools. But although these raised important questions pertaining to individual rights and personal conceptions of the good life, they first and foremost dealt with the state recognition, or support, of minority religious *institutions* (such as courts or schools). In contrast, the Québec debate over reasonable accommodation primarily revolved around *individual* claims, even though, admittedly, there is a frequent nexus between the collective and the individual whenever an argument based on freedom of religion or religious equality is made. Generally speaking, however, the primarily individual forms of accommodation that monopolized the debate in Québec barely raise eyebrows elsewhere in Canada. And assuming that the linguistic distinctness of that society cannot plausibly explain, on its own, that difference, it is worth seeking a more complex explanation.

First, although xenophobia, and in some cases, anti-Semitism or Islamophobia, may explain the attitudes of some segments of the population,[19] it would be simplistic to resort to that explanation to make sense of the Québec debate, given that there is no evidence that Quebeckers are fundamentally more intolerant of cultural diversity per se than their fellow Canadians.[20] However, there is evidence that they are clearly less comfortable with *religious* claims than other Canadians (Heinrich 2007).

19 Claims for religious accommodation have commonly been associated with non-Christian minorities in the public debate. However, a recent study of the complaints filed between 2000 and 2006 with the Québec human rights commission has shown that half of these were filed by Christians, mostly Evangelical Protestants and Jehovah's Witnesses. The other half consisted of Muslims and Jews. As well, half of the claimants were born in Canada. Although the scope of this study is limited, it suggests that Christians are as likely as non-Christians to require religious accommodations, and it is misleading to assert a causal link between claims for religious accommodation and immigration. However, the study most interestingly reveals that all of the claimants who filed a complaint with belonged to orthodox segments of their religious community (Commission des droits de la personne et de la jeunesse du Québec 2007).

20 They may be more ignorant of it, however. Besides Montréal, where half of Québec's population is concentrated and where almost all immigrants live, the rest of Québec is mostly inhabited by people of French-Canadian and Roman Catholic origins. Very often, the only historical source of ethnocultural diversity in these regions consisted in the presence of small English-speaking communities. The only source of religious diversity was, more often than not, Anglican or Presbyterian congregations. As a result, many Quebeckers outside Montréal have never experienced any form of cultural diversity, let alone 'deep diversity', in their daily lives. And ignorance breeds prejudices. A February 2008 survey revealed that while 47 per cent of Canadians outside Québec had been in contact with Jewish persons, only 28 per cent in Québec had had such contacts. Predictably, perceptions of the Jewish community were more negative and stereotypical in Québec than elsewhere in Canada. At the same time, it is worth mentioning that the image of 'the Jew' shared by those who had not had contacts with actual Jews, was possibly influenced by the image of reclusive Hassidic Jews, who where often represented in the media as regular 'claimants' of accommodations. Interestingly, the same survey showed that the level of prejudice toward Jews substantially decreased among those who had had contacts with actual Jews (Perreault 2008).

The reasons for this may be sought in Québec's particular religious evolution. Although Québec was founded as New France under the reign of the religiously liberal Henry IV, the religious policy of New France was shaped, for most of its history, by Louis XIV, who repealed the Edict of Nantes adopted by his predecessor. Louis XIV's policy of religious intolerance had one major impact on the religious make-up of New France: only Catholics could settle in the colony. French Huguenots were thus prevented from doing what English Puritans had done in Massachusetts. The outcome of this policy was to create a monoreligious colony until the British conquest of 1760, which was confirmed by the 1763 Treaty of Paris.

After the cession of New France to the British Crown, things changed, as the government now favoured non-Catholic immigration. But even though Protestants did immigrate, either from England and Scotland, or, after the American Revolution, from the former British colonies to the south, the French-speaking population, which still formed the majority, remained almost entirely Catholic, while non-Catholics were generally Anglophones. Church-influenced educational policies later ensured that all non-Catholics, even French-speaking ones, would be directed to English-speaking schools, which reinforced the association between the emerging French-Canadian identity and Roman Catholicism.

This association, which was soon presented by the Church as the 'manifest destiny' of French Canadians, did not remain unchallenged, however. In Québec as in France, a major debate shook Roman Catholicism in the nineteenth century, a debate that opposed, on the one hand, proponents of a Catholicism that would be reconciled with modernity and liberalism and, on the other, proponents of a more conservative, authoritarian, church – the 'Ultramontanes'.

Ultramontanism refers to a doctrine that rejected the separation of church and state, and advocated the church's primacy over the state on political questions carrying a moral connotation (Lamonde 2000: 290–1). Ultramontanism can only be understood in light of Gallicanism, a doctrine of French origins, which, as early as the seventeenth century, defended the autonomy of the French church vis-à-vis Rome and sought to place limits on the pope's authority, precisely in favour of national churches. The Gallican clergy tended to support, or at least acknowledge, the inevitable triumph of modern ideas, while Ultramontanes were ideologically opposed to all things modern, from democracy to human rights and industrialization.

The battle between Ultramontanism and Gallicanism proved ferocious in the first half of the nineteenth century in Québec (then called the colony of Lower Canada). In the meantime, a strong political movement had emerged in the colony advocating liberal and, sometimes, republican reforms and the separation of church and state. However, the victory of Ultramontanism in France and in Rome heralded the defeat of political liberals as well as the demise of Gallicanism in Québec. That defeat shaped Québec society for over a century, as the now predominantly conservative clergy successfully coaxed political elites into statutorily implementing the Ultramontane conception of the appropriate relation between church and state, and, most importantly, its particular conception of 'mixed' political and moral questions. Thus the church managed to obtain from the Québec legislature recognition of its preeminent role in the fields of education and health care as far as Roman Catholics were concerned. This covered the quasi-totality of the colony's French-speaking inhabitants. The church continued to occupy a central place in Québec society, until after the Second World War. Anything that could undermine the realization of the destiny of French Canadians, which was to ensure the perpetuation of a kind of agrarian island in North America where liberalism and materialism would not triumph, was either discouraged or outlawed.

However, Québec's Catholicism was closer to a 'religion of conformity' than to a 'Christianism of conviction' (Lemieux and Montminy 2000: 36). It is therefore unsurprising that, over the years, cracks appeared in the conservative wall. Some liberal reforms were made applicable due to federal initiatives. Women, for example, were granted the right to vote at the federal level in 1917, against the vigorous opposition of the Catholic church. At the provincial level, they only gained that right in 1940, again against the opposition of the church. Moreover, as of the beginning of the 1900s, urbanization allowed for a higher level of anonymity, thereby facilitating religious transgressions that would normally have been severely sanctioned (Hardy 2007). Important social changes brought about by the Second World War, especially women's work, finally offered a springboard to reformers who wanted to change the status quo.

As of the 1950s, intellectuals and artists became, often at their own risk, extremely vocal in their opposition to the alliance between state and church. Even within Roman Catholic ranks, the influence of less authoritarian conceptions of religion, such as Jacques Maritain and Emmanuel Mounier's 'personalism', increased. The death of conservative Premier Maurice Duplessis, who had reigned since the 1930s, precipitated formidable changes. In 1960, the Liberal Party, which had campaigned on a program of radical reforms aimed at modernizing Québec society, was elected and launched what has since been termed the 'Quiet Revolution'. A welfare state approach to governance was substituted for the conservative, laissez-faire approach that had prevailed for the past two centuries; the Québec government took over responsibilities previously undertaken by the church, including public instruction. Liberal values were promoted, including gender equality. In passing, religion was, at least officially, relegated to the private sphere. All this took place in the context of a drastic redefinition of the identity of the French-speaking majority of Québec. The old French-Canadian identity came to be seen as an identity of 'losers' (i.e. oppressed by the church in a 'priest-ridden province', illiberal, backwards, colonized by the English, etc.), and a new 'Québécois' political identity took shape, which implied a shift from an ethnic to a civic identity. In this process, emphasis was placed on French as Québec's *lingua franca*, irrespective of one's ethnic origin or religion, instead of on Catholicism or French origins.

Admittedly, the image of pre-1960s Québec society as essentially religious and conservative, or as completely at odds with modernity, is somewhat caricatured (Conseil des relations interculturelles 2005, Pacquet 1999, Rocher 2009), though this caricature is, or was, an integral part of the political strategy of the 1960s reformers. But within a few years, a society which, until 1960, was arguably the most religious and conservative in North America became the most liberal. This change is reflected in study after study which shows that Quebeckers of all stripes, but especially French-speaking ones, tend to be significantly more individualistic, hedonist, in favour of absolute gender equality and tolerant of alternative sexualities than their North American neighbours (Adams 2003: 81–3). Most importantly, it is in Québec that the lowest level of religious practice in North America is observable. Among those who identify as Roman Catholics, barely ten per cent actually practise this religion (Vallée 2007); there are many more 'cultural' Catholics than religious ones.

While liberal values are now central to the identity of a majority of Quebeckers of French-Canadian descent, two recurrent themes of the public discourse about that identity are the overarching importance of gender equality and a suspicion about religion as a potential locus of social oppression. The reaction in Québec against the accommodation of some religious practices cannot be properly understood absent a reference to the historical context of that society. It is as if secular Quebeckers had problems understanding why some of their fellow citizens would want to submit themselves to a set of norms – religious ones – that their collective memory views as ontologically oppressive, anti-egalitarian and illiberal. As is often heard these days, 'we have cleansed our schools and institutions of priests and nuns, why would "others" want to bring back religion at school!?' In other words, the discursive relegation of Catholicism to the private sphere has led to a growing misunderstanding of religiosity itself. The 'folklorization' of religion that took place in Québec since the 1960s has somehow rendered the religiosity of 'others' unintelligible for a majority of lapsed Catholics in the province (Larouche 2008: 103). From that perspective, claims that are construed as purporting to reintroduce religion into the public sphere become immediately unacceptable.

This redefinition of Québec's identity has taken place in the context of a nationalist recreation of a society that, because of its unique linguistic and cultural features, has always been, and remains, a kind of 'anomaly' in North America. One might argue here that, paradoxically, the 'secularism' component of that identity has become even more 'sacralized' as a result of its inscription in this particular context.

If secularism has become a tenet of the post-1960 identity reference of Quebeckers, the increasing influence, since the mid-1990s, of the French ideology of *laïcité* has arguably radicalized it. The strong institutional relations and cultural affinities between France and Québec, and the increasing mobility between the two jurisdictions, make such influences inevitable. More precisely, a very vocal minority has arguably adopted the most extreme version of the *laïcité* principle – what Baubérot (2006) designates as a form of 'republican integrism' – as a model to follow in view of managing relations between the state and religions. The problem for proponents of such an approach is that neither the Canadian nor the Québec legal order recognizes any principle similar to that of *laïcité* in France. As a state, Canada has never been truly secular (at least not in the sense given to that word in France or in the United States). Moreover, as they are construed in Canadian law, freedom of religion and religious equality would simply not allow many of the normative consequences that Québec proponents of a strong version of *laïcité* would like to draw (for example banning all religious signs from public schools). Irrespective of its actual legal status, however, the principle of *laïcité* seems to operate in some circles as a rallying point. It has been politically appropriated and turned into an ideological beacon the legal recognition of which would, according to *laïcité* proponents, accelerate the passage of Québec from a dechristianized society to a post-religious one, and this ideology has contributed to framing the debate on reasonable accommodation.

Another factor is the particular legal culture of Quebeckers. Several objections to religious accommodations expressed in the course of the Québec debate took the form of a denunciation of the 'privileges' granted to religious minorities and of the granting of such privileges by unelected judges. For sure, the 'one law for all' argument is found in most societies, irrespective of the legal tradition(s) to which they belong. However, while this argument can be, and is often, informed by a particular conception of equality where equality is understood as necessarily implying a relation of identity, it can also be buttressed by a more general conception of what law is. This is precisely where 'legal culture' is a potential source of influence.

Québec, as a mixed legal order, partakes in both the common law tradition (for public law) and the civil law tradition (for private law). In spite of that mixedness, it is the civil law component that has historically had the greatest influence on the legal culture of the citizenry.[21] This is what Friedman calls the 'external legal culture', i.e. 'the legal culture of the general population' (1975: 223). Gibson and Caldeira (1996: 59) further specify that the external legal culture encompasses the set of values, beliefs and expectations of the public toward law, its nature, its functioning and the resources it offers. One can hypothesize that the civil law, with its emphasis on codified, impersonal, general and allegedly universal norms, has left its imprint on the legal culture of many Quebeckers who tend to conceive of the law exactly in these terms. This legal culture is arguably more prone than a common law culture to value formalism, top-down approaches and legal centralism. In contrast, the logic behind reasonable accommodation is infused with pragmatism and reflects a conception of the production of the law that is organic and decentralized. Under that logic, it is the judiciary, rather than the legislature,

21 In a Canadian environment where the common law predominates, belonging to the civil law tradition is a source of distinction. This explains why the civil law has long been a central element of Québec's identity reference, alongside Roman Catholicism and the French language.

that is given responsibility for realizing discrete and modest forms of social engineering. In that context, legal culture could realistically be counted as one of the many influences explaining the turn taken by the reasonable accommodation debate in Québec.

One question remains, though: why this debate *now*? If the debate is generically the 'product of the Western world's growing anxiety about exotic religions since the destruction of the World Trade Center on September 11, 2001' (Stevenson 2008: 54), it is also, and arguably first and foremost, about Québec's identity, and its real or perceived precariousness. In other words, it is about the contours of the collective 'We', something that the Bouchard-Taylor report captures very well. Indeed, in the course of the debate, several concerns were voiced that had apparently little to do with the accommodation of religious minorities.

First, and perhaps surprisingly given the rapid secularization of Québec society since the 1960s, fears were expressed about the dilution of Québec's Catholic identity. Although these fears might not have been shared by a majority, the question of the fate of Québec's Roman Catholic heritage was posed unambiguously, and most of those who raised this question vented their frustration at the idea that at the very moment their religious heritage was made invisible in the public sphere as a result of recent decisions taken out of concern for the freedom of religion of non-Catholics, minority religions were increasingly occupying space in that very public sphere. Demands for accommodation made by members of religious minorities were thus construed as evidence of the dispossession suffered by French-Canadians of their religious heritage. Members of that majority reacted against the use of individual religious rights allegedly in view of obscuring the collective right of the majority to feel the presence of its heritage in the public sphere (Lefebvre 2008: 107).

This reaction is somewhat puzzling. Beyond evincing a possible 'nostalgia of belief' (Bouveresse 2007), the return of the 'repressed Catholic' seems to have been provoked by a misperception, that of a Christianity materially absent from the public sphere in Québec, and by a dubious assumption, that of the purely secular nature of that public sphere. However, as Seljak et al. (2008: 13) note:

> By assuming that Canadian public life is already secular and that all religious expression should remain in the private sphere, people tend to ignore the fact that our putatively-secular public sphere is in many ways residually and normatively Christian. This means that its secularity has been shaped – ironically – by Christianity and in a way to accommodate most easily the needs of Christian communities.

There is in my view a form of wilful blindness in not recognizing that Christianity provides a template for the particular type of secularized society that exists in Québec. In turn, this leads to the application of a double standard: the presence of religious minorities in the public sphere is characterized as unduly visible while that of Christian artefacts in the same society (such as the crucifix in the legislature) is downplayed (Gaudreault-DesBiens 2008: 104, Seljak et al. 2008: 18). This momentary resurgence of interest for Québec's Catholic heritage, while genuine in some cases, seems to serve a primarily political purpose, that of distinguishing a core political community from a peripheral one. As Milot (2007: 25) argues

> Au Québec, on peut supposer la prégnance d'une matrice imaginaire, sans doute non reconnue comme telle mais aisément "activée" pour redire le *nous*. Une matrice catholique, vide de son contenu dogmatique et dissociée d'une autorité normative extérieure, sécularisée, qui joue néanmoins le même rôle qu'elle le fit par le passé face aux "protestants" celui de fournir la représentation d'un ensemble de valeurs présumées partagées, quoique vaguement définies.[22]

That core political community overlaps with an ethnic one, that of 'old-stock' Quebeckers of French descent and Catholic faith. I am not suggesting that this conception of the political community is shared by a majority of citizens, but simply that it is that particular ethnic conception that hides behind the neo-Catholic discourse heard during the reasonable accommodation debate. The impact of that discourse further evinces the frailty of the now dominant representation of Québec nationalism, one that emphasizes a civic conception of nationalism. Although this conception is widely shared among elites, irrespective of their federalist or secessionist allegiances, and has been assumed to have taken root in the general population, the debate over reasonable accommodation may have proven this assumption wrong.

Predictably, those who argued in favour of a clearer recognition of Québec's Catholic heritage in the public sphere tended to adhere to a conception of the political community that emphasized the particular interests of the French-Canadian majority. But when it comes to identifying those interests, one always takes priority, whether among ethnic or civic nationalists, that is, the preservation of French as the common public language of the province. In this respect, the debate on the reasonable accommodation of religious minorities provided a forum for expressing a collective anguish about that preservation. More than anything else, it explains the emphasis on immigration that was placed by many participants to the debate.

As remote as it may seem from the problems posed by religious accommodation, the question of language was front and centre in that debate. It emerged as part of a conversation on how to integrate immigrants into a society where the majority

22 'In Québec, one may suppose the prevalence of an imaginary matrix, which is undoubtedly not recognized as such but easily 'reactivated' to reiterate the We. A Catholic matrix, emptied of its dogmatic content and dissociated from any external normative authority, secularized, which nevertheless plays today the same role that it played in the past towards "Protestants": that of providing a representation of a set of values that are deemed to be shared, even though they are vaguely defined' [my translation].

of the population itself forms a minority in Canada and in North America. Of course, the discussion about the most efficient means to facilitate the integration of immigrants in such a society also addressed the integration of *religious* immigrants who may entertain conceptions that are not always compatible with those that predominate in a liberal society. However, it soon became clear that this problem, if it exists, is not peculiar to immigrants, as other, well-established, religious groups – think of Roman Catholics, for example – also entertain values that may not always correspond exactly to what a liberal society expects. Thus, the debate over the integration of immigrants shifted in part to the linguistic variable.

Prior to the 1977 Charter of French Language, which, among other things, forced businesses to advertise in French and compelled non-Canadian residents, including immigrants, to enrol their children in French schools, most immigrants joined the ranks of the English-speaking minority of the province. Not unreasonably, English was seen as the language that would facilitate social ascent in a primarily English-speaking North America. However, the perspective of those French-speakers forming the majority in Québec was markedly different: they wanted to perpetuate a society where French would be the common public language. Hence the much-discussed language laws that were adopted to foster that objective.

To some extent, the Charter of French Language was a success. Since its adoption, immigrants to Québec do learn French, which allows them to participate more meaningfully than before in societal debates. Their integration in the French-speaking mainstream, together with a substantial influx of French-speaking immigrants (mostly from France and the Maghreb), has also had the effect of transforming the national identity of Québec, severing it, at least in part and subject to the comments I made above, from its French-Canadian origins. It is in that particular context that Québec nationalism took its 'civic' turn. But, still, a tension persists between the rationale underlying that nationalism, i.e. the blossoming in North America of a mostly French-speaking community the historical roots of which predate Canada, and the republican, if not Jacobinistic, reflexes it entails, on the one hand, and its acceptance of liberal values, on the other. As a British observer astutely puts it: 'Quebec's liberalism precariously embraces ethnic nationalism – pride in one's history and traditions – while rejecting "ethnicism" – a belief in the superiority of one's ethnic group' (Goodhart 2008: 72).

However, the reasonable accommodation debate has revived old ghosts. One is the fear of losing the French language and, with it, much of Québec's historical identity. After years of calm on this front, recent demographic indicators have rekindled that fear. First, Québec's relative weight within Canada is steadily declining. It now represents only 23 per cent of the country's population. Secondly, some statistics tend to show that only 45 per cent of immigrants actually integrate into the French-speaking mainstream. While most of them do speak French, their primary language of private interaction is either English or their ethnic language. This has been construed by some as indicating the failure of the Charter of French Language. In their view, the charter enshrined a kind of informal agreement under which Québec nationalism was to open itself to non-French-Canadians and, more broadly, to immigrants (what I earlier called its 'civic turn') provided the said immigrants were ready adopt French as their principal language. As mentioned, they did learn French, but it would be an exaggeration to say that a majority of them have made of French their primary language. Since they mostly live in the Montréal area, the sociolinguistic dynamic of the metropolis has once again become a major subject of worry. While more Montrealers than ever are able to speak French, they are also more bilingual or multilingual than ever (including the French-speaking ones). This outcome is profoundly unsatisfying for a large number of nationalists, especially those who advocate secession from Canada. They had wanted Montréal to be 'as French as Toronto is English', as some used to say in the 1970s; they now observe the daily practice of bilingualism and multilingualism on the streets of the city and pejoratively characterize it as evidence of its 'Catalanization'.[23] Beyond the linguistic debate peculiar to Québec, what this reaction highlights is the rejection by a segment of the population of a vision of Québec identity that is deeply rooted in Montréal's cosmopolitan, bilingual and multicultural environment and that is seen as the by-product of disconnected elites, federalist and secessionist alike (Rioux (2008: 61–3).

This points to another ghost that was revived in the course of the reasonable accommodation debate, that of the dilution of Québec's 'national' project. In this respect, the civic turn of Québec nationalism has been criticized for obscuring the very reason underlying Québec nationalism, which revolves around the agenda of a small substate nation on the American continent. This line of questioning is particularly acute in secessionist circles. Why, it is asked, should the project of an independent Québec be conceived as a duplicate of the Canadian multicultural, bilingual and 'identity-light' experiment; isn't there a risk if we forget why we want to become sovereign (Bock-Côté 2007, Lisée 2007, Bédard 2008)? In sum, Québec society and nationalism seem to be in a 'melancholic' phase, to borrow Maclure's expression (2000). Even Gérard Bouchard himself, one of the co-chairs of the reasonable accommodation commission, has diagnosed a crisis of Québec culture (Bouchard and Roy 2007).

In such a volatile social context, any debate that raises, directly or indirectly, questions pertaining to the co-existence or the competition of identities is likely to ignite passions. As a debate that revealed the overt or subterranean action of diverse strategies designed at constructing 'difference' (see Modood 2007: 39), the Québec debate over reasonable accommodation must thus be characterized as one pertaining to nation-building (Cairns 2008). And it has erupted only recently because of the sense, shared by many, that a cultural crisis was indeed simmering and had to be addressed. The controversies surrounding some practices of religious accommodation simply provided an opportunity to do so.

---

23 This neologism refers to the Catalan-Spanish bilingualism that is practised in Catalunya, especially in Barcelona, a bilingualism where the default language is more often than not Spanish.

Conclusion

I have provided a brief overview of the variables that may explain why the Québec debate over the reasonable accommodation of religious claims turned into a kind of social crisis. Now, what can we conclude from my 'reading' of the reasonable accommodation debate and from that debate itself?

A word, first, about the majority/minority dichotomy. Although this dichotomy is far from unproblematic, notably in that it reduces the internal complexity of both majorities and minorities and in that it tends to obscure the relative fluidity of both, the reasonable accommodation debate, for all its lack of political correctness, can be lauded for its straightforwardness. Participants, whether they belonged to the majority or to a minority, have not shied away from acknowledging that, in spite of Pollyanna-like rhetoric to the contrary, power still frames majority–minorities relations and that both majorities and minorities use various discursive strategies in conceiving of themselves and of the others. In that process, both resort to essentialism for the sake of achieving their political objectives. More particularly, both religious and non-religious groups have political agendas (Bourgeault 2002).

This straightforwardness was to be expected in the context of a debate over *reasonable accommodation*. This expression is sometimes viewed as condescending toward those, generally members of disadvantaged groups, who ask for such accommodation and who, in order to obtain it, have to remain within the bounds of the Eurocentric notion of 'reasonableness'. In other words, the legal doctrine of reasonable accommodation would be a way to 'tame the shrew', so to say. There might be some truth to that line of argument, but, all things considered, the doctrine allows calling a spade a spade. Embedded in the notion is the presumption that the norms and institutions of a particular society, even those which seem superficially neutral, reflect majoritarian conceptions. The very idea of 'reasonable accommodation' presupposes that there are sociological majorities and minorities. In sum, it does not hide the existence of power relations through an uncritical adherence to the universalist and ahistorical conception of the law that legal positivism has advocated. By doing so, it renders all parties to the debate more aware of their own limits and of the institutional limits they face, which, arguably, is a precondition to mutual tolerance (Freund 1992: 90). In the case of the Québec debate, one cannot discard outright the hypothesis that the very iteration of different, and often divergent, views during the hearings of the Bouchard-Taylor commission may have actually transformed the preconceptions that some participants initially had, as Khan argues in respect of Ontario's shari'a debate. At the very least, it may have humanized, and de-essentialized, the opponent.

Secondly, the Québec debate has shown that alleged majorities are most vociferous when they realize that they are internally fissured. In Québec, some members of the French-speaking majority seemed to believe that at least two layers of their heritage were threatened, first, the old French-Christian layer, and, second, the newer modernist secular layer. But this belief may hide a fear of what the identity of individuals composing the majority has become. Thus, the Québec debate was far from being only about defining the expectations of religious minorities and identifying the majority's threshold of tolerance within a minority rights framework, it may have first and foremost been about defining the expectations of an old majority and defining the borders of a new one against a backdrop of shared anguish. In that, the debate over reasonable accommodation showed how 'hypermodern' Québec society now is. The concept of 'hypermodernity' refers to the condition of a society which, while emphasizing 'modern' values such as human rights and democracy, fears the social fragmentation that may result from a 'radical' implementation of these values (Charles 2007).

Thirdly, while, at first glance, the Québec debate over reasonable accommodation represents a familiar case of an overwhelmingly secular liberal democracy struggling to find ways to manage the now widespread re-emergence of religious identities, the questions that it raised went beyond that. Indeed, it was peculiar in that it took place in a fragile society, not only one that is the most secular in North America, but one where the majority is a national and continental minority. A proper understanding of the particular dynamics of the debate thus requires that reference be made to the particular historical evolution *and* geopolitical position of that society. For that reason, even if parallels can be drawn with debates stirred by religion in other liberal societies, say France, Britain or Holland, we must be cautious when making comparisons. That being said, it remains to be seen whether the Bouchard-Taylor report will be of interest to such societies. We can surmise that Charles Taylor's international reputation will provide a springboard for the report. Ironically, it would not be the first time that a famous report diagnosing a deep societal malaise would come out of Québec. It is little known, but Jean-François Lyotard's famous *Postmodern Condition* (Lyotard 1979), before it became an international philosophical bestseller, was a report commissioned by the Québec government. Time shall tell.

References

Abou, S. 1992. *Cultures et droits de l'homme*. Paris: Hachette.

Adams, M. 2003. *Fire and Ice. The United States, Canada and the Myth of Converging Values*. Toronto: Penguin Canada.

Baubérot, J. 2006. *L'intégrisme républicain contre la laïcité*. Paris: Éditions de l'Aube.

Bédard, E. 2007–2008. Souveraineté et hypermodernité – la trudeauisation des esprits. *Arguments*, 10(1), 101–26.

Bock-Côté, M. 2007. *La dénationalisation tranquille*. Montréal: Boréal.

Bouchard, G. and A. Roy. 2007. *La culture québécoise est-elle en crise?* Montréal: Boréal.

Bourgeault, G. 2001. L'espace public et la dimension politique de la culture religieuse. In *Les relations interethniques en question*, edited by J. Renaud, L.

Pietrantonio and G. Bourgeault. Montréal: Presses de l'Université de Montréal, 213–27.

Bouveresse, J. 2007. *Peut-on ne pas croire? Sur la vérité, la croyance and la foi.* Paris: Agone.

Cairns, A.C. 2008. Bouchard-Taylor and Nation-building. *Inroads*, 22, 64–9.

CBC News. 2007. Quebec Politicians, Muslims Slam New Election Rules on Veils. Available at: <http://www.cbc.ca/canada/montreal/story/2007/09/06/qc-niqab0906.html> [accessed 22 October 2008].

Charles, S. 2007. *L'hypermoderne expliqué aux enfants*. Montréal: Liber.

Clément, E. and M.-A. Wolf. eds. 2008. *Le Québec sur le divan. Raisonnements de psys sur une société en crise*. Montréal: Éditions Voix parallèles.

Commission de consultation sur les pratiques d'accommodement reliées aux différences culturelles. 2008. Fonder l'avenir. Le temps de la conciliation. G. Bouchard and C. Taylor, co-chairs. Québec: Commission de consultation sur les pratiques d'accommodement reliées aux différences culturelles. Available at: <http://www.accommodements.qc.ca> [accessed 22 October 2008].

Commission des droits de la personne et des droits de la jeunesse. 1995. Le pluralisme religieux au Québec: un défi d'éthique sociale. Available at: <http://www.cdpdj.qc.ca/fr/publications/docs/hidjab.pdf> [accessed 22 October 2008].

— 2006. *Centre de recherche-action sur les relations raciales et Ecole de technologie supérieure et R.N., Résolution COM-510-5.1-1.* Available at: <http://www.cdpdj.qc.ca/fr/placedelareligion/1-documents-commission.asp> [accessed 22 October 2008].

— 2007. *La ferveur religieuse et les demandes d'accommodement religieux: une comparaison intergroupe.* Available at: <http://www.vigile.net/La-ferveur-religieuse-et-les> [accessed 22 October 2008].

Conseil des relations interculturelles. 2005. Laicity and Religious Diversity Quebec's Approach: Report to the Minister of Citizens Relations and Immigration. *Journal of International Migration and Immigration*, 6(2), 291–326. Available at: <http://www.springerlink.com/content/u240335306g47321/> [accessed 22 October 2008].

Dumont, F. 1993. *Genèse de la société québécoise*. Montréal: Boréal.

Freund, J. 1992. Conflictualité sociale et intolérance. In *L'intolérance et le droit de l'autre*, edited by G. Vincent. Geneva: Éditions Labor et Fides, 75–90.

Friedman, L.M. 1975. *The Legal System: A Social Science Perspective*. New York: Russell Sage Foundation.

Gagnon, K. and A. Gruda, A. 2006. *Les Québécois plus réticents que l'ensemble des Canadiens aux signes religieux*. La Presse, Montréal, 22 September. Available at: <http://www.vigile.net/Les-Quebecois-plus-reticents-que-l> [accessed 22 October 2008].

Gaudreault-DesBiens, J.-F. 2005–2006. Constitutional Values, Faith-based Arbitration, and the Limits of Private Justice in a Multicultural Society. *National Journal of Constitutional Law*, 19, 155–91.

— 2007. Quelques angles morts du débat sur l'accommodement raisonnable à la lumière de la question du port de signes religieux à l'école publique: réflexions en forme de points d'interrogation. In *Les accommodements raisonnables. Quoi, comment, jusqu'où? Des outils pour tous*, edited by M. Cowansville: Éditions Yvon Blais, 241–86.

— 2008. Culture Wars in Québec: Remarques à propos du débat québécois sur les accommodements religieux. *Canadian Diversity/ Diversité canadienne*, 6 (1), 103–105.

Gibson, J.L. and G.A. Caldeira. 1996. The Legal Cultures of Europe. *Law and Society Review*, 30, 55–85.

Goodhart, D. 2008. When Liberalism and Pluralism Conflict. *Inroads*, 22, 70–7.

Hardy, R. 2007. Regards sur la construction de la culture catholique québécoise au XIXième siècle. *Canadian Historical Review*, 88 (1), 7–40.

Heinrich, J. 2007. Immigrants Welcome – as Long as they Conform. *The Gazette*, September 10. Available at: <http://www.canada.com/montrealgazette/news/story.html?id=fee092fd-5859-48c7-a46e-0a0a43700b73&k=38180>[accessed 22 October 2008].

Heinrich, J. and V Dufour. 2008. *Circus quebecus. Sous le chapiteau de la commission Bouchard-Taylor*. Montréal: Boréal.

Hérouxville. 2007. *Normes d'Hérouxville*. Available at: <http://grandquebec.com/multiculturalisme/normes-en-place> [accessed 22 October 2008].

Karim, K.H. and F. Hirji. 2008. Religion and State in a Pluralist Nation: Policy Challenges in Contemporary Canadian Society. *Canadian Diversity*, 6(1), 109–12.

Khan, S. 2007. The Ontario Sharia Debate: Transformational Accommodation, Multiculturalism and Muslim Identity. In *Belonging? Diversity, Recognition and Shared Citizenship in Canada*, edited by K. Banting, T.J. Courchene, and F.L. Seidle. Montreal: Institute for Research on Public Policy, 475–485.

L'Express d'Outremont. 2007. Stationnement autorisé les jours de fêtes religieuses. Available at: <http://www.expressoutremont.com/article-69526-Stationnement-autorise-les-jours-de-fetes-religieuses.html> [accessed 22 October 2008].

Lamonde, Y. 2000. *Histoire sociale des idées au Québec 1760–1896*. Montréal: Fides.

Larouche, J.-M. 2008. *La religion dans les limites de la cité. Le défi religieux des sociétés postséculières*. Montréal: Liber.

LCN 2007. Des accommodements raisonnables à la cabane à sucre. Available at: <http://lcn.canoe.ca/lcn/infos/regional/archives/2007/03/20070319-081025.html> [accessed 22 October 2008].

Lefebvre, S. 2008. Entrevue avec Solange Lefebvre. *Canadian Diversity*, 6(1), 106–108.

Lemieux, R. and J.-P. Montminy. 2000. *Le catholicisme québécois*. Sainte-Foy: IQRC and Presses de l'Université Laval.

Lisée, J.-F. 2007. *Nous*. Montréal: Boréal.

Lyotard, J.-F. 1979. *La condition postmoderne. Rapport sur le savoir*. Paris: Éditions de Minuit.
Maclure, J. 2000. *Récits identitaires. Le Québec à l'épreuve du pluralisme.* Montréal: Québec Amérique.
Milot, M. 2007. Etre égal non en tant que semblable mais en tant que différent. *Cahiers du 27 juin*, 3(2), 23–5.
Modood, T. 2007. *Multiculturalism*. Cambridge: Polity Press.
Paquet, G. 1999. *Oublier la Révolution tranquille. Pour une nouvelle socialité.* Montréal: Liber.
Perreault, L.-J. 2008. Entre ignorance et préjugés. L'ensemble des Québécois ont peu de contacts avec la communauté juive. *La Presse*, 24 February 2008.
Rioux, C. 2008. The Quebec Language Question is Back: From Saint-Léonard to the Bouchard-Taylor Commission. *Inroads*, 22, 57–63.
Rocher, G. 2009. L'évolution religieuse de la société québécoise. In *Le droit, la religion et le raisonnable*, edited by J.-F. Gaudreault-DesBiens. Montréal: Éditions Thémis.
Seljak, D., Andréa Schmidt and Adam Stewart. 2008. Secularization and the Separation of Church and State in Canada. *Canadian Diversity*, 6(1), 6–24.
Shachar, A. 2001. *Multicultural Jurisdictions. Cultural Differences and Women's Rights*. Cambridge: Cambridge University Press.
Stevenson, G. 2008. Religion is the Elephant in the Room. *Inroads*, 22, 53–6.
Vallée, P. 2007. Un patrimoine en danger. *Le Devoir*, 7–8 April 2007.

Chapter 10
Does the Dutch Judiciary Pluralize Domestic Law?

André J. Hoekema

Introduction

Dutch judges (and occasionally public administrators and school directors) are regularly confronted with hitherto unknown or at least not officially recognized or accommodated 'distinct' legal concepts, practices and sensibilities, or with distinct patterns of family life prevailing in distinct communities living in the Netherlands. These distinct communities comprise a variety of groups of people who belong to a school of Islam, but also communities adhering to Indonesian Adat, to the Surinamese Hindu religion, to Ghanaian local customs and others.[1] As to the term 'distinct' (and 'distinct community'), some explanation is in order. Almost every society nowadays is host to many socio-culturally different encompassing societies such as 'first nations' (indigenous peoples), national minorities, immigrant communities, etc. European societies like the Netherlands are no exception to this. Clearly, these communities cannot be simply grouped under one heading, but in this contribution I use just one term for them all: distinct communities. Admittedly, there are differences between immigrant communities on the one hand and 'first nations' on the other, the latter term referring to the original peoples of some conquered territory, confined to some marginal part of that territory by a dominant group of different socio-cultural and often ethnic make-up. But in terms of the challenge for vested national law and legal scholarship, one can group these cases together. This challenge consists in a mounting pressure by members of minorities to have their distinct culture and legal sensibilities recognized not just as a kind of private property ('behind the front door of their home') but as part of the official set-up of state and national law. While not all members of such communities share this view – some are pleading for rapid assimilation – generally speaking, there is a mounting pressure for some form of recognition of this right to be legally different (in some sensitive legal domains).

The main question for this contribution will be how does the average judge cope with this challenge of diversity? In other words what empirical conflict rules – a concept to be explained below – can be detected in Dutch judicial practice?

---

1 Official data indicate some 1.7 million persons of non-Western origin in the Netherlands, c. ten per cent of the population.

Following these descriptive observations I want to develop some elements for a theory about conditions under which judges *as a matter of fact* tend to open up to the multicultural challenge or to stick to standard (dominant) conceptions and perceptions only.[2]

The object of my study is mainly domestic law, and less attention will be paid to international private law, so the stress lies on the *internal* pluralization[3] of Dutch law. However, there is some artificiality in separating the two ways through which distinct legal concepts and family patterns make their way into the Dutch legal practice. When we want to know how judges get to know, perceive, learn about and cope with these distinct legal orders and life patterns, international private law is relevant too, and will therefore be dealt with as well, albeit briefly.

All this is the subject matter of Part I of this chapter. In Part II I move briefly to another question, which is about the general effects of such internal pluralization. Can this tendency indeed be qualified as pluralization of a domestic legal order, or is it a way to assimilate a distinct legal culture into the national mainstream, a way of *incorporation* as I usually call this? It is true that the question is put awkwardly or at least highly misleadingly. Different legal orders and sensibilities, formally recognized or not, are of necessity always rubbing shoulders with each other, thereby producing new hybrid concepts, rules and meanings. This process may be intensified when judges (or the legislator) open the gates officially. But mutual interaction and penetration are always present, including outside the courts. Moreover, it is not an interaction between some well-defined blocks or entities, following some 'universal' social regularities, but a confrontation in the mind and behaviour of individuals. To begin to answer that question, one would have to look into the concrete choices people (officials or not so official) are making each day when confronted with distinct institutions, and I draw upon a concept which captures this dynamic and 'actor-oriented' approach well: 'multicultural interlegality'.[4]

2 This chapter builds on a study by my colleague Wibo van Rossum and myself, described in a contribution for a symposium in Brussels (2006), organized by and in celebration of Marie-Claire Foblets (Hoekema and van Rossum 2009). I am grateful to van Rossum for allowing me to present cases that were dealt with in that paper and generally to draw on our common work. An extended case to be presented shortly ('Hamid's case') is taken from van Rossum's research which was commissioned by the Raad voor de Rechtspraak, the Dutch Council for the Judiciary (van Rossum 2007). The interviews referred to later in the chapter were conducted by van Rossum in the course of this research.

3 A term used by various scholars who participated in the Brussels symposium, see Foblets and Renteln (eds) (2009).

4 To take the title of a special issue of *The Journal of Legal Pluralism and Unofficial Law*, 51, 2005, of which I happen to have been the guest editor (Hoekema 2005).

I Trying to Come up with Empirical Conflict Rules

The Issues

I should emphasize from the outset that my empirical material derives from instances of accommodation of cultural diversity in an *individual case*. An individual can be qualified as someone belonging to a specific community who wants to live up to the values and rules of that community, and on this basis is officially granted a specific exception to or interpretation of an existing legal rule or concept. This produces a restricted form of official (or formal) legal pluralism. An *extended* form of such official pluralism would imply granting a *collective right* to a distinct community to live by their own rules and practices in some specific domains of life, perhaps even when these rules contradict the dominant national law. Such a collective right does not legally exist in the Netherlands; group rights are hardly ever claimed,[5] particularly not by immigrant communities (except occasionally for family and personal matters[6]). This extended form of official legal pluralism is a highly contested issue as it shifts power (at least formally) from the majority to the minority and often raises very serious questions about the equal treatment of citizens. But the restricted, individual kind of official legal pluralism has also been contested fiercely, particularly in the last six or seven years. This is not *only* for ideological reasons or out of fear for social cohesion. When granting individuals special treatment, the interests of third parties are often at stake, like those of a first wife and children in an alimony case where the Dutch Supreme Court allows a man to claim making generous second marriage gifts according to local custom as a reason to reduce his alimony payment. But ideologically – or perhaps better symbolically – the case is even more sensitive when we think of the emotions concentrated in the French notion of '*laicité*'. This notion strongly suggests resisting the challenge of diversity even in individual cases. It refers to a strict constitutional separation of the state and any religious or, for that matter, distinct cultural aspect or organization. French collective identity 'has depended on the idea that citizenship should transcend community ties and define beyond all particularisms, a national "we" with which each person can identify' (Hervieu-

5 M. Berger (2007: 508) stresses the fact that e.g. under Dutch marriage law it is not possible to conduct a shari'a marriage and have shari'a family law applied (apart from international private law cases). Moreover, arbitrated or mediated conditions of marriage or divorce always have to be approved by a judge. There is no legal space for making a distinct community's 'group right' official. Obviously, people may voluntarily adhere to their proper family law.

6 Compare for instance claims in Canada for institutions which permit Muslims to conduct a shari'a marriage and live under its specific rules. This is optional only. If such a right is turned into a kind of group right which would imply that everyone belonging to a distinct community is *obliged* not only socially but also legally to follow this distinct law and procedure, more fundamental questions arise.

Leger 1998: 57). In the Netherlands, although a separation of state and religion is one of the leading constitutional principles, in practice this is not perceived as a ban on the state financially supporting religious entities nor a ban on the wearing of religious insignia during official duty (save, for example, in the judiciary). Generally, a ban on teachers wearing a headscarf is not legally upheld by the relevant decision-making body[7] (save for specific private schools and institutions), while pupils are free to wear a headscarf at school. Citizenship is not constructed along the lines of one, monocultural, typical Dutch citizen.[8]

In the wake of recent socio-political turmoil and a general stiffening of majority–minority relations, this relatively open attitude has come under severe pressure. Calls for compulsory assimilation politics have surfaced again in various European countries. In the Netherlands, quite a few judges, their advisors, public administrators and school directors continue taking multicultural diversity into account in a low key way, for example in cases of school pupils who do not want to take gym lessons or participate in a school excursion lasting several days in mixed company. Nevertheless opinions are now being voiced which are not unlike those expressed in a recent issue of the German magazine *Der Spiegel*.[9] In the leading article these innocent examples of accommodating multiculturality are set alongside darker cases like theatre directors giving in to threats by fundamentalists against staging a play which allegedly insults Islam. The article plays a rhetorical trick by suggesting that all such developments amount to the same tendency, of letting Germany be taken over by shari'a fanatics. Certainly this change in political climate will influence judges as well, but for the moment I have come to the conclusion that in concrete cases, judges usually are not adamantly set against the pluralization of domestic law and regularly take distinct legal sensibilities and family patterns seriously.

A Case

Now a case, a *kafala* case. The Dutch Child Benefit Act[10] entitles parents to a benefit for every child which they effectively raise and pay for. Adopted children and, under certain circumstances, foster children also qualify for this allowance. Therefore, Moroccan couples living in the Netherlands sometimes ask for the legal recognition of a distinct cultural institution. Moroccan Islam-based national law does not allow for adoption but has its own legal institution, the *kafala* contract.

---

7 The Commission on Equal Treatment (*Commissie Gelijke Behandeling*, CGB), which is an advisory committee only and cannot legally sanction behaviour that it deems unacceptable under the equal treatment law.

8 On *laïcité* in French practice see Eberhard et al. 2005, and also Hoekema 2005, Bowen 2006. For the Netherlands, see Vermeulen 2005.

9 *Der Spiegel*, 13/2007, 26 March 2007, under the title 'Haben wir schon die Scharia?' ('Do we have shari'a already?')

10 *Kinderbijslagwet.*

The contract obliges a family to take over care of children from other parents, pay for all the expenses, etc. without the parents losing the right to custody over the child. It is a strict Islamic prescription that parenthood is not transferred to the care taking family: no legal family relations must develop between a *kafala* child and the *kafala* parents (Wortmann 2006).

Sometimes a family living in the Netherlands acts as *kafala* parents and takes care of a child whose biological parents are living in Morocco. Such children do not qualify as adopted and therefore proper children in terms of the Child Benefit Act. But perhaps these children could qualify as 'foster' children? In the case of fostering out children, according to the general policy of the administrator of the Act, the Social Insurance Bank,[11] various requirements must be met to make the foster parents eligible for child benefit. Most importantly, if the biological parents still have official custody – regardless of the question of whether or not they really do interfere in the child's upbringing, choice of school, etc. – then the foster parents are not entitled to that benefit.

Up until recently, this formal element was decisive in the chain of legal reasoning. Obviously, *kafala* could not pass this test as the biological parents do not lose the right to custody over their children. But in 2001 the bank changed its policies and started to reason more empirically (SVB 2005: 54), asking: what about the real exclusivity of the caring relation between the *kafala* parents and the child? If the biological parents *as a matter of fact* do not interfere, foster parents can qualify for the right to a benefit *provided they bring the children up as their own* (a tight and exclusive relation, as the legal formula runs) and do this on a *durable* basis. A critical review of the bank's policy by its head of legal affairs (Vonk and Ydema-Gutjahr 2002) had an impact on the legislator; an official ruling by the State Secretary of Social Affairs in 2002 expanded the concept of foster children generally. The requirement that the biological parents should not retain custody was relaxed. The bank's new policy was codified into the regulations.[12]

I may conclude that the Dutch legal concept of a foster child has been extended (at least partially) because the public authorities applying this branch of domestic law opened up towards the norms and practices of a distinct institution. This openness was produced by a change in legal reasoning from a formal way to an 'empirical' way. Later, the legislator followed suit and settled the matter.

---

11 *Sociale Verzekeringsbank* (SVB).

12 Some *kafala* children, however, may not pass the test of foster children under the Act. Suppose that a Moroccan child is placed under a *kafala* contract in the household of some relatives, like an uncle and aunt, living in the Netherlands. It is possible that the original parents keep playing an important role in deciding educational matters. It is sometimes difficult to prove that the relation between the 'foster parents' and the child is exclusive, and durable. Cases that are accepted by the bank are mostly cases of orphans. (I refer here to an unpublished paper written by B. Benhsain for a course taught by the bank's head of legal affairs.)

There has been an interesting parallel case in England. Menski (2009) observes that the institution of *kafala* was, as he says, 'smuggled' into English law by introducing the new legal concept of 'special guardianship' in 2002. This legal concept should apply to those situations, between adoption and fosterage, where new parents receive the responsibility for raising a child without s/he becoming a full member of the new family. Argumentation in the White Paper proposing the changes (Department of Health 2000) referred to 'some minority ethnic communities' having difficulties with adoption, and to the need to 'modernise the law so it reflects the religious and cultural diversity of our country today'. 'Special guardianship' is a newly introduced legal concept, while in the Netherlands the meaning of the *existing* concept of 'foster children' was expanded. In this case the legislator pluralized English law, while in the Netherlands it was the public administrator (followed later by the legislator). In terms of judges' attitudes towards the admissibility of bold interpretations, this is an important difference, as normally judges want to be seen as loyal to the laws made by competent authorities, particularly the parliamentary legislator.

Empirical Conflict Rules

Here comes an example of such a rule, drawn from the *kafala* case. How can I best describe the regularity, the pattern an observer might detect in judges' behaviour towards multicultural challenges in matters of social security law? As already stated, judges and – perhaps to a lesser extent – public administrators want to be seen as being loyal to the law as produced by the legislator. In questions of legal entitlement to a social benefit, a rather strict legality is cherished, and therefore multiculturality does not fare well in social security law. Reformulating this, I venture to suggest the following empirical conflict rule.

In social security cases administrators and judges stick to the value of legal certainty and do not deviate from the complex of rules as it stands. But in case of concepts possibly designating an empirical complex, like 'foster child' etc., administrators may reason empirically in exceptional cases and take distinct cultural institutions into account.

This 'rule' suggests the presence of some leeway for the influx of cultural diversity in state law and purports to lay bare the matter-of-fact tendencies in legal practice to take legal diversity into account or not. These tendencies can be reconstructed in the day-to-day, factual decision-making behaviour of judges and public administrators. Let us call them social rules. They are not codified, have no formal normative validity and are not binding on judges. They are not part of the law, but are the product of our anthropological and sociological invention and imagination, generalizations from cases studied and interviews held. This empirical nature must be stressed. Although judges might recognize or affirm some of these 'rules' as plausible empirically speaking, at least for them, they will immediately comment that such a social rule has no normative standing; and that is correct.

I am instead looking for de facto ways and circumstances in which judges tend to consider a distinct cultural institution, notion or practice as relevant for the case at hand and accept it as a challenge that might be legally accommodated, or resist this challenge and decide monoculturally. I submit that regardless of the dogmatic, philosophical and political debates as to the merits of multicultural legal development, the judiciary holds one of the most important keys and acts as one of the most important gatekeepers. One might wonder if the legislator is not the most important gatekeeper. It is true that judges in this type of case regularly refuse to take a culturally distinct institution into account and refer to the legislator instead. But legal change usually starts with judges taking an unconventional, open-minded stand towards some new constellation of facts, or towards 'deviant customary norms', thereby provoking debates inside and outside the profession. Perhaps after many years the legislator follows suit. Therefore, I shall concentrate my attention on the judiciary to find out which distinct cases they accept and accommodate, for what reasons, and which ones they refuse.

Returning to the empirical conflict rule formulated above, let me stress that the notion of the primacy of the legislator over judges' possible wish to accommodate other legal sensibilities is confirmed in some other cases. Once, the highest court in these matters held that a Gypsy marriage could not justify the claim of the wife of the deceased for a widow's allowance, which is a general right for 'official' widows only, as the law says.[13] Another illuminating case[14] involved an unmarried Moroccan couple, who both held dual Moroccan and Dutch nationalities, and their child. The mother asked the court to declare officially the man to be the father of the child (which was granted) as well as order their child to take the father's name. The woman alleged that the fact that her child bears her name (which in these cases is the legal rule) suggests that she is a bad woman. The child therefore runs the palpable risk of being mistreated by schoolmates and by the Moroccan family. A request for such a change of name is legally admissible,[15] provided it comes from both parents. But here, although the father refused, the lower court granted the request, entering into a balancing of the interests of the child versus the interests of the father. The highest court quashed this decision because the relevant rule had a strict character and did not leave a space open for a judicial balancing of interests and a possible overruling of the father's objection. The legislators' intention being clear, the request had to be turned down.

---

13 See RSV (*Rechtspraak sociale verzekering*) 2001: # 54. (This is a periodical on cases in social security law.) Menski (2009) found a case in English law in which the outcome was the opposite. A marriage between Sikhs, concluded in accordance with religious rules in London in the 1950s but not officially registered, gave the woman pension rights after her husband died, as the Court of Appeal ruled. This court claims to have applied principles of equity as a result of which the case sets no precedent. Menski interprets this as an indication of the reluctance of English judges to pluralize the legal system.

14 Court of The Hague, 16 02 2005, # 925-R-04, LJN AS6769.

15 Civil Code, book 1: 5 subsection 2.

To conclude this part I would like to stress the difference between the concept of empirical conflict rules and that of conflict rules in private international law, where it denotes a complex of legally valid rules that judges have to follow in international cases when deciding what national law to apply. Why then use the same terminology? Because both notions of 'conflict rules' define the boundaries of a legal system which is supposed to be a coherent whole, a unity, vis-à-vis another system of rules. In official private international law conflict rules, the boundaries with foreign law are defined normatively, mostly in laws and international treaties or in judge-imposed rules. These rules have a normative standing, they are valid law. In empirical conflict rules, the boundaries with minority cultural practices are defined (determined) empirically. These rules do not have any normative standing.

I leave international private law for a moment, but raise the question of pluralizing a domestic legal system through the international private law cases further below.

As to empirical conflict rules in general, things perhaps have to be approached differently in cases where the official legal rules manifest open standards and therefore leave judges wide discretion. How do judges use this discretion? The next case serves to elaborate the phenomenon of empirical conflict rules and also allows me to penetrate deeper into possible conditions under which it can be presumed that judges do or do not open up to the challenge of diversity. The case is again an example in domestic law only (and not an international private law case).

Case of Hamid – 'The Interest of the Child'

Hamid's case[16] involves the divorce of a couple of Turkish origin, in which the contested points were the determination of custody over and place of residence of their two children. The wife had been living in the Netherlands for quite some time, and the husband Hamid had come over from Turkey for the wedding (an arranged marriage). They had lived in the Netherlands for several years, and the marriage went well, but after six years, when her second baby was born, the wife became depressed, the couple started to argue and finally she left their mutual home without the children for an unknown destination. The report of the Child Care and Protection Board stated that the wife wanted to 'integrate in Dutch culture' while the husband wanted her to 'stay true to Turkish culture'. The wife was absent for one and a half years, during which time the children were living with a sister of Hamid and – for over a year – with his parents in Turkey. Hamid started a divorce procedure, Dutch law was applicable, and he obtained the divorce in due course. Meanwhile, the wife had claimed custody over the children and wanted to have the children live permanently with her and not with the father. Both ex-spouses

16 The case comes from research conducted by Wibo van Rossum.

had found a new life partner, Hamid a young woman from Turkey, the ex-wife a Dutch man of Turkish origin.

Regarding the matter of custody and other decisions to be taken, the judge postponed that decision and ordered the Child Care and Protection Board to produce a report on the situation to evaluate how to serve the interests of the children best, the primary criterion which is decisive in these cases.[17] The children, however, had to return to the Netherlands first, which necessitated a court order to Hamid because he did not 'just' want to give in to his wife who had left him. The return was effected without problem. Thereupon the board officer wrote the report after having spoken to Hamid, and after having observed interactions between the two children and their mother and her new friend.

The report said that Hamid had 'mainly looked after his own interests and had neglected the interests of his children'. According to the board Hamid 'is not able to take on the primary task of raising his children'. The board attributed Hamid's behaviour of serving his own interests and arguing with his ex-wife to his Turkish cultural background in which 'his honour was damaged'. This damage to Hamid's honour was also the reason, according to the report, for the violent threats made by Hamid to his ex-wife (there were no police reports on this, however). Hamid had also once written a nasty letter to his ex-wife, after her new friend had phoned Hamid's family in Turkey and threatened them to get them to release the children. Furthermore, the wife reported to the board's officers that she was scared. Moreover, from the behaviour of the children when on the board's premises, the reporting officer 'had the feeling' that the young children did relate very well to the mother (notwithstanding that they had not seen her for years, while the young one did not even know his mother) and that they were somehow fearful of their father. There were hardly any clear patterns to corroborate this view, especially since Hamid never personally took the children to the board. Nevertheless, this interpretation of 'damaged honour' and consequent 'possible violent revenge' and even 'abduction of the children' stuck (and later the judge also adopted it). Hamid was apparently not able to give enough clues in court (he was heard separately from his ex-wife in a special session of the court) to create a contrary interpretation, even though 'he behaved correctly' according to the judge.

Eventually, custody over the children was awarded to the wife, as was the regular place of residence. One has to note here that normally custody after divorce gets shared by both parents. Moreover, one would think that the mother's long years of absence and the father's care would at least cast doubt on the decision to let the children now switch from the father's home to the mother's.

Let me concentrate now on the question of the meaning of the open legal concept 'in the interest of the child' when it comes to the decision of custody. While his 'taking care of the children' was not denied, the judge reproached Hamid

---

17 The law in Article 251 of Book 1 of the Dutch civil code provides legal custody to both parents after a divorce. The judge may deviate from this rule 'in the interest of the child'.

for his lack of affectionate behaviour. Further, there was no discussion of the possibility that in other cultures other patterns of child raising could be common, like when an aunt or a grandmother cares for children, and men go about earning the necessary money. Hamid's lawyer said in the interview that such a pattern of an 'extended family' is 'quite common' in Turkish culture. The 'interest of the children' was also not served, according to the judge, by moving them back and forth between Turkey and Holland and from one family to another. This amounted to 'a culture shock', said the judge, which would once again be the case if the children were placed in Hamid's household, where additionally the new wife was a young Turkish woman who was not a biological parent. She did not yet speak Dutch, but the judge said this had no influence on her decision.

Affective harmony, radiating from a biological parent who is permanently available in a steady household, is apparently used as the criterion for deciding custody and the household in which to place the children.[18] These elements were thought to be guaranteed better by the wife's new household (with her new friend) than by Hamid who at least in the past had not shown he could provide them. This criterion basically consists of preconceptions that have excluded the possibility of Hamid giving meaning to the open legal concept of 'the interest of the child'. A 'culture shock' for example is only experienced when the preconception is that 'steadiness' is a normal and desirable state of living. Furthermore, 'biological' parents gain importance when a restricted version of 'family' is taken into account. And 'affectionate behaviour' is a gendered term, but gender roles differ between cultures. More strongly, we can say that the unquestioned and internalized commonsense meaning among the officers of the board and subsequently judges effectively prevents the multiculturalization of the open legal concept 'the interest of the child'.

Another relevant concept in this kind of case is 'embeddedness' of the child. Its application shows the same tendency. Muslim children living in the Netherlands will be presumed to be embedded in the dominant Dutch culture. This presumption is corroborated in Hamid's case. I presume that in that case the 'culture shock' as interpreted by the judge is an argument used to favour a steady and thus a Dutch cultural embeddedness. One can catch a glimpse of yet another empirical conflict rule: in case of open legal concepts in the field of family law, as in for instance 'the best interest of the child', judges tend to value embeddedness in Dutch culture over embeddedness in different minority cultures.

It seems that judges tend to exclude the social possibility of citizens being embedded in both the dominant and a different minority culture. Note that it is not my claim that the decisions dealt with here are 'wrong' in the sense of 'legally wrong' (they are taken in accordance with the law) or in the sense of 'socially

---

18 The primary factor to determine 'the interest of the child' is 'continuity', which comes down to the rule 'if the situation of the children is satisfactory, then do not change the household they are living in'. In Hamid's case, however, there was doubt about the children's situation, which opened the door to a possible change of household.

wrong' (one would have to be able to look into the future to see whether the decisions are indeed in the interest of the children). The point is that judges should be aware of their common-sense notions influencing their decisions.

From this case, one can very tentatively infer the following empirical conflict rule: in family law judges do not deviate from the meaning of strict rules as given by the legislator and in earlier legal decisions. In the case of open legal concepts in the field of family law, like for instance 'the interest of the child', judges follow the meaning given by professional organizations. Judges and professional organizations tend in these cases to follow common-sense interpretations within the dominant culture, excluding possible interpretations from different minority cultures.

Note that this does not amount to saying that all judges act (let alone should act) according to this rule. But even though I have heard judges expressing the view that 'children growing up like in a warm bath' (i.e. in an extended sort of family) was acceptable to them, I venture to suggest that this empirical conflict rule indeed is the most common one. The 'rule' suggests that notwithstanding the presence of rather open legal standards coupled with a relatively open judicial mind-set, multiculturality does not fare well in these cases. In a way, my example is ill chosen, but its merit is that it shows an important conditioning factor to be studied in its own right, the role of the board.

The Board as an Important Actor in the Judicial Process of Decision-making

Why is the judge following standard interpretations and assimilating the case into Dutch ways of perceiving family life? To deepen our understanding of this matter, I have to delve into the impact of the advisory task of an official expert body like the Child Protection and Welfare Board. This element is hardly ever brought into play in studies of judicial behaviour in such cases. But it might be one of the more important conditions which pushes judges in a particular direction, so I shall now elaborate one element of a theory about those conditions, a topic announced in my introduction.

Judges confronted with these multicultural cases experience a notorious lack of knowledge and lack of time to fill in the blanks. Moreover, there is the element of playing safe. So, what does ultimately happen? The judge has to decide about the merits of these cultural arguments. What meaning should be given to the parents' protests and wishes and potential decisions? The juvenile judge can hardly be expected to know the distinct cultural situation or to engage in research into these matters. Sometimes when parents do not protest coherently or their lawyer is not raising these specific issues, for formal reasons alone the case is practically settled, and the board's interpretation sticks. But even in cases where a more balanced presentation of the situation is given, judges are not in a position to evaluate the 'typical distinct cultural pattern' way of arguing. In other cases, for instance, quite serious suggestions have been made as to the adequacy of some distinct cultural solutions of a child's problem, but a judge is empty-handed. Whether or not specific doctors in the country of origin or specific schools, extended family structures or specific local institutions may deal adequately with children with some specific problem, a judge cannot easily obtain and/or evaluate the knowledge about such allegations so as to feel really comfortable with an alternative, non-routine treatment (and accept it as a serious approach which shows the parents' full responsibility). In an interview, a judge stated this as follows:

> When Moroccan or Turkish parents show no insight whatsoever into the problems and also refuse to cooperate with agencies offering help, and further deny there even is a problem, then you think, 'Well, this makes no sense'. Because there will be quite a chance that things will go wrong, and then you just hold on to the licence to place the child somewhere else. Even if you know you cannot get a grip on cases like these. You don't know what's behind it all, we don't know how to find out. As with Dutch families, you talk, you ask, you probe for hidden conflicts, and of course we have a general idea of how such a family works. With these other cultures, we have no clues. We have no idea what the social pressure in these families is like, what social ties there are, what networks. We can't come up to the mark, because we don't know how best to intervene in a strange culture.

So, practically speaking, in Hamid's case a judge cannot but accept the board's interpretation, perceive the situation as serious and give custody to the mother. The board's interpretation in official reports by and large is based on the dominant Dutch culture.[19] This means that 'labels' or 'clichés' of 'typically Turkish/Moroccan cultural patterns' circulate and are reinforced in each case. One family law judge, apparently speaking also for her colleagues ('we'), specifically pointed to this issue in one of the interviews:

> When we consider the role of the Child Care and Protection Board, we don't think they pay a lot of attention to cultural differences. They basically have a quite uniform approach, 'the Dutch way' so to speak. They are scared as hell of one notion, and that is revenge for honour. You see that quite often, like 'Oh, gee! Honour!'

Another regular family problem, often involved in the matter of whom to assign custody over a young child, is the risk of 'abduction'; does this have anything to do with Muslim culture? Once a judge handled a family case in which the Dutch-Moroccan father took his wife and children with him to visit family in Morocco

---

19 The only empirical study of the board shows a contrast between what the officials say (in interviews) and what they do. In interviews these employees often have a liberal and open stance toward taking different cultural practices into account. In the reports, however, 'culture' mostly comes to the fore in the form of 'labels' and 'typologies' reinforcing a static, deterministic view of cultural backgrounds.

and then sent his wife back to the Netherlands, keeping the eldest son with him. Abduction? The judge regards child abduction as 'having something to do with the Moroccan culture, since this is indeed what we observe in certain cultures'. According to her, 'Moroccan fathers have a strong social tie with their children and bear a large responsibility for their upbringing, so I assume he wanted to keep the child under his authority.' For her this explains child abduction by Muslim fathers. These Muslim fathers are a challenge to the officers of the Child Care and Protection Board too. I submit there is a tendency for board personnel to perceive a complex situation through the lens of a cliché of 'abduction': 'active father – secret plan – submissive or unknowing mother'. This cliché, coupled with the observation of legal professionals that child abduction is a typical pattern in Muslim cultures, leads to certain directions of legal outcomes, that is to certain social rules on how to decide multicultural legal cases. The following empirical conflict rule could be put forward: in family law, judges prefer children to be raised in the Netherlands. Even when there is only a slight doubt about the possibility of abduction of children by a parent, judges give custody to the parent who prefers raising the child in the Netherlands, and they do not grant unattended parental access to the other parent.[20]

In 2003 I sat in on the occasion of a debate among judges, and one judge said (about custody, but the same goes for parental access):

> As a rule, custody after divorce is given to both parents. But when I have an Egyptian man before me in court of whom I only suspect that he could take his children to Egypt without consent of the mother, I dissent, and only the mother gets custody.

Of course much more can be said about child abduction. Especially much more to counter existing stereotypes, for example that it is not – as judges of course know – a 'Muslim' issue, and that it is not a 'male' issue.[21] In Dutch legal practice and media coverage, however, the combination of abduction to *Muslim* countries by *fathers* somehow seems to attract the most attention.

So much for empirical conflict rules – and conditioning factors – as an important topic for research into multiculturality and domestic law, both in the Netherlands and elsewhere. Let me switch to the more theoretical question of qualification.

20 I add 'unattended' because in the Netherlands there is a possibility of the father seeing his child in a 'safe environment' (safe that is for the mother and the child): The father is not allowed to leave the building with his child. He is obliged to speak Dutch only.

21 Officially, there were 77 cases (126 children) of abductions *from* the Netherlands and 31 *to* the Netherlands in 2004. Fifteen of those 77 cases probably concerned Muslim countries. In two thirds of the abduction cases, the mother is the abductor.

Part 2 Pluralizing Dutch Domestic Law or Assimilating Distinct Legal Sensibilities and Institutions?

How to qualify the judicial tendency – as far as it goes – to adopt hitherto distinct legal institutions? Is the *kafala* case bringing a multicultural change to Dutch law? And if so, on what grounds? Before I introduce the concept of interlegality, let me describe some of the problems this question throws up.

It was not only the claim by Muslim *kafala* parents which triggered a new way of applying the concept of foster child; new forms of family life and new ways of providing foster care also among the non-Muslim population challenge(d) the established concepts. The decision-maker, a public administrator, the bank, takes hitherto unknown factual circumstances into account and classifies these under a general concept – foster child – which is already well established and not specifically distinct. For judges – and public administrators applying the law – this operation is what they do all the time when facing new facts or developments. Should a *judge* have taken the *kafala* decision, he might not have perceived this case as any different from other cases of pretended foster relations brought forward by non-Muslim persons. Legal reasoning uses general concepts and norms, not norms tied to specific groups in society. The legislator likewise usually refrains from motivating a new rule or definition by referring to a specific group or culture. The legislative extension of the foster child definition was officially motivated by the general need to accommodate new family relations and not by the specific need to recognize *kafala*. A distinct institution gets stored within the existing concept and norms of the Dutch legal order and thereby loses its distinctiveness. So from this perspective there is no pluralizing at all in domestic law.

This indeed is true, at least from the point of view of legal dogmatics, in any legal system that merits the qualification legal *order*. But there is another, more empirical side to this coin. The case started off with a distinct legal institution unknown to ordinary Dutch culture. Parents, lawyers, judges, administrators certainly perceived the *kafala* as something strange, new and challenging, typically, a case that testifies to the ever more changing multicultural character of Dutch society. So, under this empirical, broader point of view, we can say that the introduction of *kafala* in Dutch domestic law, while accommodating a distinct institution into that legal order, has produced a ripple on the calm surface of legal business as usual. Judges and other officials are confronted with other ways of life, which removes the veil behind notions taken for granted, the tacit frames of meaning of judges and others. In terms of these frames of meanings, judges will surely experience a challenge, perhaps a shock, and somehow have to come to terms with it. After this confrontation they are not the same as before, and tacit assumptions are dropped. Other indicators sustain such a conclusion. For instance the bank, according to our interview with its head of legal affairs, did have the *kafala* cases in mind when it finally changed from a formal concept of foster child to an empirical one.[22] They were struggling fiercely with this problem. In the article by the head of legal affairs and another member of the bank's legal department (Vonk and Ydema-Gutjahr 2002), written *before* this change of the bank's policy, there was an explicit pleading for such a change because of the injustice done not only to the *kafala* parents but also to the biological parents who did not receive a Dutch child benefit either (as they usually have Moroccan nationality and are living in Morocco). The debate, then, suggested a rethinking of principles of good life and ordering society, embodied in legal institutions, because of the confrontation with hitherto unknown family practices.

So empirically speaking, there is indeed pluralization of the legal order. Concepts and techniques in law perhaps do not change, but hitherto disregarded distinct patterns of family life are now drawn into the legal order and do produce legal consequences. The legal order is adapted to a more plural socio-cultural situation. In particular, the frame of meaning of the judges, officials and many others has altered, which makes for a lasting change. In the minds and behaviour of people, judges included, *kafala* will ultimately be perceived as a normal, 'standard' element of the domestic legal order. Is any trace of 'plurality' left? Perhaps in the long run *kafala* is seen as a normal situation, but then the cognitive order underlying the legal order has changed already.

Interlegality[23]

The term interlegality was introduced by De Sousa Santos (2002: 437). 'Internormativé' and also 'métissage' are terms Le Roy (1999: 250, 271) uses. As a phenomenon it has been common in legal anthropology for more than 30 years, after legal anthropologists parted with the concept of and the quest for 'pure' indigenous law and after national (colonial and postcolonial) administrators quit structural and evolutionary thinking.[24] The notion has become quite common,[25] although the term 'interlegality' is a newcomer. It can be defined as a process and as an outcome. *A process of adoption of elements of a dominant legal order, both national and international, and of the frames of meaning that constitute these*

22 Jurists generally use the concept 'material' in contrast to 'formal', we prefer however 'empirical' to stress the sociological focus of the concept.

23 This paragraph is adapted from my introduction to the special issue on multicultural interlegality of *The Journal of Legal Pluralism and Unofficial Law* (Hoekema 2005).

24 This history is told by Moore (2001) and Merry (2003).

25 Apart from the authors mentioned in the text, I can point to Filip Reyntjens (1999: 676). This author writes about Belgian colonial history and after focusing on the relations between local and national law he concludes: 'this process of interaction is two-way'. Without using the term interlegality, J. Poirier (1969: 104) writing about various systems of law in African countries warns already in 1969: 'il n'y a pas un seul système, mais plusieurs ensembles interfèrent les uns les autres.'

*orders, into the practices of a local legal orde*r and/or the other way round. Or as the *outcome* of such process, a hybrid new legal order. In this way a wholesome dynamism is introduced in the matter of legal pluralism. De Sousa Santos stresses the fact that such different legal orders, like local law and national law, but also international law, cannot be said to have a separate existence as if they are elements in different social communities which are more or less sealed off from each other. On this basis I can take the study of concrete cases of interpenetrating legal (normative) orders a step further by concentrating on the process of mixing of the various orders involved. To study such a process means taking the porosity and openness of every legal (normative) order seriously. Moreover, this process is not restricted to 'elements' of a normative order like norms and concepts, making their way into the other order (and vice versa), but also covers *frames of meaning* that mutually impact on each other. I have even come to feel that this mutual interpenetration of frames of meaning is by far the more important element in trying to understand the effects of multiculturality in national and local law.[26]

Interlegality should not be perceived as a form of interpenetration which can only come about when local law is recognized as such officially. Even when state law completely ignores local law or even actively cracks down on it, a process of intermingling of distinct legal orders will still be underway. This directly suggests that, outside the world of official law, Islamic or Hindu or Adat institutions and the standard (often Christian) institutions do touch each other and mutually impact on each other.

Interlegality brings out how legal orders develop, not through the force of universal social regularities but by the way individuals define and perceive a situation and act upon it. Moreover, this concept stresses the porous character of anything called a legal order. Let us look at an illustrative case discussed by Thomas Acton (2005). He discusses the social and legal position of Kalderash Roma communities in the USA. The leadership of this distinct community changed their 'family law' in the direction of dominant US law, so as to prevent their women from going forum shopping and walking out on their own family law authorities. This example could be multiplied many times. Individuals are not the prisoners of their own supposedly integrated and homogeneous culture, but shop forums, choose among legal orders, pressure their own leaders and authorities to take other legal elements into consideration and also, the other way round, challenge national authorities to take local legal sensibilities into consideration. The way Gypsy leaders reacted to the women's new stance, bolstered by a globalizing feminism,

26 Here we touch upon an element of a legal order which Chiba (1998: 241) would call legal postulates, 'the ideas or ideology which base, orient and revise the legal rules'. So, he also distinguishes legal rules from what I call frames of meaning. Nowadays, however, the fragmented and at times even contradictory nature of the ensemble of legal postulates would be stressed more. Chiba, although not using the term interlegality is well aware of the phenomenon of interpenetration of kinds and levels of law whereby 'law' includes a variety of non-state law forms (as well as 'trans-state' law forms).

is one of the ways in which leaders of local communities nowadays try to guard their specific collective identity by taking elements of global trends into account and blending these into their own, with the hope of maintaining themselves as a distinct community. This is often called a process of ethnic reorganization (Nagel and Snipp 1993: 204).[27] Such reorganization can be observed in cases in which local law does not exist formally (and often is qualified as illegal exercise of force or pressure) *and* also in cases of some form of official recognition.

Interlegality does not only flow from the powerful to the powerless in marginalized distinct communities. Certainly, I do not want to negate the often overriding importance of such power relations, but I feel we have to bear in mind that those at the bottom, while resisting top-down pressures, sometimes see their institutions and sensibilities win a battle or two. These distinct institutions not only are occasionally taken into account by judges and public administrators but sometimes can be seen as making their way into the dominant culture (legal) on a broader scale. A well-known example is the way in which non-Western procedures geared towards reconciliation and mediation between parties, even between offenders and victims, are copied by politicians and legal professionals of the dominant order. The term 'restorative justice' is a catchword nowadays. In Canada the majority of legal professionals learn from and take over concepts and values inherent in practices of aboriginal communitarian justice (Proulx 2005). Also, conceptions of human guardianship of natural resources nowadays are slowly starting to penetrate dominant discourses challenging the relentless exploitation of such resources in a globalizing economy. Thus, a dominant elite learns to appreciate distinct institutions and views. The outcome of this *reverse* interlegality is a hybrid product, too, this time a partly intercultural national law which by this very fact loses its character as the repository of majority culture only. I consider this is a very promising way of thinking which may seem a bit optimistic but avoids the rather common notion that minority peoples are only the victims of some absolute and overwhelming power.

Hamid's Case Again

With the help of this concept of interlegality, I can now come to terms with the qualification of the wider effects of the 'open standards' case of Hamid. Before starting this analysis, I have to admit that, although theoretically this kind of 'open' legal structure offers more space for a multicultural approach, in the concrete case at hand there is not much of this to be found. For reasons I tried to expose before, it has been decided upon monoculturally. But notwithstanding this outcome, it is unmistakable that distinct legal sensibilities related to distinct patterns of family life have been raised and scrutinized. And apart from Hamid's case, there are more

27 These authors tell us that 'ethnic reorganization occurs when an ethnic minority undergoes a reorganization of its social structure, redefinition of ethnic group boundaries, or some other change in response to pressures or demands imposed by the dominant culture'.

'multicultural' cases in this domain of family matters. It is worthwhile asking the question again: are such cases pluralizing the Dutch domestic legal order?

First of all, what is the challenge of diversity in this particular example? Is it about distinct legal sensibilities, or about distinct patterns of family life? Strange question; conceptions of family life and legal sensibilities as well as norms regulating these patterns are after all intertwined. Nevertheless, what I see judges doing here is less an interpretation of a series of interrelated and well-ordered legal concepts than pondering a large series of factual circumstances and trying to fill in a standard like 'the best interest of the child'. Coming to conclusions as to the applicability of this standard is obviously not a purely factual operation. Nor is it a purely normative one, since it is heavily based on a reading of factual patterns of family life. Judges tend to perceive this kind of operation as part and parcel of their standard operations. So, if the judge in the Hamid case would have taken the distinct pattern of family life into account and ruled differently, would that have changed Dutch law? My question now sounds even stranger than in the *kafala* case. Such a balancing of interests, i.e. application of a vague, open standard on the basis of some substratum of specific facts of the case – as perceived by the judge – is precisely what a judge is doing all the time. The technique is clearly the same both in monocultural and in multicultural cases. I now refer to the view I have often heard from judges: in these kinds of cases we do nothing new, this is balancing of interests as usual.

But the definition/clarification/determination of interests involved, as well as the yardstick to use, are different in a case like Hamid. The frame of interpretation which judges apply in a Hamid-like case – if they want to take the other patterns into account – is different, broader, than before. What a judge is doing, apart from the legal technique, is definitely not business as usual, as the unknown situation poses unknown risks to be taken into account, and routine interpretations fail. This amounts to a pluralization of the Dutch legal order.

International Private Law

Through international private law – and the official legal conflict rules applied there, as well as international treaties – foreign legal institutions and sometimes distinct cultural institutions enter the Dutch territory, like the Islamic institution (codified in some national legal systems) of the repudiation of a wife by the husband. Given the fact that so many immigrant families are now living permanently in the Netherlands while keeping the nationality of their country of origin, there is a busy and lively crossing of the legal border and a lot of incoming distinct cultural institutions at the private international law gate. This is especially so in the Netherlands because the Dutch doctrine and judiciary are generally inclined to accept foreign legal institutions (due to the feeling that harmonious international legal relations should be furthered, and 'limping' legal relations prevented). Dutch official legal conflict rules are rather generous, and the test for compatibility with Dutch legal culture (the public order) is not that severe, although certainly not absent. The introduction of foreign legal institutions through the door of private international law definitely does confront the judiciary with this other law and sometimes, many times perhaps, with distinct cultural concepts and institutions. It is likely that the quantity of such cases is rising considerably. This confrontation cannot but change the general frame of mind and the know-how of judges. This in time could produce more confidence in judges to tackle the kind of purely domestic law family cases discussed before. The rising tide of private international law through these indirect means has a bearing on domestic cases. Moreover, there is cross traffic between private international law and domains of domestic law. Sometimes private international law is perceived as applicable or non-applicable according to the evaluation of the expected respective outcomes, e.g. when the judge dealing with a multicultural and multinational divorce case wants to award custody over the children to the woman only, which is a possibility in Dutch domestic law only.

Now we have to raise the second issue again. Does this practice of using international private law (and its conflict rules) change Dutch *domestic* law towards a more pluralized whole? Seen from the legal dogmatic point of view, the answer should be 'No!' The institution of 'repudiation' legally speaking has not become part of Dutch law, but is (under restrictions) legally accepted as part of a different legal system (Rutten 2005: 82–3). It is otherwise with purely domestic concepts like 'foster child' or standards like 'the interest of the child' or 'reasonable behaviour'. When these open concepts are adapted to patterns and perceptions of a distinct culture, then these distinct patterns and legal sensibilities do enter the Dutch legal order directly.

But indirectly, the wave of international private law cases is important in terms of the question of where Dutch domestic law is heading. Consider cases of people living in the Netherlands who have more than one nationality, or couples living in the Netherlands of which one partner has a foreign nationality (as well). Empirically speaking, in this kind of cases judges are learning more about distinct cultures and their legal sensibilities and/or their life patterns. Training courses will cover these topics, universities and law faculties start teaching these matters, discussion in law journals is already flaring up. Indirectly, then, such cases tend to mould judges towards a more knowledgeable position and a more willing attitude in domestic mixed cases. It is not Dutch law that changes through these international private law cases but the judges' frame of mind, and thereby, in the long run, their decisions in domestic cases towards a more plural system. Dutch legal culture is changing.[28] Frames of meaning, institutionalized in Dutch legal professional practice, are changing, get more mixed, typically a phenomenon which one perceives the moment one adopts the conceptual focus of the concept of interlegality. This conclusion confirms the one deduced from the 'open standards' case discussed previously.

28 One cannot exclude the opposite tendency: judges even the liberal ones, could close themselves off ever more. This however seems not to be the dominant trend.

Closing Remarks

From a legal anthropological point of view, the qualification of the effect of multicultural judicial decisions as an internal pluralization of the domestic order is warranted, dogmatically it is not. At least not in cases of restricted formal legal pluralism where only individual cases occasionally receive a multicultural treatment.

But also dogmatically the scene is changing. Legal professionals now widely acknowledge the existence of a relatively open structure of the legal order. Through the numerous general standards in law and other legal means, normative sensibilities of a variety of groups in society are knocking on the official door all the time and often get entry. Pluralization in a very general sense is a normal situation in legal development, even if we only take the professional dogmatic view. In the more empirical terms of frames of interpretation and concomitant behaviour, it is an empirical reality. Sure enough, norms nurtured by, for example, business networks can be accommodated more easily as they are, generally speaking, less distinct. Pluralization of the domestic legal order through incorporation of legal sensibilities of *distinct communities* is more challenging and politically far more sensitive. But it happens on a regular basis, in courts and first of all outside of courts.

References

Acton, Thomas. 2005. Conflict resolution and Criminal Justice – Sorting out Trouble. Can Legislation resolve Perennial Conflicts between Roma/Gypsies/ Travellers and 'National Majorities'? *The Journal of Legal Pluralism and Unofficial Law*, 51, 29–479.

Berger, M.S. 2007. Shari'a in Nederland is vaak keurig Nederlands ['Shari'a in the Netherlands is often very Dutch']. *Ars Aequi*, 56(6), 506–10.

Bowen, J.R. 2006. *Why the French Don't Like Headscarves: Islam, the State and Public Space*. Princeton, Princeton University Press.

Chiba, Masaji. 1998. Other Phases of Legal Pluralism in the Contemporary World. *Ratio Juris*, 11(3), 228–45.

Department of Health. 2000. *Adoption, a New Approach: A White Paper*. London: Department of Health.

Eberhard, C., M. Fernando and N. Gafsia. 2005. Droit, laïcité et diversité culturelle. L'état Francais face au défi du pluralisme. *Revue Interdisciplinaire d'etudes juridiques*, 54, 129–70.

Foblets, Marie-Claire and Alison Dundes Renteln. (eds) 2009. *Multicultural Jurisprudence: Comparative Perspectives on the Cultural Defense*. Oxford: Hart Publishing.

Hervieu-Leger, D. 1998. The past in the present: redefining *laïcité* in multicultural France. In *The Limits of Social Cohesion. Conflict and Mediation in Pluralist Societies*, edited by P.L. Berger. Boulder, CO: Westview Press, 38–83.

Hoekema, A.J. 2005. European Legal Encounters between Minority and majority Cultures, Cases of Interlegality. *The Journal of Legal Pluralism and Unofficial Law*, 51, 1–28.

Hoekema, A.J. and W. Van Rossum. 2009. Empirical Conflict Rules in Dutch Cases of Cultural Diversity. In *The Response of State Law to the Expression of Cultural Diversity*, edited by Marie-Claire Foblets, Jean-François Gaudreault-Desbiens and Alison Dundes Renteln. Brussels: Bruylant (forthcoming).

Le Roy, Etienne. 1999. *Le jeu des lois, Une anthropologie 'dynamique' du Droit*. Paris: LGDJ.

Menski, W. 2009. Law, State and Culture: How Countries accommodate Religious, Cultural and Ethnic Diversity. The British and Indian Experiences. In *The Response of State Law to the Expression of Cultural Diversity*, edited by Marie-Claire Foblets, Jean-François Gaudreault-Desbiens and Alison Dundes Renteln. Brussels: Bruylant (forthcoming).

Merry, S.E. 2003. From Law and Colonialism to Law and Globalization. *Law and Social Inquiry*, 28(2), 569–90.

Moore, S.F. 2001. Certainties Undone: Fifty Turbulent Years of Legal Anthropology. *Journal of the Royal Anthropological Institute*, 7(1), 95–116.

Nagel, J. and C.M. Snipp. 1993. Ethnic Reorganization: American Indian Social, Economic, Political and Cultural Strategies for Survival. *Ethnic and Racial Studies*, 16(2), 203–35.

Poirier, J. 1969. L'analyse des espèces juridiques et l'étude des droits coutumiers africains. In *Ideas and Procedures in African Customary Law*, edited by Max Gluckman. Oxford: Oxford University Press/International African Institute, 97-110.

Proulx, Craig. 2005. Blending justice: Interlegality and the Incorporation of Aboriginal Justice into the Formal Canadian Justice System. *The Journal of Legal Pluralism and Unofficial Law*, 51, 79–109.

Reyntjens, F. 1999. Legal and Judicial Pluralism in Africa South of the Sahara. In *60 maal recht en 1 maal wijn: liber amicorum prof. dr. Jean Van Houtte* [Sociology of Law, Social Problems and Legal Policy], edited by F. van Loon and K. van Aken. Leuven and Amersfoort: Acco, 673–81.

van Rossum, W. 2007. *Gelet op de cultuur. Reflectie op de relevantie van culturele achtergronden van etnische minderheden in de Nederlandse rechtspraktijk* [View of Culture. Reflections on the Relevance of the Cultural Background of Ethnic Minorities in Dutch Legal Practice]. Den Haag: Raad voor de Rechtspraak [The Hague: Council for the Judiciary].

Rutten, S.W.E. 2005. *Cultuur en familierecht in eigen kring* [Culture and Family Law within your own Community]. Deventer: Kluwer.

Santos, B. de Sousa 2002. *Towards a New Legal Common Sense. Law, Globalization and Emancipation*. 2nd edition. London/Edinburgh/Dublin: Butterworths.

SVB. 2005. *Beleidsregels 2005* and *Algemeen Verbindende Voorschriften* [Policies 2005 and Binding Regulations]. Den Haag: SDU Uitgevers.

Vermeulen, B.P. 2005. Religieus pluralisme als uitdaging aan de 'neutrale' rechter [Religious Pluralism as a Challenge to a 'Neutral' Judge]. *Trema, Tijdschrift voor de Rechterlijke Macht*, special issue May 2005, 243–50.

Vonk, G. and Ydema-Gutjahr, M. 2002. Over de invloed van buitenlandse culturele waarden op de juridische normering in de sociale zekerheid [About the Influence of Foreign Values on Legal Norms in Social Security Law]. In *De multiculturele samenleving en het recht*, edited by N.F. van Manen. Nijmegen: Ars Aequi Libri, 357–67.

Wortmann, S. 2006. Marokkaans en Nederlands afstammings – en gezagsrecht [Moroccan and Dutch Law of Descent and Custody]. In *Crossing Borders. Essays in European and Private International Law, Nationality Law and Islamic Law in Honour of Frans van der Velden*, edited by Paulien van der Grinten and Ton Heukels Deventer: Kluwer, 185–93.

Chapter 11

The Influence of Culture on the Determination of Damages: How Cultural Relativism Affects the Analysis of Trauma

Alison Dundes Renteln

The Role of Cultural Factors

Sometimes individuals who are injured file lawsuits in which they claim that they experienced greater trauma than the ordinary plaintiff because of their cultural or religious background. As a consequence, they contend in civil litigation that they ought to be entitled to larger damage awards. In one case, for example, after Gypsies in Spokane, Washington, were subjected to an illegal police search that rendered young Roma girls unmarriageable, they filed a civil rights lawsuit in which they sought forty million dollars.[1] As there was no question about liability because the city admitted that the search was illegal, the sole issue on appeal was the size of the damage award.[2] While anyone subject to an illegal police search can seek monetary damages, the claim here is that the impact of the misconduct was more devastating to the plaintiffs than it would have been to non-Gypsies. In short, the injury was ostensibly more severe because of their belief that the girls, touched beneath the waist by the police, were *marime* or polluted and hence incapable of ever marrying.[3] This type of argument is part of a larger trend in the legal system of individuals making claims based on cross-cultural differences (Levinson and Peng 2004).

With increasing migration across borders, states are realizing that the newly arrived raise new types of legal questions. In many instances, individuals commit acts which are considered acceptable in their countries of origin but apparently

---

1 Bill Morlin, 'Expert Says Raids Were Catastrophic to Gypsy Families', *Spokesman Review*, 17 September 1992. For more detailed discussion of the case, see Renteln 2004: 120–1.

2 After eleven years, when the case settled out of court, the Marks family received $1.43 million.

3 The argument was based on the ideology of defilement known as '*marime*'. It is unclear whether the *marime* sanction is always permanent. See Miller (1975).

violate the law of the new country. These matters of criminal law involve the question of whether defendants should be entitled to raise a cultural defense (Renteln 2004, and Foblets and Renteln 2009). Sometimes, when these cultural conflicts can be anticipated, legislatures may decide to carve out exemptions from statutes to avoid unnecessary prosecution of individuals whose actions involve no threat of harm to others. Even though the cases that involve criminal acts have, to date, attracted the most attention, there are matters of civil law that deserve attention as well. Consequently, although there are many fascinating issues of cross-cultural jurisprudence, in this chapter I focus on the question of whether cultural and religious considerations should influence the calculation of damage awards.

Cultural factors play a role in the assessment of damages in tort cases as well as civil rights actions. Although this issue affects indigenous peoples, particularly where there is harm to cultural property, here I consider mainly cases involving immigrants. And while there is growing attention to religious harassment in the workplace, I do not deal with this phenomenon. Although most of the cases discussed are from the United States, the types of issues they illustrate should be relevant to the European experience. In general, there appears to be relatively little discussion of the general question of the influence of cultural factors on damage awards in the scholarly literature.[4]

One may wonder why the question of culture affecting damage awards merits our concern. Although one may have the intuition that contextual factors in legal disputes elucidate the nature of the problem, some may object on the ground that all litigants should be treated alike. This raises the question of what is the best way to interpret equal treatment in a multicultural society. There is also the practical question as to whether there is anything in the jurisprudence of damages that may preclude the consideration of cultural and religious factors.

Calculating Damages

To those unaccustomed to the inner workings of the legal system, the process of calculating damages awards seems quite mysterious. There is apparently no uniformity in the assessments. The courts themselves acknowledge that they cannot rely on any single mathematical formula. If decisions about the amount of damage awards are left to the discretion of judges and juries, at least in common law jurisdictions, they must take into account contextual aspects of particular cases (*American Jurisprudence* 2003, Volume 22, *Damages*). The question then is whether any specific contextual factors, like culture and religion, are deemed inappropriate for this analysis.

4 One thoughtful analytic essay on this topic is Villarreal (1991, especially 1221–42).

Despite what is apparently a flexible system, it is not as though any award is acceptable. If a judge finds that a jury has awarded what seems to be an extravagant amount, the judge may reduce it through the device known as *remittitur*. If, by contrast, the award is too paltry, the judge can increase it through *additur*. Insofar as there is no 'right answer' regarding the calculation of damages, there does not appear to be any insurmountable barrier to the consideration of cultural dimensions of disputes.

As there are various types of damages awards, it may turn out that it is easier to incorporate cultural considerations in some as opposed to others. In some cases the question that arises is whether there are obstacles to increasing damages based on culture because of a duty to mitigate or other defenses. In this context the analogy drawn between the eggshell skull doctrine,[5] i.e., more generally understood as 'you take the plaintiff as you find him', and religious worldview will be of interest.

One challenge in cases involving religious and cultural factors is the reluctance of courts to allow for recovery for psychic injuries. To the extent that judges feel it is hard to ascertain the value of emotional or mental distress, this may complicate efforts to obtain damages in cases involving a cultural dimension.

While in most of the cases it is the plaintiff whose religious or cultural divergent worldview is crucial for the disposition of the case, in some it is rather the defendant's outlook that is the crux of the matter. Therefore, I will also touch on the use of cultural arguments by the defense. To see how cultural factors figure into the assessment of damages, let us turn now to the cases themselves.

Cases

Increasing the Damage Award

In 2006 an EgyptAir plane tragically crashed, and all 217 on board died. The relatives of 28 year-old Sami Makary, one of those killed, filed a suit under the Death on the High Seas Act (DOHSA) in which they advanced an argument based on Egyptian culture.[6] They said that because Makary was the eldest son, he held a special position in the family. Consequently, there was a strong expectation that he would support his parents in their old age and other relatives as well, and he had apparently already begun to do so. The court remarked that the testimony of his father, a distinguished advocate and former member of the Egyptian Parliament was 'particularly credible'.[7]

---

5 I discuss the analogy between the eggshell skull doctrine and the use of cultural factors in the assessment of damages below on p. 206.

6 *In re Air Crash near Nantucket Island, Massachusetts v EgyptAir*, 462 F. Supp. 2d 350 (E.D.N.Y., 2006). As EgyptAir did not contest liability, the only issue was the amount of the damages (p. 362).

7 Ibid. 362.

One issue that arose concerned who was entitled to bring the action and whether that included siblings and cousins. The federal judge in New York attempted to clarify which relatives qualified as 'dependent relatives' under DOHSA. Evidently case law supported the proposition that the siblings could recover as the law authorized those who relied on support to make claims.[8]

On 23 August 2006 the judge conducted a bench trial to determine what the damages should be.[9] As Sami Makary was only 28 years old when he died and conceivably would have supported his relatives for many years, the judge took this into account in calculating the damages. The judge awarded $3.6 million in pecuniary and non-pecuniary damages. Afterwards, the lawyer representing Makary's estate was quoted as saying that while the award was 'atypical', it was 'justifiable under the circumstances'. The attorney commented on the influence of the cultural argument: 'The judge very sensitively appreciated the role of the firstborn son in an Egyptian family'.[10] The judge acknowledged that the amount of the damage was not precise: 'Mathematical certainty is unnecessary to prove the amount of the pecuniary loss, but there must be some evidence from which the court can estimate future support without engaging in conjecture' (p. 366). There is no question but that the cultural background of the plaintiffs played a role in this case.[11]

In *Salinas v Fort Worth Cab & Baggage Co.* the plaintiff's cultural background was also was part of the argument advanced for a larger damage award.[12] In this case a taxi cab driver threatened to kill a woman and her two infant daughters

---

8 'In order for a relative to be dependent under the law the pecuniary contribution from the decedent must have been in whole or in part a means of maintaining the relatives in the manner in which they had been living. And you must also consider whether the relative looked forward to and relied upon the continuance of decedent's contribution to maintain that standard of living' (ibid. 365).

9 Judges and juries award damages. The calculation of what payment should be made is governed by formulae that vary by jurisdiction. Treatises in the field specify various types including punitive damages, compensatory damages, special damages, and others.

10 John Marzulli, 'Air Crash Victim's Kin Win $3.6M award', *New York Daily News*, 8 December 2006.

11 There are other cases in which cultural factors were introduced, e.g., in Re Air Crash Disaster Near New Orleans, 789 F. 2d 1092 (5th Cir. 1986), *Saavedra v Korean Air Lines*, 93 R.3d 547 (9th Cir. 1996). In Canada judges have considered filial piety in assessing damage awards in lawsuits concerning the death of a son or daughter in families of Chinese and Vietnamese ancestry. See, e.g., *To v Toronto (City) Board of Education* (2001), 55 OR. (3d) 641 (C.A.), *Lian v Money* [1994] 8 W.W.R. 463 (B.C.S.C.), rev'd [1996] 4 W.W.R. 263 (B.C.C.A.), *Lai v Gill* [1980] 1 S.C.R. 431, [1868] B.C.J. No. 1988, [1978] B.C.J. No. 300. I am indebted to Professor Jennifer A. Chandler, Law Faculty, University of Ottawa, for bringing these cases to my attention.

12 *Salinas v Forth Worth Cab & Baggage Company, Inc.* 725 S.W. 2d 701 (Tex. 1987).

if she did not submit to sexual intercourse. During the trial there was testimony about the impact of the assault on her family:

> Dr Brown testified about Maria's prior marital relationship and the effect this incident had on her marriage. Dr Brown related in some detail that Maria came from a traditional family in Mexico with a conservative religious background. He testified that: Maria's husband was the only man with whom she had ever had sexual relations; prior to this incident they had a normal, stable family life; as a result of the rape, Maria suffered post-traumatic stress disorder causing her to have frequent sleep disturbances, nightmares, depression, obsessive rumination about the rape, exhibited regressive behavior; and that the marriage relationship suffered because of this incident.[13]

Her husband later left his wife and children. In essence her attorney argued that her relationship with her husband was more drastically affected because of her background than would have been the case for other wives.

The jury found the cab company grossly negligent for allowing Jenkins, a man with a criminal record, to operate a cab. The jury awarded five million in actual and punitive damages to the mother and her two daughters, but the judge reduced the actual damages by $300,000. The Court of Appeals reversed because one element of damages was not proved and remanded the case for a new trial. The Texas Supreme Court, in a decision by Justice Alberto Gonzales, reversed: 'We hold that the court of appeals erred when it held that there was no evidence these damages resulted from the event in question.'[14] The court declined to rule on the question of whether the damages were excessive because it lacked jurisdiction over this question of fact. For a decision on this question the case was remanded to the trial court.

In this decision by Justice Gonzales, the court ruled implicitly that her cultural values concerning 'impairment of familial relationships' were relevant to the analysis of the scope of the damages.[15] Villareal criticizes the court for failing to take the opportunity to reshape the legal doctrine. In his view the Texas Supreme Court should have offered guidance as to which kinds of causes of action are legitimate and which are not.[16] Discussing cultural factors directly, he contended, would give this type of analysis legitimacy.

---

13 Ibid.

14 Ibid. 704.

15 Ibid.

16 'While Justice Gonzalez's opinion in *Salinas* provided individualized justice which took into consideration the plaintiff's culture, the opinion failed to offer a more direct explanation on the significance of testimony regarding the effect of Salinas' culture on the scope of recoverable damages' (Villareal 1991: 1226). 'The failure of courts to candidly address the role of culture in their decisionmaking has undermined the legitimacy of making the cultural inquiry. By failing to articulate the relevance of culture in tort

International tribunals have at times been influenced by cultural considerations. For instance, in *Aloeboetoe et al. v Suriname,* a case decided by the American Court of Human Rights, the calculation of damages centred on cultural difference.[17] Confronted with incontrovertible evidence of a massacre of Saramacan people, the government conceded liability, and so the issue to be decided was the amount of the damages. As fair compensation is required under the American Convention on Human Rights, the Human Rights Commission asked the court to find that Suriname should pay the Saramaca tribe compensation for moral damages based on the group's conception of a family as reflected in customary law:

> in traditional maroon society, a person is a member not only of his or her own village community and tribal group … the villagers make up a family in the broad sense. This is why damages caused to one of its members also represent damages to the community, which would have to be indemnified.[18]

This meant taking into consideration the multiple families each man had, thereby increasing substantially the number of relatives to whom the government was obligated to pay damages. The InterAmerican Court of Human Rights had to decide what was the appropriate method for assessing damages after the Suriname government massacred the Saramacas, an indigenous group. In the end the court determined that it was appropriate to use the concept of extended family that operated in the indigenous community.[19]

In European cases plaintiffs have also argued that their injuries are more traumatic because of their cultural background. For instance, in *Bakhtiari v the Zoological Society of London* a court considered cultural factors in deciding on the appropriate size of the damage award in the case of an Iranian girl whose three fingers were bitten off by a chimpanzee when she visited the zoo. The court awarded a larger award to because of the social significance of the stigma that she would purportedly experience.[20] One possible consequence of the disability might be limiting her prospects of marriage.

In some instances the plaintiffs contend that they suffered an injury that would not constitute as significant an injury for others. For instance, Hindus discovered

---

law decisionmaking, the courts have failed to develop a general norm to guide future determinations' (pp. 1223–4). This means that there is a risk in subsequent litigation that culture will be ignored (p. 1227).

17 The decision has persuasive authority in the United States and in the European Union. Regardless of its official juridical status, it is widely cited as supporting the use of culture in the calculation of damages. See, e.g., Shelton (2005).

18 *Aloeboetoe et al.* Case, InterAmerican Court of Human Rights, Reparations, Judgment of September 10, 1993: 23.

19 For a discussion of the case, see Padilla (1995).

20 *Bakhtiari v The Zoological Society of London* (1991), cited in Poulter (1998: 64; text available at <www.lexisnexis.com>). Poulter notes the sexist nature of the decision. For an analysis of cultural relativity as it relates to disability, see Renteln (2003).

that McDonald's was surreptitiously seasoning French fries with beef flavouring without disclosing this information, a practice which obviously violated the Hindu dietary prohibition against the consumption of beef. One of the plaintiffs was said to be horrified when he found out: 'I feel sick in the morning every day, like I want to vomit … Now it is there in my mind that I have done this sin'.[21] Although the effect of this practice was especially problematic for Hindus, it was also repulsive for the vegetarians who decided not to eat meat as a matter of personal conscience.[22] Even though the practice was equally deceptive for all consumers of the McDonald's French fries, the consequence of this was much more severe for the plaintiffs in this case.

When vegetarian law students joined forces with the Hindus, they first filed a lawsuit in Seattle. Following this, additional suits were filed in other states. Eventually McDonald's, though denying it had ever claimed that the French fries were 'vegetarian', settled the suit by paying each of the 11 named plaintiffs $4000 each, by donating ten million dollars to Hindu and other groups, by creating a dietary advisory board and by posting an apology on the McDonald's website.[23] The plaintiffs' attorney, Harish Bharti, described the settlement as 'a landmark in corporate accountability'.[24]

Similarly, when a Hindu ordered a bean burrito at Taco Bell and was mistakenly given a beef burrito, he was traumatized to such an extent that he had to travel to India to bathe in the Ganges to purify himself.[25] These cases demonstrate how a simple mistake would not give rise to a cause of action in most instances but does so for religious individuals.

I have considered cases in which plaintiffs have sued for damages after they suffer an injury whose impact is tied to a cultural or religious difference. Even though individuals from the dominant culture would also have a cause of action, the basic notion is that the magnitude of the harm is greater because of an individual's cultural or religious background. For example, when medical examiners perform an unauthorized autopsy, the 'next of kin' could sue, regardless of the religious identity of the deceased. However, those who believe that the relative will be forever mutilated in the afterlife as a consequence of the improper

21 Laura Goodstein, 'For Hindus and Vegetarians, Surprise in McDonald's Fries', *New York Times*, 20 May 2001.

22 The plaintiffs' lawyer explained: 'any reasonable person who hear that McDonald's fries are prepared in '100 per cent vegetable oil' and read the list of ingredients would assume the food is suitable for vegetarians', cited in 'US Hindus Take on McDonald's over French Fries', *The Times of India*, 4 May 2001.

23 Herbert G. McGann, 'McDonald's Settles Beef Over Fries', *CBS News*, 5 June 2002 (AP).

24 Ashfaque Swapan, 'Supersize This – McDonald's Disburses $10 Million as French Fries Fallout', *India West*, 23 May 2005.

25 Richard Beigel, 'Hindu Served Beef at Taco Bell', *Los Angeles Times*, 1 February 1998; Davan Maharaj, 'Taco Bell Settles Suit with Hindu Over Meal Order', *Los Angeles Times*, 11 February 1999.

procedure contend that their psychic injury is greater (see Renteln 2001 and 2004: Chapter 9).

In short, the unfortunate event was arguably more traumatic for them. In some cases the relevance of cultural factors relates to particular types of defenses. The question is what is the scope of the defendant's responsibility under the circumstances.

Duty to Mitigate Damages

One type of case involves an argument that there is a duty to mitigate the damages. In tort law there has been considerable debate about the so-called eggshell skull doctrine (see Bahr and Graham 1982, Linden 1969, Rowe 1977, Shinkle 1967). The basic idea is that one takes one's plaintiff/victim as one finds him, whether that means a physical condition, a religious conviction or a cultural sensitivity. Some treatises describe the thin skull rule as an exception to the forseeability requirement of proximate cause. According to the Restatement of Torts:

> The negligent actor is subject to liability for harm to another although a physical condition of the other which is neither known nor should be known to the actor makes the injury greater than that which the actor as a reasonable man should have foreseen as a probable result of his conduct.[26]

Shinkle elaborates on the meaning of the doctrine:

> There are certain areas of tort law where the courts hold that once negligence is established, the defendant must take the circumstances as he finds them and be liable for consequences that arise even though a reasonable man might not have anticipated them. Even the courts that would appear to be committed to the 'foreseeable risk' limitation discard it in the 'impact on the person of the plaintiff' cases. The reason for the application of this so-called liability beyond the risk rule to this type of case seems to be a feeling on the part of some courts that as between the entirely innocent plaintiff, and the defendant who has been negligent, natural justice is better served if consequences beyond the risk fall upon the wrongdoer and not on the innocent injured party. The courts assign a great deal of importance to contact in determining damages. It is as if the plaintiff is in a circle, and if the defendant breaks it even to inflict minor harm to the person therein, he becomes liable for all resulting harm to the party, even emotional disturbance and death. (Shinkle 1967: 49–50)

26 Restatement (Second) of Torts S. 461 (1965).

The case of *William v Bright* illustrates how the doctrine is applied in the case of a religious plaintiff.[27] A woman who was seriously injured in an accident happened to be a Jehovah's Witness. Although she would have made a much more complete recovery if she had undergone surgery, she refused to do so as this would have required blood transfusions which are proscribed by her religion. The court had to ascertain whether her refusal to submit to medical procedures represented a shirking of her duty to mitigate the damages. The precise issue was the conflict between religious freedom and the duty to mitigate damages. The judge instructed the jury that:

> The law provides, with respect to damages, that a person who has been injured is not permitted to recover for damages that she could have avoided by using means which a reasonably prudent person would have used to cure the injury or alleviate the situation … The reason Mrs. Robbins rejected the surgery in the past and the recommended surgery in the future, is not because of the physical risk, but because of her strongly held religious beliefs that there can be no blood transfusion. Now, in making your determination as to whether she has acted reasonably to mitigate the damage, I will instruct you that under no circumstances are you to consider the validity or reasonableness of her religious beliefs that there can be no blood transfusion. …[28]

The judge proceeded to consider whether there is a religious exception to the duty to mitigate and, in the absence of case authority on point, he concluded that a court may not evaluate the reasonableness of another person's religious beliefs in this context. The judge distinguished the assessment of damages from other areas of law, concluding that no compelling state interest existed to justify questioning a plaintiff's religious beliefs:

> What compelling governmental interest in the amount of tort recovery which is permitted one private individual against another outweighs the need to forbid any governmental agency from passing on the soundness or reasonableness or religious beliefs? There always remains an obligation of official neutrality. By recognizing the special circumstances and conditions of one litigant, we may individualize justice.[29]

---

27 *Williams v Bright*, 167 Misc. 2d 312, 632 N.Y.S.2d 760 (NY.Sup.,1995). For commentary, see Loomis 2007. Loomis (n. 119) cites a British criminal case that in which eggshell skull doctrine was applied – *Regina v Blaue* [1971] 1 W.L.R. 1411.

28 *Williams v Bright.*, pp. 316–17.

29 Ibid. 326. See also Note (1978), Pomeroy (1992).

Despite the strong pro religious position accompanied by an endorsement of the 'eggshell skull doctrine',[30] the judge ironically decided that the damages the jury had awarded exceeded reasonable limits. After reducing the amounts initially given, he stipulated that he would order a new trial on the issue of damages unless the plaintiff agreed to the damage award.[31]

Even if one is convinced that it is possible to extend the 'thin skull' rule to apply to religious plaintiffs, one must acknowledge objections to the doctrine itself. Bahr and Graham (1982) not only reject the application of 'thin skull' rule to other than pre-existing physical conditions but also catalogue a series of criticisms. They note that the doctrine relies too much and unjustifiably on the moral status of the defendant, that it is used much more widely throughout tort law than many realize and that it shifts from a negligence standard to one resembling strict liability. Despite the existence of such criticisms, attorneys and judges seem inclined to expand the scope of the rule to include religious and cultural worldviews.

Duty to Warn

Another question is whether other sorts of duties should be construed differently under tort law in a multicultural society. For instance, although manufacturers do have a duty to warn about the potential risks of products, must they provide warning in languages other than the dominant one?[32] A case that turns on this linguistic issue is *Ramirez v Plough*.[33] The defendant, St Joseph's Aspirin for

30 'We sometimes make reference to the egg-shell skull doctrine – the fact that the person injured may be more fragile or more susceptible than most is a consequence the tortfeasor must accept, for it was his wrong which set off the train of injuries, unusual and unanticipated though they may be. The universally accepted doctrine is that if a person has a special condition or predisposition which results in greater than normal damages the defendant remains legally responsible [citations omitted] When we consider the condition of a plaintiff as she is, while it is true that the doctrine is generally construed in the light of pre-existing conditions, it can also extend to latent mental instability and mind-sets, i.e., psychological conditions. There is no compelling reason (other than potential fraud) to draw the line there and hold that we may not consider others aspects of an individual persona. Conscience and religious belief are not passing whims, but guide human beings to life and death decisions.' *Williams v Bright*: 326.

31 The legal issue was whether the judge should grant the motion to set aside the jury verdict and direct a new trial. The judge attempted to reduce the award thereby avoiding the necessity of having another trial.

32 For an astute analysis, see Maciejewski (1994:144): 'The determination of whether manufacturer of over-the-counter drugs should be required to provide warnings in foreign languages requires analysis of two issues: (1) whether warning in foreign languages is required under a duty of ordinary care; and, (2) whether a warning printed only in English is adequate under the circumstances.'

33 *Ramirez v Plough*, 6 Cal. 4th 539, 25 Cal. Rptr. 2d 97, 863 P.2d 167 (Dec. 1993). To my knowledge, this was the first case of its kind in the United States.

Children (SJAC), put labels warning of Reyes syndrome because some children who took aspirin for the illness developed extremely serious health problems. In this case Spanish-speaking parents who could not read English gave their son, Jorge, aspirin, and he subsequently developed Reyes syndrome which left him with severe disabilities ('cortical blindness, spastic quadriplegia, and mental retardation'). With the assistance of the American Civil Liberties Union (ACLU), the parents sued the company.

The trial court granted summary judgment for the defendant. The California Court of Appeals reversed on the ground that the question whether a product warning was adequate was a question of fact that should go to a jury. Given the circumstances involved, i.e., the language barrier, the appellate court concluded that the question as to whether not labelling SJAC with a Spanish-language warning was reasonable was a triable issue of fact. It is possible that the court was influenced by the fact that the company had spent a great deal of money marketing the product in Spanish-speaking media.

The case then went on appeal to the California Supreme Court. In reaching a decision the California Supreme Court noted that there was no clear-cut doctrine: 'In most cases, courts have fixed no standard of care for tort liability more precise than that of a reasonably prudent person under like circumstances.'[34] The California Supreme Court then held as follows:

> We granted review in this case to determine whether a manufacturer of nonprescription drugs may incur tort liability for distributing its products with warnings in English only. Recognizing the importance of uniformity and predictability in this sensitive area of law, we conclude that the rule for tort liability should conform to state and federal statutory and administrative law. Because both state and federal law now require warnings in English, but not in any other language, we further conclude that a manufacturer may not be held liable in tort for failing to label a nonprescription drug with warnings in a language other than English.[35]

The court relied on the Health and Safety Code provision requiring that package warnings on non-prescription drugs be in English only and inferred that the legislature had chosen not to require them in foreign languages. The court effectively accepted a statutory defense based on the failure of legislatures to provide expressly for multilingual warning labels. Even though providing the warnings in Spanish would have protected Jorge, broadening the scope of a duty to warn, the court concluded that an interpretation of the scope of the rule was a policy decision better left to the legislature. The court may have been influenced by the fact that California has a constitutional requirement of 'English only'.

34 Ibid. 546.
35 Ibid. 542.

The decision was subject to much criticism (Baldwin 1995). The American Civil Liberties Union ACLU attorney, Edward Chen, chastised the court for 'abdicating its responsibility' to protect non-English speaking citizens.[36] Another advocate found it unfair that the company could spend money for Spanish-language advertising to promote the sale of the aspirin, but refuse to pay for warnings to inform consumers about the risks of the product.[37] One commentator underscores this point: 'If a manufacturer cultivates demand for its product in the native language of a significant minority group, then that manufacturer may assume the duty to warn in that language' (Maciejewski (1994: 153). One counterargument is usually that it is prohibitively expensive to impose on businesses the cost of making multilingual warning labels. Another is that there is not enough space on the label to accommodate warnings (Cox 1993).

In the final analysis one must consider the cost to the families of not having warning labels as well as the cost to the manufacturer of having to provide warning labels in other languages. As for the question of symbols and sufficient space, government agencies have considered proposals to simplify labels to aid all consumers.[38] The challenges of cost and space hardly seem insurmountable.

With globalization the issue of warning labels is likely to become a salient one. Although it may not be practical to create multilingual warning labels for all products, there are some that have inserts in several languages. Another possibility would be to use pictorial representations such as the skull and bones used on toxic household products (Maciejewski (1994: 150–1). This is not a panacea, however, as some images may not be understood or else may have different meanings.[39]

It is worth noting that the challenge of interpreting the duty to warn is by no means limited to drugs. Such a duty may apply in other areas, as, for example, Minow and Rakoff show (1998). They cite a late nineteenth century negligence case involving a warning about a fragile bridge. The plaintiff did not read English and crossed the bridge safely in the morning, but the bridge collapsed when he returned. His horses were killed and his wagon damaged. This example suggests that the scope of a duty to warn will have much wider repercussions than simply for the pharmaceutical industry.

36 Jennifer Warren, 'Bilingual Warnings Rejected by Justices', *Los Angeles Times*, 10 December 1993.

37 'Former Justice Grodin Argues: Drug Company Must Issue Warning Labels for Non-English Speaking Consumers', *ACLU News*, (S.F.), November–December 1993.

38 David Stout, 'U.S. Acts to Simplify Medicine Labels: Effort Is Being Made to Eliminate Small Letters and Dense Prose', *New York Times*, 26 February 1997.

39 'Labels in English Pose Risk in Multilingual Nation', *New York Times*, 20 May 2001.

Defendants' Use of Cultural or Religious Arguments

In some of the civil litigation it is the defendant who attempts to use cultural background as a basis for avoiding having to pay damages. One case involved allegations of sexual harassment, and one basis of the appeal was the failure of the lower court to award punitive damages. In *MacKinnon v Kwong Wah Restaurant* the defendants ostensibly made reference to cultural and linguistic barriers in order to escape punitive damages.[40] Two women, Charissa McKinnon and Beatric Poulin, filed lawsuits alleging that they endured sexual harassment while they worked as waitresses at the Kwong Wah Chinese restaurant.[41] The plaintiffs were dissatisfied with an award of $2500 each for compensatory damages and claimed the district court erred in declining to award punitive damages. Evidently, the women did not persuade the lower court that the defendants' misconduct met the standard for paying these damages as the lower court explained:

> There is no question that Defendants' repeated sexual harassment was offensive. In fact, in many cases, this behavior might be strong evidence of malice or, at least, reckless indifference to Plaintiffs' rights. In this case, however, the Court believes that the behavior of at least some Defendants was influenced by language, cultural, and educational barriers. With this consideration and all of the other evidence in mind, the Court concludes that Defendants were not acting with malice or reckless indifference to Plaintiffs' rights. No award of punitive damages is therefore appropriate.[42]

The plaintiffs attacked the logic underlying the trial court's decision saying that 'the ethnic background [of most of the defendants] is not an excuse negating malice or reckless indifference …' but the Court of Appeals for the First Circuit rejected the premise of their claim:

> A defendant's cultural background is not irrelevant in evaluating the appropriateness of punitive damages. In certain circumstances, a defendant's background will likely have an impact on his consciousness of wrongdoing. In the instant case, however, the district court's only explicit reason for denying punitive damages was the cultural, ethnic, and educational background of the defendants, and this is not the dispositive factor. The court did not point to any evidence in the record to support its assumption that the defendants were not acting with reckless indifference to the plaintiffs' rights. In the context of this case and on this record, primary reliance on cultural and educational background is tenuous and appears unsupported. Although the court also considered 'all the

40 *MacKinnon v Kwong Wah Restaurant* (1996), 83 F. 3d 498.

41 This conduct allegedly violated Title VII, the Maine Human Rights Act and state tort law.

42 *McKinnon v Kwong Wah Restaurant*: 508.

> other evidence,' it is not clear from the record what 'other evidence' the court considered.[43]

The appellate court remanded to the district court to clarify the basis of its decision to deny punitive damages. Although it left the door open to a cultural argument justifying a denial of punitive damages, the explanation had to be sufficiently elaborated, which was not the case here.[44]

In another case religious background might have been raised as a defense in a civil rights suit. Two blind Oakland, California, residents, Claude Everett and Constance Kelly, claimed that taxi drivers from Friendly Cab had refused repeatedly to give them a ride because they had their dogs with them.[45] On one occasion Everett waited 45 minutes for a Friendly Cab to pick him up. He called the company several times and finally the dispatcher informed him that the driver 'had refused to stop because he had a guide dog'.[46] After that Everett decided to sue, and the Disability Rights Education and Defense Fund (DREDF) filed suit on his behalf against Friendly Cab on 10 July 2001.[47] Even though the company said it had no policy against taking service animals or dogs specifically, they asserted that drivers have discretion as independent contractors as to whether they will allow dogs in their cabs. The case was settled out of court two years later, so there was no judicial determination as to the relative importance of religious freedom versus disability rights.[48] It is unfortunate that the case did not generate

---

43 Ibid. 509.

44 Although the court here is somewhat receptive to cultural arguments, in a criminal sexual harassment case a Korean immigrant man was convicted of criminal contempt (2nd degree) and aggravated harassment, despite an attempt to raise a cultural defense. See 'Sociologist's Testimony on Culture is Precluded in Harassment Case', *People v Jaechoel Yi*, Criminal Court. *New York Law Journal*, 3 November 1995. In an unreported sexual harassment case the jury considered the plaintiff's cultural background when computing her compensatory emotional distress damages. The employment of Ling Kheit Luu, a woman of Vietnamese ancestry, was terminated as retaliation for reporting misconduct and experienced loss of reputation and shame. 'Plaintiff's shame was so great that could not bring herself to tell her family of her termination. She explained that, in her culture, losing a job brings a shame upon the terminated employee and the employee's family.' *Luu v Seagate Technology*, F. Supp. 2nd (not reported), 2001.

45 Friendly Cab Company is owned by Baljin and Surinder Singh.

46 Daniela Mohon, 'Cab Company Sued for Refusing Service to Blind with Guide Animals', *Berkeley Daily Planet*, 12 July 2001.

47 Lisa Fernandez , 'Advocates Say Case is Latest Evidence of Growing National Problem: Cab Firm Accused of Snubbing Blind Pair's Suit alleges that Friendly Cab Discriminated by Refusing to Give Rides to Them and Their Guide Dogs. Some Say Drivers' Ethnicities May Be the Cause', *San Jose Mercury News*, 12 July, 2001.

48 Under California law whether religious organizations are subject to the Unruh Civil Rights Act, the state anti-discrimination law, is an unsettled question of law. In the US the federal law, the Americans with Disabilities Act, contains an exemption for religious organizations.

any precedent as, according to DREDF, taxis throughout the United States refuse to pick up passengers with guide dogs, even though this is a blatant violation of civil rights laws.[49]

In other countries persons with disabilities have experienced similar difficulties as taxi drivers have refused to transport blind individuals who have service animals.[50] In England, for example, a campaign begun in 2000 resulted in successful enactment of provisions in 2002 affording protection to persons with guide dogs.[51] Even where laws exist, it is hard to find actual cases in which courts or government agencies imposed sanctions on the drivers. This is because of enforcement problems. As the victims of the discrimination are blind, they cannot see the licence plate or other identifying features of a particular taxi to report it. Unless someone is present with them when the refusal occurs, it is unlikely they will be able to report the incidents. In Australia a disability rights advocate explained this challenge: 'We asked the driver for his accreditation number and he gave us the wrong one. It was only because an airline staff member had accompanied us that we got the right number and could properly complain about being refused.'[52]

In a Canadian case a Muslim taxi driver, Behzad Saidy, refused to pick up Mr Bruce Gilmour because of his golden retriever guide dog. Saidy's contention was: 'that his Muslim religious beliefs will not allow him to take dogs in his taxi, because Muslims can't associate with dogs'.[53] According to documentation filed with the British Columbia Human Rights Tribunal, approximately half of available taxi drivers are 'unable to take animals into their taxis due to medical or

49 DREDF, 'Disability Rights Lawsuit Against Oakland Taxi Company. Friendly Cab Company Refuses to Pick Up Passengers with Guide Dogs'. Press release, 12 July 2001.

50 'Guide Dog Taxi Controversy', BBC News, January 12 2000. Available at: <http://news.bbc.co.uk/1/hi/health/600187.stm> [accessed 4 November 2008]. This story reports that a transport minister told the House of Lords he favoured measures 'to prosecute drivers who refuse to carry dogs for the disabled'. However, at that time legislation had not yet been enacted.

51 'The law extended the Disability Discrimination Act to make it illegal for minicab drivers, as it is for licensed taxi drivers, to refuse to carry guide dog owners just because they are accompanied by their dogs.' Available at: <http://www.guidedogs.org.uk/index.php?id=1668#c9268> [accessed 4 November 2008]. See Section 37a of the Disability Discrimination Act which came into force in March 2003.

52 'Biased Cabbies Face Fines', *Daily Telegraph*, 24 May 2007. Available at: <http://www.news.com.au/dailytelegraph/story/0,22049,21782513-5001021,00.html> [accessed 4 November 2008].

See also Lincoln Wright and Ian Haberfield, 'Muslim Cabbies Refuse the Blind and Drinkers', *Herald Sun*, 8 October 2006. In Minnesota-St Paul Int'l Airport officials noted the cabdrivers, three-quarters of whom are Somalis, have often refused to transport passengers carrying alcohol.

53 Jane Seyd, 'Tribunal to Rule on Guide Dog vs. Religion', *North Shore News*, 15 November 2006.

religious reasons'. As part of his religious defense that religious employees should be accommodated, Mr Saidy submitted a cleric's statement explaining that 'Islam holds some restrictions towards certain animals, including dogs'.[54] As Islam may permit exceptions to the rule in order to help people, the tribunal could not resolve this question on the basis of the documents submitted and scheduled the matter for a full hearing.

Three days before the scheduled hearing the case was settled.[55] Mr Gilmour received $2500 and the North Shore taxi cab company agreed to abide by a new policy.[56] In the future cab drivers, if unable to transport passengers because of a sincere religious belief or allergies, must call for another cab, provide the passenger with his cab number, inform the passenger of the wait time and then stay with the passenger until the next cab arrives.[57] Although this settlement appeared to recognize the rights of persons with disabilities, it also provided for religious accommodation. In any event, it did not establish a precedent and affected only the policy of one taxi cab company. That no general policy has resolved this type of conflict is unfortunate, as those who commented on this case note that this form of discrimination is widespread.

On occasion, taxi cab drivers have been subject to fines. In England a legal officer with the Royal National Institute for the Blind appeared on the BBC news programme after which she was to take a 'BBC-contracted car' home. Because the minicab driver, Abdul Rasheed Majekodumni, would not allow her dog in the car because his religion considered dogs 'unclean', he was fined £200 and also ordered to pay another £1200 for failing to comply with the Disability Discrimination Act. He was quoted in the *Daily Mail* as saying that he: 'remained defiant and insisted that he would continue refusing passengers accompanied by guide dogs'.[58] In Australia government transport ministers have threatened to impose hefty fines as well.[59]

The occurrence of disability discrimination against the blind with guide dogs is a worldwide phenomenon. Furthermore, those who object to dogs on religious grounds may advance this argument when they exclude the blind and their dogs

---

54 *Gilmour v North Shore Taxi and Others*, 2006 BCHRT 529 (Oct. 31, 2006), File 3775: 2.

55 Kelly Sinoski, 'Taxi Firm Settles with Blind Man Refused Ride because of Guide Dog', *Vancouver Sun*, 16 August 2007.

56 Laura Paynton, 'Blind Man Wins Human Rights Case against Taxicab Company', *The Province*, 16 August 2007. Gilmour announced he would give some of the money to the Az-zahraa Islamic Centre because its imam was providing cultural information in this case, and some to British Columbia Guide Dog Services.

57 Joanna Habdank, 'Taxi Firm Settles with Blind Man', *North Shore News*, 17 August 2007.

58 See UK Taxi News. Available at: <http://uktaxinews.the-cabby.com/41/uk-minicab-drivers> [accessed 4 November 2008]. See also 'Taxi Driver Fined for Refusing Blind Couple; *UK Taxi News* 14 June 2007. Available at: <http://www.taxiblog.co.uk/2213/taxi-driver-fined-for-refusing-blind-couple> [accessed 4 November 2008].

59 Heath Aston, 'Biased Cabbies Face Fines'. *The Daily Telegraph*, 24 May 2007.

from hotels, restaurants, or grocery stores.[60] Consequently, it is likely that the use of religious defenses in civil rights suits will recur. Although as a matter of law the plaintiffs should prevail, difficulties associated with enforcement may thwart the potential protection the civil rights laws should be able to provide.

The Relevance of Culture for Damage Awards

The theory of cultural relativism[61] suggests that individuals, because of their enculturation, perceive and react to phenomena differently. The issue in these cases is that individuals may experience varying degrees of trauma when they are injured as a consequence of the misconduct of others. The law ought to acknowledge variation in individual reactions, based on their cultural background, and consequently there should be explicit policies authorizing the consideration of cultural and religious factors in appropriate cases.

Although I have concentrated on civil cases in which courts award damages, the distinction between civil and criminal cases is somewhat artificial. The standard view is that in criminal prosecution the penal sanction is incarceration whereas in civil litigation the remedy is monetary damages or an equitable remedy like an injunction. The reality is that criminal cases can lead to the payment of restitution or fines; money is not limited to civil litigation. In *People v Keichler*, the California Court of Appeals had to decide whether it was proper for the trial court to order the payment for a Hmong healing ceremony in a criminal case.[62] The court ruled that it was:

> We conclude the trial court's award of the expenses arising out of this traditional Hmong healing ceremony was proper. The court establishes these victims underwent these traditional Hmong healing ceremonies because the defendant injured them. ... this ceremony is the Hmong equivalent of western medical expenses.[63]

Moreover, it can be problematic to distinguish between criminal and civil matters since the same set of facts can also give rise to both criminal and civil cases. It is somewhat arbitrary whether the societal response to the harm leads to a criminal or civil matter. However, since the law makes distinctions, we are

---

60 Lisa Fernandez (source cited in footnote 47) refers to cases in New Orleans, Cincinnati and Ottawa where Muslims object to having dogs in taxis or grocery stores.

61 For an overview of the issues associated with the theory of cultural relativism, see Renteln (1988). For a thoughtful treatment of enculturation, see Shimahara (1970), Markus and Kitayama (1991).

62 *People v Keichler*, Cal. App. 3 Distr., 2005. [Citation 129 Cal.App.4th 1039]

63 Ibid. 1046.

compelled to examine how matters of cultural difference can be introduced into these categories.

The question is whether cultural factors can influence decisions about damage awards? There are no doctrinal barriers to this. Despite this, the reluctance of judges to admit that cultural considerations affect their decisions suggests that this may be a controversial practice. As there are likely to be increasing numbers of plaintiffs invoking cultural arguments in their lawsuits, governments would do well to devise policies appropriate for this analysis.

Formulating a useful policy should take into account the potential misuse of the cultural factors. To avoid the concern about fraud, courts could use the cultural defense test, which I have discussed elsewhere (Renteln 2004: 207):

1. Is the litigant a member of the ethnic group?
2. Does the group have such a tradition?
3. Was the litigant influenced by the tradition when he or she acted?

As this test can be applied in both criminal and civil cases, let us consider how it works in a civil case. There was case in which a young Orthodox Jewish woman, Ruth Friedman, found herself trapped in a ski lift chair with a young man as it was beginning to become night. She became hysterical because some Orthodox Jews believe it violates religious law to be left alone with a man unchaperoned at night. When she catapulted out of the chair, she was injured and sued for damages. If we apply the test we ask the following questions:

1. Was Ruth Friedman an Orthodox Jew?
2. Can Orthodox Jewish law be interpreted to disallow a young girl from being with a man after dark?
3. Was she influenced by this belief when she catapulted off the ski lift?

Having verified the claims advanced, courts should proceed to include this consideration in the calculation of damages.

Another crucial question is whether there is any way to stipulate in all cases how much the cultural factor should influence the size of the damage award. Although it would be ideal to have a way to do this, there is, in fact, no way to devise a rule by means of which to make this determination. Courts will simply have to proceed to make assessments of damage awards in cases involving cultural factors on a case-by-case basis. Nevertheless, there should at least be some effort made to legitimize the use of cultural analysis in civil litigation. This could be achieved by providing judges with official authorization of the use of cultural evidence in their decision-making process. This will indeed become a necessity to ensure that adjudication is fair in increasingly pluralistic societies.

References

American Jurisprudence. 2003. 2nd edition. St Paul, MN: Thomson/West.

Bahr, Gary L. and Bruce N. Graham. 1982. The Thin Skull Plaintiff Concept: Evasive or Persuasive. *Loyola of Los Angeles Law Review,* 15, 409–30.

Baldwin, Linda. 1995. *Ramirez v Plough,* Inc.: Should Manufacturer of Nonprescription Drugs have a Duty to warn in Spanish? *University of San Francisco Law Review*, 29, 837–74.

Cox, Kelly. 1993. The Duty to Warn: should California Extend the Duty to Include Foreign Language Warnings. *San Diego Justice Journal*, 1, 517–540.

Foblets, Marie-Claire and Alison Dundes Renteln. (eds) 2009. *Multicultural Jurisprudence: Comparative Perspectives on the Cultural Defense*. Oxford: Hart Publishing.

Levinson, Justin D. and Kaiping Peng. 2004. Different Torts for Different Cohorts: a Cultural Psychological Critique of Tort Law's Actual Cause and Foreseeability Inquiries. *Southern California Law Journal*, 13, 195–226.

Linden, Allen M. 1969. Down with Forseeability! Of Thin Skulls and Rescuers. *The Canadian Bar Review*, 47, 545–72.

Loomis, Anne C. 2007. Thou shalt Take thy Victim as thou Findest him: Religious Conviction as a Pre-existing State not Subject to the Avoidable Consequences Doctrine. *George Mason Law Review*, 14, 473–511.

Maciejewski, Christopher S. 1994. The Dilemma over Foreign-language Labeling of Over-the-counter Drugs. *The Journal of Legal Medicine*, 15, 129–54.

Markus, Hazel Rose and Shinobu Kitayama. 1991. Culture and the Self: Implications for Cognition, Emotion, and Motivation. *Psychological Review*, 98, 224–253.

Miller, Carol. 1975. American Rom and the Ideology of Defilement. In *Gypsies, Tinkers and other Travellers*, edited by Farnham Rehfisch. London: Academic Press, 41–54.

Minow, Martha L. and Todd D. Rakoff. 1998. Is the 'Reasonable Person' a Reasonable Standard in a Multicultural World? In *Everyday Practices and Trouble Cases*, edited by Austin Sarat, Marianne Constable, David Engel, Hans David and Susan Lawrence. Evanston, IL: Northwestern University Press, 40–67.

Note. 1978. Medical Care, Freedom of Religion, and Mitigation of Damages. *Yale Law Journal*, 87(7), 1466–503.

Padilla, David J. 1995. Reparations in Aloeboetoe v Suriname. *Human Rights Quarterly*, 17, 541–55.

Pomeroy, Jeremy. 1992. Reason, Religion, and Avoidable Consequences: when Faith and the Duty to Mitigate Collide. *New York University Law Review*, 67, 1111–55.

Poulter, S. 1998. *Ethnicity, Law and Human Rights: The English Experience*. Oxford: Clarendon Press.

Renteln, Alison Dundes. 1988. Relativism and the Search for Human Rights. *American Anthropologist*, 90(1), 56–72.

— 2001. The Rights of the Dead: Autopsies and Corpse Mismanagement in Multicultural Societies. *South Atlantic Quarterly*, 100(4), 1005–27.

— 2003. Cross-cultural Perceptions of Disability: Policy Implications of Divergent Views. In *Different but Equal: the Rights of People with Intellectual Disabilities*, edited by S. Herr, L. Gostin, Lawrence and H. Koh. Oxford: Oxford University Press, 59–81.

— 2004. *The Cultural Defense*. New York: Oxford University Press.

Rowe, P.J. 1977. The Demise of the Thin Skull Rule? *Modern Law Review*, 40, 377–88.

Shelton, Dinah 2005. *Remedies in International Human Rights Law.* 2nd edition. New York: Oxford University Press.

Shimahara, Nobuo 1970. Enculturation – a Reconsideration. *Current Anthropology*, 11(2), 143–54.

Shinkle, Anna. 1967. Taking the Plaintiff as you Find him. *Drake Law Review*, 16, 49–56.

Villarreal, Carlos. 1991. Culture in Lawmaking: a Chicano Perspective. *U.C. Davis Law Review*, 24, 1193–242.

Chapter 12

Jews and Muslims in France: Changing Responses to Cultural and Religious Diversity

Martine Cohen

Introduction

Over the last few decades, Western European societies have been facing a newly reinforced pluralism, due to the massive presence of Muslims and, more generally, to a broader process of globalization. This situation calls into question their national identity, which was supposed until then to foster a neutral liberal State.

In France, after a period of openness to cultural diversity (in the 1970s and the 1980s), a new social debate has emerged on the subject of secularism, which has been oscillating between two extreme positions. On the one hand, a strict secularism maintains religious identities in the private sphere, helping to preserve individual freedom and civil society as a whole from religious groups' pressure; this position is identified by its adherents as the 'true' secularism, the uniqueness of which is strongly correlated with France and the term *laïcité*. On the other hand, secularism affords a more prominent place in the public sphere to religious identities, allowing them to participate in public moral issues; this position is also referred to as French *laïcité* but rather highlights its historical liberal trend toward religion – all the more as its contemporary evolution makes possible to relate it to other forms of associative and cultural engagement. In this case, *laïcité* is often associated with multiculturalism.

I propose to analyse the national and international factors of this growing debate on secularism, expressed here as '*laïcité vs* multiculturalism' – although I know this formulation tends to adopt the first position on the 'uniqueness' of 'French *laïcité*' against 'Anglo-Saxon multiculturalism'. I will first highlight, in a short historical overview, the background of this debate with discussion of the respective positions of Jews and Muslims in France before World War II. In conclusion, I will ask the question: how do multiculturalism and globalization destabilize secularization processes in 'old' national identities?

Jews and Muslims in France before World War II: A Limited Religious Pluralism

A legal framework for religious pluralism was set up in nineteenth century France, more precisely during the Restoration period (1814–30). But this pluralistic framework, which included Protestants and Jews in the French dominant Catholic society by offering them equal rights, showed some limitations, either on the legal level or on the factual level. It was a limited religious pluralism.

For Jews, a full legal equality was not achieved before the middle of the nineteenth century. Among the examples of this long-lasting legal process, was a Napoleonic discriminatory decree of 1808 against Jews (actually, only Alsatian Jews were concerned, but they were the vast majority of them); this so-called 'loathsome decree' was revoked only in 1818. Furthermore, rabbis were paid by the state (like others clerics) only in 1831, and a selective courtroom oath was required from Jews until 1846.

Under the Second Empire and the Third Republic, Jews went through a process of socio-economic betterment and gained access to civil positions in the army, the judiciary and governmental positions. But continuing social discriminations lasted until the end of the nineteenth century, and two major shocks called into question Jewish social integration: the Dreyfus Affair (1894–1906) and, to an even greater extent, the Vichy regime of the Second World War.[1]

The Dreyfus Affair occurred at a moment of fragility for the Republic. Anti-Semitism gathered together anti-modernist Catholics, anti-German patriots (especially in the army) and anti-capitalist left movements. The ideological battle turned into an opposition between two conceptions of French identity; a monolithic vision of a Catholic France – which evidently excluded the Jews – or a Republican regime. Fortunately for the Jews, supported by a new group of intellectuals (among them the writer Emile Zola, the sociologist Emile Durkheim, the French-Jewish Anarchist Bernard Lazare), the ideals of justice and equality overcame the 'ethnic' conception of French identity. This victory led Jews to a reinforced adhesion to the Republic. They continued to be involved in the building of a strong centralized State, whose authority was supposed to protect them from the forces of anti-Semitism.[2] Jews benefited from the Law of Separation between church and state (1905), which removed the legal monopoly of the Consistory (see below), and allowed the creation of an independent Reform congregation, founded by open-minded intellectuals who aspired to counter assimilation.[3] Moreover, a cultural

1 For a history of French Jewry in the nineteenth and early twentieth centuries, see: Albert-Cohen (1977), Berkowitz (1989), Graetz (1996), Hyman (1998), Hermon-Belot (1999), Malinovich (2008).

2 See Birnbaum (1992).

3 More generally, the Law of Separation erased the unequal status between 'recognized' and non-recognized religions (essentially small Protestant groups), creating a newly pluralistic situation.

Jewish revival sprang up in the 1920s, which shaped a new sense of Jewish pride among the intellectuals and the associative realms. But anti-Semitism flourished again a few years later in the context of economic crisis, and the Vichy regime which ruled France under the Nazi occupation succeeded in legally expelling Jews from the national frame for four long years. Opposing the principle of pluralism, the Vichy crisis showed the continuing marks of a racial-Catholic conception of French identity. For a second time, Republican values were at stake; and fortunately again, Jews found common interest with the French Resistance, as well as with the numerous French non-Jews who helped them to escape from deportation. The final victory over Nazism and the Vichy regime allowed Jews to re-integrate in France on the basis of these Republican values. Thirty years later, facing the upsurge of a renewed anti-Semitism and the trials of personalities who were involved at a high level of the Vichy regime, they broke the silence.[4]

As for Muslims, it is in colonial Algeria that their unequal condition was evident, as contrasted with the legal status of the Jews. After the incorporation of Algeria into the French State (three French departments were constituted in 1858), Algerian Jews, but not Muslims, were offered full citizenship by the 'Crémieux Decree' (1870). This exclusion of Muslims contradicted the principle of religious pluralism and, as is well known, even if Muslims converted to Catholicism, they maintained inferior 'subjects' rather than full French citizens. If the majority of the Algerian Jews accepted their distinction from the other '*indigènes*', it was not without ambivalence. They indeed cherished their new enfranchisement from a '*dhimmi*'/protected condition, but they continued to feel close to Muslims by their strong communitarian religiosity. Besides, with the further reinforcement of a local European anti-Semitism – during the Dreyfus Affair and the Vichy regime[5] – Jews could have common interests with Muslims and a majority of them were indeed close to left Republican parties. However, only a few fought openly for equal rights for Muslims.[6] Their own *political fragility* might have determined this hesitation and, later on, their final choice in favour of France and its ideals, when France finally had to leave Algeria in 1962.

A Denominational Pattern of Integration

Being newly considered as a religious group, Jews (or 'Israelites', as they have been called since the nineteenth century) were required to integrate on the basis of a 'denominational pattern'. The Jewish *global identity* – associated with the pre-

4 In the 1970s, the memory of this dramatic period supported a new Jewish activism, first condemning France in general for its anti-Semitism and then requiring France to take into account this moral condemnation within the national memory.

5 The abrogation of the Crémieux Decree was maintained until 1943, one year after the Allies arrival in North Africa. See Weil (2004) chapter entitled 'Les crises ethniques de la nationalité française').

6 On this complex history, see Benjamin Stora (2006).

modern conception of a 'nation' – was transformed into a *religion* which implied an individual adhesion to a faith (beliefs) and to practices. Based on a distinction between religious and civil rules, the Jewish practice thus constituted *just one sphere of Jewish life*, organized within *a separate institution*, the 'Consistory', with its two heads: a chief rabbi for the spiritual matters and a president for the administrative management. A third feature may be added to this picture: toward the end of the nineteenth century, when the 'social utility' of religion was questioned and an autonomous secularized morality was independently elaborated (*morale laïque*), religion was more and more supposed to be *confined to the private sphere*. This meant restrictions on religion in the public sphere and on religious interference in political life, although no absolute legal prohibition existed. This *denominational pattern* can therefore be seen as consistent with the 'Jacobin model' which dictates that the only identity allowed to be asserted in the public sphere by individuals or groups is the national one. Religious affiliation or regional belonging are considered thus as 'secondary' identities, not at all relevant in the realm of political life. This ideological hierarchy is the basis of the individualistic principle of the French Republic, where no communitarian body can interfere between the state and the individual.[7]

Accepting Diversity. Changes in French Political Tradition and within the Jewish Community after World War II

As previously mentioned, a Jewish cultural revival spread in France in the 1920s, in the aftermath of the Dreyfus Affair, encouraged by the strong Jewish identity of East European immigrants. This 'Réveil Juif' – note the return to the adjective 'Juif' as a source of pride – flourished essentially in the literary world, the press and youth movements. The support of some writers or leftist leaders for Zionism was another expression of this new Jewish pride. By supporting the cause of a 'homeland' for their persecuted brothers, these French Jews tried to carve out a secular, left-wing Jewish identity in France, without giving it a Jewish-national expression *within* the French political sphere. They linked their pro-Zionist attitude with a strong sense of belonging to France.[8] Indeed this French-Jewish revival,

7 The case of the Alliance Israelite Universelle may appear as contrary to this model. Founded in 1860 by Jewish scholars and intellectuals in order to defend their 'brothers' persecuted in Russia and the Middle East, this organization intervened on the international scene. As such, it has been analysed by Graetz (1996) as a renewed expression of Jewish peoplehood, a 'proto-Zionism'. But this political activism intended also to promote the French model of emancipation and its universalistic culture outside of France, especially among the Jews. By doing so, it also supported France's interests in colonial or protected countries. This ideological synthesis between French patriotism and Jewish engagement is known as 'Franco-Judaism'.

8 On this period, see Charbit (2005) and Malinovich (2008).

which also comprised a blossoming of Jewish associational life, was forced later on to focus on the renewed battle against anti-Semitism during the 1930s and the Vichy regime. However, the existence of numerous secular Jewish associations may be seen as a quasi-political background that would favour, later on, a first shift toward institutional and political changes within the Jewish community.

First Steps toward Changes within the Jewish Community.

Although reintegration of the Jews into post-war French society took place along the former denominational pattern, *a first and limited shift from this denominational pattern* occurred on the institutional level, with the constitution in 1943 (officially in 1944) of a Jewish political body, a federation of all Jewish organizations *including* the Consistory, the Representative Council of Jews in France (in French, CRIF).[9]

Why a 'limited' shift ? Because it was decided that the chairman of the CRIF would be, by right, the President of the Consistory. Thus, the religious body formally remained the chief umbrella of French Jews, preserving a religious definition of Jewish identity and the centrality (although not the monopoly) of the Consistory as its representative institution. The CRIF was devoted to settling claims relating to confiscated property and to fighting anti-Semitism, but its influence was in fact very limited until the 1970s.

Another new secular institution was created in 1949, the Fonds Social Juif Unifié (FSJU), which was devoted to social and cultural work among the Jews. It would increasingly have more and more impact on Jewish cultural life, as it coordinated and fundraised in order to create several 'Jewish community centres', based on a North American model, where secular cultural and political activities became prevalent.

During the 1950s and the 1960s, intellectual and demographic factors also laid the groundwork for a larger shift from the denominational pattern. The so-called 'Ecole d'Orsay', a sort of Jewish learning centre functioning as a community headed by a charismatic leader (Léon Askenazi), was founded in 1947 by the leaders of a the Jewish Scouting movement (Eclaireurs Israélites). Actually this Ecole would function, during its twenty-year life-span, as a training ground for many future institutional leaders. In addition to this informal 'school', a Jewish intellectual revitalization would also develop around the figures of the philosopher Emmanuel Levinas and other Jewish thinkers (such as André Néher), who organized annual meetings of French-speaking Jewish intellectuals since 1957.[10] On the demographic level, the arrival after Algerian independence of

9 The first full name of the CRIF was 'Conseil Représentatif des Israélites de France' but immigrant organizations pushed to change it into 'Jews of France', while keeping the same abbreviation. It became hereafter the 'Conseil Représentatif des Institutions juives de France'.

10 Colloque des Intellectuels juifs de langue française.

close to 200,000 North African Jews involved a profound transformation of the Jewish community, whose population doubled while the rebuilding of many local communities implied a new Jewish visibility in French society. Thus, the coming of these 'Sephardic' Jews constitutes only one of the factors explaining the Jewish revival of the 1970s, and not the sole one as it is commonly thought. Furthermore, it may be noted that a similar revival occurred during the same period in other countries (England, United States) where Sephardic Jews were not present.

The Jewish Revival of the 1970s: A Shift from the Denominational Pattern

The shift from the denominational pattern which took place in the 1970s can be illustrated by several phenomena, both *political* ones (public expressions of solidarity with Israel after the Six Day War, fight against the denial of the Jewish genocide) and *cultural* ones (Festivals of Jewish and Israeli cultures, new interest in Jewish history and folklore, the development of Jewish studies in universities and of a publishing sector), as well as new *religious* public expressions of Orthodox groups.[11]

These processes can be synthesized as having *three main features*, still relevant today. Firstly, Jewish identity is no longer exclusively religious, but rather openly cultural and/or political as well. One may notice here the diversity and the complexity of this identity assessment: solidarity with Israel is not exclusive of a strong defence of a diasporic existence and culture; secular involvement is not contradictory to some religious practice, sometimes deliberately adopted in a selective and secular way. Secondly, although Jews are officially considered as a religious group represented by the Consistory, 'Jewish interests' in other domains than religious affairs are de facto recognized, related to two other institutions: the CRIF and the FSJU. The CRIF's autonomous political role was affirmed with its institutional reorganization in 1977 and 1981, which submitted the position of chair to an election by the federated associations, taking it over from the president of the Consistory. This political role grew when the first elected president, Théo Klein, instituted an annual 'CRIF Dinner' in 1985, regularly inviting the prime minister of the standing government.[12] The FSJU informally took the place of a cultural representative institution vis-à-vis public authorities (in the schooling domain, for instance, although the FSJU is not the main founder of the numerous schools networks). Finally if the Consistory, as the mainstream religious institution, still

11 For a precise description of this many-sided revival and its historical background, see Cohen (1993 and 2000).

12 Among other factors of this growing political influence of the CRIF, one can evoke the involvement of Théo Klein in the resolution of the 'Auschwitz Carmel' affair (1985–7) when Catholic women wanted to maintain their Carmel Monastery inside the Auschwitz Campus. Good relationship with religious leaders of the Catholic churches in France and Poland helped to resolve this problem. See Ghiles-Meilhac (2007).

includes the majority of Jews in France, it is now challenged by other religious groups, both orthodox and reform. Consequently, although it remains the official religious partner institution, other religious bodies *do have* their own contacts with French political authorities.

A plurality of Jewish identity models, a plurality of Jewish representative institutions and a plurality of religious institutions: these were the threefold changes which are still in effect today within the organized Jewish community. This principle of separate organizations delineating three main domains (religion, culture and politics) is generally accepted – in spite of a new competition for Jewish leadership which has recently developed, as we shall see hereafter – and can be said to express the *secularization* of the whole of Jewish community life, as well as its diversity. These profound changes in organized Jewish life could not have occurred without a simultaneous change within French society and French political tradition.

Changes within French Society and French Political Tradition

Many pragmatic moves toward an enlarged religious pluralism can be noticed before and after World War II, with administrative arrangements facilitating religious practices for some minorities.[13] This was followed, as in other Western societies in the 1960s, by a deep cultural shift toward cultural diversity. Critics of the 'cultural uniformity' of the 'Jacobin model' originated in regionalist movements. In addition, an individualistic morality developed with the refusal of all forms of authority (in family or at school). Secularization continued, as Catholic norms were increasingly dismissed in the domains of family and sexual life (laws establishing equality between men and women, permitting contraception, abortion). Diversity became a value in itself, as formulated later on by the slogan 'the right to difference'.

These changes in French political tradition towards public affirmation of minorities allowed Jews to adopt a global conception of their identity, going beyond the previous denominational pattern for defining their place in French society. One can speak also of an 'ethnic' model.

Debating Multiculturalism. From the 1980s to the 2000s: Toward a Fear of Social Fragmentation

In the last decades of the twentieth century, two major changes led to a new perception of diversity as a potential risk for social cohesion: the presence of Muslims in France – and in Western societies in general – and globalization, which implies bolstered exchanges between 'North' and 'South'. This multifaceted

13 See in particular Messner (1993), Basdevant-Gaudemet (1996) and the so-called 'Machelon Report' (2006).

turmoil – labour migrations, delocalization of business enterprises, mass tourism, new technology and mass-communication, etc. – involves a new intertwining of secularized and non-secularized societies, as well as religious and political issues. Furthermore, formerly colonized populations became a constituting part of the nation states that once ruled over them. This radical mutation implies another confusion, a sort of historical backlash, with the upsurge of memories of these 'others' within the normative national narrative. As a consequence, the place of the Jews in France has been somehow destabilized. This is not to say that their integration is questioned, but rather that they are no longer the historic 'other' of a Christian majority society.

Religion and Politics Intertwined on the National and the International Scenes

Settlement of Arab migrant families in French society and persisting discrimination against them led to their new perception as a religious group, but also to a 'politicization' of Islam, reinforced by the emergence of a radical political Islam on the international scene. While such a politicization can be seen also among the Jews, it is far from being a similar process.

Towards a Denominational Pattern vs Politicization of Islam

With the settlement of Arab migrants' families during the 1970s, diversity was first conceived along a cultural pattern, associated with left ideals (François Mitterrand was elected as president in 1981). The slogan of 'the right to difference' was adopted by young Arabs during their first 'March for Equality' in 1983 and by the anti-racist association 'SOS-Racisme' which was created in 1984 by Jews and Maghrébins together, many of them being socialist supporters. But persisting discrimination against Maghrébins (notably in the socio-economic and housing fields) as well as police brutality against them, which has led to recurrent urban riots since the summer of 1981, cast doubts on this 'right', which gradually gave way to another slogan: the 'right to similarity' – e.g. invisible identity in the public sphere.

This first move back to the 'Republican model' was associated with a new political objective: the building up of a 'French Islam'. With the first attempt to organize Islam into an institutional religious frame in 1990 by the Socialist Pierre Joxe, religious affiliation began to appear as a more legitimate collective identity than ethnicity.[14] A denominational pattern was thus proposed to immigrants and their children, whereas it was perceived at that time as old-fashioned among Jews. But those 'Muslims' who were secularized did not want to be ascribed a religious identity,[15] and some voices asked publicly if religion was a suitable frame for

14 Joxe created the 'CORIF' (Organizational and Reflexive Council for Islam in France); it was just one year after the first 'headscarf affair' in 1989.

15 See the survey conducted by Brouard and Tiberj (2006).

'Muslims'. Referring to the Jewish CRIF and the existence of secular Jews, they created secular Muslim associations, thus claiming another ground of legitimacy for their representation.

As a matter of fact, the Islamic reference became for some a means of personal identity searching (several leaders of the 'March for Equality' became religious activists as early as 1985) and newly created Muslim associations took over the former fight against discrimination. Besides, the French government did not follow through on its own call to create a 'French Islam' and often turned to foreign Muslim governments (specially in North Africa) in order to get control over these new activists. Political interests thus interfered all along the process of creation of the French Islam 'representative' body, which was finally achieved in 2003, under pressure from the then Minister of the Interior, Nicolas Sarkozy.[16] This multiple process of the 'politicization of Islam' increased with the growth of the extreme-right party (National Front) during the 1980s, which denounced the alleged danger of Islam for French national identity. The theme of immigration still continues to be a political issue connected to Islam on both the left and right sides of the French political spectrum, with political leaders pandering to a 'Muslim vote'.

The Emergence of a Radical Political Islam and its Impact on European Societies

As we know, Islamic parties succeeded in conquering state power in Iran (1978) and later in Afghanistan. This gradually had political consequences within European societies. The beginnings of international Islamic terrorism showed the reality of a political, violent Islam, which was 'confirmed' by the Rushdie Affair (1989) and later on by Al Qaeda terrorism. The Palestinian revolts against the Israeli occupation also expressed themselves more and more in religious ways. These various religious-political causes have been somehow 'reunified' by Al Qaeda leaders into an Islamic struggle against 'the Western world', gaining here and there supporters *within* European societies.[17]

If Muslim diaspora communities may help develop a new sense of transnational solidarity – different from the previous national belonging of the first migrants – they can also give room to Islamic radical tendencies, even if this constitutes a minority phenomenon. In France, young Muslim generations aspire to their incorporation into French society, but they are sometimes regarded with a fair amount of suspicion. Although the majority of them are secularized and individually

---

16 Sarkozy insisted that the first chairman of the French Council for Muslim Cult (CFCM) would be the rector of the French-Algerian Mosque of Paris, Dalil Boubakeur, for political reasons (links with the Algerian government) as well as for religious motives: Boubakeur is supposed to belong to a 'reform' wing of Islam.

17 The Fall of the Berlin Wall in 1989 ended a world polarization against communist ideology, but it also opened the way to other expressions of ideological confrontations, in religious or 'civilization' terms.

integrated, the religious activism of some Islamic organizations or leaders among them triggers the fear of an ambivalent transnational (global) community: is the *Ummah* a spiritual 'community of believers' or a political transnational group which opposes loyalty to the French nation?

Within the French Jewish Community: The Impact of Israeli Policy and Religious Radicalization

During the 1970s and the 1980s, similar fundamentalist tendencies appeared in the Jewish realm. But it was not on the same scale and it did not endanger the democratic State of Israel, nor the integration of French Jews. Furthermore, these evolutions involved neither the emergence of an international Jewish terrorism nor a threat towards West European countries.

The recovering of 'sacred' territories by Israel during the Six Day War (1967) favoured there a religious revival focused on the new political-religious slogan of 'Great Israel'. A religious Zionism linked to right-wing parties gained more and more influence in the governmental spheres (the first victory of the right-wing Likud party occurred in 1977), enhancing the religious legitimacy of settlement in the occupied territories. These developments led to increasing conflicts in Israel, concerning these settlements as well as the justification of military operations since the Lebanon war in 1982. They also echoed among French Jews. They actually became a matter of controversy *within and outside* the Jewish community. Hence Jewish solidarity with Israel, which was previously consensual among Jews and encouraged by sympathy from the larger French society, became more complex and problematic. The political role of the CRIF grew and appeared to some as a pro-Israeli lobby.

Toward the end of the 1980s, changes occurred too within the French religious sphere. A new chief rabbi who was close to ultra-orthodox circles was elected in 1987 (in office in 1988). He began to integrate some of their members into the Consistory or to associate them with its public actions. This religious radicalization, which enhanced the 'sectarian' (religiously exclusive) character of the Consistory, provoked notably the surge of new 'secular Jews' organizations (1989 and later on). One may analyse this polarization as a classical battle between anti-clerical movements and radical religious groups. But it also shows a sort of politicization of the French Jewish realm, since the chief rabbi is now competing with the CRIF over Jewish leadership. Hence, while the previous distribution of roles between the three Jewish institutions did not give a prominent place to any and somehow restrained the political implication of the CRIF, the competition now enhances the perception of a strong collective Jewish entity whose nature may be either political or religious.[18] This may be analysed as *a political step toward ethnicity*, beyond

18 The competition has grown over and over during recent years, leading the CRIF to engage in religious matters (encounters with Muslims, Catholics and Buddhists), while

the former cultural or religious activism, at a distance from the denominational pattern and the previous 'Franco-Judaism'.

The Headscarf Affairs: Multiculturalism against Laicité*?*

The first headscarf affair occurred in October 1989 and sparked several questions. An 'old' debate first concerned two principles both associated with French *laïcité* but which suddenly appeared as contradictory: guarantee for individual religious freedom *or* 'religious neutrality' of the public sphere imposing 'invisible' identities? When this latter principle was globally consensual, no major claim went to contradict it in state schools (all the more as religious expressions did fade away with the general process of secularization). But since the 1970s, individual rights gained supporters in many domains, including free expression of pupils at school. For those who were more accustomed to *political* youth movements, the upsurge of religious expression at school raised surprise and opposing positions, either in favour of a complete freedom (even if it was contrary to their own secular option) or in favour of a strict *laïcité* – which appeared then for the first time as opposed to individual rights. When Prime Minister Jospin asked the State Council for its opinion on this affair, it responded by affirming the principle of free religious expression for pupils *but not for teachers as civil servants*, thus adding to the confusion.

A second and new debate was also triggered, which concerned the issue of emancipation. It was framed either in *gender terms* – does the headscarf mean a real free choice or inferiority of women? – or in *more general terms*: how can individual choice lead to religious involvement, contradicting our modernization scheme based on the principle of progressive liberation from religious values and norms? If former identity movements were based on individual choice against 'Jacobin uniformity', this new form of 'differentialism' based on inherited identities did not appear clearly as a 'progressive' step, since it seemed to encourage 'archaic' and holistic identities. In other terms, the question was: in the name of multiculturalism, would it be possible to imagine *different ways of emancipation*? This disturbing question led some activists of *laïcité* to oppose multiculturalism, when others rather highlighted the complex processes of individualism in different cultures or societies.[19]

The subsequent headscarf affairs were analysed also as a mixed political-religious issue. They were linked by public opinion (with reason or not) to international Islamic political movements which tried to reinstall (or reinforce) the religious law (the shari'a) in Muslim countries. Then the renewed question of *laicité* guaranteeing *individual* religious freedom came to the fore, as opposed to

the chief rabbi organizes meetings and popular trips to Israel to support its settlement policy in the occupied territories.

19 These activists were also close to post-colonial perspectives, when refusing the exclusive model of Western modernization.

hypothetical pressures from religious-political groups on Muslim individuals and on French society. Although this reality has not been statistically studied as yet, the supposed growing influence of these international pressures added motives for the reassessing of the 'principles of *laïcité*'.

A Growing Ethnic Perception of French Society and the Return to a Restricted Laïcité

The already conflicted international scene became dramatically worse at the beginning of the new millennium, and this had political repercussions in France. The renewed Palestinian–Israeli conflict (the 'second Intifada', since autumn 2000) and the Durban Conference in September 2001 (where Arab countries concentrated their harsh criticism on Israel), which was immediately followed by the terrorist attack against the World Trade Center on 9/11, crystallized previous oppositions between French Jews and Muslims. Anti-Semitic slogans were heard during the pro-Palestinian demonstrations, physical attacks increased against the Jews or Jewish buildings, to a point where a fear of social fragmentation became a dramatic issue of concern. Added to the visible contradictions of multiculturalism (also related to the new debates which arose in England after the July 2005 terrorist attack), it called into question the previous positive French attitude toward the celebration of 'diversity'.

Furthermore, while the incorporation of the memory of the Holocaust within French national memory was seen as a positive way to think anew about a contested period of French history,[20] new claims of Muslims activists about reconsidering colonial domination sounded like an accusation against France as a whole and provoked strong oppositions. As anti-Muslim discriminations continued, the idea of 'privileges' attributed to the Jews by French society and public authorities became more or less widespread among Muslims milieus. Could we speak of 'jealousy' toward 'well-integrated' and 'successful' people?[21] An old, and probably not conscious, resentment may have nourished this jealousy with regard to the privileged status Jews acquired in Algeria during the colonial period with the Crémieux Decree. In this climate, while many Jews thought a new anti-Semitism has emerged (a 'judeophobia', according to some scientists),[22]

20 It was in 1993 that President Mitterrand decided to establish a new national celebration related to the memory of the French participation of the Vichy regime in the Jewish genocide; President Chirac went further in 1995 when he officially recognized the 'collective fault' of the French state.

21 The murder of the young Jew Ilan Halimi by a 'barbarian gang', in 2006, revealed such a jealousy toward 'rich people', as the gang wrote in their letters.

22 Taguieff (2002) invented the term 'judeophobia' to designate the way anti-Semitism was now hiding behind 'anti-Zionism' and critics against Israel. According to scientific surveys, most of the attacks were attributed to Arabs/Muslims, but they were not necessarily analysed as anti-Semitism. Due to their close relationship to the periods of Israeli

Muslims spoke of 'islamophobia' to qualify their own numerous discriminations. A competition between victims thus developed and worsened with the claim about reconsideration of black slaves' traffic by European countries.[23]

The ethnic perception of French society thus increased and was even implicitly confirmed by positive initiatives such as the creation, in 2004 by a rabbi, of the Jewish-Muslim Friendship Association and its circulating 'Fraternity Bus'. The positive attitude toward 'diversity' could remain the slogan for some political steps (for instance the creation of the French Council for Muslim Cult in summer 2003), or the true preoccupation of new managers, but it also had to face strong oppositions to any assessment of 'ethnic' groups within the national frame.

As a matter of fact, religious signs, especially the headscarf, became the core of the ideological battle against these 'ethnic' quarrels. New headscarf affairs led the French government to create in July 2003 the 'Stasi Committee on *Laïcité*', which published a report with twenty-five proposals at the end of the year.[24] But none of them was adopted except one: a new law forbidding any 'conspicuous' religious sign at school (March 2004), which is often seen as having the unique purpose to suppress the 'Islamic veil'.

On the ground, the interpretations of this law now go far beyond its strict expression. The ban on the headscarf in school is often taken as a general ban, with several cases of women excluded from a city hall during a wedding celebration or from places of work (private and public). Other cases of inequality regarding Muslims have been recently noticed: while mayors frequently agree to rent municipal land cheaply to religious groups (Catholics, Protestants, Jews and even Muslims) who wish to build a place of worship, members of a nationalist party (a dissident one from the National Front) locally challenged the Muslims' right to benefit from this same advantage in three places (Marseille, Roubaix and Montreuil); the judicial contest was grounded, it was said, on a strict interpretation of the Separation Law of 1905 forbidding any financial support to religious groups from public authorities.[25]

Other recent cases put into question the financial state support previously given for the social activities of religious groups (youth camps for Catholics and Protestants as well as for Muslims and Jews); this led the French Protestant Federation to address a protest, in 2006, to the new French authority officially

---

assaults against Palestinians, some scientists like Mayer (2005) thought that this motive would disappear with the end (or the weakening) of the conflict; others like Wieviorka (2005) insisted on the economic and social frustrations of non integrated young people. Laurence and Vaïsse (2007: Chapter 9) give a good synthesis of these studies, concluding however on the persistence of a 'structural' anti-Semitism.

23 Chaumont (1997) was the first who spoke of a 'competition between victims'.

24 Commission Stasi (2003).

25 In one case (Marseille), the mayor and the Muslim association negotiated a new price; in the two other cases (Montreuil, Roubaix), the Muslim associations appealed against the judicial contest; the cases are not over.

established for fighting against discrimination (Halde).[26] Concerning particularly the Jews, previous individual arrangements facilitating religious practice were called into question (the wearing of the *kippa* at school, permission to be absent on Saturdays). By making this parallel with Muslims' demands, it is implicitly assumed that Jews' requests, which were previously granted on the basis of individual practical accommodation, now could ultimately be also a threat to republican values as well as to national unity.

The former processes of enlargement of the scope of pluralism are thus being put into question, in contradiction with the liberal understanding of secularism which was practiced from1905 up to the 1980s. Due to its long and rich history, French secularism is a complex and multiple site of memory. When facing radical changes regarding the nature of the public space, in the context of international political tensions, some activists of *laïcité* tend to remember the 'old battles' of the republican regime against the Catholic church and to call for a new vigilance toward all religious requests.

Conclusions

From Religious Pluralism to Cultural Diversity: France Facing the Fear of Social Fragmentation

The historical overview first showed us the progressive enlargement of *religious pluralism* to the sole non-Christian religion which was present in France in the nineteenth century, Judaism. But the non-respect of this principle concerning the Muslims in colonial Algeria demonstrated the reluctance of a culturally (religiously) Christian France, when facing 'others' who were demographically in a position to oppose its colonial power if they had been given full citizenship. Algerian Jews (between 15,000 and 20,000 people in 1831), by contrast, were given the same political status as French Jews, namely that of fully fledged French citizens. However, the two major crises which endangered their place within the national frame or even excluded them from it for several years (the Dreyfus Affair and the Vichy regime) showed the persisting conception of a Catholic-French identity. When post-war France reintegrated them, the explicit acceptance of secularism by the Catholic church did reassure the republican regime, which began to enlarge the principle of religious pluralism and to include other minority groups. Later on, the continuing process of secularization, as well as economic welfare and moral individualism, allowed a new openness of French society to *cultural diversity*.

But persistent discrimination against Arab-Muslims immigrants cast doubt on the efficiency of the 'right to difference' model as a means to integration. The wish to return to the 'republican model' and to consider the immigrants and their children as 'Muslims', along the old denominational pattern, was then reinforced in public

26 To this date, no proper response has been given.

opinion by new factors: the upsurge of a political Islam on both the international and national scenes, as well as the growing impact of religious-political conflicts in the Middle East on relationships between French Muslims and Jews. The fear of social fragmentation along 'ethnic' or religious differences has now resulted in a new debate on *laïcité* as opposed to multiculturalism, a term which has become a synonym for 'separatism'.

Multiculturalism in a Global World vs Secularization in 'Old' National Identities

Secularization implies not only the limitation of religion to one specific sphere of social reality and the decline of religious practice, but also the possible transformation of some religious symbols and celebrations into secular festivals or patrimonial signs. These secularization processes are now questioned by *globalization* and by the *rise of a political radical Islam.*

With globalization, Western societies develop tight relations with non-secularized societies, from where immigrants may either partake in the secularization process of their new national frame (this seems to be the case for the majority of them), or not. Thus, secularized symbols like the Christmas tree, for example, might be now contested as 'non-neutral' and related to their Christian background, as it is the case in several Western countries (France, Italy, England, United States, etc.). In response, public opinion may reconsider this symbol either as part of a common collective identity – and defend its use – or as the survival of a religious sign which must be removed in order not to offend the newcomers – this has been done, for example, by turning 'Merry Christmas' wishes into 'Happy Holidays'.

Thus, 'religious' signs may be used by Western societies as part of their cultural background, defining a more or less open national identity (as well as on the local or the European level), and thus including or conflicting the immigrants' cultures. This possibility of conflict may be in turn exploited by political radical Islam, specially (but not only) when the integration of Muslim immigrants is difficult or even fails (because of discrimination, economic crisis, or the weakened integration capacities of the state). Confronting this proposed alternate Muslim transnational identity, the debate on 'religious symbols' has turned into a debate on 'national identity'. *Global religious identities have become a possible competing frame to that of the national states.*

In a global world, multiculturalism destabilizes 'old' national identities. It questions the supposed neutrality of the modern liberal states which were built up in the Western world – especially in France where the political model of a nation built up on civic bounds 'covered' the social reality of a cultural Catholic majority. Thus, if we pretend to preserve the existence of a national frame, how can we elaborate new cultural 'compromises' in the context of a conflicted global world? How can democracies continue to maintain and manage their existing pluralism – which includes the right of every individual to exit from his primary group – against extremists' attacks and radical identities?

References

Albert-Cohen, P. 1977. *The Modernization of French Jewry: Consistory and Community in the Nineteenth-century*. Waltham, MA: Brandeis University Press.

Basdevant-Gaudemet, B. 1996. Le Statut juridique de l'islam en France. *Revue de Droit Public*, 2-1996, 355–85.

Baubérot, J. 2000. *Histoire de la laïcité en France*. Paris: PUF.

Berkovitz, J.R. 1989. *The Shaping of Jewish Identity in Nineteenth-Century France*. Detroit, Wayne University Press.

Birnbaum, P. 1992. *Les Fous de la République. Histoire politique des Juifs d'Etat, de Gambetta à Vichy*. Paris: Fayard.

Brouard, S. and V Tiberj. 2006. *Français comme les autres ? Enquête sur les citoyens d'origine maghrébine, africaine et turque*. Paris: Presses de Sciences Po.

Charbit, D. 2005. Déclinaisons du franco-judaïsme. In *Les Cultures des Juifs. Une nouvelle histoire*, edited by David Biale. Paris: Editions de l'Eclat, 1003–42.

Chaumont, J-M. 1997. *La Concurrence des victimes: génocide, identité, reconnaissance*. Paris: La Découverte.

Cohen, M. 1993. Les Juifs de France. Affirmations identitaires et évolution du modèle d'intégration. *Le Débat*, 75(mai–août), 101–15.

— 2000. Les Juifs de France. Modernité et identité. Vingtième Siècle. *Revue d'Histoire*, 66(avril–juin), 91–106.

Commission Stasi. 2003. *Commission de Réflexion sur l'Application du Principe de Laïcité dans la République*. Rapport au Président de la République, 11 Décembre 2003. Available at: <http://www.ladocumentationfrancaise.fr/rapports-publics/034000725/index.shtml> [accessed 22 October 2008].

Ghiles-Meilhac, S. 2007. La politique étrangère du Conseil Représentatif des Institutions Juives de France, la communauté juive organisée: une force diplomatique? Mémoire de Master 2 d'Histoire, l'École des hautes études en sciences sociales.

Graetz, M. 1996. *The Jews in Nineteenth-Century France: From the French Revolution to the Alliance Israelite Universelle*. Stanford: Stanford University Press.

Hermon-Belot, R. 1999. *L'émancipation des juifs en France*. Paris: PUF.

Hyman, P. 1998. *The Jews of Modern France*. Berkeley: University of California Press.

Laurence, J. and J. Vaïsse. 2007. *Intégrer l'Islam. La France et ses musulmans: enjeux et réussites*. Paris: Odile Jacob.

Machelon Report. 2006. *Commission de réflexion juridique sur les relations des cultes avec les pouvoirs publics*. Paris: Ministère de l'Intérieur. Available at <http://www.islamlaicite.org/IMG/pdf/Rapport_machelon_20_septembre-2.pdf> [accessed 22 October 2008].

Malinovich, N. 2008. *French and Jewish. Culture and the Politics of Identity in Early Twentieth Century France.* Oxford-Portland: Littman Library of Jewish Civilization.

Mayer, N. 2005. Les opinions antisémites en France après la Seconde Intifada. *Revue internationale et stratégique*, 58(été), 143–50.

Messner, F. 1993. Laïcité imaginée, laïcité juridique. Les évolutions du régime des cultes en France. *Le Débat*, 77(nov–déc), 88–94.

Stora, B. 2006. *Les trois exils des Juifs d'Algérie*. Paris: Stock.

Taguieff, P-A. 2002. *La nouvelle judéophobie*. Paris: Fayard-Mille et Une Nuits.

Weil, P. 2004. *Qu'est-ce qu'un Français?* Paris: Grasset, Folio-Histoire.

Wieviorka, Michel. 2005. *La Tentation antisémite. Haine des Juifs dans la France d'aujourd'hui*. Paris: Robert Laffont.

Chapter 13

L'affaire du foulard in the Shadow of the Strasbourg Court: Article 9 and the Public Career of the Veil in France

Claire de Galembert

Introduction

This chapter deals with the role that Article 9 of the European Convention for the Protection of Human Rights (ECHR) has played in the French *affaire du foulard*, the 'headscarf affair'.[1] This is part of a larger research project concerning what I call the 'public career of the Islamic veil in France'. By using the term 'public career', I refer both to the process through which the Islamic veil has become a public issue and to the successive developments of this issue from 1989 until 2004 (Galembert 2007, 2008). Although this story was clearly about politics, it immediately turned out to be about law, too. Indeed, in the autumn of 1989, barely a month after it began, the so-called *affaire du foulard* was brought before the Conseil d'État, the highest administrative court in France, by the Minister of National Education asking for a legal opinion on the issue.[2] Since then, law and politics have remained intertwined as this enduring and sometimes heated controversy has unfolded. A famous result was the adoption in March 2004 of a law banning from state schools signs or clothing by which pupils overtly manifest a religious affiliation,[3] a law that led de facto to the prohibition of headscarves. Any sociological account of the public career of the Islamic headscarf in France

1 The French word *foulard* refers to what is usually called the *hijab* or headscarf. Although the term *voile* (veil) is often used in France it is generally applied to the headscarf, and not the *niqab* or other head/face covering.

2 The Conseil d'État is both the supreme administrative court and a legal council of the executive branch. In this second role the Conseil d'État can be officially consulted (as has been the case with the veil) by the government on a specific issue. Moreover bills proposed before the legislature and decrees promulgated by the executive branch must be submitted to the *Conseil* so that it can recommend changes.

3 *Loi n°2004-228 du 15 mars 2004 encadrant, en application du principe de laïcité, le port de signes ou de tenues manifestant une appartenance religieuse dans les écoles, collèges et lycées publics* (2004). Available at <http://legifrance.gouv.fr/affichTexte.do?cidTexte=JORFTEXT000000417977> [accessed 27 November 2008]. It stipulates: 'In public schools, the wearing of symbols or clothing by which pupils conspicuously (*ostensiblement*)

would therefore be deemed incomplete if it focused only on the politics of the veil without emphasizing the extent to which these politics had been 'legalized'.

International and European law has also played a very prominent role in the public career of the veil in France. Stating as a general rule that 'everyone has the right to freedom of thought, conscience and religion' and setting the conditions under which national restrictions to this right may be permitted,[4] Art. 9 ECHR, in particular, eventually became a kind of unexpected 'hero' in a national debate that unfolded in the shadow of the Court of Strasbourg. Such a national public debate framed by European law is a fascinating instance of legal 'constitutionalization' and 'internationalization'. The intrusion of international law into a very specific domain, *laïcité*, a domain constitutive of French political culture and history, as the difficulty in translating the term amply demonstrates, reveals a new feature of the power of the judicial branch over the political activity. There is no doubt that the importance of Art. 9 in the career of the Islamic veil in France resulted from the confluence of the Europeanization of national law and the ever-increasing relevance of human rights within positive law. With regard to the absence of a clear-cut distinction between municipal and international law, between international norms binding states and international rights with which individuals are endowed, *l'affaire du foulard* appears to have occurred in the larger context of the 'cosmopolitanization' of law. However, it is one thing to notice this cosmopolitanization, it is quite another to delve into the concrete process *in progress*. In this respect, examining how the dispute about Art. 9 interfered with the dispute about the veil in France is relevant.

The role of Art. 9 in the public career of the veil in France has been not only very prominent, but also intensely discussed. Indeed, almost as soon as *l'affaire du foulard* became a topic of legal discussion, the meaning of Art. 9 became a crucially contested issue. From its departure from the legal limbo marking the government's request for a legal opinion from the Conseil d'État in November 1989, in the midst of the *affaire du voile*, to the debates relating to the law of 15 March 2004, which sought to prohibit the veil, different actors have not ceased discussing the meaning of Art. 9. This legal norm has been invoked by legal professionals, militant secularists and feminists, Islamic activists, veiled

manifest a religious belonging is forbidden. Internal regulations state that the initiation of disciplinary proceeding must be preceded by a dialogue with the pupil.'

4 'Everyone has the right to freedom of thought, conscience and religion; this right includes freedom to change one's religion or belief and freedom, either alone or in community with others and in public or private, to demonstrate one's religion or belief, in worship, teaching, practice, and observance. Freedom to manifest one's religion or beliefs shall be subject only to such limitations as are prescribed by law and are necessary in a democratic society in the interests of public safety, for the protection of public order, health or morals, or for the protection of the rights and freedoms of others.' Available at <http://www.echr.coe.int/NR/rdonlyres/D5CC24A7-DC13-4318-B457-5C9014916D7A/0/EnglishAnglais.pdf> [accessed 27 November 2008].

girls, school administrations, administrative judges, journalists, intellectuals and scholars either as an argument in favour of allowing the wearing of the veil at school or of prohibiting it. These controversies involve complex configurations of technical, ideological and strategic considerations, of individual destinies, of social movements, collective entities (the Republic, the French Nation, the Muslim Community, women), and diverse and sometimes rival institutions and causes (Islam, the veil, the republican integration model, *laïcité* and sexual equality). If for the militants this is about making Art. 9 speak for their cause, these attempts to instrumentalize law do not clash any less with the doubts shared by a number of actors (including legal professionals) over what authorizes or prohibits Art. 9 and what its authorized interpreters, particularly the judges in Strasbourg, may make it say. The intersecting careers of the veil and Art. 9 are in this respect characteristic of the incertitude that has long surrounded the normative impact of a text written in 1950, which crystallized strong tensions between different European political-religious traditions (Gonzalès 1994: 8).

The interest in studying these controversies lies in the way they highlight the shaky path of the law. Although it looked like an ally of the veil, in the sense that it seemed to impede the legislature bent on prohibiting it, Art. 9 eventually became one of the legal justifications for the law of 15 March 2004. But these controversies also show how, at a given moment, the actors succeed in determining the meaning of a legal norm. The elaboration of a national understanding of the meaning of Art. 9 offers thus a privileged opportunity to examine a process of 'domestication' of European law in the sense that the national actors, in particular the legislature,[5] reaffirm their autonomy in creating and interpreting the law. Analysing how doubts are raised about what this norm 'says' permits us to understand the process according to which the law, whatever its contingencies, affirms at any given moment its resistance to things and to actors: the 'objectivation of the law' (Latour 2002).

The approach in terms of 'career' which orders the articulation of what follows in this article, responds to the concern for observing the dynamic evolution of the interpretation of a legal norm, relating this interpretation to the activity of various actors, not only legal professionals who participate in its production. In order to follow the transformation of Art. 9's meaning through the manner in which the actors appropriate and discuss this legal norm and the 'tests' to which it is subjected, I will distinguish three principal sequences. First, how the veil and Art. 9 linked their destinies after the Conseil d'État's opinion was delivered in November 1989. In this legalization of the controversy a new playing field emerges and there is incertitude surrounding the normative reach of Art. 9. Secondly, the sequence of 'judiciarization' during which, Art. 9 seems to have been transformed into an ally of veiled girls to the point of being presented as an obstacle to a law prohibiting the headscarf at school advocated by supporters of *laïcité* and women's rights. The

5 I follow Bourdieu (1986: 17) in treating the legislature not in a strictly institutional perspective, but as an ensemble of agents.

third sequence highlights the 'domestication' of Art. 9 by the legislature and the locking in of a new interpretation that transforms it as a legal weapon against the veil in state schools.

Legalization of the Islamic Veil Affair and Birth of the Controversy Concerning Art. 9

The legalization of the *affaire du voile* occurred only weeks after the affair surfaced in October 1989. It shifted the problem to a new discursive space that reconfigured, in part, the meaning and the stakes at issue. In analysing the manner in which the government, Islamic organizations and jurists begin to explore, invest in and appropriate this new context of meaning, I will show how they reshape it.

Opening of a New Space of Judgment and International Law Arrives on Stage

There is no reason to recapitulate why three veiled girls were expelled from a middle school [*collège*] in Creil, north of Paris, in October 1989, nor why this situation, led to the first '*affaire du voile*' (Kepel 1994, Khosrokhavar and Gaspard 1995, Bowen 2006). For our purposes, it is sufficient to recall that the legal translation of the question resulted from the Minister of National Education's initiative. Indeed the legalization of *l'affaire du foulard* resulted not so much from the mobilization of social actors as from a governmental strategy to deal with the political crisis which it caused. The government itself, in asking the Conseil d'État to render a legal opinion as to whether or not the wearing of religious symbols is compatible with the principle of *laïcité*, provoked this legalization. Placed in difficulty by the virulence of a debate that divided the government as well as the political parties and social movements, the minister tried to regain control of the controversy by addressing the Conseil d'État, an official request for a legal opinion regarding the 'compatibility of wearing symbols demonstrating adherence to a religious community in public teaching with the principle of laïcité' (Rivéro 1990: 1). The debate pitted people like Michel Rocard (the prime minister) and Lionel Jospin (the Minister of National Education), who thought that veiled girls should be persuaded to remove their headscarves rather than be expelled, against those who were convinced that the toleration of Islamic scarves at school represented an unacceptable act of treason against the republican tradition.

Shifting the debate from the political to the legal arena, the Minister of National Education was not so much asking for a legal opinion about what was permissible or not, as attempting to gain legal justification for the political approach he had chosen to deal with the veil issue (Jospin 1990: 15). In other words, his goal was to restore his contested political legitimacy by providing proof that his policy was fully compliant with the principle of *laïcité*. As Jospin declared, 'this procedure will allow us, above passions and polemics, to guarantee, through dialogue and in conformity with fundamental principles as they are recognized by the Republic that the school's *laïcité* is fully respected, in conformity with the national tradition' (*Le Monde*, 6 November 1989). In this context of political crisis, referring to legality, in particular to the *État de droit*, became a political resource to oppose legal arguments by those who denounced his policy in the name of the republican tradition. The reference to the *État de droit*, which has been increasingly evoked in French political rhetoric since the 1980s (Chevallier 1999, Agrikoliansky 2005), opened a new space. It enabled the redesignation of the veil issue as a matter of civil rights, and specifically of freedom of conscience and of religion, a dimension till then largely absent from the controversy. As a result, the Conseil d'État was made the ultimate interpreter of the essence of the principle of *laïcité*, which nobody questioned in 1989.

Giving unusual publicity to the consultative procedure of the Conseil d'État, which can play the role not only of governmental advisor but also of legal censor, the government was showing itself bound by legality. Although it had chosen to pose the question in legal terms the government, by addressing itself to the Conseil d'État instead of to the legislature, assumed that the solution of the veil issue was in legal interpretation rather than law creation. It attempted to reduce the scope of the discussion, and temporarily it succeeded in doing so. Indeed, as the legal translation of the veil issue occurred far from the public gaze (the Conseil d'État deliberated in secret in its chambers at the Palais-Royal), the object of discord was provisionally removed from the clash of values and principles. This alliance with the Conseil d'État reduced the government's dependency on public opinion and on the political class, both of which were momentarily excluded from the decision-making process.

The request to the Conseil d'État for a legal opinion was formulated in terms of three issues (McGoldrick's translation 2006: 69): 'Was the wearing of religious symbols compatible with the principle of *laïcité*? If so, under what conditions was regulation of such wearing permissible? Could refusal to follow such regulations result in the expulsion of the offending student from the school?' These questions helped to reduce and (partly) recast the scope of the terms of the discussion. Considering the veil as a sign of religious community affiliation excluded from the start any other interpretation such as one based on gender. This generated an important shift, posing the issue in terms of liberty rather than gender equality.

In its opinion, rendered on 27 November 1989, the Conseil d'État stated that wearing religious garb in a school 'is not in itself incompatible with the principle of *laïcité*' but must not 'constitute an act of pressure, provocation, proselytism, or propaganda'. It continues:

> It results from the constitutional and legislative texts and from France's international engagements cited above (the visas) that the principle of *laïcité* in public education, which is one of the elements of the *laïcité* of the state and of the neutrality of all public services, requires that education be dispensed with respect, on one hand, for this neutrality by the programs and teachers and, on the other hand, for the students' liberty of conscience. This freedom on the students'

> part includes the right to express and to manifest their religious beliefs inside educational establishments, (so long as such expression is done) with respect for pluralism and for the freedom of others, and without detracting from the (school's) educational activities (and) the content of (its) programs.[6]

Thus although none of the texts quoted by the Conseil d'État went as far as the Conseil did in positing that the school had an obligation to respect the expression of the religious freedom of the students, the opinion did not allow for unconditional protection for the wearing of headscarves. Their ban from the schools (1989–2004) was legally permissible if headscarf-wearing threatened public order or endangered a student's safety.

The opinion did more than justify Jospin's policy against exclusion of veiled schoolgirls. In the wake of this legal translation of the veil question, a new way of resolving problems emerged in which the Conseil d'État played the role of ultimate arbiter in cases involving a school administration and veiled girls. Moreover, the opinion recast the interpretative framework in which the veil had until then been considered. Previously, wearing the veil was principally considered a symbol of political-religious extremism, an infringement on school secularism or alienation of women; wearing the veil at school was widely seen as a deviant practice. With the legal opinion, the veil qualified as a religious symbol was blessed with the grace of the law (Bourdieu 1986). As a corollary, veiled teenagers, previously almost exclusively regarded as submissive to the fathers', brothers' or the Islamic community's dictates, suddenly became entitled to rights as 'subject of law'. Girls even became entitled to *international* rights since they might expect not only national but international judges (the Court of Strasbourg) to protect them. This redesignation certainly did not neutralize the pejorative views of the veil, but it softened their impact by calling into question the justifications upon which the republican and feminist condemnations of the veil rested.

Henceforth, then, wearing the headscarf was no longer a matter of tolerance, but stemmed from a law with which the school administration must reckon and which the state is obliged to protect. The legal translation redesignating the veil as a religious symbol, thereby associating it with the freedom of conscience and inscribing it in the protected and valourized domain of human rights, had the effect of transforming the dominant discursive opportunity structure. While imposing new constraints on the school administration, the legalization of the veil issue offered support to those who, in the name of the Muslim community, a new faceless collective entity that established itself in the public scene in the 1980s, call for mobilization in favour of the veil and those who wear it (Galembert 2009).

6 Translated by Beller (2004: 611); French version in Rivéro 1990.

Pro-veil Legal Mobilization in its Infancy

Associating the veil with freedom of conscience tended to reinforce the credibility of new Islamic organizations that denounced the exclusionary measures pronounced against veiled girls as a new injustice against Islam. These organizations, which contested the legitimacy of the Mosque of Paris as the historical representative of Islam in France, did not await the filing of the case with the Conseil d'État before using legal weapons to defend the expelled veiled girls. In the work of representing the Muslims of France, the law became a new resource. Indeed, in their race to represent the Muslim organizations used the mobilization of the law to distinguish themselves from others such as the Voice of Islam, who, it was believed, stigmatized Islam and undermined its respectability. The National Federation of French Muslims (Fédération Nationale des Musulmans de France, or FNMF), for example, brought a criminal case for racial discrimination against the school principal, Ernest Chénière, and entrusted the case to Jacques Vergès, a controversial star of the French bar.

Yet the entrance of the Conseil d'État contributed to a change of scale and resulted in an 'increase in generality' of the veil's cause (Boltanski 1984). Bringing the case to the Conseil d'État offered a new resource for the constitution of a pro-veil cause. In the eyes of everyone it was a case about justice and religious freedom. Assuming centre stage, the FNMF sent the Conseil d'État a quasi-memorandum[7] before it pronounced its legal opinion, a gesture it publicized through the media. Similarly, the day after the opinion, the defenders of the young veiled girls publicly saluted the accomplishment of a 'duty of republican justice … the first act of justice rendered in favour of the Muslim community [by] a voice of the state apparatus, founded on laws, effected in complete neutrality' or 'the concretization of the traditions, of welcoming reception, of tolerance and of liberty that constitute the grandeur of France' (in *Le Monde*, 29 November 1989). It was no longer in the name of the Muslim community but in the name of the rule of law, the Republic, that these new spokespeople could henceforth justify their cause. At the same time, by offering new venues for bringing cases to court, e.g. legal recourse against the state's abuse of power, the Conseil d'État's opinion carried in embryonic form a redefinition of the identities of the conflicting parties. The shift from judicial courts to administrative courts[8] implied a transformation of the impact of the conflict and of the parties' status: the issue is no longer about sanctioning individuals (the fathers of the Creil girls subpoenaed a principal for racist speech) but about protection from the state bureaucracy's excesses.

---

7 Letter of the FNMF to members of the Council of State apropos the headscarf affair in Creil, November 1989, signed by Dr Abdallah-Thomas Milcent. P.O. the administrative council of the FNMF, nine pages. Unpublished document.

8 This differentiation between administrative courts and civil courts reflects the particularity of the French judicial system which is marked by a dichotomy separating administrative from judicial judges.

With the Conseil d'État's presentation of its opinion to the government at the end of November 1989, the ECHR, one of four international conventions referred to in the text, appeared on stage. It is impossible to ascertain if these international texts dictated the liberal position of the Conseil d'État. One can observe, however, that those international conventions are mentioned to justify the Republic's obligation to guarantee religious non-discrimination, and to protect freedom of thought, conscience, religion and the public demonstration of one's religion. Upstream from the transmittal of the case to the Conseil d'État, not a single actor implicated in the debate seemed to have anticipated that international law could have a say on the question: neither the minister in the formulation of his request to the Conseil d'État, nor in his official declaration justifying his way of dealing with the issue,[9] nor the journalists from the national newspapers following the affair,[10] nor the FNMF in its pre-opinion letter to the Conseil d'État, nor even an eminent constitutional scholar, François Goguel, interviewed by *Le Figaro* (8 November 1989).

From the Veil Controversy to the Emergence of the Controversy over Art. 9

If at this stage the social and political actors who began to populate the new playing field produced by the legalization of the veil affair paid no attention to the resources and constraints of incorporating international norms in French law, these norms were immediately at the heart of the debate among scholars specialized in public law. The attention to the ECHR and the Strasbourg Court brought forward a new protagonist heretofore ignored by everyone. The first commentaries on the Conseil d'État's opinion, published in a specialized journal of administrative law (Rivéro 1990, Durand-Prinborgne 1990, Costa 1990), point out the new stakes introduced by the entrance of the ECHR. The professional position and trajectories of the authors of these first commentaries made them distinctively authorized interpreters of the legal opinion, although there are disagreements between the commentators which are not simply the product of a national competition for 'the law's monopoly to speak the law' (Bourdieu 1986: 4), but also the result of the vagueness of the national and European judges' relative positions on a question newly affected by the Europeanization of law: *laïcité*.

The positions they took, and trajectories they followed, were not unrelated to their different conceptions and interpretations of *laïcité*. Jean Rivéro (1910–2001), professor emeritus of public law, was the author of the only book treating different

9 In Lionel Jospin's communiqué relating to the case submitted to the Council of State: 'this procedure must guarantee by dialogue and by application of the Fundamental Principles recognized by the laws of the Republic that the public school's laïcité is clearly respected in accordance with the tradition of the nation', in *Le Monde*, 6 November 1989.

10 See notably the articles in *Le Monde* (7 November 1989), *Le Figaro* (8 November), and *Libération* (7 November) engaging in a mapping of legal texts susceptible of orienting the work of the Conseil d'État.

legal aspects of *laïcité* available at that time (Rivéro 1960). He was not only a renowned specialist of public law but also a reputed defender of public liberties and of the memory of René Cassin. According to him, the opinion about the veil confers 'an incontestable legal basis to a [liberal] tradition (of *laïcité*) that dates from the origins of the secularization of public education and [it] has not ceased to be corroborated ever since' (Rivéro 1990: 6). Younger in age, Claude Durand-Prinborgne (b. 1928) and Jean-Paul Costa (b. 1941) position themselves less as scholars than as practitioners of school administration. Professor of public law at the University of Paris I, the former has several times been rector and was general director at the Ministry of National Education (1984–6). Certainly he anticipates the resistance in the educational world to the legal position of the Conseil d'État allowing the wearing of headscarves, and he wonders whether 'the act of admitting the expression of religious convictions in school milieu ... at the end of this bicentennial year [represents] an infidelity to 1789 or an enrichment of its message' (Durand-Prinborgne 1990: 20). Yet for him the Conseil d'État 's position is nothing but the result of a rigorous legal analysis dictated by the state of the law. The judges would have been only the voice and not the authors of the law.

Jean-Paul Costa's position is quite different. Currently a member of the Conseil d'État, Costa was from 1981 to 1984 the *chef de cabinet* for Alain Savary, Minister of National Education, when Mauroy's socialist government project to create a unified and secularized teaching system failed because of the resistance of the Catholic church. In his commentary on the legal opinion, Costa does not hide his disappointment nor his attachment to the idea of religious neutrality in schools. He does not wonder whether the Conseil d'État's position is justified or not; he challenges it. Indeed, in his commentary, which looks like a dissenting opinion, he argues that the Conseil d'État possessed some leeway in asserting a stricter conception of *laïcité*. Thus, he suggests that the opinion was typical for the historical political function as 'pacifier of *laïcité*' traditionally attributed to the Conseil d'État (Costa 1990).

The critique led him to interpret the legal impact of the international norms, particularly of the ECHR, differently from Rivéro and Durand-Prinborgne. For them, these norms imposed the recognition of a law to exteriorize religious convictions, even in schools. For Rivéro, there is no doubt that 'if an expelled veiled girl brought her case before the judicial authorities of Strasbourg [then] they could hardly have avoided censuring her expulsion' (Rivéro 1990: 5). Having had the opportunity to examine the report that contributed to the writing of the Conseil d'État's opinion, Costa confirms the role played by international texts and the 'particular pressure' exerted by Art. 9. There he even sees the reflection of a 'less French' inclination of the Conseil d'État hitherto renowned for its 'legal nationalism'; recent rulings would, according to him, attest to this evolution (Costa 1990: 44). Yet he definitely rejects the idea that the ECHR would force French *laïcité* to allow the wearing of scarves at school. 'The national law [can] impose neutrality ... without disregarding Art. 9', he writes (ibid.) .Of the three authors he is the only one who explicitly refers to the Strasbourg case law. Doing this, Costa sets out to reverse what seemed to Rivéro and Durand-Prinborgne to be evident, and he insists that Art. 9 recognizes 'the right of restraint (of freedom of thought and of religion) in order to protect others' rights and freedoms' (ibid.).

The critique made by this future judge (1998), vice president (2001–2006) and president of the Strasbourg Court (2007) found an echo in the articles of Jean-François Flauss (1992, 1993), one of the earliest French public law professors to specialize in European human rights law. According to him there is no alternative but to support Costa's point of view that the national law would have permitted the prohibition of headscarf-wearing. Flauss voices loudly what is more or less implicit in Costa's article: the interpretation of the Conseil d'État was not constrained by positive law, be it municipal or international, and its interpretation was actually constructive in causing to prevail a liberal conception of *laïcité* that overturned the republican tradition (Flauss 1993). As he puts it: 'It would be hard to find any decision rendered by the European Court or even by any of the ECHR States parties' national Courts in support of the Conseil d'État's interpretation of Art. 9' (Flauss 1992 : 21).

In his opinion, such an interpretation illustrates the 'methodological pitfalls that accompany the internationalization and Europeanization (of) domestic law' (ibid.). Breaking with a 'nationalist' legal tradition, both law professors and judges would, according to Flauss, now be tempted by a 'loose interpretation of international norms, one sometimes made easier by the lack of genuine international pronouncements or more often by the (conscious) ignorance of the genuine international interpretation' (ibid.). According to him, the legal opinion of the Conseil d'État exemplifies the 'perverse usage ... of the international rule's superiority to make the domestic law evolve in a direction neither required nor implied by the treaty' (ibid.).

Although European human rights law tends to assert itself as a new specialization, the dearth of knowledge in this new legal hinterland, as well as the jurisprudential lacuna of the Strasbourg Court dealing with the interpretation of the convention's religious articles (Gonzalès 1994), as was still the case in 1989, complicates the determination of Art. 9's impact.[11] The disagreements over the impact of Art. 9 do not reveal a simple doctrinal controversy; instead, they expose more general uncertainties regarding the new economy of powers emerging around the mounting intensity in the 1980s of a new supranational legal centre, the European Court of Human Rights.

During this sequence of legalization of the veil affair, a new playing field opened up and actors began to explore it. There were, nonetheless, several sources of uncertainty. For sure, the government, in November 1989, temporarily succeeded in exiting from the political impasse by referring to the Conseil d'État's

11 The books on the ECHR are rare and out-of-date. The two references in the *Bibliographie de la langue française* date to 1964 (Lanarès 1964, Vasak 1964). Quite remarkably, one of the first articles on the religious dispositions of the ECHR is based largely upon transnational sources (Goy 1991).

version of the law and in depoliticizing the *affaire du foulard*. Yet the progression of events depended on the manner in which the protagonists, the schools and their administration and the Muslims and their spokespersons appropriated this new legal opportunity structure. This means that the analysis must pay attention not only to the manner in which the actors adjust to the new rules of the game (Lascoumes and Serverin 1986), but also to what they make the rules do and say. In this indecisive context Art. 9, because of its supra-legal status and its undetermined interpretation, constitutes a particularly favourable terrain for lawyerly quarrels and for battles between actors and causes opposed to or supporting the veil.

Judiciarization of the Veil Affair and Transformation of Art. 9 into Headscarf Ally

It is time now to consider how Art. 9 has been used by litigants and interpreted by administrative judges and how those protagonists have contributed to the construction of its meaning. Whereas Art. 9 was an object of scholarly speculation, it also became a legal outlet for the pro-veil Islamic actors in the court room. In this sequence of judiciarization, while the legal impact of Art. 9 has been neutralized by the administrative jurisdictions, it nevertheless becomes the object of polemics and criticism outside of the legal arena.

The Uncertain Enlistment of Art. 9 in the Pro-veil Legal Mobilization

Transformed into a legal justification for the girls' claims in the litigation with the school administration, Art. 9 became one of the vehicles allowing the problem of the veil to pass through the doors of the administrative jurisdictions. From the first appeal (*Antar* case 1990), the article effectively figures alongside other French legal norms used to attack the decision to expel the veiled girl. The growing body of cases brought before the administrative tribunals reveals constant references to the ECHR from 1990 to 2005.

Essentially concentrated in Strasbourg, Lille and the Paris region, the geography of the tectonic 'plates of litigation' confirms that the progression of litigation is certainly not foreign to the legal mobilization orchestrated by the defenders of the veil. Dr 'Abdallah' Thomas Milcent, a physician who converted to Islam, spearheaded this mobilization. The author of the quasi-memorandum addressed to the Conseil d'État on behalf of the FNMF in November 1989, in which legal arguments in favour of the right to wear the headscarf at school were presented, he also wrote an evocatively titled book: *Le foulard islamique et la République Française: mode d'emploi* (1994). It was published shortly after François Bayrou (Minister of Education 1994–7) attempted to ban veiled girls from state schools. In a circular (Bayrou 1994), which contradicts the case-by-case approach proposed by the legal framework implied in the Conseil d'État's opinion, Bayrou wrote that every ostentatious religious symbol should be forbidden in schools. As a result, several hundred veiled girls were expelled and increasing numbers of controversial cases taken to the courts.

Milcent's book sets out not only to convince its readers of the religious obligation to wear the headscarf, but also to persuade young women and 'the Muslim community' to make litigation a weapon against what he considers the State's abuse of power.[12] In his advice on legal strategy, Milcent (known as 'Dr Abdallah') does not fail to cite Art. 9. He especially insists on the importance of this legal text, thanks to which, he writes, 'the inhabitants of signatory countries possess a veritable tribunal, the European Court of Human Rights, which can eventually sanction the governments that do not respect the convention' (Milcent 1994: 85). While indications about the functioning of the Strasbourg Court and the modalities of introducing a petition are provided, they are relatively abstract and the Strasbourg case law is neither evoked nor receives any comment.

The success of this judicial pro-veil mobilization remains precarious, limited by the unfavourable position of the potential litigators, the majority of whom were of immigrant background, at least at the end of the 1980s and the beginning of the1990s. The Islamic associations' inadequate legal and organizational competences, a lack of familiarity with the political culture of a country that remains for them predominantly foreign, and the intensity of the public disapproval of the veil at school, combine to predispose the concerned populations to forced loyalty rather than to contesting decisions of a school administration unfavourable to the wearing of the veil. Thus, while David grabs hold of the sling, Art. 9, the doubts concerning the effectiveness of this weapon still persist. Dr Abdallah's comments attest to this. Fearing a 'verdict armed with the law' (Bourdieu 1986: 4) unfavourable to the veil and without appeal, he refused to move up the European hierarchy of proceedings:

> I have always been opposed to the utilization of the ECHR. Why? It's an important question. The case arose in 1997. It was an affair in a suburb of Nancy in which we had obtained a lot of money in appeal and we had been dismissed by the Conseil d'État. Naturally, we had six months to appeal before the ECHR and I made an appeal in this sense to the Islamic associations. Do we do it or not? To do it requires considerable means in terms of money and lawyers. In six months one must make operational sufficient legal means. One has to play it American style. I mean, when you want to play, you pull out all of the stops because when

12 The book, which is distributed by Muslim organizations such as the *Union des Organisations Islamiques de France* (UOIF) and is accessible on the Internet, also indicates legal norms that are supposed to guarantee the right to wear the headscarf at school, practical advice on the procedure and manner to construct a relevant dossier, how best to manage relations with the school administration, the media and the close entourage, and how to avoid providing an outlet for all interpretations that anti-veil adversaries could put to legal use against the veil (propaganda, making a public disturbance, proselytizing, truancy, etc.).

> you appear before a court, you must know that court's jurisprudence by heart. We are no longer before the Conseil d'État; we are dealing with the ECHR's case-law: this requires an enormous investment legally speaking. This raises extremely complex questions. We don't need one lawyer, we need ten! It's the leader and when one is the leader, you watch your step. Thus, I ask this question: must one go or not? Secondly, I plead that one cannot. How come suddenly Dr Abdallah, who was such a scrapper [*castagneur*] before the Conseil d'État, doesn't want to go? Simply because a decision by the ECHR sets the precedent for all the countries that come within its field of jurisdiction. So if you obtain a negative decision, it concerns all the Muslims of Europe ... This legal position established the legal status quo that scarf-wearing at schools was legally acceptable. Then the stakes are considerable and in this sort the case is not meaningful enough.[13]

The social isolation of orchestrators of the legal mobilization doubles the entry costs in the European judicial arena. They fail to create alliances with potential supporters such as the anti-racist or human rights associations (*Ligue des Droits de l'Homme*, *Mouvement contre le Racisme et l'Amitié entre les Peuples*, and SOS-Racisme), which, without supporting the cause of the veil, protested against the exclusion of veiled girls. Organizations that could have brought them legal expertise and symbolic credit remain deeply divided on the question of the headscarf and deaf to the solicitations of religious actors with corrosive reputations.

The Domestication of Art. 9 by the Administrative Judge

Systematically transformed into a legal argument in the cases brought before the French administrative courts, the enlistment of Art. 9 for the veil's cause was submitted to examination by the administrative judges. We do not have access to case files, to the hearings or to the final deliberations since they are protected by judicial secrecy. The only data available are the conclusions of the *Commissaire du gouvernement*, a member of the Conseil d'État, assigned to give an independent opinion on each case, in order to highlight the issues and to help the judges to reach their decision. These conclusions[14] act as a hinge; they clarify the exegesis of the judgment, echo the condition of the legal scholarship *ad intra*, and provide indications about the legal reasoning *ad extra*. In the discussions about Art. 9, there is a 'jurisdictional claim' with regard to the university, and especially the specialists of what became a new domain of expertise in the 1990s.[15] Clearly,

13 Interview, May 2005. Full text available in Galembert 2008: 183–98.

14 Although the *Commissaire du gouvernement*'s conclusions are not systematically published, they are generally published when associated with decisions marking a milestone in administrative law.

15 In this respect, the trajectory of Jean-François Flauss is exemplary. Then professor in Strasbourg, he offered the first assessment of the international sources of French law vis-à-

the *Commissaire du gouvernement* has become an 'essential cog of the "judges dialogue"' (Genevois 2005: 103–104) in a context where it is vital to position oneself in regard to the Strasbourg Court. The domestication of Art. 9 implies discussion of the case law of the Strasbourg Court. For the judges dealing with cases involving veiled girls, the web of precedents thus not only encompasses a Franco-French war about *laïcité*; but as a result of the European judiciarization also crosses national borders, and puts the veil case in the context of rulings in the heterogeneous political and legal traditions of the forty member states of the Convention.

The first case, the *Kherouaa* case, was brought before the Conseil d'État in November 1992. The Conseil quashed the decision of the administrative court of first instance that had confirmed the legality of the expulsion of the veiled schoolgirls. It was an important moment in the legal history of the Islamic veil in France, because for the first time the Conseil had the opportunity to implement its legal opinion, which until then had simply been a legal advisory opinion providing a 'virtual', but non-binding, legal framework. This decision was a very important step in the consolidation of the legal meaning of the opinion, in restricting the range of the legal possibilities, and in thus creating a path of dependency for future cases. It firmly stated as a general rule that wearing a headscarf at school could not be regarded as a violation of the principle of *laïcité* per se, but, on the contrary, it amounted to the exercise of a freedom protected by the law. Moreover, it appeared to confirm the 'liberalism' of the opinion, although the directives derived from it and sent by Jospin to school principals had interpreted the text in a stricter direction.

What role did Art. 9 play in this first judgment? In the laconic text of the judgment the article seemingly played an insignificant role in the construction of the legal argumentation that led to the order to reinstate the expelled girls. In fact, Art. 9 is not even explicitly mentioned; there are only references to 'international conventions' as a whole. The decision derives more from national law (in particular Article 10 of the *Déclaration des Droits de l'Homme et du citoyen*, Article 2 of the 1958 French Constitution and Article 10 of the 1989 law on schools) than from international law. The *Commissaire du gouvernement's* conclusions in the case

vis religion in *Les Petites Affiches* (Flauss 1992), based on findings presented in the context of a newly created research group concerned with the confluence of French law and religion. Since 1994, he has regularly published analyses of Strasbourg Court case law in the journal *Actualité Juridique. Droit Administratif.* In the meantime, he has become a professor at the University of Paris 2, secretary-general of the Institut International des Droits de l'Homme (International Institute for Human Rights) created by René Cassin, and the author of several key works about the ECHR. The trajectories of professors Sudre and Gonzalès are similar. A new specialization was born; the creation of courses of study dedicated to international human rights in French law schools, new journals such as the *Revue Trimestrielle des Droits de l'Homme*, the inclusion of international law in administrative law textbooks, publications concerning the ECHR in key public law journals, and the editorial success of books on this subject all confirm this spectacular breakthrough.

confirms this view (Kessler 1993). The *Commissaire*, David Kessler, explicitly emphasizes his disagreement with Rivéro's and Durand-Prinborgne's position (as expressed in their articles published in 1990), that the opinion would have been required to comply with public international law. According to him, the *Kherouaa* decision implies a reversal of the 'overly rigorous approach of certain defenders of French *laïcité*' that 'nevertheless reflects the liberal spirit of the texts and protagonists that inspired the school secularization' (Kessler 1993: 114). On this point, he writes 'we disagree with Durand-Prinborgne's article because we think the freedom of religion has been recognized from the beginning by our [national] law' (ibid.). In other words, according to his argumentation, there is no need to invoke public international law to defend the right to express one's religious affiliation through dress codes, as long as wearing the Islamic headscarf does not disturb a school's normal functioning. The principle of *laïcité* mandates that freedom of religion (and not just freedom of inward religious belief) be respected except when it clashes with another significant educational interest.

Although the *Kherouaa* decision did not provoke much reaction outside the legal sphere, aside a few articles in the national press, it did generate a series of new legal commentaries drawing a sharper line between those favourable to the liberal position of the Conseil d'État (Lebreton 1993, Tedeschi 1993, Sabourin 1993) and those sceptical, if not critical (Schwartz and Maugüe 1993, Koubi 1994, Flauss 1992, 1993). In this discussion, Art. 9 is once again a bone of contention. Noteworthy is the commentary made by Schwartz and Maugüé (1992), two members of the Conseil d'Etat, which is similar to Costa's. Like him, they oppose the idea that the opinion was a mere statement of the law as it was then. They insist on the fact that a stricter interpretation of the principle of *laïcité* was conceivable, and that such a conception had prevailed until then, ensuring the pacification of the conflict between church and state as well as the proper functioning of schools.[16] Rémy Schwartz and Christine Maugüe are not content with exposing the administrative court's logic of argumentation and present it as an unquestionable outcome; they take advantage of this discussion to present the existing legal means that may justify restricting religious expression in public institutions.

A series of new case law references, likely to become resources for those who would defend the cause of a stricter *laïcité*, enter the developing drama of the controversy. Schwartz and Maugüe do not simply point out the legal resources existing within national law. In the wake of what Costa began to argue in his own commentary a few months earlier, they tend to disqualify the thesis according to which Art. 9 would be a resource exclusively in favour of the recognition of the right to wear the veil at school. Developing this argument they devote a few paragraphs to Art. 9. According to the authors Art. 9 does not offer an unconditional

16 They argued that 'an interpretation that obliges the users of public services to strictly respect their neutrality by refraining from overtly expressing their beliefs' would have been legally acceptable since the freedom of religion is guaranteed by the existence of chaplains within public institutions such as schools, jails and hospitals.

guarantee to express one's religious conviction. Moreover, they seek to clarify the Strasbourg Court's case law concerning the freedom of conscience and religion in public services, such as jails and schools, to show that the court would accept, under specific conditions, some restrictions to the expression of one's religion in public services.

Although in *Kherouaa* David Kessler did not devote much time to examining the impact of the European Convention, he did so when in 1994 he had to give his opinion as *Commissaire du Gouvernement* on a new veil-related case, *Yilmaz*. As Kessler explains to his peers:

> since your *Kherouaa* decision, something new happened on the strict level of law when the ECHR, intervening after a decision of the Turkish constitutional court declared unconstitutional, in the name of the principle of *laïcité*, a provision authorizing the wearing of the Islamic headscarf in state universities ... interpreted the exteriorization of one's religious belief as that represented by wearing an Islamic headscarf as an act of pressure on students who do not practice Islamic religion nor identify with it. (Kessler 1994: 5)

Kessler's reference to this recent decision was due to the publication in the interim of a commentary criticizing the Conseil d'État's legal position. In this article entitled 'The European Human Rights Commission rescues *laïcité* in state schools' (Flauss 1993), Flauss went on to discuss what seemed to him a strategic use of international law by national legal actors to shape the law in a certain direction. In a critical manner, he confronted the position of the Conseil d'État with the recent Strasbourg Commission decision of *Karaduman v Turkey* (1993)[17] to demonstrate not only the 'antagonism' between both courts but also to defend the idea that the French Administrative Court made a constructive interpretation of Art. 9 in favour of a liberal conception of *laïcité.* Contesting Flauss's position, that this recent ECHR decision should lead the Conseil d'État to a judicial reversal as far as the veil is concerned, Kessler develops two arguments. He denies the legitimacy of the comparison between France and Turkey, and disputes Flauss's assertion that Art. 9 would have been used by the Conseil d'État as an 'alibi'. He reaffirms to his peers what he had said in his *Kherouaa* conclusions: 'Your opinion presents an interpretation of religious freedom founded as much on texts of municipal law [including, as he points out, the 1789 Declaration of the Rights of Man] as on texts of international law, including the Convention' (Kessler 1994: 4).

He then points out that neither the European Court nor *a fortiori* the Commission has any interpretative monopoly on the European Convention. His riposte is thus the occasion to assert the idea that an administrative judge is competent to interpret

17 In this decision the Commission acknowledged that the manifestation of the observance and symbols of the religion of the great majority, without restriction as to place and manner, might constitute 'improper pressure on students who do not practice that religion or those who adhere to another religion'.

the European Convention in a 'constructive' manner, or to assert his interpretive autonomy in regard to the Strasbourg Court. Asserting his role as authorized interpreter of European human rights law, the administrative judge refuses a relationship of simple dependence on the Court.

Since 1994, this defusing of the impact of Art. 9 has been accompanied by an interpretation highlighting its potential for limiting the freedom of public display of religious convictions. As a result, the relevant case law is examined to affirm that the European judge does not conceive of the Convention as an absolute recognition of the rights of conscience and religion. In the *Aoukili* case (1994), the *Commissaire du gouvernement* estimates thus that 'it is rather imprudently that the claimants (veiled girls' parents) cite Art. 9' in order to contest schools decisions to expel their children (Aguila 1995).

Art. 9 as Fulcrum of the Legislative Re-problematizing

This neutralizing of the legal impact of Art. 9 or transforming it as a justification against the veil does not end criticism on the subject, or the public declarations by members of the Conseil d'État, including the vice-president[18] who sometimes invoke among other things the ECHR to justify the liberal position of the Conseil d'État. The controversy unfolds outside the legal arena, and changes in scale to the extent that the anti-veil mobilization is reborn as a consequence of the administrative judge's annulations of the exclusionary decision in 1996 and 1997.[19] While new participants appear, it is the organization of the framework in which the controversy must be resolved that is questioned: it is no longer the

18 See Raphaël Haddas-Lebel, *Le Point*, 18 November 1993 and especially the declarations of Vice-President Renaud Denoix de Saint Marc justifying the position of the council: 'mores have evolved and the freedom of thought today goes to admit this right (demonstration of one's religious sympathies at school). Even more so, France has contracted international engagements, like the European Convention of Human Rights, that involve the right to display these sympathies'. *La Croix*, 7 November 1996.

19 At the Lycée Racine in Paris, a philosophy teacher refused in the name of freedom of conscience to teach in the presence of a young veiled girl, who had been readmitted following a decision by the Administrative Tribunal of Paris; a Committee to Defend the Republic's Schools was created and supported the teacher, declaring its determination 'not to compromise the principles of the Republic'. In Vendôme, south-west of Paris, the contentious decisions sparked the creation of a Vendômois Committee for the Defence of *Laïcité* headquartered at the city hall which formed an alliance with elected officials to call for a law. In Albertville, 500 people protested before the under prefecture against the readmission of four young veiled girls which had been ordered by the Administrative Tribunal of Grenoble; a petition addressed to the deputy mayor François Grosdidier (member of the Gaullist Rassemblement pour la République or RPR), who joined with Ernest Chénière, principal of the Creil middle school in 1989, and then RPR deputy, to introduce a bill in November 1996 that would prohibit wearing the veil and penalize 'differentialist behaviour' (*conduites différentialistes*).

veil that is submitted to the judge's decision but the law spoken by the judge that is submitted to the court of public opinion. It is no longer just the jurists who debate the impact of Art. 9, but also more heterogeneous actors who denounce the Conseil d'État's perverse use of and 'ideologization of the law' that could put the Republic in peril. The denunciation is accompanied by appeals to the legislature in order to dispossess the administrative judge of the 'propriety of the problem' (Gusfield 1981).

While in 1989 none of the social and political actors hostile to the veil discussed the legal validity of the opinion rendered by the Conseil d'État, its position is now *legally* questioned by those actors. Ernest Chénière, the former principal of the Creil middle school turned deputy in the National Assembly and author of an early bill to prohibit the veil, is one of the first to contest the council on its own ground by criticizing the ignorance by the Conseil d'Etat of the international protective conventions of women's rights. While the sociologists Kosrokhavar and Gaspard, in their book *Le foulard et la République*, opposed to the expulsion of veiled girls, refer to the ECHR as a legal obstacle to such expulsions, certain anti-veil intellectuals attacked the administrative judge's 1994 interpretation of the ECHR. For example, Guy Coq, frequently quoted by the national dailies, philosopher, member of the editorial board of the journal *Esprit*, and early critic of the Conseil d'État's jurisprudential position:

> The argument for the international engagement that would be put in place if France were to clarify her law on *laïcité* is not serious ... It is significant from an anti-republican and *anti-laïque* reading that an entire current of international law influences the French jurists ... French *laïcité* is not going to disappear when faced with transnational (*inter-étatiques*) texts, of which the goal was clearly not to deliberate the question. The general principles of religious freedom must be inscribed in the framework of French *laïcité*. It is quite imprudent to depart from the principle of interpretation that postulates *a priori* a contradiction, between *laïcité* and signed treaties. This points to one of the problems hypocritically unfurled by the dominant elite: is this signification of Europe for this elite the erasure of France, of the Republic? (*La Croix*, 27 November 1996)

Other 'militant intellectuals' take up this cause (e.g. Kaltenbach and Tribalat 2002, Pena-Ruiz 2003), as do certain journalists writing for publications with editors openly hostile to the wearing of the veil to school, such as *Le Point* or *Le Figaro*. The argument gains new allies and wins plausibility to the extent that the appeals to the legislature multiply as the increased number of bills sent to the National Assembly show. Yet, public support for legislating for the prohibition of the headscarf collides with Art. 9 of the ECHR. Even if these demands for legislation were heard favourably by the executive branch in 1995 and one bill even received greater attention in the Senate in 1997, they misfired. Whereas the executive branch did not pursue the project, the examination of the bill by the Commission of Social and Cultural Affairs in the Senate, the first collective and concerted examination of such a project, ended in a flat refusal. The measure appeared to the commission as 'neither desirable nor useful'. Moreover, even its *legal* feasibility was put into doubt because of a risk of unconstitutionality (*Le Monde*, 28 March 1997).

When the controversy of the headscarf returned to the public stage in 2003,[20] after a gap of six years, it was not so much the obstacle of the Constitution as the ECHR with which the proponents of a legislative solution almost instantly collided. The legislative sequence marked a new step in the career of Art. 9: the conflict over its interpretation moved from the judicial to the legislative arena.

The Domestication of Art. 9 by the Legislature

The *affaire du foulard* revealed a new dimension in the growing integration of European law into French domestic law. The legal constraint of this convention not only weighs on the judges' interpretative work, but also on the work of legislators, who, in principle, possess the freedom to create the law. As a result of this new legal context, the evaluation and then bypassing the risk of Strasbourg's censure has become one of the key stakes in the debate over the law.

Art. 9 and the Veil are put to the Test

The creation of two commissions, the Debré Mission, May 2003, headed by Jean-Louis Debré (President of the National Assembly), and the Stasi Commission, established by President Chirac in July 2003 and assigned the task of organizing a public debate over the application of the principle of *laïcité*, stemmed from a new attempt to gain political control of the '*nouvelle affaire du voile*'.

A new arena on the question of wearing the veil at school then began to take shape. Contrary to the judges' deliberations in 1989 when the government asked the Conseil d'État to render a legal opinion, this new arena was open to a plurality of actors from different social spheres including members of social movements, activists, social scientists, legal scholars or experts and representatives of the political milieu and of the administration. A plurality of arguments and justifications were not only accepted but expected in order to provide a realignment between the law and different interests.

The 'conventionality'[21] of the law prohibiting the headscarf was certainly questioned by actors openly hostile to it (such as Abdallah Milcent), or simply sceptical of its appropriateness (notably Luc Ferry, the Minister of National Education). The issue of its conventionality also exercised the law's defenders. Doubts about this arose during the first meeting of the Debré Mission and continued

20 About the background of this resurgence see Galembert 2007, Lorcerie 2005.

21 'Conventionality' here means in accordance with, or compliant with, or not in contradiction to, the ECHR.

to surface throughout the hearings in the comments of jurists, representatives of teachers' unions, school administrators and even an Islamic specialist like Mohamed Arkoun. The deputies' questions demonstrated that uncertainty persisted until the end of the hearing. In what appeared to be a 'judiciarisation of the legislative process' (Stone 1992: 4), it was not the shadow of the constitutional judge but the shadow of the ECHR that hung over the legislature's sovereignty, as expressed by the exasperated Jean-Louis Debré:

> Each time that we want to legislate, we are told that we cannot because there is case-law ... Between the case-law of the Conseil d'État and the European Court of Justice, one asks oneself if we haven't returned to the Parlements of the *Ancien Régime* ... It is fascinating that we, the legislators, are obligated to ask jurists if we can borrow legislative channels at the risk of interfering with the judges who originated the jurisprudence! (<http://www.assemblee-nationale.fr/12/rapports/r1275-t2-6.asp> [accessed 27 November 2008])

Confronted with a legal context over which they had partially lost control, the actors of this legislative sequence pursued its exploration through their debates, scrutinizing the new horizon and attempting to discern the jurisprudential politics of the Court of Strasbourg. They not only discovered this new legal world, but they tried to shape it by attempting to impose their own interpretation of it.

The Transformation of Art. 9 into Legislative Support

Perceived in May 2003 as a potential obstacle to the law, Art. 9 was transformed over four months of debate into one of the key arguments justifying the legislature's intervention. The reports of the Debré Mission (2003) and the Commission Stasi (2003) offer convergent positions in this respect. This was corroborated by the Law Commission's report concerning the bill introduced by the government barely weeks after Debré and Stasi completed their work (Clément 2004).

This reversal occurred as much on the legal level as the social and political. A re-interpretation and redesignation of the significance of wearing the veil, heretofore considered not only through the prism of the freedom of conscience but also of gender equality, took place by invoking the women's cause. Denouncing the Conseil d'État's legal precedent, certain feminists compared the rights of women to the freedom of conscience, the international convention of New York to the ECHR, and even Article 5 (sexual equality) of the ECHR to Art. 9. The widely disseminated criticism of wearing the veil in the name of women's rights, *laïcité* and the future of schools and the Republic is based on the condemnation of those who invoke the administrative case law to justify legal mobilization on behalf of the veil, presented as an exemplary demonstration of the instrumentalization of the law for the benefit of bad causes, This became one of the privileged targets for attack by defenders of women, of the Republic, of *laïcité*, etc.

This vigorous condemnation of the 'Islamist' misuse of human rights has a corollary in the disparagement of the guardians of the operative law. Among many other testimonies, that of Neslinur Yilmaz, proposed by a militant feminist member of the Stasi Commission, was recognized in this respect by several members of the commission (including the former vice president of the Conseil d'État, Marceau Long) as determinant. This young woman was not presented simply as the victim of a fundamentalist and violent father, who threatened to forcibly veil her. As 'victim' of one of the first decisions of the Conseil d'État (*Yilmaz* 1994), wherein an expulsion was rejected precisely in the name of respecting one's freedom of conscience and religion, Ms Yilmaz incarnated, for the commission, all of the victims of an alleged lack of reality of the administrative judges. Over the course of these hearings, the meaning and the value of wearing the headscarf changed: the headscarf was perceived more and more as an infringement on the freedom of conscience and a menace against law and order.

As the succession of hearings made this menace evident and justified the legislature's meddling in the domain of fundamental freedoms, the evidence of three ECHR experts constituted the decisive moments in the building of a consensus in the commissions and in the progress of the legislative process from a technically legal point of view. The expertise of the practitioners of the ECHR was preferred to that of the European law professors. It was not so much their legal competency as their official functions within the court that made their evidence authoritative and that, in turn, contributed to the reduction of uncertainty over the law's conventionality. Michele De Salvia, legal consultant at the ECHR, and Ronny Abraham, director of legal affairs at the French Foreign Office and the legal attorney for the French Republic, as they were heard by the Debré's Mission, both interpreted the Strasbourg case law in order to determine precisely what was possible. In doing this they not only confirmed the possibility of a law, but also offered a considerable argument to justify it: in effect, by way of Art. 9, the restrictions of religious freedom are not admissible except on the condition of being anticipated by the law (Debré Mission 2003, Tome II, Part 4: 81 ss).

Jean-Paul Costa, Vice President of the Court since 2001, stood before the Stasi Commission and deemed the legal regime in force to be 'very suspect from the point of view of its compatibility with the (ECHR)'. He pleaded and convinced his audience that the law cannot be ignored.[22] In contrast to the little attention paid by the media to the hearings held before the Debré Mission, the press instantly commented on Jean-Paul Costa's evidence. Although a professor of public law considered Costa's intervention as technically approximate and deontologically hazardous (Flauss 2003: 100), it has nonetheless been interpreted as a certificate of conventionality. This evidence (in closed hearing) was perceived as the position of an official spokesperson of the court and it became irrefutable proof that a law, now

22 Interviews with the reporter of the commission, Rémy Schwartz, two members of the staff, Pascale Flammant and Séverine Calazel and two of its members, Gaye Petek and Jean Baubérot.

considered safe from censure by Strasbourg, was inevitable. Constantly evoked in parliamentary and legal media circles,[23] the Strasbourg Court Vice-President's evidence became the authority of reference in the public debate.

The uncertainties about the impact of the Art. 9 also affected the formulation of the proposed bill. While the Debré Mission recommended risking the censure of Strasbourg by prohibiting 'visible symbols', the Stasi Commission stood by the more prudent qualification of 'ostensible'. In favour of the latter, the government's arbitration left the door open for 'discreet' demonstrations of religiosity, while the bill envisioned the interdiction of 'ostensible symbols and clothing by which pupils demonstrate their religiosity'. This formulation, filed with the Conseil d'État, was transformed into 'symbols by which pupils ostensibly demonstrate religiosity'.

The introductory report to the parliamentary debate on the bill shows well how, as a result of the commissions' work, Art. 9 became a decisive argument in favour of a law banning the headscarf from schools. As the reporter explained, such a bill would be necessary not only from a social but also from a legal point of view (Clément 2004). Its purpose was certainly to send a solemn signal to halt the *communautarianisation* (i.e. ethnic and religious division) of France. From the legal point of view this legislation would be the only legal means enabling restrictions on fundamental liberties without risking censure from the Strasbourg Court. Legislation would provide a predictable framework, this predictability being required to comply with the ECHR obligations.

Consequently, if the law's conventionality did not disappear from the parliamentary arena, it remained pertinent only in relation to the content of the law rather than its legal feasibility.[24] Opposition parties argued that the ECHR hinders both the prohibition of visible symbols and the imposition of a 'strict *laïcité*' in schools, while the government and the political right invoked the risks of censure by the Court for defending gains of an 'open *laïcité*'. This enlistment of Art. 9 in the ritualized left/right conflict, however, did nothing to prevent the deputies' support for a law deemed indispensable and hugely popular by a 494-to-36 vote.

Jurisprudential Immobilization, Alignment of Judges and Failure of Legal Mobilization

While the vote on the law on 15 March 2004 did not mark the end of judicial mobilization on behalf of the veil, it favoured its defeat. Different associations were created with the goal of proposing legal assistance to potential and real victims of the new text: the Collectif contre l'islamophobie and, above all, the Comité 15 mars et libertés, established by Dr Abdallah Milcent, which offered

23 In certain cases, the media continued to support the argument by placing at the disposition of its readers clarification of the jurisprudential orientations of the Strasbourg Court, see notably Rivais (2004).

24 The parliamentary debate is available at <http://www.assemblee-nationale.fr/12/dossiers/laicite.asp> [accessed 26 November 2008].

material and legal support to young women, e.g., with the creation of a toll-free hotline and updated legal advice regarding the new legal constraints. Even before the beginning of the school year, the first contentious offensive before the Conseil d'État took the form of a motion to annul the law's letter of application (*circulaire d'application de la loi*) called the 'circulaire Fillon' (Union Française pour la Cohésion Nationale, 2004). The motion contested the clause stipulating that 'the symbols and clothing that are prohibited are those which by being worn are immediately recognizable for their religiosity such as the Islamic veil'. This clause would betray the interdiction in the law of 'wearing of symbols or clothing by which the pupils ostensibly demonstrate their religiosity' (Keller 2004). Through this appeal, in which Art. 9 was again upheld as grounds, it was the application of the law that was subject *ex post* to an assessment of conventionality. In investigating the Strasbourg jurisprudence to see if the explicit prohibition of the Islamic headscarf was compliant with its case law, the *Commissaire du gouvernement* set out to remove the last uncertainty concerning the impact of Art. 9. He proposed to his peers that the ruling validate the legislative reversal. Arguments unfavourable to the claimant are drawn from the most recent Strasbourg court decisions. As a result, the *Commissaire* concluded that the court not only admits limitations on the freedom of religion, but also recognizes each country's margin of judgment, considering that no uniform conception of religious freedom and the forms it can take exists at the European level.

Among the several decisions cited[25] the *Leyla Sahin* case played a decisive role in his argumentation. Despite the *Commissaire*'s own admission that the transposability of these decisions is debatable (one concerns a female teacher and not a pupil, the others deal with Turkish political Islam), he concluded 'that they do not shed any less light that appears favourable to the French regulations [forbidding the headscarf in schools]' (Keller 2004: 4). Indifferent to criticisms in certain specialized law journals that the reasoning was 'hasty' (Burgorgue-Larsen and Dubout 2006) or disappointing (Rolin 2005), the administrative jurisdictions aligned themselves on this ruling of the Conseil d'État.[26] All requests for a

25 *Dahlab vs. Switzerland* (15 February 2001); *Refah Partisi vs. Turkey* (13 February 2003); and the very recent *Leyla Sahin*. The first of these concerns a veiled Swiss teacher who was forbidden to teach: 'difficult to reconcile the message of tolerance, of respect of others and the non-discrimination that, in a democracy, each teacher must transmit to the pupils'. The second accepts the Turkish authorities' position in which they pronounced the dissolution of the Prosperity Party in 1998, of which certain leaders made political speeches with religious content and theocratic tones. The third confirmed the expulsion of female medical student from the University of Istanbul for having refused to take off her veil during her classes and examinations. Eur. Court of Hum. Rights (4th section). (*Le Monde*, 1 July 2004, *Le Figaro*, 11 November 2005).

26 During the academic year 2004–2005, the Ministry of National Education counted 639 instances where students wore ostensible religious symbols (out of ten million pupils) versus 1465 the previous year. Of those 639, there were: 626 Islamic veils, 11 Sikh turbans and two large crosses. 240 cases were deemed severe and led 143 girls to quit school either

legal decision invoking Art. 9 as legal justification were in effect rejected in the courts of first instance, testifying to a new immobilization of the jurisprudence, unfavourable to the pro-veil mobilization. This had implications for Sikhs, whose attempts to assert, in the name of Art. 9, the right to wear their turbans, also ran up against what became a veritable legal obstacle, the 15 March 2004 law.

This vertical alignment of administrative jurisdictions on the Conseil d'État's position was coupled with a horizontal alignment between the national supreme courts (the Conseil Constitutionnel and the Conseil d'État) and the ECHR. The dynamic of this jurisprudential immobilization was also characterized by an economy of legal production that was no longer inscribed in a uniquely pyramidical perspective, but also in a network (Ost and Van de Kerchove 2002). In effect, the press, the legal journals,[27] and the Conseil d'État are no longer alone in interpreting the *Leyla Sahin* ruling as the symbol of a Strasbourg jurisprudential policy unfavourable to the headscarf and a validation of the law of 15 March 2004. The Constitutional Council lent its authority to this interpretation of Art. 9's meaning. In November 2004, while examining the draft of the Treaty Establishing a Constitution for Europe, whose negotiation collided notably with the problem of France's singular *laïcité*, the council judged the clauses recognizing everyone's right to publicly demonstrate his or her religious convictions compliant with the first article of the French Constitution, which clearly states that 'France is a secular Republic'. Relying on the *Leyla Sahin* ruling, then in appeal, the constitutional judge concluded that:

> Art. 9 of the Convention has been consistently applied by the European Court of Human Rights, and lastly by its decision (*Leyla Sahin*), harmoniously with the constitutional tradition of each member State; that the Court has thus taken note of the value of the principle of *laïcité* recognized by several national constitutional traditions and that it leaves to the State a large margin of judgment to define the most appropriate measure, taking into account their national traditions, in order to reconcile the freedom of religion with the principle of *laïcité*.[28]

If certain commentators have underscored the temerity of the constitutional judge's argument, based on a decision in appeal, the second *Leyla Sahin* decision, handed down in January 2005, has contributed to the closure of discussion of the meaning of Art. 9. This ruling, in which commentators saw a principled decision covering a 'communal importance for the member states', is seen as the validation

spontaneously or following expulsion (47 for 44 veils and three turbans) prompting 28 court cases. The year 2005 confirms the reduction in litigation (Toulemonde 2005).

27 According to Flauss (2003: 111) it is 'nevertheless obvious that the conventionality of the law's dispositions prescribing the interdiction of wearing religious conspicuous religious symbols is no longer disputed'.

28 He cites this in the *visa* of his decision. *Décision N° 2004-505 DC du 19 novembre 2004 relative au traité établissant une Constitution pour l'Europe.*

of a 'restrictive and prohibitive conception of laïcité' (Burgorgue-Larsen and Dubout 2006: 214), as an *a posteriori* 'certificate' of conventionality of the 15 March law.

While the judiciary arena, as a result of this mutual support of the administrative, constitutional and Strasbourg judges, was no longer accessible to the cause of the veil, the cause itself was publicly discredited (Galembert 2009). Its defenders failed to create a united front in spite of the newly created collectives protesting the law, such as the Ligue française de la femme musulmane, Une école pour toutes et pour tous (based on the Ligue Communiste Révolutionnaire), figures from the anti-globalization movement, the Greens, the Mouvement contre le Racisme et l'Egalité entre les Peuples, and the Collectif des Musulmans de France. The anti-law rallies, presented in the media as proof of political-religious manipulation framed by men at the expense of women and of the Republic, attracted little support. Moreover the defenders of the veil turned out to be powerless in relying on the international condemnations of a 'liberticidal law', in particular that of the UN's Commission of Human Rights (September 2004). When the Islamic Army took the journalists Chesnot and Malbrunot hostage in Iraq at the end of August 2004 and demanded the repeal of the law, this act rendered impossible all protest against the law by the spokespersons of Islam in France and muzzled certain pro-veil militant actors like Dr Abdallah Milcent and the Union des Organisations Islamiques de France, who, meanwhile, had become the official representatives of Islam in France through their election to the French Council of the Muslim Religion (Conseil Français du Culte Musulman).

The reversal of Art. 9's normative impact resulted notably from a legal redesignation of the headscarf. Justifying the headscarf's interdiction in public schools, the legal redesignation was inseparable from a social and political redesignation. This demonstrates the asymmetry of resources at the disposal of the winners and losers of the *affaire du voile*, resources that include mastery of the media and public discourse, alliances with human rights associations, legal competence and proximity to the political-administrative world that partly controls the logic of law creation and of the evolution of a Franco-European jurisprudence.

Conclusion

When it was seized by the law, the *affaire du voile* brought onto the French stage a new text, Art. 9, with an uncertain normative impact. During the judiciarization sequence, it seemed that this article from an international convention constituted a constitutional point of support for the veil's cause in France, a structural element of a legal opportunity favourable to the veil's defenders who had not otherwise failed to grasp the law to emphasize their claims before the administrative jurisdictions. The legislators' enlistment of Art. 9 revealed how much making sense of European law is dependent on what the national actors are capable of making it say.

In fact, the analysis of the birth, deployment and closure of the controversies surrounding Art. 9 and the Islamic veil shows how the actors, by the manner in which they make reference to and interpret European law, define the legal context in which they operate. This recontextualization involves not only the appearance of new texts drawing their validity from new legal sources as much as new resources and pressures, but also the arrival of new actors such as the Strasbourg Court, specialists of European law and human rights, and a re-evaluation of the relative authority of different loci of law production, legislative and judicial, French and European. An international norm of supra-legislative value, Art. 9 does not impose itself as such in the domestic legal order; the domestication of European law and judges testifies to the importance of the national actors in the Europeanization of the law. The controversies related to the legal impact of this norm are also telling of the conflicts and power relationships that underlie the interpretation and national appropriation of European law. In this work of recontextualization the effects of symbolic domination cannot be ignored. The resources allowing us to make sense of the veil and of the law as well as the applicable norms and their 'true' interpretation, and, furthermore, the political order in which they are inscribed, are unequally distributed between the actors. The failure of the judicial mobilization in favour of the veil testifies to difficulties in embracing and defining the law while denouncing an injustice (the expulsion of veiled schoolgirls), in representing a 'victim' group (Muslims), and in creating a collective cause (equating the freedom to wear the veil with freedom of conscience). If the state has clearly lost its monopoly on the sources of the law, the fact remains that it is in the national public space that the inseparably legal, political and moral construction of human rights plays out. This is particularly true for *laïcité*, which is such a central issue to the integration of the national political order.

References

Agrikoliansky, E. 2005. Liberté, Liberté chérie … : la gauche et la protection des libertés publiques dans les années 1970. Hypothèses sur la résurgence de la notion d'Etat de droit. In *Sur la portée sociale du droit,* edited by L. Israël., G. Sacriste, A. Vauchez and L. Willemez. Paris: CURAPP/PUF, 235–40.

Aguila, Y. 1995. CE, 10 mars 1995, AOUKILI, conclusions. Actualité Juridique – Droit Administratif, avril, 332–5.

Bayrou, F. 1994. *Circulaire n° 1649 du 20 septembre 1994 relative au port de signes ostentatoires dans les établissements scolaires*. Available at: <www.cndp.fr/doc_administrative/laicite/93-316.htm> [accessed 15 November 2008].

Beller, E.T. 2004. The Headscarf Affair: the Conseil d'Etat and the Role of Religion and Culture in French Society. *Texas International Law Journal*, 39(4), 581–623.

Boltanski, L. 1984. La dénonciation. *Actes de la Recherche en Sciences Sociales*, 62, 3–40.

Bourdieu, P. 1986. La force du droit. Eléments pour une sociologie du champ juridique. *Actes de la Recherche en Sciences Sociales*, 64, 3–19.

Bowen, J. 2006. *Why the French Don't Like Headscarves*. Princeton: Princeton University Press.

Burgorgue-Larsen, L. and E. Dubout. 2006. Le port du voile à l'université. Libres propos sur l'arrêt de la grande chambre. Leyla Sahin c. Turquie du 10 novembre 2005. *Revue Trimestrielle des Droits de l'Homme*, 66, 183–215.

Chevallier, J. 1999. *L'Etat de droit*. 3ème edition. Paris: Montchrestien.

Clément, P. 2004. Au Nom de la Commission des Lois Constitutionnelles, de la Législation et de l'Administration Générale de la République sur le Projet de Loi (n° 1378) Relatif à l'Application du Principe de Laïcité dans les Écoles, Collèges et Lycées Publics, No. 1381. N° 1381. Available at: <www.assemblee-nationale.fr/12/rapports/r1381.asp> [accessed 26 November 2008].

Commission Stasi. 2003. *Commission de Réflexion sur l'Application du Principe de Laïcité dans la République*. Rapport au Président de la République, 11th December 2003. Available at: <http://lesrapports.ladocumentationfrancaise.fr/BRP/034000725/0000.pdf> [accessed 24 October 2008].

Costa, J-P. 1990. Le principe de laïcité et les signes d'appartenance à une communauté religieuse. *L'Actualité Juridique – Droit administratif*, 20 January, 39–45.

Debré Mission. 2003. Rapport n° 1275 de M. Jean-Louis Debré au nom de la mission d'information sur la question des signes religieux à l'école. Available at: <http://www.assemblee-nationale.fr/12/rapports/r1275-t1.asp> [accessed 24 November 2008].

Durand-Prinborgne, C. 1990. La circulaire Jospin du 12 décembre 1989. *Revue Française de Droit Administratif*, 6(1), 10–22.

Flauss, J-F. 1992. Les sources internationales du droit français des religions. *Les Petites Affiches,* 95(7 August 1992), 22–4.

— 1993. La Commission Européenne des Droits de l'Homme au secours de la laïcité de l'enseignement public. L'affaire Karaduman c/Turquie. Requête n° 16278/90. *Les Petites Affiches*, 142(26 november 1993), 11–13.

— 2003. Les signes religieux. In *La liberté religieuse et la Convention Européenne des Droits de l'Homme*, edited by Christophe Pettiti and Thierry Massis. Brussels: Némésis-Bruylant, 98–112.

Galembert, C. de. 2007. La fabrique du droit entre le juge administratif et le législateur. La carrière juridique du foulard islamique (1989–2004). In *La fonction politique de la justice*, edited by J. Commaille and M. Kaluszynski. Paris: La Découverte, 94–118.

— 2008. Le voile en procès. *Droit et Société*, 68, 11–31.

— (forthcoming) 2009. Cause du voile et lutte pour la parole musulmane légitime. *Sociétés Contemporaines*.

Genevois, B. 2005. Le Commissaire du gouvernement devant le Conseil d'Etat statuant au contentieux ou la stratégie de la persuasion. In *Théorie des contraintes juridiques*, edited by M. Troper, V. Champeil-Desplats and C. Grzegorczyk. Paris/Bruxelles: LGDJ-Bruylant, 91–108.

Gonzalès, G. 1994. La Convention Européenne des Droits de l'Homme et la Liberté des Religions. Paris: Economica.

Goy, R. 1991. La garantie européenne de la liberté de religion. L'article 9 de la Convention de Rome. *Revue de Droit Public*, 5–60.

Gusfield, Joseph. 1981. The Culture of Public Problems: Drinking-Driving and the Symbolic Order. Chicago: University of Chicago Press.

Jospin, L. 1990. Le moment ou jamais. *Le Débat*, 58(janvier), 3–19.

Kaltenbach, J.H. and M. Tribalat. 2002. *La République et l'islam entre crainte et aveuglement*. Paris: Seuil.

Keller, R. 2004. Conclusions sur Conseil d'Etat, 29 septembre 2004, Union française pour la cohésion nationale. N° 269077 et 269704. Unpublished.

Kepel, G. 1994. *A l'Ouest d'Allah*. Paris: Seuil.

Kessler, D. 1993. Neutralité de l'enseignement public et liberté d'opinion des élèves (à propos du port de signes distinctifs d'appartenance religieuse dans les établissements scolaires). Conclusions sur Conseil d'Etat, 2 novembre 1992, M. Kherouaa et Mme Kachour, M. Balo et Mme Kizic. *Revue de Droit Administratif*, 9(1), 112–19.

— 1994. Conclusions sur Conseil d'Etat, 14 mars 1994, Melles Neslinur et Zehranur Yilmaz. Unpublished.

Khosrokhavar, F. and Gaspard, F. 1995. *Le foulard et la République*. Paris: La découverte.

Koubi, G. 1993. Conseil d'Etat, 2 novembre 1992, Kherouaa et al. *Recueil Dalloz Sirey*, 9ème cahier, 108–11.

Lanarès, P. 1964. La liberté religieuse dans les conventions internationales et dans le droit public général. Paris: Horvath.

Lascoumes, P. and Serverin, E. 1986. Le droit comme activité sociale: pour une approche wébérienne des activités juridiques. *Droit et Société*, 9, 171–90.

Latour, B. 2002. La fabrique du droit. Une ethnographie du Conseil d'Etat. Paris: La découverte.

Lebreton, G. 1993. Port de signes religieux et laïcité de l'enseignement public. Cons. d'État, 2 novembre 1992, M. Kherouaa et Mme Kachour, M. Balo et Mme Kizic. *Les Petites Affiches*, 24 mars, n° 62, 4–10.

Lorcerie, Françoise. 2005. La politisation du voile, en France, en Europe et dans le monde arabe. Paris: L'Harmattan.

McGoldrick, D. 2006. *Human Rights and Religion: the Islamic Headscarf Debate in Europe*. Oxford and Portland, Oregon: Hart.

Milcent, Thomas-Abdallah. 1994. *Le foulard et la République française: mode d'emploi*. Bobigny: Editions de l'intégrité.

Ost, F. and M. van de Kerchove. 2002. *De la pyramide au réseau? Pour une théorie dialectique du droit.* Bruxelles: Publications des Facultés Universitaires Saint-Louis.

Pena-Ruiz, H. 1999. Dieu et Marianne. Philosophie de la laïcité. Paris: PUF.

Rivais, R. 2004. La jurisprudence de la Cour européenne de Strasbourg n'est pas favorable au port du voile. *Le Monde*, 8 January 2004.

Rivéro, J. 1960. *La laicité.* Paris: PUF.

— 1990. La laïcité scolaire et signes d'appartenance religieuse. L'avis de l'Assemblée générale du Conseil d'Etat en date du 27 novembre 1989. *Revue Française de Droit Administratif*, 1990, 1–6.

Rolin, F. 2005. Le Conseil d' État abandonne la doctrine de l'avis de 1989 sur la laïcité. *Actualité Juridique- Droit Administratif*, 43–5.

Sabourin, P. 1993. *CE, 2 novembre 1992, KHEROUAA et autres*: note de jurisprudence. *Revue de Droit Public*, January–February, 220–31.

Schwartz, R. and C. Maugüé. 1992. CE 2 novembre 1992, Kherouaa et autres, req. n. 130394, *Actualité juridique, droit administratif*, 790–4.

Stone, A. 1992. *The Birth of Judicial Politics in France*. Oxford: Oxford University Press.

Tedeschi, P. 1993. Cons. d'Etat, 4ème et 1ère Sous-sect., 2 décembre 1992, Kherouaa et autres, req. n. 130394, *La Semaine Juridique (JCP)*, Ed. G, N° 6, 61–5.

Toulemonde, B. 2005. Le port de signes d'appartenance religieuse à l'école: la fin des interrogations? *Actualité juridique, droit administratif*, 2044-2047.

Vasak, K. 1964. *La Convention Européenne des Droits de l'Homme*. Paris: LGDJ.

Chapter 14
The Changing Position of Religious Minorities in English Law: The Legacy of *Begum*

Russell Sandberg[1]

Introduction

The school is often seen as a microcosm of wider society. It is therefore fitting that decisions made by schools have made a significant impact on the debate concerning the extent to which religious and racial diversity should be accommodated, a question that has dominated public discourse in the wake of 11 September 2001. Three cases concerning schools reflect the changing extent to which, and means by which, English law accommodates religious and racial difference. This chapter seeks to explore the changing face of English law by reference to these three decisions: *R v Secretary of State for Education and Employment and others ex parte Williamson* in 2005 (hereafter '*Williamson*'), *R (on the application of Begum) v Headteacher and Governors of Denbigh High School* in 2006 (hereafter '*Begum*') and *R (on the application of Watkins-Singh) v The Governing Body of Aberdare Girls' High School* in 2008 (hereafter '*Watkins-Singh*'). Building upon previous work (Hill and Sandberg 2006 and 2007, and Sandberg 2008), it contends that the reasoning of *Begum* has set an unfortunate and flawed precedent that has constrained religious liberty in England and Wales.

The Human Rights Act 1998

The face of English law had already been changed before these cases (Doe and Sandberg 2009). The Human Rights Act 1998 had ushered in a more rights-driven approach to civil liberties. The largely negative but flexible protection provided by the common law was superseded by the protection of religious liberty as a positive right. A previous legislative and judicial stance of passive accommodation

1 I am grateful to my colleagues at the Centre for Law and Religion at Cardiff University, especially Professor Norman Doe (the centre's director), Professor Mark Hill, Frank Cranmer, Paul Colton and Layla Wilkie-Buckley for their invaluable assistance in refining the ideas expressed here.

had been replaced by prescriptive regulation (see King 2007: Chapter 5, Hill and Sandberg 2006, 2007: 490). The Human Rights Act 1998 largely incorporated the European Convention on Human Rights (ECHR) into English law. Previously, the ECHR simply had the status of a treaty obligation under international law; although individual petition to the European Court in Strasbourg had been permitted since 1966, domestic courts lacked the 'jurisdiction directly to enforce the rights and freedoms under the Convention' (*R. v DDP ex p. Kebeline*).

During this period, Articles of the Convention, including Article 9 which protects freedom of thought, conscience and religion, were simply regarded as an aid to interpretation; although English courts sought to ensure that their decisions conformed to the ECHR, they were under no obligation to follow it, and the decisions of the European Court of Human Rights, slavishly to the letter (Hill and Sandberg 2007: 491). This is well illustrated by the case of *Ahmad v Inner London Education Authority* in 1978 concerning a Muslim school teacher, who was employed full time but sought to take 45 minutes off every Friday for prayer. He left his employment claiming constructive unfair dismissal. The Court of Appeal dismissed his claim, holding that the termination of employment was consistent with domestic education and employment law. Scarman LJ dissented, holding that domestic law should be construed broadly against the ECHR. He commented that:

> society has changed since 1944: so also has the legal background. Religions, such as Islam and Buddhism, have substantial followings among our people. ... This calls not for a policy of the blind eye but for one of understanding. The system must be made sufficiently flexible to accommodate their beliefs and their observances. (at 48)

His fellow judges, however, were less enthusiastic about following the ECHR. Lord Denning, in particular, questioned whether reference to Article 9 would help the claimant and doubted more generally whether reference to the style and form of the convention would be helpful and sufficiently flexible if followed to the letter:

> The convention is not part of our English law, but, as I have often said, we will always have regard to it. ... We will do our best to see that our decisions are in conformity with it. But it is drawn in such vague terms that it can be used for all sorts of unreasonable claims and provoke all sorts of litigation. As so often happens with high-sounding principles, they have to be brought down to earth. (at 41)

The Human Rights Act 1998 incorporated the positive right to religious liberty provided by Article 9 into English law and required courts to take into account – though not necessarily follow (*R (Alconbury Developments Ltd) v Secretary of State for the Environment, Transport and the Regions*) – the decisions of the

European Court at Strasbourg. However, whilst at first the impact of the Human Rights Act 1998 in matters of religious and racial difference seemed to fulfil the predictions of Scarman LJ, the decision in *Begum* suggests that it was Lord Denning's comments which were prophetic.

Article 9 in Strasbourg Jurisprudence

The changing interpretation of the Human Rights Act 1998 found in *Williamson*, *Begum* and *Watkins-Singh* needs to be understood in the context of the Strasbourg case law on Article 9. The European Court of Human Rights at Strasbourg generally takes a formulaic approach to religious liberty cases. In line with similar international human rights instruments on religious liberty, Article 9 ECHR provides an absolute right to both the freedom of thought, conscience and religion (known as the *forum internum*) and a qualified right to manifest religion or belief (the *forum externum*). The right to manifest one's religion or belief is qualified by Article 9(1) in that the manifestation must be 'in worship, teaching, practice and observance' and by the possible limitations in Article 9(2) which permits the state to interfere with the right if the three tests in Article 9(2) are met: the interference needs to be 'prescribed by law', be 'necessary in a democratic society', and have a 'legitimate aim' as spelled out in the Article.

Most cases are concerned with the latter qualified right. In dealing with such cases, Strasbourg organs invariably begin by stressing the importance of the right, citing the leading case, *Kokkinakis v Greece*, which elucidated how 'Freedom of thought, conscience and religion is one of the foundations of a "democratic society" within the meaning of the Convention'. Although they then ask whether Article 9(1) has been interfered with or has been engaged, this is often a formality and the focus shifts to the Article 9(2) limitations, which are used to determine whether the limitation by the state was justified. Since the Article 9(2) limitations have an 'elastic character' (Sandberg 2006: 455) this allows the court to consider the merits of the case, before reaching an appropriate conclusion.

The Strasbourg focus is upon whether the interference with the right to manifest is justified rather than whether there was an interference with the right to manifest. The threshold in relation to interference is low. The battleground is generally Article 9(2) rather than Article 9(1). This is particularly true in relation to more recent decisions of the Strasbourg Court. Earlier decisions tended to rely more upon filtering devices to exclude superfluous claims. Three such devices were developed: first, the definition of belief filter, stating that Article 9 would only protect a worldview held with 'a certain level of cogency, serious reflection and importance' (*Campbell and Cosans v United Kingdom*); second, the manifestation/motivation requirement that the claimant's actions manifest their religion or belief as opposed to being merely motivated by it (*Arrowsmith v United Kingdom*); and third, the specific situation rule, recognizing that a person's Article 9 rights may be curtailed by the particular situation of the individual claiming that freedom (*Ahmad v United Kingdom*).

These devices are relied upon less and less by Strasbourg organs. The manifestation/motivation requirement is not always applied and when it is the test has often been rephrased as requiring, for example, that the action is 'intimately linked' to the claimant's religion or belief (Knights 2007: 44); a requirement which is seemingly more elastic and less strict. The specific situation rule has limited application, applying only where someone has voluntarily submitted to a voluntary system of rules, typically by voluntarily submitting to military service or a contract of employment (Hill and Sandberg 2007: 495). Although Strasbourg institutions seemed to go further in *Jewish Liturgical Association Cha'are Shalom Ve Tsedek v France* by imposing an 'impossibility test' requiring that an 'alternative means of accommodating religious beliefs had ... to be "impossible" before a claim of interference under article 9 could succeed', later Strasbourg decisions have not followed this (Hill and Sandberg 2007: 495).

Indeed, more recent cases have seen a change in approach with Strasbourg taking 'a broader view of what amounts to an interference' (Knights 2007: 44) and giving more attention to the Article 9(2) limitations rather than the semantics of Article 9(1). In *Thlimmenos v Greece*, for example, the court simply accepted that the 'set of facts' complained of 'falls within the ambit' of Article 9 since it was 'prompted' by the claimant's religion or belief and noted that it did 'not find it necessary' to examine whether the facts 'amounted to interference with his rights under Article 9(1)'. In *Sahin v Turkey*, the court proceeded on the assumption that the regulations in issue, which placed restrictions of place and manner on the right to wear the Islamic headscarf in universities, constituted an interference with the applicant's right to manifest her religion. These cases convey a preference on the part of Strasbourg institutions whereby the use of filtering devices is minimized and attention is paid instead to the question of whether the interference was justified.

The Impact of *Williamson*

The incorporation of Article 9 into domestic law effective from October 2000 originally led English courts to follow the trend set by Strasbourg. This was epitomized by the House of Lords decisions in *Williamson*. The case was brought by head teachers, teachers and parents of children at four independent schools where discipline was enforced by the use of mild corporal punishment. They contended that the ban on corporal punishment in schools (Education Act 1998, s. 548) was incompatible with their belief that physical punishment was part of the duty of education in a Christian context and so infringed, *inter alia*, Article 9 ECHR. While lower courts sought to exclude the claim largely by reference to the Article 9(1) right, the House of Lords focused on the Article 9(2) limitations and specifically ruled out the use of filtering devices.

Lord Walker of Gestingthorpe, doubted whether it was right for courts, except in extreme cases, 'to impose an evaluative filter' at the stage of identifying whether there was a belief, 'especially when religious beliefs are involved' (para. 57). Lord Nicholls was adamant that while courts may be concerned with whether the claim of religious belief was made *in* good faith, they are not concerned whether the religious belief professed is *a* good faith in terms of judging the validity of that faith (para. 22; Sandberg 2008). Although both Lord Nicholls and Lord Walker defended the use of the Strasbourg manifestation rule, they seemed to support the re-formulated and relaxed version of this rule focusing upon whether the act is '"intimately linked" to the belief' and clarifying that this does not mean 'that a perceived obligation is a prerequisite to manifestation of a belief in practice' (see paras 31 and 62). Lord Nicholls also rejected the application of the 'specific situation' rule as in this case the rule did not apply on the facts since there was 'no comparable special feature affecting the position of the claimant parents' (at para. 39). He also rejected as unrealistic the submission of the Secretary of State that there has been no interference: the law 'left open to the parents several adequate, alternative courses of action' (para 40–1).

After considering but rejecting all three filtering devices, the House followed a typical Strasbourg approach finding that although there had been interference with the applicants' Article 9 rights, this was justified under Article 9(2) as being prescribed by law, necessary in a democratic society for the protection of the rights and freedoms of others, and as having a legitimate aim to protect children as a vulnerable group and promote their well-being. The House of Lords attracted much praise for following 'a classic human rights approach' (Langlaude 2006: 345). Lord Walker, in particular, contended that a holistic approach to the Article should be taken since 'the issues of engagement, interference and justification are in truth closely linked together' (para. 57). This approach and that of Lord Nicholls has been welcomed (Langlaude 2006, Hill 2007: 31). By contrast, the different approach of Lady Hale focusing upon 'children's rights' has been criticized (Langlaude 2006: 344–5): as Hill (2006) has noted: 'The purposive sociology of Baroness Hale may inspire liberal attitudes but it makes advising clients in Swindon County Court next to impossible.'

Following *Williamson*, the lower courts began to develop a considered jurisprudence on Article 9, following the trend set by Strasbourg. The High Court in *Khan v Royal Air Force Summary Appeal Court* recognized this, noting that while in 'earlier years the Commission in particular has often appeared to take a rather formal approach to Art.9(1)' and there appeared 'to have been some unwillingness to allow for the possibility of the engagement of Art.9(1) and thus to get into the question of justification under Art.9(2)', it was possible to detect a 'new preparedness to allow for possibilities that state interference under Art.9(1) may have to be justified' (para. 95). This change in English jurisprudence was demonstrated by the decision of the Court of Appeal in *Copsey v WBB Devon Clays Ltd*. Although the claimant was unsuccessful in his claim that his dismissal for refusing to agree to a contractual variation in his working hours to introduce a rotating shift procedure which included some Sunday working was unfair, the court provided a refined analysis of Article 9, stressing the importance of considering Article 9(2) and singling out the Strasbourg specific situation rule for criticism. Mummery LJ, for instance, noted that the 'specific situation' rule was simply constituted of 'repeated assertions unsupported by the evidence or reasoning that would normally accompany a judicial ruling' which were 'difficult to square with the supposed fundamental character of the rights' (para. 35); he declared that if there had been no such authority, he would have thought it necessary to examine the arguments under Article 9(2) (para. 30).

Other cases, however, did not follow the approach in *Williamson*. For example, whilst some ecclesiastical court decisions on exhumation and Article 9 (such as *Re Durrington Cemetery*) were exemplary, the judgment of Chancellor Bursell in *Re Crawley Green Road Cemetery, Luton* seemed to overstate the importance of Article 9 by presenting it as an absolute right which trumps domestic law (Sandberg 2006). Nevertheless the general trend was that lower courts followed the Strasbourg-compliant approach favoured by the House of Lords in *Williamson*. However, this trend was upset by another House of Lords decision, that of *Begum*.

The Impact of *Begum*

The case concerned Begum's wearing of the long *jilbab* coat in a state school contrary to the school's uniform policy; she contended that she had been 'excluded/suspended' from the school in breach, *inter alia*, of Article 9. At all three levels, the courts struggled with the interpretation of Article 9 (Hill and Sandberg 2006). The High Court focused on the issue of exclusion but noted that if she had been excluded, she would have been 'excluded for her refusal to abide by the school uniform policy rather than her beliefs as such', and since this would only have been 'motivated by religious beliefs', there had been no interference with her Article 9(1) right (paras 72–4). This assertion that insistence on wearing religious dress does not constitute a manifestation of one's religion or belief per se seems questionable (Hill and Sandberg 2007: 496).

The Court of Appeal, in holding that there was a breach of Article 9, took a different approach. Its treatment of Article 9(1) was exemplary; the court held that there was interference with Article 9 and noted that the specific situation rule had no application. Brooke LJ claimed that he was unable to derive any assistance from the cases the court was shown which related to employment disputes (para. 62) while Mummery LJ concurred, noting that it was no answer that she could have attended school if only she had worn the uniform and that it was irrelevant that she could have changed schools to accommodate her religious beliefs since she was not in the same position as an employee; rather there was a statutory duty to provide education and the school did not follow the proper statutory procedure for excluding her (para. 84).

However, the Court of Appeal erred in relation to the application of Article 9(2).

Rather than deciding whether the restriction on the right to manifest prescribed by school uniform could be justified as being necessary in a democratic society, Brooke LJ outlined the decision-making structure which the school should have used since, on his findings, the onus lay on the school to justify its interference with the Convention right (paras 75–6). This rests on a basic mistake; whilst courts apply such a proportionality test when reviewing decisions of public authorities after they have been made, there is nothing in the Human Rights Act 1998, the ECHR or Convention jurisprudence that requires public authorities themselves to adopt a proportionality approach to the structuring of their own decision-making (Poole 2005). The Court of Appeal hid 'under the blanket of procedure' producing a regrettable and erroneous approach imposing 'a stifling culture of formalism on public administrators that is quite at odds with the substantive objectives' of the Human Rights Act 1998 (Poole 2005: 694).

The House of Lords decision corrected the Court of Appeal's overly formulaic interpretation of Article 9(2). However, rather than following the Court of Appeal's exemplary treatment of Article 9(1) the majority of the House repeated and compounded the error originally made by the High Court (Hill and Sandberg 2007: 497). Lords Bingham, Hoffmann and Scott held that there had been no interference with the applicant's rights under Article 9(1). Lord Bingham held that although Article 9(1) of the ECHR was 'engaged or applicable' because Begum sincerely held the religious belief which she professed to hold (para. 21), Article 9 does not protect all acts motivated or inspired by belief (para. 22). He summed up the 'specific situation' rule developed by Strasbourg thus:

> The Strasbourg institutions have not been at all ready to find an interference with the right to manifest religious belief in practice or observance where a person has voluntarily accepted an employment or role which does not accommodate that practice or observance and there are other means open to the person to practise or observe his or her religion without undue hardship or inconvenience. (para 23)

This ignores the move against such filtering devices in Strasbourg jurisprudence and suggests that the interference requirement is rarely met. No reason was given for the application of the specific situation rule to the school environment where there is no contractual relationship between the pupil and the school (Hill and Sandberg 2006). Moreover, although Lord Bingham's elucidation of the specific situation rule required both voluntary acceptance of a rule *and* an alternative means to manifest religion or belief, Lord Bingham seemed to place great emphasis upon this second limb; he held that there was no interference with Begum's right to manifest her belief in practice or observance since Begum's family chose the school from outside their own catchment area and that there was 'no evidence to show that there was any real difficulty in her attending' another school (para. 25).

This conclusion, supported by Lords Hoffmann and Scott, suggests that provided there is a choice then an applicant's Article 9 right to manifest is not even engaged. This point brings domestic law in line with the much-criticized Strasbourg case of *Jewish Liturgical Association Cha'are Shalom Ve Tsedek v France*. This is particularly disturbing since both Lord Hoffmann and Lord Bingham followed *Williamson* in questioning the correctness of this case.

Lord Bingham's further elucidation of the rule proved even more suspect. Quoting selectively from numerous Strasbourg and domestic cases on the 'specific situation' rule, Lord Bingham omitted to mention references to the caveats to the rule, and applied the rule to the facts of the case without explanation (Hill and Sandberg 2007: 497). Although he recognized the view of the Court of Appeal in *Copsey v WBB Devon Clays Ltd*, he effectively gave the specific situation rule general application by concluding that:

> Even if it be accepted that the Strasbourg institutions have erred on the side of strictness in rejecting complaints of interference, there remains a coherent and remarkably consistent body of authority which our domestic courts must take into account and which shows that interference is not easily established. (para. 24)

This very broad proposition that 'interference is not easily established' seems to over-state the law. The Court of Appeal judgment in *Copsey v WBB Devon Clays Ltd* and more recent Strasbourg decisions question whether the body of authority should be followed as being coherent and consistent. Reliance on the specific situation rule was also unnecessary since if it was simply accepted that Article 9 was engaged, the claim could nevertheless be defeated by the use of one or more of the Article 9(2) limitations (Sandberg and Hill 2006, 2007).

The preferable reasoning is that of the minority, who concurred with the majority in the ultimate disposal of the appeal (Hill and Sandberg 2007: 498, Knights 2007: 48). Lord Nicholls and Lady Hale recognized that Article 9 had been engaged but that the interference was justified under Article 9(2). However, it is unfortunate that their speeches did not explain why their approach was the consistent interpretation of the Strasbourg jurisprudence. Although the House of Lords judgment in *Begum* includes helpful *obiter dicta*, such as passages correcting the Court of Appeal's procedural approach and hinting at a domestic 'margin of appreciation' (see paras 34, 63–4) it is a matter of regret that the *ratio* of the case is flawed. Giving universal effect to the specific situation rule and then rigidly applying it as a filtering device was likely to be problematic in terms of precedent. Although the speeches of the majority considered Article 9(2) in *obiter* and thus gave consideration to the merits of the case, a future court would not be obliged to do so. The majority's unnecessary and erroneous treatment of Article 9(1) had the clear potential of undoing the legacy of *Williamson*.

The case law following *Begum* suggested that the reasoning of the majority had undone the legacy of *Williamson*, with the overly narrow approach of the majority being adopted uncritically by lower courts and tribunals (Hill and Sandberg 2007: 498, Hill 2007: 31, Sandberg 2008). In *R (on the application of X) v Y School* the High Court regarded the *Begum* decision as an 'an insuperable barrier' (para. 100) to a claim for judicial review by a twelve-year-old schoolgirl who wished to wear a *niqab* veil while she was at school and being taught by male teachers, or when she was likely to be seen by men (Hill and Sandberg 2007: 498–9). Drawing on Lord Bingham's elucidation of the 'specific situation' rule in *Begum*, Silber J interpreted this as meaning that there would be no interference *either* where a person has voluntarily accepted an employment or role that does not accommodate that practice or observance *or* where there are other means open to practise or observe that religion without undue hardship or inconvenience (para. 26). Although this goes further than Lord Bingham who said that both requirements were needed, this is not unsurprising since it takes the majority's reasoning in *Begum* to its natural conclusion by giving general effect to the specific situation rule, bringing English law in line with the discredited 'impossibility' test provided in *Jewish Liturgical Association Cha'are Shalom Ve Tsedek v France* (Hill and Sandberg 2007: 448).

Although more recent civil cases have not gone quite as far as *R (on the application of X) v Y School*, they have shown a stricter approach to Article 9(1) than was the case prior to *Begum* (Sandberg 2008). In *R (on the Application of Playfoot (A Child) v Millais School Governing Body* the High Court rejected an application for judicial review on behalf of a schoolgirl who had wanted to wear a 'purity' ring at school as a symbol of her religiously motivated commitment to celibacy before marriage. Michael Supperstone QC, sitting as a deputy High Court judge, held that Article 9 was not engaged since the wearing of the ring was not a manifestation of her religious belief; it was not 'intimately linked' to the belief in chastity before marriage because the claimant was under no obligation, by reason of her faith, to wear the ring. This seems at odds not only with the more liberal application of the motivation/manifestation distinction found in the speech of Lord Nicholls in *Williamson* and recent Strasbourg jurisprudence but also runs the risk of infringing the well-established principle emphasized by Lord Nicholls in *Williamson* that courts should not be concerned whether the religious belief professed is a good faith in terms of judging the validity of that faith (Sandberg 2008). Determining whether an action is a manifestation of a person's religion or belief by determining whether that action was mandated by that person's religion as interpreted by a deputy High Court judge seems inappropriate.

Moreover, the High Court in *Playfoot* also invoked the post-*Begum* version of the specific situation rule. The judge held that there was no interference with Article 9 since the claimant had voluntarily accepted the school's uniform policy and there were other means open to her to practise her belief without undue hardship or inconvenience (para. 32). This conclusion not only follows *Begum* in accepting that the rule applies to schoolchildren but also follows *Begum* in casting the rule as one of general application. The judge placed emphasis upon this argument, noting that the claimant could have expressed her belief in another way, for example by attaching the ring, a key ring or other visible signs to her school bag or by transferring to another school which would allow the wearing of the ring. These comments suggest that the 'specific situation' aspect of the 'specific situation' rule is increasingly broader in domestic case law than in the Strasbourg jurisprudence. The rule has moved beyond its original contractual setting and the scope of the rule is now unknown (Sandberg 2008). The reasoning of the High Court is a matter of regret, given that the same decision could be made in a more Strasbourg-complaint manner by simply holding that there had been interference with Article 9 and that interference would have been justified under Article 9(2). Although the High Court to date has followed the House of Lords in *Begum* in undertaking some analysis of Article 9(2), this analysis has been purely *obiter*, allowing courts in the future to base their decisions solely on the less-convincing *dicta* concerning whether or not Article 9 was engaged.

It is also of concern that commendable elements of the House of Lords judgment in *Begum* have been forgotten. This is clear from High Court and Court of Appeal decisions in *R (on the Application of Swami Suryananda) v Welsh Ministers* concerning whether the slaughter of Shambo, a bullock at the claimant's Hindu temple, which had tested positive for the bacterium that causes bovine tuberculosis (TB), breached the claimant's human rights (Sandberg 2008). In the High Court, whilst the applicability of Article 9(1) was quickly accepted, confusion arose in relation to the application of Article 9(2) in that the judge quashed the decision by the Welsh ministers (to order the slaughter) on the basis that they had failed to approach the balancing exercise required under Article 9(2) since they had not identified a public interest to balance against the individual rights of the community; rather, they had defined their legitimate object too narrowly to be a proper public interest objective for the purposes of Article 9(2). The Court of Appeal unanimously allowed the appeal, criticizing the High Court for erroneously focusing upon the 'whether the decision maker proceeded in the right way', when the focus should have simply been on 'whether the decision taken does or does not infringe the relevant rights' (para. 103). The High Court had made the same mistake as the Court of Appeal in *Begum.* The Court of Appeal, however, followed a classic human rights and Strasbourg-compliant approach by using the Article 9(2) limits to hold that the interference was justified, thereby setting aside the order quashing the slaughter notice (Sandberg 2008). However, despite the decision of the Court of Appeal in *Swami Suryananda v Welsh Ministers*, the decision in *Watkins-Singh* was to demonstrate that the effect of *Begum* was to leave Article 9 moribund.

The Impact of *Watkins-Singh*

The case concerned Sarika Angel Watkins-Singh, a fourteen-year-old girl of Punjabi-Welsh heritage, who attended Aberdare Girls' High School. After being asked to remove her *kara*, defined judicially as 'a plain steel bangle which has a width of about 50 millimetres' (para. 1), since it contravened the school's uniform policy, she sought an exemption from the policy on the basis that her *kara* was a matter central to her ethnic identity and religious observance. When this exemption was refused she was at first taught in isolation at the school, but later moved to Mountain Ash School, which permitted the wearing of a *kara*. The governing body of the school had refused the request for an exemption on Article 9 grounds. Invoking the language of the post-*Begum* domestic specific situation rule, the governing body originally refused on the basis that it has 'not been convinced that, as part of her religion, it was a requirement that the *kara* be worn on the wrist, that if it were allowed this may result in bullying from other pupils and the wearing would give rise to health and safety issues' (para. 16). The appeal committee of the governing body was even more specific, refusing a subsequent appeal on the basis that 'article 9 of the ECHR does not require that one should be allowed to manifest one's religion at any time and place of one's choosing' (para. 17). Watkins-Singh challenged the decisions of the governing body of the school contending that they were based on errors of law.

Crucially, whilst the school saw the case as concerning Article 9 and therefore likely to be unsuccessful due to *Begum*, Watkins-Singh's legal team did not argue the case on Article 9 grounds. Rather, it was argued that the refusal to allow Watkins-Singh to wear the *kara* at school was unlawful as indirect unjustified race and religious discrimination contrary to the Race Relations Act 1976 and the Equality Act 2006. A number of other claims were also made, most notably that the defendant had not complied with the general statutory duty under Section 71 of Race Relations Act 1976, but the only human rights based claim was a contention that the segregation of Watkins-Singh contravened her rights under Articles 8 and 14 of the ECHR.

The difference between *Watkins-Singh* and the previous religious dress cases was elucidated by Silber J at the start of his judgment. He noted that unlike the previous cases of *Begum*, *X v Y* and *Playfoot* which were 'founded largely, if not solely on the provisions of the Human Rights Act 1998', the claim in the present case was 'based mainly on the totally different provisions' of the Race Relations Act 1976 and the Equality Act 2006, 'provisions on which the claimants in the previous case were unable to rely on' (para. 3). The previous claimants had been unable to rely on race discrimination laws since adherents of Islam and Christianity are not seen as races whilst Sikhs and Jews are (*Mandla v Dowell Lee*; *Seide v Gillette Industries Limited* cf. *J H Walker Limited v Hussain and Others*). Part 2 of the Equality Act 2006 which extended religious discrimination to cover goods and services and the exercise of public functions was not in force at the time of the earlier cases.

The claim for indirect discrimination on grounds of religion and race was upheld. In so holding Silber J employed a much more generous approach to religious symbols which are not mandated by the religion in the discrimination law context, than the High Court did in *Playfoot* in the human rights context. In *Watkins-Singh*, the question of whether the wearing of the *kara* was obligatory to the claimant was sidestepped. Although the expert evidence suggested that it was initiated Sikhs who observed all five Ks, of which the *kara* was one, and Watkins-Singh was an observant non-initiated Sikh, the expert also suggested that of the five Ks, the *kara* was the symbol most commonly worn. Silber J held that in relation to claims of indirect discrimination, he was unable to accept the defendant's contention that there would be a disadvantage *only* where a member of the group is prevented from wearing something that they are *required* to wear (para. 51). This threshold was too high: the language of the provisions does not suggest such a threshold; such an interpretation would require rewriting the legislative provision, would be inconsistent with the approach in recent Strasbourg jurisprudence, has no authority and has no valid reason of principle. Silber J commented that 'the court should not impose too high a threshold in seeking to establish *prima facie* discrimination as to do so would undermine the intension of the legislation' (para. 67).

He therefore concluded that disadvantage would occur – but would not *only* occur – where a pupil is forbidden from wearing an item where 'that person genuinely believed for reasonable grounds that wearing this item was a matter of exceptional importance to this or her racial identity or his or her religious belief' and where 'the wearing of the item can be shown objectively to be of exceptional importance to his or her religion or race, even if the wearing of the article is not an actual requirement of that person's religion or race' (para. 56B). Both the subjective and objective elements are satisfied on the facts: nothing had been suggested to undermine the truthfulness of Watkins-Singh's comments and the wearing of the item can be shown to be of exceptional importance to her religion and race as a Sikh even if not a requirement of that religion or a race. The reasons given by Silber J are strong and raise the question why the same conclusion ought not to be applied in the human rights context. By relying on Strasbourg cases for the 'exceptional importance' test Silber J's judgment questions the sharp distinction drawn in *Playfoot*.

Moreover, ironically in this case agued on discrimination grounds, the High Court cited and followed the *dicta* in *Williamson* concerning how a court should decide whether a claimant is genuinely manifesting a religious belief; Silber J noted that whilst the court may inquire into the genuineness of a claimant's belief as an issue of fact, it is not for the court to inquire into its validity. This again questions the decision in *Playfoot*. Furthermore, unlike the cases argued on Article 9 grounds, questions of justification were not mere *obiter* statements in *Watkins-Singh*. Interestingly Silber J again sought to distinguish the instant case from the Article 9 case law: 'decisions on justification which were successfully used by schools in the *Begum*, *X v Y School* and *Playfoot* cases' did not apply since 'many of the aspects of justification relied on in those cases are related to the extremely clearly visible and very ostentatious nature of the religious dress ought to be worn' (para. 78). However, this distinction is suspect. Silber J contended that it could not be said that allowing pupils to wear a *kara* causes substantial difficulties because they may stand out and that it undermined the uniform policy's aim of fostering a community spirit because the *kara* is small and is usually hidden by a long-sleeved sweater. This may be true in relation to the cases on Muslim dress but this was hardly true of the ring in *Playfoot*. The argument that the *kara*, unlike a ring, could be covered up is erroneous on two grounds. First, the *kara* was seen by the teacher on the day in which Watkins-Singh was asked to remove it; second, as Silber J's language conceded, it was simply the case that it was 'usually' covered by a long sleeve as opposed to always covered. Surely, obtrusiveness was ultimately irrelevant to the issue. Silber J sought to distinguish the justifications put forward in *Playfoot* on the grounds that in the instant case it could not be said that the ban was justified in that it minimized pressures resulting from wealth and style. However, this sees the purity ring in *Playfoot* as simply a fashion accessory, a conclusion undermined by the fact that the lifestyle it symbolizes is, if anything, out of fashion. A watertight distinction between the justifications accepted in the previous cases and the justifications rejected in the instant case is unsustainable.

Silber J also rejected the 'floodgates' argument on the basis that it was far from obvious that other pupils would be able to invoke this exception which is dependent on two factors: the first is that both the subjective and objective tests would have to be met: 'the belief of the pupil justified by objective evidence that the wearing of the article is a matter of exceptional importance as an expression of race and culture'; the second is the 'unobtrusive nature of the *kara*' (para. 92). However, this need for 'objective evidence' also raises the risk of courts engaging in issues upon which *Williamson* establishes that they should not tread since determining that 'evidence' invariably stretches if not defies the *Williamson* principles concerning the role of the court. *Watkins-Singh* is preferable to the Article 9 case law in that it does not fail at the interference stage. However, although *Watkins-Singh* is welcome in that it does not say that a religious manifestation has to be mandatory to be protected, *Watkins-Singh* disappoints in setting a high threshold for protection in the case of a religious manifestation which is not mandatory which suggests that both an objective and subjective test is required. It would be far preferable for the question of justification to be decisive.

It is of interest that all the other various claims made in *Watkins-Singh* succeeded apart from the human rights based one. The segregation of Watkins-Singh did not contravene her rights under Articles 8 and 14 of the ECHR; it was necessary to proceed on the basis that she was content at school, Article 8 was not infringed. This claim did not add anything to the claim of indirect discrimination (para. 137). This was telling of the approach generally taken: *Watkins-Singh* was not argued on Article 9 grounds because it is likely that on Article 9 grounds it would have failed, as the school governors readily understood. The case was successful because it seemed that the school, its teachers or its governors had not been informed, let alone instructed, on the significance of discrimination law generally and particularly to the dispute. Although the new law on religious discrimination offers a means of protecting religious freedom *in lieu* of Article 9, the restriction of Article 9 post-*Begum* remains lamentable. Silber J's comments concerning whether a religious undertaking needs to be mandatory and the proper role of the court in *Watkins-Singh* are to be welcomed. However, the threshold imposed in relation to interference still seems too high.

Many cases – even those argued on discrimination rather than Article 9 grounds – will continue to fall at the first hurdle. Surely the preferable approach would be to focus on the question of justification rather than saying that a religious practice must be mandatory or virtually mandatory (which is what Silber J's 'exceptional importance' test amounts to) before their religious freedom is infringed. Focusing on the question of justification would mean that if *Watkins-Singh* was successfully decided, then the decision in *Playfoot* is suspect. The mere fact that Article 9 was not argued in *Watkins-Singh* is important. It seems to suggest that *Begum* has restricted the application of Article 9 to such an extent that it has become moribund, at least in relation to claims concerning religious dress.

Conclusions: The Legacy of *Begum*

The actions of the assistant head teacher of Denbigh High School on the first day of the school term in September 2002, in telling Shabina Begum to go home, change and return wearing school uniform, must have seemed at the time to be rather mundane and ordinary. Yet, the judicial deliberations that followed provided 'a confusing and unhelpful precedent' that constrained religious liberty in England and Wales (Hill and Sandberg 2007: 498), being regarded as an insuperable barrier by the judiciary (*X v Y School*, para. 100) and being disregarded by litigants (such as the claimant in *Watkins-Singh*) who now, it appears, seek to rely on anything *but* Article 9.

Given the traditional judicial reluctance to intervene in matters of religion (Hill 2001), it is not surprising that the judiciary has struggled with the effects of the Human Rights Act 1998. The significance of the change is underscored by comparative reference with the even later incorporation of the ECHR in Ireland (European Convention on Human Rights Act 2003) which has had less effect and has led to little case law because of the pre-existing constitutional protection of religion. Even after the incorporation of the ECHR into Irish law, 'the principal (if not all) cases involving questions of religious freedom or religious issues *per se* have been determined in Ireland with reference to the provisions of *Bunreacht na hÉireann* rather than to the ECHR' (Colton 2007). The UK's Human Rights Act 1998, by contrast, provided a constitutional and cultural shift. It was thus unsurprising that the judiciary in this new task became entangled quite unnecessarily in the semantics of the right rather than the merits of the case. The focus on questions of interference rather than justification led judges to rely unduly upon filtering devices, most notably the general application of the specific situation rule in *Begum*.

Whilst prior to *Begum*, lower courts and tribunals generally followed the 'classic human rights approach' taken by the House of Lords in *Williamson* (Langlaude 2006: 345), after *Begum*, lower courts and tribunals generally adopted an overly restrictive interpretation of the Article 9(1) right, with domestic courts falling into problems which have largely been avoided by Strasbourg institutions

(Sandberg 2008). The arguments deployed in *Watkins-Singh*, their success and Silber J's reasoning are all part of the legacy of *Begum*, a case important not so much for its actual decision but for the reasoning of the majority. It remains to be seen how the legacy of *Begum* will affect subsequent higher court decisions on religious freedom.

Reference to the changing face of English law, as demonstrated in the cases of *Williamson*, *Begum* and *Watkin-Singh*, provides a deeper understanding of issues of cultural difference which are reduced to 'moral panics' (Cohen 1972) by the media. Such legal analysis is of particular importance at a time in which the legal framework appears to have changed (Doe and Sandberg 2009), and further change to the constitution is mooted (see Cranmer 2009). Reference to changing legal interpretations provide a valuable insight into the complex relationship between religion, law and society, or to be more precise, religions, laws and societies (Bradney 2001: 81). However, a legal approach in isolation may not be sufficient (Sandberg 2009). For instance, in *Begum* wider political and social trends – such as the fact that it was clear that the girl in question had come through her brothers under the influence of *Hizb u Tahrir*, an extremist religious organization, in particular, and the backdrop of September 11 and July 7, in general, – shaped the bringing of the claim, the way in which it was argued and the response of the judiciary. Analysis of the reasoning provided in law reports in isolation cannot provide a complete picture of changing social norms, yet it does provide a valuable and often neglected contribution to wider debates (Twining 1994). In the ongoing debate concerning the extent to which religious and racial diversity should be accommodated in England and Wales, these three cases concerning schools are of considerable importance.

References

Bradney, A. 2001. Politics and Sociology: New Research Agenda for the Study of Law and Religion. In *Law and Religion*, edited by R. O'Dair and A. Lewis. Oxford: Oxford University Press, 83–100.

Cohen, S. 1972. *Folk Devils and Moral Panics*. New York: St Martin's Press.

Colton, P. 2007. Ireland, the European Convention on Human Rights and Freedom of Religion. Paper submitted to the European Consortium for Church and State Research, November 2007.

Cranmer, F. 2009. Human Rights and the Christian Tradition: a Quaker Perspective. In *Law and Religion: New Horizons*, edited by N. Doe and R. Sandberg. Leuven: Peeters.

Doe, N. and R. Sandberg. 2009. Conclusion: New Horizons. In *Law and Religion: New Horizons*, edited by N. Doe and R. Sandberg. Leuven: Peeters.

Hill, M. 2001. Judicial approaches to religious disputes. In *Law and Religion*, edited by R. O'Dair and A. Lewis. Oxford: Oxford University Press, 421–42.

— 2006. Freedom of Religion in Contemporary English Jurisprudence. Unpublished lecture to the Oxford Society for Law and Religion, delivered at Balliol College, University of Oxford on Thursday 16 March 2006.
— 2007. *Ecclesiastical Law*. 3rd edition. Oxford: Oxford University Press.
Hill, M. and R. Sandberg. 2006. Muslim Dress in English Law: Lifting the Veil on Human Rights. *Religión y Derecho/Law and Religion*, 1, 302–28
— 2007. Is Nothing Sacred? Clashing Symbols in a Secular World. *Public Law*, 2007(3), 488–506.
King, A. 2007. *The British Constitution*. Oxford: Oxford University Press.
Knights, S. 2007. *Freedom of Religion, Minorities and the Law*. Oxford: Oxford University Press.
Langlaude, S. 2006. Flogging Children with Religion: a Comment on the House of Lords' decision in Williamson. *Ecclesiastical Law Journal*, 8, 339–45.
Poole, T. 2005. Of Headscarves and Heresies: the Denbigh High School Case and Public Authority Decision Making under the Human Rights Act [2005]. *Public Law*, 685–695.
Sandberg, R. 2006. Human Rights and Human Remains: the Impact of Dödsbo v Sweden. *Ecclesiastical Law Journal*, 8(39), 453–7.
— 2007. Flags, Beards and Pilgrimages: a Review of the Early Case Law on Religious Discrimination. *Ecclesiastical Law Journal*, 9, 87–91.
— 2008. Controversial Recent Claims to Religious Liberty. *Law Quarterly Review*, 124, 213–17.
— 2009. Religion, Society and Law: An Analysis of the Interface between the Law on Religion and the Sociology of Religion. Doctoral thesis: Cardiff University.
Twining, W. 1994. *Blackstone's Tower: The English Law School*. London: Sweet and Maxwell.

Chapter 15
Approaches to Diversity in the Domestic Courts: Article 9 of the European Convention on Human Rights

Samantha Knights

Introduction

'Is London's Future Islamic?' So ran the front cover of the June 2007 edition of *Time Out London* and title of an article that argued that an Islamic London would be a better place (Hodges 2007). The article caused relatively little by way of public reaction at the time or subsequently. However, just over six months later, the Archbishop of Canterbury unleashed a veritable torrent of furies with remarks he made, subsequently quoted out of context in the media, about the uses of shari'a law in the UK in a nuanced and scholarly lecture on the subject of civil and religious law in England (Williams 2008). The tabloids called for his resignation evoking images of women being stoned to death for adultery, men having their hands cut off for theft or indiscriminate floggings being inflicted as examples of shari'a justice. The reaction was informative more as an example of stereotyping of Islam rather than furthering any meaningful debate on the issues raised in the speech.

Underlying the manipulation of religious identity are serious issues about multiculturalism, diversity politics, and accommodation in the UK. There is little doubt that the political climate has changed since 11 September 2001 and again since 7 July 2005. Prior to this, the UK's government position on multiculturalism and diversity although far from consistent was at least not an overt promotion of the 'assimilation' model encouraged by the French state. One only has to look at the heterogeneity of the British state-maintained education system to see diversity in practice as regards religion in schools – whether through admission on faith-based criteria, religious teaching, worship, exemptions from the national curriculum (e.g. sport and swimming classes) or the variety in school uniforms.[1] But the recent issues surrounding Muslim extremism and anti-terrorism policies and legislation have become conflated with diversity politics in a way that arguably

1 See acknowledgement of the legitimate aim of faith-based admission criteria in *R(E) v The Governing Body of JFS & Ors* [2008] EWHC 1535/1536 (Admin) at [187–8].

damages society as a whole and the image of minorities in the UK in particular (see, for example Grillo 2005).

This chapter examines the role of both the higher domestic courts in the UK as well as the European Court of Human Rights (ECtHR) in Strasbourg in dealing with diversity issues principally in the context of Article 9 ECHR. It argues (1) that the UK and Strasbourg courts have made some positive statements regarding diversity and pluralism but that it is far from clear how and whether these principles are applied coherently in practice; (2) in the context of education and employment and freedom of religion cases (Article 9 ECHR) the courts have narrowed the ambit of application of Article 9 by effectively excluding it where applicants are found to have 'chosen' their situation; (3) in so doing the courts have dealt with Article 9 cases far more restrictively than those involving freedom of expression (Article 10) and freedom of association (Article 11); and (4) that law cannot be divorced from the socio-political context and that it is necessary to have continual regard to this in considering issues involving religious freedom and all areas of law – criminal and civil.[2]

Diversity Politics in the UK

It is important to say something at the outset about the changing and inconsistent language of diversity politics in the UK. Although courts do not invariably refer to the political climate in which a case is brought, it must be acknowledged that a decision-maker's individual perception of what is going on in the socio-political backdrop will no doubt impact on the decision-making process, particularly in cases involving broadly defined rights.

In 2004 the Home Office stated that 'integration is not about assimilation into a single homogenous culture and there is space within the concept of "British" for people to express their religious and cultural beliefs' (Home Office 2004: 5). However, this must be compared with a former Home Secretary's comments in 2002 that immigrant families should speak English at home even if it is not their mother tongue (Hinscliff 2002), and an earlier Home Secretary's statement in 2006 that he would rather Muslim women did not wear veils at all (Sturke 2006). More recently, Lord Goldsmith, the former Attorney General, has produced a report on citizenship and its meaning and significance in British society (Goldsmith 2008). This report highlights the lack of clarity and coherence in legislation and policy on citizenship, the rights and responsibilities of citizens, and notions of Britishness. In short, there is no clear current government policy on the way forward for diversity

2 This chapter focuses on the ECHR rights enacted in UK law by the Human Rights Act 1998. It should be noted that protection from religious and race discrimination is also provided by the Race Relations Act 1976, the EC Race Equality Directive and Framework Employment Directive of 29 June 2000 and 27 November 2000 respectively, and the Equality Act 2006.

– and what form it should take – accommodation, integration, assimilation or something else.

The position of the Commission on Racial Equality (now merged into the Equality and Human Rights Commission from 1 October 2007) on diversity also shifted under its chair, Trevor Phillips, who adopted a stance that multiculturalism is bad for minorities and that everyone should strive towards a form of accommodation. In the spring of 2004, Phillips sparked off a heated public debate on the meanings of integration, Britishness, core values, cohesion and multiculturalism. In a series of interviews and articles, he challenged what he saw as outdated concepts of multiculturalism – the ideology of difference as opposed to the fact of diversity in country that has been socially, culturally and ethnically diverse for centuries. He then advocated that he was not in favour of assimilation but, rather, an integrated society where people were free to be different but where citizenship with core common values for all was recognized.[3]

Alongside the public debate, it is important to recognize the changing demographic picture of the UK and the relative importance which religion has for different groups. In religious terms, Christianity, in its active form of worship, has been on the decline for some time, although in the last census the majority of the population identified themselves as Christian.[4] By contrast, there is apparently a continuing rise in the proportion of religious minorities in the UK, and evidence that religion is a far more significant factor for such minorities than for the majority (O'Beirne 2004: 20). Thus whatever form the policy of co-existence takes, it will need to be subject to continuing negotiations between groups within society and reflective of the fluid and changing culture of the population. This is not simply a question of accommodating music, literature, and food, but also the landscape of religion – planning permission for places of worship – mosques, gurdwaras, temples; the education system – choice of religious curriculum, forms of teaching; and religion in the public sphere generally (see further Knights 2007a).

Legal Approaches to Diversity

Tolerance of others has long been considered a fundamental principle in society in the UK and has found expression in a number of judicial decisions. In *Singh v Entry Clearance Office New Delhi*,[5] a case involving an adoption of an Indian Sikh

3 See website of the Equality and Human Rights Commission at <www.equalityhumanrights.comcre.gov.uk> for a fuller discussion.

4 See 2001 Census at <www.statistics.gov.uk>. A YouGov poll commissioned by the *Daily Telegraph* in 2004 reported highly contradictory results including that only 44% of those questioned believed in God. Available at <http://www.yougov.com/uk/archives/pdf/STI040101003_2.pdf> [accessed 5 November 2008].

5 [2004] EWCA Civ 1075 at [67].

boy and its recognition in the UK for the purposes of immigration law, Munby LJ in the Court of Appeal stated:

> We live, or strive to live, in a tolerant society increasingly alive to the need to guard against the tyranny which majority opinion may impose on those who, for whatever reason, comprise a weak or voiceless minority. Equality under the law, human rights and the protection of minorities have to be more than what Brennan J in the High Court of Australia once memorably described as 'the incantation of legal rhetoric'.

The same judge in that case recognized the de facto position that England was becoming increasingly secular and increasingly religious at the same time and further stated:

> [T]here have been enormous changes in the social and religious life of our country. The fact is that we live in a secular and pluralistic society. But we also live in a multi-cultural community of many faiths.[6]

In 2007 in *Khan v Khan*,[7] a case concerning a partnership agreement settled in the UK in Punjabi as part of a Muslim family arrangement between parties of Pakistan origin, Arden LJ in the Court of Appeal said:

> Where the parties are members of a particular community, then in my judgment the court must bear in mind that they may observe different traditions and practices from those of the majority of the population. That must be expected and respected in the jurisdiction that has received the European Convention on Human Rights. One of the fundamental values of the Convention is that of pluralism: see Kokkinakis v Greece [1994] 17 EHRR 397. Pluralism is inherent in the values in the Convention. Pluralism involves the recognition that different groups in society may have different traditions, practices and attitudes and from that value tolerance must inevitably flow. Tolerance involves respect for the different traditions, practices and attitudes of different groups. In turn, the court must pay appropriate regard to these differences.

In *R (Watkins-Singh) v The Governing Body of Aberdare Girls' High School & Anor*,[8] Silber J said in the context of a claim under the Race Relations Act 1976 and Equality Act 2006 about the wearing of a *kara* (Sikh bangle) in a school:

> [T]here is a very important obligation imposed on the school to ensure that its pupils are first tolerant as to the religious rites and beliefs of other races and

6 Ibid. at [62].
7 [2007] EWCA Civ 399 at [46].
8 [2008] EWHC 1865 (Admin) at [84].

> other religions and second to respect other people's religious wishes. Without those principles being adopted in a school, it is difficult to see how a cohesive and tolerant multi-cultural society can be built in this country.

The ECtHR has also made clear statements about the importance of pluralism, broadmindedness and tolerance of minorities in a democratic society. In *Young, James and Webster v United Kingdom*[9] it said in this context:

> Although individual interests must on occasion be subordinated to those of a group, democracy does not simply mean that the views of a majority must always prevail: a balance must be achieved which ensures the fair and proper treatment of minorities and avoids any abuse of a dominant position. Accordingly, the mere fact that the applicants' standpoint was adopted by very few of their colleagues is again not conclusive of the issue now before the Court.

And in *DH & Ors v Czech Republic*,[10] a case involving discrimination against Roma, the ECtHR said:

> [I]n Chapman, … the court also observed that there could be said to be an emerging international consensus amongst the contracting states of the Council of Europe recognizing the special needs of minorities and an obligation to protect their security, identity and lifestyle, not only for the purposes of safeguarding the interests of minorities themselves but to preserve a cultural diversity of value to the whole community.

So from the perspective of the UK domestic courts and the ECtHR there are at least some clear statements about the importance of pluralism, tolerance and fair treatment of minorities as fundamental applicable principles in a democratic nation. However, how do these principles work in practice in cases involving competing interests of parties? And do the principles apply differently depending on the area of law concerned?

Religion in the Public Sphere

By way of preface it is worth commenting briefly on the specific relationship between religion and the state in the UK. Unlike the constitutional arrangement in France and Germany, the UK has an established church in the Church of England. This creates an interesting paradox for minority groups. On the one hand, the

9 (1982) 4 EHRR 38 at [63]. See also *Serif v Greece* (judgment of 14 December 1999) at [53]; *Moscow Branch of the Salvation Army v Russia* (2006) 44 EHRR 912 at [57]. [61].

10 [2008] ECHR 922 at [181].

Church of England stands in a position of legal privilege. It is not directly funded by the state but its bishops are entitled as of right to sit in the House of Lords, the monarch is head of the Church of England and may not marry a Catholic, and the church conducts certain public ceremonies such as the coronation. In the sphere of education many state-funded schools are Church of England schools and the national curriculum reflects the culture of the majority of the population. There is, for example, a legal requirement enshrined in the Education Act 1988 that there be a daily form of worship in school 'wholly or mainly of a broadly Christian character'.[11] On the other hand and importantly for minority religions, this establishment of the Church of England means that the UK state is not hostile to religion in the public sphere per se. To advocate wholly secular principles in the public arena would in fact be in contradiction to the existence of the established church.

Another significant feature of the church–state relationship for minority religions in the UK is that the particular form of establishment is relatively weak by comparison with for example the church-state arrangement in Greece.[12] So to date there have been relatively few examples of religious groups in the UK which have experienced difficulties in recognition as a religious organization per se. Notable exceptions have been the Unification Church (commonly referred to as Moonies) and the Church of Scientology, which are not recognized as religions for the purposes of the immigration rules. This prevents members of these religious groups from entering the UK under the category of religious ministers.[13]

That said, given the religiously diverse make-up of the population of the UK today, evidence of increasing secularism of the majority and increasing religiosity among certain minority groups, the established church is arguably an anomaly. It is, for example, hard to justify the position of Church of England bishops who sit in the House of Lords as of right, without representatives of other religious groups being granted a similar privilege. Certainly there are a number of forceful advocates of disestablishment in the UK such as the Fabian Society, yet seemingly little political will to effect such a change. And equally there are fierce defenders of the status quo.[14] In this regard it should be noted that the EU and ECtHR have made it clear that the existence or lack of an established church in a state is not of itself a violation of the ECHR.[15] Plainly, however, the practical effects of the

11 Education Act 1988, Sch 20 paras 3(2) and (4).

12 See Constitution of Greece, 7 June 1975, Art 3.

13 IDI, Ch 5, s 6 para 1 (August 2004). Text available at <http://www.bia.homeoffice.gov.uk/sitecontent/documents/policyandlaw/IDIs/idischapter5/06section6/annexq.pdf?view=Binary> [accessed 5 November 2008].

14 See Ahdar and Leigh (2005: 127–54), Knights (2007a: 1.45). See also Modood (1997) for a perspective from different faiths and secularism on the question of disestablishment.

15 See Declaration (No 11) on the Status of Churches and Non-Confessional Organisations to the Final Act of the Treaty of Amsterdam, signed 2 October 1997. See

particular arrangements within a state may give rise to claims of discrimination, and lack of equal treatment.[16]

Case Law: Civil

Along with the jurisdictions of other states (and in particular Canada and the United States) the English judiciary has on the whole astutely avoided wading into the murky waters of weighing religion. That is made unnecessary by the wording of Article 9 ECHR which covers 'thought, conscience and religion', and its broad application by the ECtHR.[17] The weighing of religion has also been thought of as an inappropriate exercise for secular courts, as was recognized by Lord Nicholls in *R (Williamson) v Secretary of State for Education*,[18] who said:

> [T]he court is concerned to ensure an assertion of religious belief is made in good faith neither fictitious, nor capricious and that it is not an artifice … emphatically it is not for the court to embark on an inquiry into the asserted belief and judges its 'validity' by some objective standard such as the source material upon which the claimant founds his belief or the orthodox teaching of the religion in question or the extent to which the claimant's belief conforms to or differs from the views of other professing the same religion … the relevance of objective factors such as source material, is at most, that they may throw light on whether the professed belief is genuinely held.

This was further recognized by Munby LJ in *Sulaiman v Juffali*:[19]

> Although historically this country is part of the Christian west, and although it has an established church which is Christian, I sit as a secular judge serving a multi-cultural community of many faiths in which all of us can now take pride, sworn to do justice 'to all manner of people'. Religion – whatever the particular believer's faith – is no doubt something to be encouraged but it is not the business of government or of the secular courts. So the starting point of the

---

Darby v Sweden (1991) 13 EHRR 774.

16 See further Monaghan (2007: 5.142 –5.153). See also *R(E) v The Governing Body of JFS & Ors* [2008] EWHC 1535/1536 (Admin); *R (Sarika-Watkins) v The Governing Body of Aberdare Girls' High School & Anor* [2008] EWHC 1865 (Admin) for two cases considering discrimination within the meaning of RRA 1976 in the context of religion.

17 But note *R (Playfoot (A Child)) v Millais School Governing Body* [2007] EWHC 1698 (Admin) at [23] (wearing of a purity ring not intimately linked to belief in chastity before marriage).

18 [2005] 2 AC 246 at [22].

19 [2002] 1 FLR 479 [47]. See also *R(E) v The Governing Body of JFS & Ors* [2008] EWHC 1535/1536 (Admin) at [4], [107].

> law is an essentially agnostic view of religious beliefs and a tolerant indulgence to religious and cultural diversity. A secular judge must be wary of straying across the well-recognised divide between church and state. It is not for a judge to weigh one religion against another. All are entitled to equal respect, whether in times of peace or, as at present, amidst the clash of arms.

Similarly, in *Moscow Branch of the Salvation Army v Russia*,[20] the ECtHR observed:

> The State's duty of neutrality and impartiality, as defined in the Court's case law, is incompatible with any power on the State's part to assess the legitimacy of religious beliefs.

In practice, however, in the areas of law where religious issues are particularly prevalent – namely education and employment – it can be seen that the domestic courts have developed a restrictive approach to the application of freedom of religion in Article 9 ECHR. They have essentially done this by the adoption of a so-called 'clear line of authority' from Strasbourg and have rejected the notion of interference with Article 9 ECHR in a situation where an applicant is said to have voluntarily placed themselves.[21] This approach can be readily distinguished from that where other rights such as free speech and freedom of association are involved. In deciding that there has been no interference with an individual's rights, the court does not have to go on to consider the importance balance between the respective rights in any case.[22]

The high water mark of this approach was set out by a majority of the House of Lords in *R (Begum) v Headteacher and Governors of Denbigh High School*,[23] where they found no interference with Article 9 ECHR in a case where a schoolgirl voluntarily accepted a place at a school with knowledge of its uniform policy that did not permit the wearing of a *jilbab* and where that pupil could have chosen to attend another school where the *jilbab* was permitted. The House of Lords acknowledged that the line of Strasbourg authority had been criticized by the Court of Appeal in *Copsey v VWB Devon Clays Ltd*,[24] a case involving a devout

20 (2006) 44 EHRR 912 at [58], see also [92].

21 See *Kontinnen v Finland* (1996) 87 DR 68; *Stedman v United Kingdom* (1997) 23 EHRR CD 168; *Kalac v Turkey* (1997) 27 EHRR 552. But note *Ivanova v Bulgaria* (App. 52435/99) 12 April 2007 where a teacher was dismissed on account of her religious beliefs and an interference was found by the ECtHR.

22 Note that in *R (Sarika-Watkins) v The Governing Body of Aberdare Girls' High School & Anor* [2008] EWHC 1865 (Admin) a successful challenge was made to the school policy of refusing pupils to wear jewellery other than a watch and ear studs under the RRA 1976 and EA 2006. This was held to indirectly discriminate against a Sikh pupil who wished to wear a *kara* (bangle).

23 [2006] UKHL 15 at [23] (per Lord Bingham).

24 [2005] EWCA Civ 932 at [31–9].

Christian who regarded work on Sundays as conflicting with his religious beliefs. Nevertheless, the majority stated that even if it were accepted that Strasbourg had erred on the side of strictness in rejecting complaints of interference under Article 9 ECHR, there remained a 'coherent and remarkably consistent' body of authority that supported its view.[25]

The approach is problematic for a number of reasons and the line taken by the minority (Baroness Hale and Lord Nicholls) to the effect that there was an interference but that in the circumstances of the particular case it was justified is a far more principled and satisfactory approach. First, it is far from certain that there is such a clear line of authority from Strasbourg. The House of Lords relied heavily on decisions involving employment situations, whereas in examining the Strasbourg case law on education, interferences have been found by the ECtHR and Commission in a number of cases although the interference may well have been justified.[26] Employment cases have, in any event, frequently involved private parties whereas the school in *Begum* was state-maintained (see Knights 2007a: 2.71–2.74).

Secondly, the concept of freedom of choice does not sit easily with the practicalities of finding a school (or indeed employment) in many places. Baroness Hale recognized this much in her dissenting judgment. A survey by the *Guardian* newspaper suggested that local authorities failed to give one fifth of parents their first preference of school in admissions for 2008, showing that freedom of choice is simply a fiction in many areas (Lispett 2008). Even where (as was the case in *Begum*) another school may offer a child the opportunity to have its particular religious requirement respected, he or she may not wish to transfer to that school for a variety of good reasons such as academic performance, proximity to home and settled social life in existing school.

Thirdly, the approach here is at odds with that taken in other areas of ECHR rights. For example, in the case of freedom of expression the fact that someone could choose another form of media, area, country in which to express their views does not provide a complete answer such that it can be said that there is no interference. The underlying purpose of the ECHR is to protect the individual against the state. The fact that a person has placed himself in a particular situation should not necessarily affect the question of interference, although it will no doubt be relevant to the issue of whether interference is justified. So for example, in the case of an individual who volunteers for army service and who for reasons of army regulations may not pray freely at all times of day, it can be argued that there is an interference but that it is justified on grounds of public order, and/or the protection of rights and freedom of others. In all cases it must be remembered

25 [2006] UKHL 15 at [24]. See also *X v Headteacher and Governors of Y School* [2007] EWHC 298 (Admin).

26 See e.g. *Dahlab v Switzerland* (App. 42393/98) 15 February 2001; *Sahin v Turkey* (2005) 41 EHRR 8; *Casimiro & Ferreira v Luxembourg* (App. 44888/98) 27 April 1999.

that regulations, rules and norms adopted by the state are themselves culturally specific. There are few (if any) that are inevitable or immutable.

Although the majority in *Begum* stated that there had been no interference, it nevertheless went on to consider whether the interference could have been justified in any event. It should be pointed out that in the relatively few cases involving school regulations that have reached the domestic courts, the judiciary has been keen to underline that the primary decision-making is taken at a lower level (e.g. by the school or local authority) but that this does not preclude proper scrutiny by the courts. An important principle in any case is 'proportionality'. The House of Lords in *Begum* rejected the procedural approach adopted by the Court of Appeal below in that case and said that the court had to decide for itself whether there was a violation of an ECHR right. In that context Lord Bingham said:

> There is no shift to a merits review, but the intensity of review is greater than was previously appropriate, and greater even than the heightened scrutiny test adopted by the Court of Appeal in R v Ministry of Defence, ex p Smith [1996] QB 517, 554. The domestic court must now make a value judgment, an evaluation, by reference to the circumstances prevailing at the relevant time … Proportionality must be judged objectively by the court … [I]t is in my view clear that the court must confront these questions, however difficult. The school's action cannot properly be condemned as disproportionate, with an acknowledgement that on reconsideration the same action could very well be maintained and properly so.[27]

The majority, citing the Grand Chamber[28] decision in *Sahin v Turkey*[29] as recognizing the importance of Article 9, the value of religious harmony, and the need for compromise and balance, found that any interference with Article 9 in the case was justified. Lord Bingham noted that the school had taken advice, had been told that its uniform policy conformed with the requirements of mainstream Muslim opinion and the uniform policy, which allowed for an alternative *shalwar khameez* to be worn, was thought to contribute to harmony and success in the school.[30] The minority agreed that the interference was justified on the facts of the case. Baroness Hale, however, acknowledged that a distinction may be drawn between adults and young girls and the inherent difficulty of understanding the cultural background in play in a case. Citing a number of academic articles, she

27 Ibid. [30].

28 The Grand Chamber is the second and final tier of the ECtHR. It will hear cases considered to be of great importance.

29 (2005) 41 EHRR 8.

30 Contrast the position of the school in *R (Watkins-Singh) v The Governing Body of Aberdare Girls' School* [2008] EWHC 1865 (Admin) which was found to have failed in its duties to have an appropriate racial equality policy as required under s 71 RRA 1976.

noted the complexity of cultural issues surrounding the wearing of the *hijab* and the ensuing competing interests. She noted in particular:

> In deciding how far to go in accommodating religious requirements within its dress code, such a school has to accommodate some complex considerations. These are helpfully explained by Professor Frances Radnay[31] in 'Culture, Religion and Gender' [2003] 1 *International Journal of Constitutional Law* 663:
>
> 'genuine individual consent to a discriminatory practice or dissent from it may not be feasible where these girls are not yet adult. The question is whether patriarchal family control should be allowed to result in girls being socialised according to the implications of veiling while still attending public educational institutions ... A mandatory policy that rejects veiling in state educational institutions may provide a crucial opportunity for girls to choose the feminist freedom of state education over the patriarchal dominance of their families. Also, for the families, such a policy may send a clear message that the benefits of state education are tied to the obligation to respect women's and girls' rights to equality and freedom . . . On the other hand, a prohibition of veiling risks violating the liberal principle of respect for individual autonomy and cultural diversity for parents as well as students. It may also result in traditionalist families not sending their children to the state educational institutions. In this educational context, implementation of the right to equality is a complex matter, and the determination of the way it should be achieved depends upon the balance between these two conflicting policy priorities in a specific social environment.[32]

It is interesting to compare the approach taken to Article 9 ECHR in the context of education and employment disputes with that taken in the area of freedom of expression (Article 10 ECHR). There have been a number of cases before the Strasbourg courts involving the balance of interests between an individual's right to express himself and the rights of others. Although the right not to be offended is not recognized as such under the ECHR,[33] cases concerning the expression of religious views may give rise to fears of public disorder or security such that member states may be justified in placing restraints on such expression.[34] Similarly in the area of freedom of association for example in cases involving employment

31 Sic. The author's name is Frances Raday.

32 Ibid. at [98].

33 See in the context of an attempt by a member of a Christian group to bring a private prosecution for criminal blasphemy relating to a theatrical work, *Jerry Springer: the Opera*: *R (Green) v City of Westminster Magistrates' Court* [2007] EWHC 2785 (Admin).

34 See e.g. *Otto-Preminger-Institut v Austria* (1995) 19 EHRR 34; *Klein v Slovkia* (App 72208/01) 31 October 2006.

law and trades unions the ECtHR has not relied on the doctrine of freedom of choice.[35]

However, in these cases the approach of the ECtHR has generally not been to consider whether an individual could choose to express himself in another forum that may have less impact or may not offend in the same manner. The rationale is obvious in that the very purpose of the rights exercised in this area may be to impact on the particular group targeted. The other principle at play may be the fundamental importance attributed to the marketplace of ideas and hence to freedom of expression. However, the ECHR contains no hierarchy of rights and in principle Article 9 is no more or less worthy of protection than Articles 10 or 11.

In the domestic context, in *Church of Jesus Christ of Latter Day Saints v Price*,[36] the administrative court considered the balance between the corresponding rights of a preacher and those of residents and local churchgoers under the law of tortuous nuisance and unlawful harassment. The court in that case did not approach the issue of interference as a matter of freedom of choice. It should also be noted that the Human Rights Act 1998 makes express provision for the protection of both Article 9 and 10 rights over and above the incorporation of the ECHR rights themselves.[37] Although it does not appear that these express statutory provisions add anything as a matter of practical effect in terms of the balancing exercise that the court is required to perform in any case, it is an indication of the concern for proper protection of victims of violations in both areas.[38] The point remains that as a matter of general principle there is no particular reason for the court to use the doctrine of freedom of choice in deciding the question of interference (as opposed to the issue of justification). For this reason, future cases are more likely to be argued under the provisions of the RRA 1976 and EA 2006 where the issue of discrimination is live.[39]

Cases: Criminal

While in civil cases it is far easier to raise the issue of Article 9 ECHR, in the area of criminal law an appeal to Article 9 ECHR is unlikely to succeed as a

35 See *Sorensen and Rasmussen v Denmark* (11 January 2006); *Sibson v United Kingdom* (1994) 17 EHRR 193; *Young, James & Webster v United Kingdom* [1981] IRLR 408.

36 [2004] EWHC 3245 (Admin).

37 Human Rights Act 1998, ss 12–13.

38 See *R (Williamson) v Secretary of State for Education and Employment* [2002] EWCA Civ 1820 [49] (per Buxton LJ). Note these dicta were not disturbed in the House of Lords' subsequent judgment.

39 See e.g. *R(E) v The Governing Body of JFS & Ors* [2008] EWHC 1535/1536 (Admin); *R (Sarika-Watkins) v The Governing Body of Aberdare Girls' High School & Anor* [2008] EWHC 1865 (Admin).

defence. The balance of interests between state and the individual is likely in this area to weigh far more heavily in favour of state interest. The reasons for this are obvious in the sense that arguments supporting public order and state security are very powerful, and particularly so in the current climate. So, for example, in cases involving prosecutions for drugs, it has been held by the UK courts on two occasions that religious beliefs are no defence to a criminal charge.[40] Moreover, in cases involving the most serious of crimes, e.g. rape or murder, there is no room as such for a religious defence although cultural and religious factors may be taken into consideration at the sentencing stage by way of mitigating features[41] or referred to in relation to a person's character.[42]

However, English law has for a long time provided for statutory exceptions to criminal law provisions, including provisions whose primary rationale is not merely the protection of the individual concerned but also the protection of the public. So, for example, Sikhs have been granted an exemption from the general requirement to wear a helmet when riding a motor cycle,[43] and from the prohibition on carrying offensive weapons to allow the wearing of a *kirpan* (a ceremonial sword).[44] Additionally Muslims and Jews have been able to obtain exemptions from meat slaughter regulations to allow them to prepare and sell kosher and halal meat.[45]

Importantly a number of criminal law provisions contain an element of lack of 'reasonable excuse' as part of the case which the prosecution must prove, or alternatively provide for 'reasonable excuse' as part of a defence which may be raised by the accused. One such area involves prosecutions for noise nuisance under the Environmental Protection Act 1990. The courts have stated that the concept of 'reasonable excuse' is not to be narrowly defined and in principle religious and cultural background may be taken into account but have so far have not held that a religious defence could be considered as a reasonable excuse on the facts of any case.

In a notable case, *London Borough of Hackney v Rottenberg*,[46] an Orthodox Jewish rabbi and member of the Hasidic community ran a school and synagogue in one of the most religiously and culturally diverse boroughs in London. The school was relatively small with only twenty boys attending and was in a street with a

40 See *R v Andrews* [2004] EWCA Crim 947; *R v Taylor* [2001] EWCA Crim 2263. See Renteln's chapter, this volume, for a discussion of the so-called 'cultural defence'.

41 Note conversely that in *Re Attorney General's Reference* (No 51 of 2001) [2001] EWCA Crim 1685 at [17] , Mantell LJ in sentencing had regard to the fact that the victim of a rape was a Muslim woman who had been a virgin and had lost a degree of respect in her own community, and had suffered damage to her marriage prospects and self-esteem.

42 See e.g. reference to the defendant's 'deep and sincerely held religious beliefs' in *R v Faqir Mohammed* [2005] EWCA Crim 1880 at [29].

43 Road Traffic Act 1988, s 17.

44 Criminal Justice Act 1988, s 139.

45 Slaughterhouses Act 1976, s 36.

46 [2007] EWHC 166 (Admin).

far larger synagogue opposite, a noisy local public house and a hostel for asylum seekers among other buildings. A Muslim woman had lived next door to the rabbi without complaint for a number of years but had started to complain about noise during the Sabbath worship on Friday night. Environmental health officers employed by the London borough recorded noise nuisance on six occasions for very limited periods of time. Three of these occasions were during Sabbath prayers on Friday evenings, one was during religious prayers during school hours, another was during Passover celebrations and the final one involved a large organized one-off celebration of the Induction of the Scroll which had been granted prior authorization by the police and was accompanied by a police presence (Knights 2007b).

In cross-examination of the environmental health officers it emerged that Hackney had no specific policy on dealing with noise emanating from religious buildings, the officers themselves were not all aware that the building concerned operated as a school or a synagogue, and few of them were aware of the significance of the Jewish festivals and worship in question. They all agreed, however, that noise nuisance was context-specific and that it was important to have regard to the cultural diversity of the neighbourhood, the reason for the noise and the nature of the area i.e. whether it was wholly or partly residential. The London Borough of Hackney also accepted that the dates and times in question involved religious celebrations.

The Crown Court, on appeal from the magistrates court (where the rabbi had been convicted of all six charges), held on the facts that there was no statutory nuisance under the provisions of the Environmental Health Act 1990, as the London borough had not satisfied the court to the requisite standard of proof. It was accordingly not necessary to consider in any detail the impact of Article 9 ECHR or whether the rabbi had a reasonable excuse. However, the court stated that, had it been satisfied that there had been a statutory nuisance, it would not have considered the prosecution to be disproportionate in violation of Article 9 ECHR. The London Borough of Hackney appealed to the divisional court which upheld the decision of the lower court finding that there was no statutory nuisance. As regards Article 9 ECHR issue the divisional court stated:

> [I]t is not necessary for us to decide the second point as a discrete issue; the matters are closely inter-related. I would hold that the fact that the noise is created in the course of religious worship, in premises registered and with planning permission for that use, would inevitably be a relevant consideration, both in considering whether noise constitutes a nuisance and whether there is reasonable excuse for it. But, for myself, I would share the Crown Court's provisional view that, if the service is conducted in such a way that the court, exercising its own judgment, finds that a statutory nuisance exists, then the fact that the nuisance was created

> in such circumstances would be unlikely to amount to a defence of reasonable excuse, nor would a prosecution be disproportionate.[47]

Although the court's dicta indicated that it did not think that the religious defence would likely prevail in a case in which the constituent elements of the offence were otherwise established, they did not rule it out.

Conclusions

It is clear that there has for some time been recognition in English law of the de facto changing religious and cultural diversity in the UK. Pluralism, broad-mindedness and tolerance have been long regarded as fundamental principles in a democratic society. There is also recognition of the need to protect minorities against the tyranny of the majority on the basis that minorities' views will not necessarily be reflected in legislation passed in a democracy. With the advent of the Human Rights Act 1998, EC directives on race and religious discrimination and the Equality Act 2006, additional protection is given to minorities. However, the approach to religious diversity under Article 9 ECHR in particular areas of civil law is not universal and has been severely curtailed in education cases by the approach taken by the House of Lords in the *Begum* case. This sets an unfortunate precedent at a moment when the balance of cultures and diversity in society is particularly acute. Along with the raft of restrictive measures contained in anti-terrorism legislation it may serve only further to alienate minorities from the majority of the population.

When the case law is examined as a whole and a comparative view is taken of the approach to Article 9 ECHR in different contexts, as well as the approach to other rights in the ECHR, it is clear that important distinctions can be drawn. While there are obvious and strong public policy reasons for ensuring that a uniform set of criminal laws exist, it is far less clear why there should be different approaches to the various rights contained in the ECHR in civil law. Given the lack of hierarchy in rights in the ECHR and in domestic law, it is not clear that such differences in approach can be justified. In any event, it is important to recognize the underlying socio-political context in any given case and not simply to make assumptions, silent or otherwise, in decision-making. Diversity should be not only acknowledged in spirit but also in practice. In the words of Montaigne: 'There never were in the world two opinions alike, no more than two hairs or two grains; the most universal quality is diversity' (cited in Hazlitt 1853: 363).

---

47 Ibid. at [90].

References

Ahdar, R. and I. Leigh, I. 2007. *Religious Freedom in the Liberal State*. Oxford: Oxford University Press.

Goldsmith, P. 2008. *Citizenship: Our Common Bond*. London: Ministry of Justice. Available at <www.justice.gov.uk/docs/citizenship-report-full.pdf> [accessed 22 October 2008].

Grillo, R. 2005. *Backlash Against Diversity? Identity and Cultural Politics in European Cities*. Centre on Migration, Policy and Society, Working Paper 14. Oxford: COMPAS, University of Oxford.

Hazlitt, W. ed. 1853. *The Works of Montaigne*. London: Templeman.

Hinscliff, G. 2002. Speak English at Home Blunkett tells British Asians. *Observer*, 15 September.

Hodges, M. 2007 Is London's Future Islamic? *Time Out*, 5 June 2007.

Home Office. 2004. *Strength in Diversity. Towards a Community Cohesion and Race Equality Strategy*. London: Home Office.

Knights, S. 2007a. *Freedom of Religion, Minorities, and the Law*. Oxford: Oxford University Press.

— 2007b. Noise Nuisance under EPA 1990 and Article 9 ECHR: London Borough of Hackney v Rottenberg. *Environmental Liability*, 3, 150.

Lipsett, A. 2008. School Admissions show 'Lack of Choice'. *Guardian*, 4 March 2008.

Modood, T. (ed.) 1997. *Church, State and Religious Minorities*. London: PSI.

Monaghan, K. 2007. *Equality Law*. Oxford: Oxford University Press.

O'Beirne, M. 2004. *Religion in England and Wales: Findings from the 2001 Home Office Citizenship Survey*. London: Home Office Research, Development and Statistics Directorate.

Raday, F. 2003. Culture, Religion and Gender. *International Journal of Constitutional Law*, 1(4), 663–715.

Sturke, J. 2006. Straw: I'd Rather No One wore Veils. *Guardian*, 6 October 2006.

Williams, R., The Rt. Rev. 2008. Civil and Religious Law in England: A Religious Perspective. Speech at the Royal Courts of Justice, 7 February 2008. Available at: <http//www.archbishopofcanterbury.org/1575> [accessed 22 October 2008].

Chapter 16

Human Rights in Contexts of Ethnic Plurality: Always a Vehicle for Liberation?

Roger Ballard

Introduction

Human rights occupy a central role in contemporary legal and socio-political discourse. Having been given concrete form in the American Constitution, and reinforced in revolutionary France's Declaration of the Rights of Man and the Citizen, all flavours of Euro-American social, cultural and political thought have since been conditioned by a powerful conceptual trope: the expectation that individual freedom, underpinned by a legally guaranteed charter of human rights, provides the most effective means of constructing a just and equitable social order. This vision was further strengthened when the United Nations adopted the Universal Declaration of Human Rights in 1948, in the hope that it would provide a universal legal bastion against exploitation and oppression.

In so far as it provides (at least in principle) a means whereby the citizens of any state can challenge the legitimacy of the unbridled application of totalitarian power, the doctrine has undoubtedly had many beneficial consequences. Its agenda is deemed to be inherently progressive, and it is assumed that efforts to implement its premises will bring unqualified social and cultural benefits, regardless of the context, the distinctive cultural commitments and historical experiences of those on whose behalf such initiatives are undertaken. In a world where humanitarian intervention is being widely deployed to justify legal, political and military interference in the lives of others, can we be sure that such initiatives will always and everywhere be as favourable as their advocates declare? Or are there circumstances in which the outcome of such efforts is seriously dysfunctional, especially when they provide a means whereby a privileged few can throw a veil of legitimacy over initiatives which do more to reinforce their own position than to advance the interests of those whom the intervention was nominally designed to assist?

This not to suggest that the discourse of human rights is everywhere and always deployed for such purposes; but it is to insist that the current discourse has been ordered in such a way that it can readily be so utilized. Nor are such outcomes uncommon. In international contexts the discourse of human rights has been turned into a political football, with the result that it is as often used to justify initiatives whose consequences (intended or not) are as likely to reinforce, rather than undermine, established patterns of inequality and injustice.

My concern with these matters is, however, more narrowly focused. I write as anthropologist rather than lawyer or political scientist, in response to a delimited set of empirical concerns: the social, political and legal conundrums which have emerged from the pluralizing consequences of post-war non-European labour migration.

The Enlightenment and Ethnocentrism

During the course of the past half century Britain has witnessed the rapid growth of ethnic colonies, within which settlers have made strenuous efforts to rebuild the personal and domestic lives on their own distinctive terms, whilst making all manner of strategic adaptations to cope with the external challenges they were facing. As the post-war economic boom developed, migrants began to arrive in Europe's industrial cities in increasing numbers to fill the gaps which had emerged at the bottom of the labour market. The response of the indigenous population was distinctly uneasy. At one level their presence was regarded as welcome, since it enabled indigenes to move into better-paid sections of the expanding labour market, leaving the immigrants to perform a host of necessary but menial tasks, often for lower wages than they themselves once received. But it was not long before more negative reactions came to the fore. As the settlers' colonies grew in size, so the competition which they were seen to be offering to indigenous interests, not just in the labour market, but with respect to scarce public resources such as housing, hospital beds and school places, began to be regarded as deeply unwelcome. The resultant contradictions were further exacerbated as the early pioneers (virtually all of whom were male) called their wives and children to join them, and the locally-born segment of the minority population began to burgeon.

Much has changed since these processes initially took off. Ethnic colonies continue to thrive, and it is increasingly inappropriate to describe them as 'immigrant', since in many cases well over half of their members are now in principle 'indigenous', in terms of birthplace and citizenship. But no matter how much of an integral component of the surrounding social order settlers and their offspring have become, they still find themselves alienated by and from their surroundings. No matter how substantial their material achievements, the degree of hostility they encounter remains significant, particularly since it has broadened in character and now focuses as much on their commitment to maintaining a personal sense of ethnic alterity as on the unwelcome competition for access to scarce resources which those who differ are still held to represent.

To what extent has the European Convention on Human Rights (ECHR) served to counter such developments? In principle one might expect that such a pan-European commitment would bring unqualified benefits to members of minority groups who found themselves subjected to powerful forces of marginalization. In part that expectation holds good. Insofar as it insists that all humans are beings of intrinsically equal worth, the discourse provides unequivocal support for the proposition that all forms of unequal and discriminatory treatment predicated on hereditary difference, such as those of race and gender, are *ipso facto* illegitimate. As a result it is widely assumed that this provides a sufficient basis around which to construct comprehensive and universally applicable policies of anti-hegemonic and anti-oppressive practice.

But idealistic aspirations are one thing, and empirical outcomes another. Close inspection of the conceptual foundations of current discourse reveals several alarming *lacunae*. One of the most serious is its failure to take cognizance of one of the most salient features of the human condition, our capacity to order our inter-personal relationships on the basis of our own self-constructed conceptual premises. Locked within the iron cage of the conceptual premises which its liberally minded Euro-American authors took for granted, the current discourse has nothing to say about our capacity to act as cultured beings, and hence *to create the terms of our own existence*. Yet despite, indeed because of, the ongoing rush of globalization it should be self-evident that the cultural universes which we humans inhabit are anything but uniform; on the contrary, our conceptual and linguistic frameworks are bewilderingly diverse, and likely to remain so into the foreseeable future.

Even if current discourse takes little if any cognizance of this dimension of the human condition, it wrong to assume it remains unaffected by this deficiency. Like all other human constructions, the discourse is a cultural product, and its conceptual foundations require scrutiny. Rooted in ideas generated during the course of Europe's eighteenth-century Enlightenment, it still takes the commonplace premises of that period largely for granted. One such notion is the prospect of social progress, with the result that one of the driving forces behind development of the discourse was, and remains, an effort to chart a course towards a freer, more open and more rationally grounded future, with the object of facilitating steady progress towards a *singular* vision of social perfection (Gray 2000). Thus the discourse is underpinned by a conceptual trope which is culturally grounded, and structured in such a way as to impose an evolutionary perspective on culture itself. If culture is perfectible, as eighteenth-century savants assumed, then it should in principle be possible to place all given instances of cultural practice along a spectrum ranging from less to more perfect. Yet although this view further underpinned the assumption that the discourse was nominally universal in scope, this was immediately contradicted, no less in the eighteenth century than today, by a further assumption that the arena within which such rights could be enjoyed would be spatially delimited, namely by citizens resident within the boundaries of the nation state. The circle was completed by an assumption that responsibility for their enforcement would fall on those who had been democratically elected to exercise authority on their behalf.

However reasonable (if ethnocentric) these assumptions may seem when considered separately, their consequences can be toxic when combined. Once it is assumed that society (or rather the set of cultural premises within which the citizens of any given state democratically decide that their interactions should be ordered) is perfectible, as did the French revolutionaries and their successors, cultural plurality will tend to be perceived as a threat, not just to 'progress', but to national integrity. Tensions arising from contradictions of this kind can readily be observed throughout the contemporary world. No matter how 'universal' the discourse of human rights may proclaim itself to be, contradictory premises embedded in its roots combine in such a way as to render it difficult, if not impossible, for its exponents to champion what can reasonably be argued is the most fundamental human right of all: *the right to differ,* not just on an individual, but also on a *collective* basis.

Despite claims to universal applicability, the contemporary discourse of human rights is far more *emic* than *etic* in character, its 'accounts, descriptions, and analyses are expressed in terms of the conceptual schemes and categories that are regarded as meaningful and appropriate by the actors themselves', rather than by 'the community of scientific observers' (Lett 1996: 382–3). Far from standing above and beyond its authors' taken-for-granted, parochial conceptual premises, the contemporary discourse is a product of a specific conceptual tradition, an individualistic, liberal and consciously evangelistic ideological and philosophical outlook which emerged from the Enlightenment. As such it is not just Euro-centric but enshrines a civilizing mission which seeks to put all aspects of humanity's unenlightened past behind it, and to promote progress towards a rosier, but necessarily singular, future.

This vision suited the political purposes of the instigators of the eighteenth-century Euro-American Enlightenment. Seeking to liberate themselves from the power of monarchy, they adopted a revolutionary philosophy: that the only legitimate source of state power was that which flowed from its citizens, rather than from divinely ordained monarchs. The notions of liberty in which this proposition was grounded flagged an equally far-reaching revolution in their assumptions about the human condition. Social actors were seen as drawing their social being not from subordination to a master, membership of a corporation, a monarch, or God, but from their capacity to act as autonomous but *responsible* individuals. Hence as Blackstone famously put it in his *Commentaries on the Laws of England*, 'The first and primary end of human laws is to maintain and regulate the absolute rights of individuals', on the basis of a further assumption that those who made and administered such precepts were persons who had capacity to act 'as a free agent, endowed with discernment to know good from evil, and with power of choosing those measures which appear to him to be the most desirable' (Blackstone 1765: 119).

Nevertheless it would be a mistake to assume that Blackstone or his fellow-commentators believed that the capacity to act with moral discrimination was universally distributed. Rather, as Hunt emphasizes, settled opinion in the eighteenth century took the opposite view: 'Women, children foreigners and those who paid no taxes should be "passive" citizens only' (Hunt 2007: 148). If the republic was to be governed by its citizens, participation in the process of government should be limited to those with the capacity to exercise individual judgement. Thus along with foreigners, servants, slaves and 'savages', the immediate familial dependents of independent citizens of revolutionary France were excluded from the franchise. Lacking a sufficient degree of moral discernment to exercise political responsibility in their own right, it followed that their interests were best safeguarded by the patriarch. The gendered character of the declaration of 'The Rights of Man and the Citizen' was no slip of the tongue, as Mary Wollstonecraft (1792) underlined. The revolutionaries were not universalists: the rights they had were deliberately constrained by gender, class, race and nationality.

Much has changed since then. Thanks to political battles during the nineteenth and twentieth centuries, classist, sexist and racist restrictions on access to citizenship have been removed as a result of the application of a more universalistically oriented vision of *Human* rights. But why has plurality proved to be such a sticking point? If progress has been made with respect to class, gender and race, absence of progress on other fronts can best be traced to a further salient feature of eighteenth-century discourse, a dual commitment to methodological individualism on the one hand and methodological nationalism on the other; and as Beck (2006), Grey (2002) and Wimmer (2002) all emphasize, those premises still remain largely unchallenged.

Alternative Perspectives

From an extra-European perspective it has long been self-evident that civilization is no European monopoly. Certainly, Euro-Americans may have developed some extraordinary technical and organizational skills which those subjected to their hegemony during the course of the past two centuries have been only too keen to borrow. But to those operating within other traditions, the untrammelled commitment to individualism which is such a salient feature of Euro-American ideology inverts their own premises regarding the proper foundations of civilized behaviour, and they have long been doubtful as to whether social orders constructed on that basis are in any way worthy of emulation. Two brief examples serve to highlight the grounds on which they reach such conclusions.

A core premise of the Confucian tradition is that righteousness (*shu*) is best sustained through the maintenance of relationships of hierarchical reciprocity as between benevolent patriarchs (ranging from the head of the family up to the emperor himself) and their respectfully pious filial subordinates. Individual self-interest and autonomy are consequently placed at a discount. *Reciprocity*, articulated in the midst of a necessary condition of hierarchy, is the starting point of Confucian social philosophy. The Hindu vision of *dharmic* order is similarly structured, holding that the multitudinous components of the cosmic order, from the macrocosm of the entire universe, through all parts and levels of the natural and social order down to the microcosm of the human body, function as internally differentiated but hierarchically integrated wholes. This vision rejects the idea that each is merely the sum of its parts. Instead it insists that the meaning and purpose of all the differentiated parts derives from their participation in, and contribution to, the operation of the wider *dharmic* whole, *varnashramdharma.* Hence from both Hindu and Confucian perspectives a viewpoint which prioritizes the personal rights of autonomous individuals, but with nothing to say about maintaining the integrity of the corporate whole, appears positively bizarre.

The contrast between this perspective and that of the heirs of the Enlightenment could hardly be starker. Whilst the former holds that personal rights arise as the result of the fulfilment of one's obligations within a pre-existing web of binding reciprocities, the ideologues of the Enlightenment argued that a progressive social order is the outcome of a consciously deliberated agreement between autonomous and free-standing individuals to come together on a collective basis to pursue their common interests. Few authors have articulated the consequences of this revolutionary ideology more fully than Rousseau. Bitterly hostile to all forms of hierarchy, he urged citizens deliberately to throw off the yoke of duty, so enabling them to generate 'a form of association which will defend and protect with the whole common force the person and goods of each associate, and in which each, while uniting himself with all, may still obey himself alone, and remain as free as before' (Rousseau 1762: I, vi). No matter how much the ideologues of the Enlightenment may have championed the prospect of unbridled personal freedom, their vision of freedom and equality was intensely partial, qualified by the assumption that such freedom was only available to those able to exercise moral discernment. Hence the capacity to form the associations which Rousseau identified as the institutional framework within which the social contract would be implemented was gender and class specific.

All this exposes a fundamental paradox in the thinking of eighteenth-century savants. Whilst the revolutionary enterprise eliminated all forms of corporate entity operating over and above the level of the citizen on the grounds that such institutions were inherently tyrannical, at a microcosmic level inter-personal relationships within domestic regimes which were in principle equally tyrannical in character were left untouched. Still subject to the yoke of duty, servants, slaves, women and children were excluded from the new freedoms, since they were incorporated into the new order by virtue of their subordination to and dependency upon the familial patriarchs to whom they were responsible, and who were in turn responsible for protecting their individual and collective interests. Hence whilst the Declaration of the Rights of Man and the Citizen may have radically reformed the structure of relationships in public domain, it left those within the private domain of corporately and hierarchically structured households virtually untouched.

Yet there is an obvious reason for the revolutionaries' reluctance to extend their arguments downwards. Had they done so, they would have risked atomizing a crucial social institution: the family. In the eighteenth century no less than today, the family was regarded as an unqualified social good. As well as forming the domain within which we express our most powerful and passionate interpersonal emotional, social and physical relationships, it is and remains the locus within which to satisfy everyday material needs. As such it is indeed a *universal* phenomenon, and one which can only function when it is held together by a network of relationships of comprehensive as between its members. A corporation, no less.

Family Life: Mutual Support or Threat to Personal Freedom?

Since the end of the eighteenth century the Euro-America socio-political order has changed dramatically. The right to vote is no longer confined to men of property, and restrictions which formally excluded women from the public domain have been eroded. The gendered terminology of the 'Rights of Man and the Citizen' has been rendered archaic, and when the Universal Declaration was promulgated by the United Nations its in 1948 *Human* Rights became the order of the day. The rights of women and children have been brought within the scope of public law, and no longer relegated to the private domain. Moreover the Declaration also gave explicit recognition to the institution of the family, and to what has since been glossed as 'the right to family life'. Nevertheless the precise way in which the Declaration, as well as its successor the European Convention, actually did so deserves careful examination.

Article 16 of the Universal Declaration of Human Rights says:

1. Men and women of full age, without any limitation due to race, nationality or religion, have the right to marry and to found a family. They are entitled to equal rights as to marriage, during marriage and at its dissolution.
2. Marriage shall be entered into only with the free and full consent of the intending spouses.
3. The family is the natural and fundamental group unit of society and is entitled to protection by society and the State.

This formulation contains some worrying *lacunae*. Although it recognizes the family as 'the natural and fundamental group unit of society', it does not identify the range of persons who might be regarded as belonging to an institution which it goes on to declare is 'entitled to protection by society and the State'; nor does it seek to specify the range of reciprocal rights and obligations which its members might be expected to owe to one another. Most strikingly whilst it underwrites the *right* to found a family, it says nothing about an obligation to *sustain* the institution, once founded. Thus the text stays true to its heritage in the Enlightenment, overlooking the *corporate* character of any meaningful family unit, and instead focuses almost exclusively on the relationship which contemporary Euro-American conventions regard as the keystone of family life: marriage. Even then it says nothing about the obligations which spouses might owe to one another, other than to emphasize that they stand as equals; nor does it have anything to say about the couple's obligations to offspring arising from their relationship, or to the elderly parents of whom the spouses are themselves the offspring.

Instead the Article is primarily concerned with *individual* rights: to marry, or not to marry if one so chooses; to 'start a family'; and the right of each partner to remove themselves from the marital relationship as and when they choose. Inspection of the Article's wording, especially the way 'starting a family' is presented almost as an afterthought, suggests that the framers of the text were operating within Euro-American assumptions wherein the nuclear family is the conventional norm; marriage and 'starting a family' are presumptively coterminous. However such assumptions are far from universal. In traditions in which families are normatively constructed on a corporate basis, relationships of descent, as opposed to marriage, typically form the backbone of the corporate whole. Nevertheless from a historical (and Eurocentric) perspective one of the most significant features of Article 16 was that it established divorce as a human right. In so doing it unpicked the long standing Christian view that marriage was sacramental in character, which served to bind wives to their husbands on a life-long basis. Hence the inclusion of divorce in an article nominally guaranteeing a right to family life undermined one of the last remaining planks which sustained the formal subordination of women and which had been so carefully enshrined in the Rights of Man.

It would be idle to suggest that the wording of a single article in the Declaration had an immediate impact on popular practice or social policy with respect to the family and kinship. It was nevertheless a harbinger of future developments in Euro-America where during the latter part of the twentieth century the eighteenth-century consensus on such matters has largely disintegrated. As a result of growing pressure from libertarian and feminist sources, restrictions on the dissolution of marriage have steadily been set aside. The most immediate consequence was an upsurge in the incidence of divorce, but the process did not stop there. Before long the assumption that marriage was a prerequisite to cohabitation was abandoned, as was the notion that such a formalized union was a necessary precursor to 'starting a family'. With far-reaching changes in popular practice, together with the impact of statute law on well-established legal premises, the edifice of marriage as it was once understood is currently being comprehensively dismantled.

With gender equality taken for granted (at least in principle), marriage law is currently being further revised. Efforts are being made to accommodate homosexual partnerships in such a way as to ensure that they have the same degree of social and legal respect as those contracted on a heterosexual basis; likewise as new reproductive technologies and DNA analysis have become more sophisticated, the tendency to understand maternity and paternity as strictly biological (rather than as socially constructed) relationships has become steadily more widespread. As a result family courts have begun to take the view that connections revealed by DNA tests should be accorded greater legal substance than those which have arisen through emotional reciprocity within close-knit family units, Consequently, the rights of genitors may well be deemed to out-trump those of paters. These tendencies have been further reinforced by numerous statutory initiatives which give the authorities a right (and indeed a duty) to intervene in family affairs to protect children from neglect and women from domestic violence. Eighteenth-century caution about state intervention in citizens' domestic affairs has now been abandoned, at least in Euro-American contexts. As the 'yoke of duty' has been cast off, so has the privacy which domestic relationships previously enjoyed: family law has become ever more public, and hence individualistically oriented, in character. So even though the institution of the family still survives in Euro-American contexts, it has in many ways become a shadow of its former self. 'Progressive' individualism, operating both from within and without, has steadily eroded its corporate foundations.

Nevertheless there are few signs that current Euro-American assumptions with respect to the rights and duties associated with matters of kinship and marriage are gaining universal acceptance. Indeed, the developments to which they have given rise are the subject of critical comment throughout the non-European world, especially in those societies whose ancestral traditions are such that they continue to construct their personal and domestic lives on a corporate basis. It is not that competitive individualism is unknown in the non-European world: business and commerce is conducted on just as much a cut-throat basis there as anywhere. But in more personal and domestic contexts, individualism is typically placed at a discount rather than a premium, not least in the light of a growing awareness of the personal chaos that can be so easily precipitated by the unbridled pursuit of hedonistic self-interest in a manner which has become such a salient feature of the contemporary Euro-American socio-cultural order. Seeking actively to distance themselves from such trends, the pursuit of 'tradition', or at least social cohesion, is beginning to trump the attractions of Western-style 'progress', most especially with respect to the organization of domestic affairs. The reasons for this are ultimately pragmatic. When times are hard and/or when novel opportunities begin to open up, making the most of ties of reciprocity with one's immediate associates, and especially the fulfilment of obligations towards one's immediate kinsfolk, regularly offers the most effective route towards personal, domestic and familial satisfaction.

Where such conventions still hold, marriage is less likely to be the sole locus of reciprocity around which family life is constructed. This is not to suggest that conjugal partnerships become insignificant in such contexts. Not only do the reciprocities which normally develop between conjugal couples give rise to an extremely powerful dyad, but their ongoing relationship is the only legitimate the source of offspring who will carry a corporate family forward by a further generation. But because such dyads are set within the context of a wider corporate whole, the selection of a suitable bride is too important in strategic terms for the choice to be left to the whims of the would-be spouses. Instead, such decisions are taken on a collective basis, not least to ensure that all members of the corporate whole feel they have a stake in the success of the project. In such circumstances the institutional backbone of family life is likely to be as strongly grounded in ongoing reciprocities of descent and siblingship, together with those negotiated as between mothers- and daughters-in-law, as it is in relationships of conjugality per se.

Kinship Reciprocity as a Critical Diasporic Resource

It is not hard to discern why multi-generational corporate extended families are proving to be such resilient institutional features in the contemporary world, at least within communities of non-European origin. The economic advantages which can accrue to those who organize their domestic affairs on this basis can be substantial, especially when they are transnationally extended. Once it is taken for granted that family assets are held collectively, it follows they can and should be distributed (and redistributed) amongst family members according to the principle of 'from each according to their ability, to each according to their need'; the group can readily order itself as a miniature multinational corporation, shifting assets, ideas and personnel across borders in such a way as to maximize their collective advantages. Nevertheless interpersonal relationships within such collectivities are frequently far from egalitarian; superordinates are expected to offer support and guidance to their subordinates, whilst subordinates, typically defined in terms of gender, generation and age, are expected to respect and obey their elders. However membership of such a collectivity brings substantial benefits. The capacity to facilitate access to every potential resource of which any network member may become aware, no matter how spatially distant, enables extended networks to maximize members' material, financial and emotional security when times get tough; they also provide the foundations for entrepreneurial springboards whenever and wherever more positive opportunities arise (Ballard 2003).

For those seeking to move upwards through the unequal structures which characterize the contemporary global order, access to, and/or the capacity to construct, such translocal networks is a valuable source of cultural capital. Besides providing innumerable escalators of chain migration along which millions of migrants have moved from specific locations in the poverty-stricken South to labour-hungry locations in the prosperous North, those stepping off such escalators have made equally extensive use of this resource to construct thriving ethnic colonies at their many destinations, and to recycle ideas, assets and personnel on a global scale, regardless of national boundaries (Ballard 2003, 2005, 2008). Their progress on this front seems virtually unstoppable. No matter how actively national authorities may seek to control such cross-border traffic, migrants and their offspring are making ever more active use of these strategies to challenge established, but grossly unequal, opportunity structures (Bhagwati 2003, Raj 2003). In constructing these networks reciprocities of kinship, and failing that of quasi-kinship, have proved to be crucial. Whilst also drawing on ties of lineage, clan, sect and caste to construct yet wider alliances, reciprocities maintained within corporately-structured families, have been the key to such initiatives. Transnational extension has in no way undermined established patterns of kinship reciprocity; indeed, their strength has for the most part been reinforced.

Contradictions

Nevertheless such successes have been accompanied by a down-side. When migrants are perceived to be 'aliens' pushing their way unacceptably upwards, virulent anti-immigrant hostility has regularly emerged amongst members of the indigenous populations within whose territories they had established themselves. Such concerns have been articulated along two complementary vectors: first that the settlers' success constituted unwelcome, indeed unfair, competition; and that their maintenance of cultural alterity, together with the emergence of ethnic colonies, constituted an unacceptable threat to the integrity of the established socio-cultural order. As ethnic polarization has sharpened, the balance between these vectors frequently shifts from the former to the latter. In the face of protests that complaints of 'unfair competition' were essentially racist in character, arguments to the effect that the newcomers' religious and cultural alterity threatened national integrity frequently proved to have greater moral traction than complaints about the unacceptability of their physical appearance. This has certainly been the case in Western Europe. Although the precise course of such developments has varied from country to country, nationalistic and xenophobic criticisms of the consequences of the minority presence have steadily hardened. One argument has proved particularly appealing: that their presence threatened the Christian foundations of the European civilization. This opened the way for popular demands that the new minorities should be expelled forthwith, on the grounds that the lifestyles which they brought with them, and to which they perversely remained committed, were inherently uncivilized, as the barbaric fashion in which they allegedly treated their women-folk serves to demonstrate.

By tapping into well-established tropes about the innate barbarity of 'primitive' peoples, lurid accounts of honour killing, forced marriages, female genital mutilation and the repression of female autonomy under the veil, rabble rousers have legitimized popular hostility to the minority, and especially the Muslim, presence. Moreover as those pressing such agendas soon realized, xenophobic policies and practices of this kind could be readily justified as a form of humanitarian intervention. The use of a *rights* agenda for such purposes has caused much confusion amongst liberal-minded anti-racists and multiculturalists, not least because they found moral arguments which they had once launched against their opponents being used against them. More disturbingly, many radical feminists also took the opportunity to swap sides, on the grounds that they could not overlook the barbaric patterns of patriarchal tyranny to which so many of their black sisters found themselves subjected. These processes eventually had a far-reaching impact on social policy, and on legal provisions regarding ethnic plurality.

Professional Practice in Contexts of Plurality

In the early days of settlement the authorities mostly sought to overlook the conundrums created by migrant workers' tendency to order personal and domestic lives in terms of alien cultural premises. So long as the newcomers made few demands on public services, they could argue that members of this section of the population were well capable of looking after themselves, and in no great need of such services.[1] But as minority populations grew, and ethnic colonies became a salient feature of the urban landscape, this view became increasingly difficult to sustain. When it came to developing policies which would actively address the cultural dimensions of the challenges with which they were confronted, service providers regularly found themselves nonplussed.

Although they were undoubtedly committed to anti-racist and anti-oppressive practice, as ethnic colonies grew in size professional practitioners rapidly discovered that such nostrums provided little guidance on how to cope with the real-life challenges with which they found themselves confronted. In the absence of the linguistic and cultural skills which would enable them to deal with minority clients on their own terms, front-line service providers found themselves, and often still find themselves, out of their depth, especially when dealing with knotty problems precipitated by physical and mental ill health, issues of child care or the breakdown of interpersonal domestic relationships. A fundamental source of their difficulties was the lack of congruence between the familiar conceptual frameworks in terms of which they had been trained to order their professional practice, and those in terms of which their minority clients, patients and pupils ordered their domestic lives (Ballard and Parveen 2008). Should service providers seek to adjust the terms and conditions of their professional practice to take into account their clients' preferred linguistic, conceptual and behavioural conventions? If so, how far should they be prepared to go? Could such issues be resolved with the assistance of interpreters? Or do they reach much deeper, such that they engage with, and often challenge, the conceptual foundations around which professional practice is normatively constructed?

Such problems are widespread. My own observations suggest that they are likely to arise whenever professionals whose practice requires them to engage in some way with the personal, familial and domestic dimensions of their clients', patients' or pupils' lives. Unless such practitioners have acquired a sufficient degree of cultural competence to engage positively with those whose personal lifestyles differ significantly from their own, there is in my experience a strong probability that they will do their clients a disservice, no matter how excellent the technical dimensions of their professional competence. On the basis of the experience I have acquired in the process of preparing expert reports in several hundred cases in

1 *Émigré Journeys* (Abdullah Hussein 2000) is a tragicomic account of early settlers' self-help efforts to dispose of the corpse of one of their compatriots who had died of pneumonia.

which British South Asians have found themselves involved in proceedings before the criminal, civil, family or administrative courts, it is quite clear that lawyers are no exception to this generalization. Nevertheless there are several features of legal practice which are exceedingly helpful to researchers such as myself. In legal contexts all aspects of dispute resolution are normally agued out in explicit detail, and in writing. The resultant plethora of documentation (largely absent in non-legal contexts) provides an invaluable resource for researchers seeking to explore how legal practitioners respond to the challenge of ethnic plurality.

Nevertheless so far as I can see the broad character of the challenges and the conundrums with which lawyers find themselves in these circumstances do not differ significantly from those encountered by their colleagues in other human professions. Hence whilst the issues nominally at stake in the proceedings in which I have been instructed to prepare reports have been bewilderingly diverse, the range of cultural phenomena on which I found myself focusing have been far more restricted. Likewise, in explaining that patterns of behaviour which might otherwise appear deluded, bizarre, inappropriate, unreasonable or downright criminal can be rendered much more meaningful (although by no means necessarily forgivable) once set in the context of the actors' conceptual logic, I have regularly found myself returning to a limited number of themes. These include the significance of honour, modesty and shame, and above all the logic of relationships of mutual reciprocity and the consequences of their disruption, especially where issues of family, kinship and marriage loom large.

Before exploring the specifically legal dimensions of these issues, it is worth considering why issues of plurality prove so troublesome to well-educated professionals, no matter their field of practice. My experience, whether acting as a teacher, an advisor or an expert, suggests that those whom I am addressing have rarely, if ever, given much consideration to the prospect that the conceptual order which underpins their own thinking and behaviour, no less in professional than in everyday personal and social contexts, *might itself be culturally coded*. Instead their default assumption is that it is only the thoughts and behaviour of others which are significantly culturally conditioned, such that the conceptual premises which they themselves deploy can safely be regarded as 'normal', 'natural' and 'rational'. Given such a perspective it is all too easy to reach the mistaken conclusion that the European conceptual categories that implicitly frame their practice are not only *a*cultural in character, but of universal applicability (Ballard and Parveen 2008).

That there should be such limited awareness of the distinction between emic and etic categories and concepts amongst members of the indigenous majority, no matter how extensive their professional qualifications may be, should be no surprise: 'Anth 101' is not part of the regular undergraduate curriculum in British universities. If the premises of the Enlightenment encourage the maintenance of such a stance, it is also clear that those who have long enjoyed a condition of de facto global hegemony have as yet had little if any reason to query the emic character of their everyday assumptions. Hence when asked to provide objective (and hence etic) definitions of such commonplace concepts such as 'family', 'marriage' or 'fate', most professionals find themselves nonplussed, since they have never been required to step outside their own taken-for-granted assumptions.

This may be illustrated by the nominally straightforward queries about the commonplace institution which we casually identify as 'the family' that arise when the people in question organize their domestic affairs in terms of conventions which differ radically from those which constitute the contemporary Euro-American norm:

- If a household contains two conjugal couples, should it be considered to be composed of one family or two?
- Just what body of persons might or should 'a family' include? What rights and obligations do those so included have towards one another?
- How far should family members be entitled to redistribute property amongst themselves in such a way as to minimize their exposure to taxation, and to maximize their access to social benefits?
- What is the legitimate scope of parents' rights over and obligations to their children, and vice-versa? Is it right and proper for these rights and obligation to be extended to include all members of an extended corporate family?
- Whom may one marry, and in what circumstances? What are the prerequisites for a legitimate marriage? In what sense, if any, is mere cohabitation illegitimate?
- How extensive a role can parents legitimately play in choosing spouses for their offspring? In the light of this, how can arranged marriages be distinguished from those deemed to be 'forced'?
- What is the status of a polygamous marriage?
- In what circumstances can divorce occur? When it occurs, how should rights over and responsibilities for children be redistributed? How should assets be divided?
- Should the rights and duties of paternity be ordered according to the community's understanding of the marital status of the child's parents, or should biological linkages, if they should prove not to be congruent with those conventions, be given just as much weight?
- Are parents who insist that their older children should take active responsibility for the welfare of their younger siblings restricting such youngsters' capacity to explore their own individuality?
- Are parents who have brought their children up in this way acting irresponsibly if and when they leave young children temporarily in the care of their older siblings?
- How should the disposal of the dead be handled? To whom and on what basis should the assets of the deceased be handed?

However challenging such conundrums may seem, they can at least be described within the context of a familiar terminology of family, marriage, parents, divorce, siblings and so forth, even if their meaning may be subject to all sorts of subtle shifts when deployed within unfamiliar cultural contexts.[2] Problems of comprehension become more acute when family members assert that their behaviour has been conditioned by concepts and considerations that do not engage in any obvious way with contemporary English ideas and experiences. For instance, when domestic disputes run seriously out of hand in South Asian contexts, my experience suggests that initiatives driven by, or at least alleged to be driven by, most of the following phenomena are likely to have been in play:

> *Rista*: The set of reciprocities (*lena-dena*) between corporate families to which relationships of kinship, and most especially of marriage, give rise.
> *Qurban*: Sacrifice: hence *kushi se qurban* is to voluntary sacrifice one's own interests (e.g.) in marriage for the benefit of the family.
> *Izzat*: Honour, personal self-esteem, as well as the standing of the family in the eyes of the community at large.
> *Sharam*: Modesty, or more specifically the preservation of one's own and one's family's *izzat* by taking care not to flaunt oneself inappropriately in public spaces.
> *Be-sharam*: Shameless behaviour which compromises one's own and one's family's *izzat*.
> *Badlah*: Feud, normally engaged in to restore one's own besmirched *izzat* by undermining the *izzat* of one's opponent, and in extreme cases by compromising the modesty of one's opponent's female dependants.
> *Nazar*: Occult distress caused to another (and most especially to children) as a result of the observer's sub-conscious feelings of jealousy.
> *Jadoo-tuna:* Occult distress deliberately launched to cause disaster and distress, most usually to some other closely related person.
> *Churail:* One of a number of evil-minded spirits who may take possession of a person (most usually a woman) causing her to behave in bizarre, aggressive and immodest ways.
> *Tawiz:* An amulet containing verses from the Qur'an, empowered by the blessings (*barakat*) of a Pir, with the capacity to keep occult forces of the kind listed above at bay.

Those who operate within a South Asian conceptual universe will be familiar with such terms which are deployed in vernacular discourse, especially when interpersonal tensions and contradictions within large extended families have begun to get out of hand. Moreover those familiar with Ioan Lewis's classic text *Ecstatic Religion* (1971) will recognize that the apparently 'superstitious' elements of the vocabulary are less irrational than they might seem. They enable those pressed into

2 Apparently straightforward kinship terms are a ready source of confusion. Punjabi distinguishes between two sets of five distinct categories of relationship which English boils down to 'aunt' and 'uncle'.

a tight corner to articulate feelings of fear, anger, jealousy and distress in a manner which does not bring the whole corporate structure tumbling down, providing an effective means whereby junior (and consequently the most vulnerable) members of a large extended family can 'say the unsayable' to a husband or a mother-in-law whose demands have made their lives unbearable (Ballard 2000: 17ff).

If one is in a position to crack the code, discourse which outsiders dismiss as bizarre, irrational and superstitious provides immediate insight into the likely location and character of the most severe sources of contradiction within the familial network, and an indication of how those contradictions might best be resolved. But if these concepts (or more usually the actions and reactions to which their deployment gives rise) attract the attention of observers who lack the capacity to interpret symbolic discourse appropriately, the consequences can be disastrous. Unable to translate the concepts or the actions they have precipitated into the procrustean framework of their own conceptual premises, it is easy for external observers to conclude that those who deploy such notions must be deranged, wicked or criminal. Such judgements are rarely helpful in moving towards an accurate identification of the contradictions which precipitated such outbursts, let alone facilitating interventions which might ameliorate them.

Matters are rendered more chaotic when external observers assume that given the 'patriarchal' character of the conceptual order within which such 'medieval' notions are deployed, all power must lie in the hands of men, and female family members are helpless pawns, lacking the capacity to exercise any kind of agency which would enable them to act in their own cause. Circumstances and personalities may sometimes combine to precipitate such an outcome, but the assumption that this will *invariably* be the case is grossly misleading. Given the emotional power which they are able to exercise over their husbands and above all their offspring, mothers frequently operate as the real power behind the patriarchal throne, no matter how much they may be content to allow public appearances to suggest the reverse.

A significant number of cases in which I have been instructed to prepare reports have involved homicide; many more have arisen as a consequence of marital breakdown. In virtually all I concluded that matters had come before the court as a result of interpersonal contradictions within the family getting so far out of hand that established patterns of dispute resolution had been overwhelmed, with disastrous consequences. But in the absence of a relevant degree of cultural competence, courts and lawyers frequently find themselves perplexed as to how to make sense of such cases. They are far from being alone; police officers and guardians *ad litem* responsible for collecting the evidence to be set before family courts find themselves just at much at sea, as do the psychiatrists, psychologists and social workers to whom the courts turn for expert advice on behavioural matters. In these circumstances the equitable delivery of justice is rendered just as problematic as is the delivery of other public services.

The Development of Public Policy: Violence Hits the Headlines

There is now increasingly widespread recognition that the provision of such services in contexts of plurality is an exceedingly challenging task. This stands in sharp contrast to the position during the early years of settlement, when the majority of migrants were fit young men. As families arrived and ethnic colonies grew more mature, so the range of services to which their members sought access become wider and are now closely congruent to the patterns of demand from the indigenous majority. But whilst those demands have consequently become less distinctive in *quantitative* terms, the *qualitative* difference remains substantial, if only because they are conditioned by a range of linguistic, cultural, religious and conceptual conventions with which the vast majority of established service providers are unfamiliar.

Providing an adequate response to the resultant challenges has proved to be far from easy. The conceptual perplexities with which professional service providers are confronted have been exacerbated by a fevered debate about the degree to which it was (and is) legitimate for the providers of public services to make *any* positive response to minority alterity. Three lines of argument have emerged. Firstly, if service provision to the minorities is proving to be problematic, the fault lies with the minorities themselves, their inadequate command of the English language and their failure to adopt more reasonable and acceptable behavioural and cultural conventions; secondly that beyond the difficulties precipitated by their ongoing commitment to alien ways, the very presence of minorities places an unjustifiable strain on the public purse, and meeting their distinctive interests and concerns does not deserve to be prioritized; and thirdly that the unequal status of women within such communities leads them to being subjected to unacceptable, all too often hidden, levels of domestic violence. As a result the press has had a field day with stories about the experience of pupils of indigenous origin isolated in schools where ninety per cent of pupils are Muslims or about doctors and midwives overwhelmed by mothers with little knowledge of English.

Few stories have attracted more attention than accounts of forced marriages and honour killings. Whilst the reality of such incidents is undeniable, as is the fact that they are regarded as 'newsworthy', close inspection of the facts of such incidents invariably reveals that in most cases their core characteristics are less unique than is popularly supposed. In all societies interpersonal relationships with the family occasionally get so far out of hand as to lead to incidents of homicide; and as ethnic colonies have grown in size, all aspects of established patterns of family life, negative no less than positive, have begun to manifest themselves overseas. Against that background the main feature which distinguishes such incidents of domestic violence, up to and including homicide, within such families is not their greater frequency as compared to that found amongst the indigenous population, but rather the cultural context within which they occur. As a result they can readily be identified as incidents of 'honour-related violence' which can in turned be ascribed to the influence of a further pathogenic characteristic of minority communities: parents' propensity to subject their unwilling children to 'forced marriages' (see, for example, Allen 2008). So whilst the pendulum of opinion may have swung from benign neglect to agitated alarm, there is little evidence that policy-makers, let alone the media-driven popular opinion to which they have felt forced to respond, have any greater understanding of the ways in which these incidents are *conditioned* (as opposed to *determined*) by cultural factors.

A further striking feature of these developments, by no means exclusive to Britain, is the extent to which they have relied on systematic efforts to pathologize the corporate family structures which most of the new minority groups continue to deploy, as well as the alleged plight of women within them. Hence in the course of efforts to construct strategic remedies to reduce the (much hyped) incidence of forced marriages and honour killings, police and Home Office officials relied on suggestions that they were advancing human rights when they published a ground-breaking report entitled *Forced Marriages: A Wrong not a Right* (Forced Marriage Unit 2006). The result of these initiatives, which are still ongoing, is the emergence of what can only be described as *cultural crimes*, in which cultural factors are held to aggravate existing criminal offences such as child neglect, assault and homicide.

Developments of this kind are by no means limited to the issues highlighted above. Whilst there was a brief 'multicultural' interlude during the 1980s and early 1990s, during which tentative efforts were made towards taking more positive cognizance of minority lifestyles, virtually all such initiatives soon ran into the sand. If they were to be more than cosmetic, a prerequisite for their success was the willingness of professional service providers to make significant revisions to the conceptual premises which underpinned the norms of professional practice. Such challenges invariably encountered vigorous opposition. Indeed, most professionals took the view that such 'concessions' to ethnic plurality were unnecessary and intolerable. The public agreed, and financial support declined. The argument that many of the challenges confronting service providers might be significantly reduced if they gained the capacity to approach them from a more ethno-sensitive perspective fell away. Instead, the favoured explanation was that the difficulties which they encountered were primarily the outcome of the alien, unhelpful and ultimately pathogenic behaviour of those standing on the far side of the ethnic divide.

These developments were reinforced by popular reactions to much publicized incidents such as the forced retirement of the headmaster of a Bradford school where ninety per cent of the pupils were Muslim, as a result of his opposition to the local authority's commitment to multicultural policies, the uproar following the Rushdie Affair, the so-called 'northern riots' in 2001, and not least the suicide bombings in London in July 2005, which led to a tsunami of hostility (Ballard 2007b). Multiculturalism was deemed to have failed, and a new consensus emerged, building on arguments outlined in a report on the 'northern riots' (Cantle Report 2002): 'community cohesion', together with numerous anti-terrorism initiatives, would be the priority for all public policy in this sphere. As a consequence, efforts to accommodate the de facto presence of ethnic plurality were abandoned, attempts to amend the structures of public service provision in response to minority alterity thought misguided; alterity was an obstacle to be eliminated, rather than a resource to be negotiated with. This switch to an explicitly anti-pluralist policy was welcomed by members of the indigenous majority. By contrast the response of the great majority of those who differ has been to batten down the hatches in the hope that the storm will eventually subside.

Plurality and the Delivery of Justice

How have those responsible for the delivery of justice charted their way through these stormy seas? In broad terms lawyers now find themselves confronted by much the same conundrums, as well as being subjected to much the same pressures, as colleagues in other human professions, although analysis of professional decision-making in legal contexts is a good deal easier to undertake, because more transparent. Sebastian Poulter's publications, culminating in *Ethnicity, Law and Human Rights* (1998) must be regarded as ground-breaking. No other profession has yet produced such a thoroughgoing attempt to grapple with the issues in this field. But his approach was anything put pluralist. Although he accepts that public policy should make every effort to tolerate diversity, he nevertheless argues for caution:

> On *precisely* what basis are exceptions to the pluralist philosophy to be admitted in practice? How can it adequately be determined whether minimum national standards are breached by a particular traditional practice, which therefore needs to be suppressed? Another way of posing the dilemma is to ask exactly where the limits of tolerance lie. (1998: 21)

As he goes on to demonstrate, such matters have long been a bone of contention; although it was suggested that a clause guaranteeing minority rights should be included in the 1948 Declaration, no agreement could be reached about its wording. The matter was passed to a UN sub-commission, eventually emerging as Article 27 of the International Convention of Civil and Political Rights, which in principle indicated that members of minority groups should not be denied the right to enjoy their own culture, to profess and practice their own religion, or to use their own language. But as Poulter rightly emphasizes, the wording of the article is such that its contents are shot through with reservations:

> First, while the Article is clearly intended to recognize the claims of groups or communities within a state, the right is not spelt out, in terms, as a collective right. The right is expressed as adhering instead to individuals who belong to minority groups, and is thus of the same nature as the other rights guaranteed in the Covenant, which are accorded to individuals rather than to other entities.

> In the light of this individualistic approach, the minority itself cannot be said to possess a right of its own to the preservation of its separate identity. Secondly, the opening words of Article 27 display a hesitancy, almost a trepidation, about mentioning the possible presence of minority communities within a state. An earlier draft began in much more robust fashion with the phrase 'Persons belonging to ethnic, religious or linguistic minorities shall ...' Several states ... were unwilling even to recognize the existence of minorities within their borders. France went so far as to ... declare that Article 27 was 'not applicable so far as the Republic is concerned'. Thirdly, the guarantee is expressed in negative terms, in the sense that members of minorities are not to be 'denied' the specific rights allotted to them. These 'cultural' rights are not spelt out in the same assertive vein as are, for example, the rights to life and liberty or to freedom of assembly and association. (Poulter 1998: 79, 81)

Poulter also notes that the wording makes no attempt to address the *political* issue which comes to the fore in contexts of ethnic plurality, namely how and where and on what basis a balance should be struck as between the minority interest in cultural preservation and the interest of the state and the majority in maintaining social cohesion, minimum standards and national unity. With this in mind Poulter turns to the European Convention for inspiration, but finds little on which to rely. Like the Declaration, the Convention contains no clause which offers members of minorities any kind of explicit protection. As he rightly notes, all the Articles which address issues which are of particular concern to members of minority groups, such as the right to family life, freedom of religion, freedom of expression and freedom of assembly, are accompanied by caveats to the effect that:

> There shall be no interference by a public authority with the exercise of this right except such as is in accordance with the law and is necessary in a democratic society in the interests of national security, public safety or the economic well-being of the country, for the prevention of disorder or crime, for the protection of health or morals, or for the protection of the rights and freedoms of others.

As Poulter notes, the text of the ECHR, like that of the Declaration, is primarily oriented towards protecting the rights of individuals, whilst the caveats can be interpreted as prioritizing the rights and interests of the democratic majority over those who differ. Unfortunately Poulter did not live long enough to see just how far the UK government would twist these provisions to the disadvantage of members of extended families with significant overseas connections. In interpreting the provisions of Article 8 the Home Office Immigration Service defines 'family life' as being an arena which extends no further than a conjugal couple and their dependent children. It insists that the UK has no obligation to facilitate their right to live collectively in Britain if one of the spouses is a citizen of and resident in some other country, and that in the light of developments in modern communications, family life can readily be enjoyed by electronic means. Poulter's analysis reflected a time when efforts to exploit these loopholes in the ECHR were far less blatant than has subsequently been the case.

Unable to find any clear guidance from human rights discourse as to how his dilemmas might be resolved, Poulter turned to the resources of the English law, especially the strategies devised by Britain's colonial judiciary to respond equitably to cases set in unfamiliar (i.e. non-European) cultural contexts. In doing so he highlights the way in which a formula to the effect that 'local customs and conventions should be accepted as legitimate, always provided they were *not contrary to justice, equity and good conscience, and had not been declared void by any competent authority*' initially articulated in the Punjab Laws Act of 1872 was taken up in numerous other colonial jurisdictions, and ultimately confirmed as a legitimate approach to such matters by the Judicial Committee of the Privy Council (Poulter 1998: 38–42, my italics).

With this yardstick he examines a series of high profile confrontations in which such issues subsequently came to a head in the UK, including controversies over Jewish methods of religious slaughter, Gypsies' efforts to maintain their nomadic lifestyles, Muslim demands for the recognition of their distinctive forms of personal law, Hindu temples and planning regulations, the right of Sikhs to wear turbans, and the right of Rastafarians to dreadlocks and the consumption of cannabis. In most instances he finds himself unimpressed by the minority arguments in favour of exceptional treatment. As a result he was able to reach a liberal-sounding but otherwise thoroughly innocuous conclusion that:

> While English law should broadly approach other cultures in a charitable spirit of tolerance and, when in doubt, lean in favour of affording members of ethnic minority communities freedom to observe their diverse traditions here, there will inevitably be certain key areas where minimum standards, derived from shared core values, must of necessity be maintained, if the cohesiveness and unity of English society as a whole is to be preserved intact. (Poulter 1998: 391)

No matter how confidently Poulter may have grounded his arguments in the common-sense assumption that the 'shared core values' of the indigenous majority must trump those of deviant minorities, there are now clear signs that the judiciary is becoming less and less certain as to whether such an anti-pluralist perspective is compatible with equitable decision-making. An initial straw in the wind could be found in Lady Arden's powerfully expressed opinion in *Khan v Khan [2007] EWCA Civ 399*, a case involving the legal status of a customary form of dispute resolution within a Pakistani family. Drawing on the provisions of Article 6 of ECHR (which provides a caveat-free right to a fair trial) she argued that:

> Where the parties are members of a particular community, then in my judgment the court must bear in mind that they may observe different traditions and practices from those of the majority of the population. That must be expected and respected in the jurisdiction that has received the European Convention

> on Human Rights. One of the fundamental values of the Convention is that of pluralism: see *Kokkinakis v Greece [1994] 17 EHRR 397*. Pluralism is inherent in the values in the Convention. Pluralism involves the recognition that different groups in society may have different traditions, practices and attitudes and from that value tolerance must inevitably flow. Tolerance involves respect for the different traditions, practices and attitudes of different groups. In turn, the court must pay appropriate regard to these differences.

Whilst Lady Arden follows Poulter insofar as she pitches her argument within a discourse of human rights, her approach to the issues is more hard edged. By grounding her argument in the provisions of Article 6, rather than the heavily qualified rights set out in Articles 8 to 11, she is able to conclude that courts have an inescapable obligation to make a positive response to plurality: hence her employment of '*must*'. In doing so she leaves no space for the ethnocentric caveats whose origins can be traced to the Punjab Laws Act. Nor has she been alone in striking out in this way. In a further case which arose as a result of a Sikh pupil finding herself barred from attending school as a result refusing to conform to its uniform regulations by wearing a *kara*, a steel bracelet, Mr Justice Silber handed down an equally decisive pro-pluralist judgment *[2008] EWHC 1865 (Admin)* of more general applicability:

> There is a very important obligation imposed on the school to ensure that its pupils are first tolerant as to the religious rites and beliefs of other races and other religions and second to respect other people's religious wishes. Without those principles being adopted in a school, it is difficult to see how a cohesive and tolerant multi-cultural society can be built in this country

In a subsequent paragraph he also went on to criticize

> the repeated failure of the school to consider the important aspects of [the policy] to which I have referred to in the paragraph above. In particular the school and the defendants failed in its duty of (a) 'fostering respect for people of all cultural backgrounds'; (b) 'respect'[ing] the values of cultures [with] which they are unfamiliar'; (c) 'ensure [ing] that every pupil develops a sense of identity that is receptive and respectful to other cultures'; (d) 'promote [ing] the respect of other cultures, celebrates diversity and educates against racism, our teaching challenges racial prejudice and stereotypes and fosters critical awareness of biased, inequality and injustice'.

However the discourse of human rights, on which both judges in the cases cited above grounded their arguments, is by far from being the only available source of inspiration when it comes to dealing with the challenges of plurality. A distinctive feature of the English common law tradition is its long-standing commitment to the view that judicial finders of fact should set the evidence before them within their appropriate context, and then to seek out the appropriate yardsticks against which to assess its significance. Unfortunately this ancient libertarian tradition is currently subject to increasingly severe pressure from the centralizing proclivities of the state, further reinforced by popular majoritarian hostility to the pluralizing consequences of religious and ethnic diversity. Indeed these tendencies attracted the attention of Lord Bingham, then Senior Law Lord. As efforts by the judiciary to deal with cases involving 'immigrants' and 'terrorists' on an equitable basis have begun to attract demands that judges not be allowed to reach judgments which compromised the will of Parliament and hence, so it is said, 'the law of the land', Lord Bingham felt impelled to highlight the other side of the coin. In a magisterial speech entitled *The Rule of Law* (2006) he launched a blistering critique of the way in which statutory and executive interventions have begun to undermine many of the ancient liberties enshrined in English law, concluding: 'We are not, as we are sometimes seen, mere custodians of a body of arid prescriptive rules but are, with others, the guardians of an all but sacred flame which animates and enlightens the society in which we live.'

But what is the precise character of the sacred flame of which Bingham and his colleagues are the ultimate custodians? To modernist libertarians the proper answer may seem obvious: the values of the Enlightenment, the discourse of human rights to which it has given rise, and the consequent opportunities for individuals to enjoy access to liberty and personal freedom. Whilst Lord Bingham in no way ignored this source of inspiration, his arguments were far from being predicated upon it. Rather, his critique of hyperactive legislative activity by Parliament highlighted the ease with which nominally enlightened governments can all too easily set forth statutory initiatives which prove in due course to reinforce patterns of injustice instead of relieving them.

Humanitarian Concern for the Vulnerable?

Let me explore some examples of how this is achieved. If there are two points on which all lawyers agree it is that justice should be open to all, and judicial decision-making should go out of its way to protect the interests of the vulnerable. Such assumptions are as deeply embedded in the values of the Enlightenment and the discourse of human rights as they are in the Hindu and Confucian systems discussed earlier. However, there is a further distinctive feature of current Euro-American thinking which can best be described as a double-edged sword: its evangelical commitment to the universal applicability of its ideological premises. That commitment can have paradoxical consequences: nominally humanitarian efforts to rescue vulnerable others from tyranny and oppression can readily be utilized to legitimize structures of social, colonial and imperial hegemony. With such considerations in mind it is worth considering how the moral and ideological arguments currently being utilized to legitimate popular hostility towards rising levels of ethnic plurality in metropolitan heartlands parallel those deployed by nineteenth-century missionaries seeking support for their proselytizing activities in Britain's imperial possessions. Doing so exposes all manner of parallels, especially with respect to the frequency which such interventions have focused on the social, cultural and religious conventions around which family life is organized, and on the allegedly horrific barbarities to which women and children consequently found themselves exposed.

A graphic example of the power and popularity of initiatives of this kind can be found in missionary efforts to justify their evangelization of the population of Calcutta in the early decades of the nineteenth century. Pennington (2005) demonstrates how those involved legitimized and then financed their activities by producing ghoulish accounts of female infanticide, child marriages, paederastic husbands abandoning teenage widows whom Hindu custom deemed permanently unmarriageable, and most horrifically, the practice of *suttee*. Nor did the monotheistic Muslims escape the missionaries' moralistic scorn: commonplace tropes suggesting that Muslim women were hidden away in the *harem*, constantly exposed to the lascivious attentions of sex-crazed menfolk soon began to be widely circulated.

The missionaries received little if any support from the East India Company in the early years of the nineteenth century. However when the British Raj came into being after the 1857 uprising officers of the Indian Civil Service took a more activist view of their role, on the grounds that they were engaged in a 'civilizing mission' which required them to root out 'social evils' of this kind. Oldenburg (2002: 41ff.) has shown how a group of evangelistically minded British administrators in the Punjab became acutely concerned about high levels of female infanticide which they believed they had identified within the population for which they were responsible, whose causes they concluded were the outcome of a toxic mixture of two major social evils: 'caste pride' and excessive dowry payments paid at daughters' marriages. The immediate outcome of their efforts was the passage of the *Prevention of Murder of Female Infants Act of 1870*. Besides providing the authorities with unprecedented opportunities to scrutinize the internal operation of Punjabi families in every case of neo-natal death, the Act also criminalized all aspects of family life which they adjudged to stand in contravention of civilized conventions of justice, equity and good conscience, the very phrase in the Punjab Laws Act of 1872, and subsequently picked up by colonial administrators elsewhere, and by Poulter. Not that the Act had any great effect on popular practice. As Oldenburg notes, it was repealed in 1906: by then the ideological debate had moved on to other issues.

For the Sake of Women and Children?

Contemporary European administrators currently find themselves confronting similar challenges to those faced by nineteenth-century predecessors in at least three senses:

- to devise legal and administrative structures within which to accommodate the personal and domestic lifestyles of large bodies of people who organize their familial affairs in terms of conceptual premises radically different from those deployed by the indigenous majority;
- to respond to popular demands from the indigenous majority to root out all such 'uncivilized' practices;
- to find a means of cloaking any initiatives they might take with a veneer of legitimacy.

In contemporary Europe (compared with the United States) tropes grounded in the presuppositions of evangelistic Christianity no longer cut much ice. Nevertheless an equally effective source of inspiration has emerged as a means of justifying initiatives of the same kind: the list of *Harmful Traditional Practices*, including female genital mutilation, son preference, female infanticide, early marriage, dowry, early pregnancy, nutritional taboos and practices related to child delivery, set out by the Office of the High Commissioner on Human Rights (no date). Linked as they are to the Convention on the Elimination of all Forms of Discrimination against Women, these provisions ensure that unreflective feminists can be recruited to the cause with relative ease, and provide legislators with a ready legal bastion on the basis of which to introduce novel statutory initiatives.

But on just what issues do such initiatives focus, and in what circumstances? One has already been mentioned 'honour-related violence', which is formally classified as a 'hate crime' in English law, despite the fact that Article 12 of the Universal Declaration explicitly indicates that 'Everyone has the right to the protection of the law against such interference or attacks upon his honour and reputation'. However statutory interference has been most active in the spheres of immigration law and rights of access to citizenship. Given that popular hostility amongst members of indigenous majorities is directed as much at continued inflows of settlers as at the growth of ethnic colonies, and that such ongoing inflows are largely kinship-driven, immigration legislation introduced in the name of 'migration management' has borne down with particular force on the kinds of marriage which are frequently executed within transnational communities of non-European, and especially of Muslim, origin: those in which conjugal partnerships are contracted early, organized by the spouses' parents and arranged as between cousins.

Migration managers for many years sought to query the legitimacy of migrants' marriages as a means of curbing the incidence of family reunion, although they met with limited success (Sachdeva 1993). However, a more recent set of initiatives originally developed in Scandinavia are currently proving to be rather more effective. Influenced by a report of the Oslo-based Human Rights Service entitled *Feminine Integration* (Storhaug and Human Rights Service 2003, see Hagelund 2008), a head of steam built up behind the view that marriages within such communities were frequently 'forced', since they were rarely the outcome of a free choice on the part of both spouses, especially when spouses were young and closely related. Storhaug argued that the most effective way in which the incidence of forced marriages, violence and abuse within marriage, and the use of marriage for immigration purposes could be minimized, was by altering immigration rules to incorporate:

- a ban on entry in the case of transnational marriages between cousins;
- a limit on the number of family unifications through marriage one person can obtain, set at once every ten years (to counteract repeated cycles of marriage and subsequent divorce, either through *pro forma* marriages for immigration purposes or to establish polygamous families);
- a ban on family unification for those with a history of marital violence;
- a requirement that foreign marriage contracts should contain a clause which guarantees equal divorce rights to both spouses before it could be regarded as a valid basis for family unification in Scandinavia.

These recommendations were swiftly taken up by both the Danish and the Norwegian authorities, and are currently being emulated elsewhere in the EU.

However, one of the key driving forces behind these Scandinavian developments closely paralleled nineteenth-century missionary-inspired pamphlets: a much publicized monograph by Unni Wikan (2002, originally published in Norwegian in 1995) highlighting the plight of Muslim women unfortunate enough to find themselves trapped within the oppressive framework of immigrant families who established themselves in Norway. Although Wikan writes as a social scientist, and takes her ideological inspiration from individualistic feminism rather than from evangelical Christianity, her analytical methodology is at another level remarkably close to that of her predecessors. Like them, she builds her argument around detailed commentaries on a small number of individual case studies, each of which she deploys as a means of highlighting the potentially horrific outcomes which can occur when young female members of corporate and hierarchically structured extended families find themselves at odds with the interests and priorities of its senior members.

I do not quarrel with her observations, in so far as they go. They are familiar enough to all those who have experienced the consequences of the implosion of normative patterns of reciprocity within families of this kind (Ballard 2008: 53). What is striking about Wikan's analysis, and those of all the others commentators who make their case within the same kind of emic and hence ethnocentric perspective, is the lack of any significant effort to appreciate the conceptual universes of those responsible for treating such 'victims' in the way that they did. Instead she simply asserts that their behaviour was so far beyond civilized expectations, and hence so barbaric, that such motivations do not merit consideration. This is not to suggest that their motivations were necessarily acceptable: rather the core of my argument is that it is unsound to attempt to make such judgments without taking careful and sympathetic cognizance of the conceptual universe within which those involved in the incident in question were operating. Whatever horror stories may be circulated about the barbaric character of Muslim law, in historical terms justice *insaaf* has always played at least as much of a central role in the delivery of Islamic law as it has done in the Judaeo-Christian tradition.

A Plural Future?

It is not my purpose to dismiss the utility of a discourse of human rights per se. My concerns in this chapter are threefold. Firstly to emphasize the profoundly emic character of the conceptual foundations of the current discourse; secondly to highlight the ease with which its non-universalistic deficiencies can be utilized as a means of doing *in*justice to those whose behavioural and conceptual premises are out of step with those underpinning Europe's Judaeo-Christian Enlightenment; and thirdly to underline how such alleged moral deficiencies are once again being used for hegemonic purposes: namely to de-legitimize, and in some instances actively criminalize, the familial strategies deployed by entrepreneurially minded migrants seeking to challenge established patterns of Euro-American privilege by engaging in strategies of globalization from below. The contradictions precipitated by these developments are becoming more severe. Whilst Enlightenment-driven efforts to promote national homogeneity, reinforced by the impact of education, literacy and mass media, once led to a decline in ethnic plurality in Europe's nascent nation states, the recent upsurge in migration 'from below' has subverted that tendency. Given that the majority of contemporary newcomers are carriers of non-European cultural traditions, and that most are Muslims to boot, the plurality to which their presence has given rise is particularly sharply articulated, and likely to remain so for the foreseeable future.

All systems of law, whether statutory, customary or nominally universalist, are products of the social, cultural and ideological contexts from which they have emerged. If a given set of rules, conventions and expectations has been generated and applied within what appears to be a homogenous socio-cultural arena, then it will probably seem to its users to be of universal applicability. Moreover, so long as the arena within which any given legal system is applied is as homogenous as its users believe, its etic (or non-universalistic) character will be of little significance. However the moment that presupposition is rendered false, either as a result of the recognition (or resurgence) of hitherto overlooked patterns of internal plurality, or as a result of newcomers' construction of ethnic colonies, or indeed of a general shift towards globalization, the parochial character of the conventional assumptions within which the system operates will have immediate consequences, especially for those who differ. In contexts of de facto plurality the imposition, indeed legal enforcement, of expectations of homogeneity and uniformity, even if implemented on nominally humanitarian grounds, will lead to many components of their everyday behaviour being identified as inappropriate at best, and as illegitimate, subversive or even criminal at worst. Such a situation is in no way compatible with equity or justice.

Approaching the issue from this perspective poses a very different set of questions to those which Poulter or Wikan confront. Philosophical questions about our capacity to tolerate diversity are no longer meaningful. The issues which current developments have thrown up are much more hard-nosed: how can legal systems currently based on implicit assumptions of homogeneity respond on an equitable basis to the existence of de facto patterns of ethnic and religious plurality? And if contemporary legal systems consequently have no alternative but to pluralize themselves, how can this best be achieved?

My core argument is that the most serious current obstacle to making progress on this front in Euro-American jurisdictions stems from a deep-rooted commitment to the philosophical assumptions of the Enlightenment, and the consequent, profoundly mistaken, assumption that the premises within which such jurisdictions operate are of universal validity. So long as lawyers and social policy-makers remain committed to that position, any steps they take towards recognizing the legitimacy of ethnic plurality will encounter the tripwire set by their nineteenth-century predecessors: that practices contrary to justice, equity and good conscience, in other words to the premises of the European Enlightenment, will be deemed unacceptable. Indeed in a remarkable parallel with eighteenth-century assumptions, the prospect of access to citizenship is currently being rendered dependent on the ability of applicants to manifest a sufficient degree of moral discernment before they can achieve such a status. Hence Baden-Württemberg has recently introduced what is popularly described as a 'Muslim test'[3] including such questions as:

- How do you view the statement that a woman should obey her husband, and that he can beat her if she doesn't?
- You learn that people from your neighbourhood or from among friends or acquaintances have carried out or are planning a terrorist attack; what do you do?
- Some people hold the Jews responsible for all the evil in the world, and even claim they were behind the attacks of 11 September 2001 in New York. What is your view of this claim?
- Imagine that your son comes to you and declares that he's a homosexual and would like to live with another man. How do you react?

If the applicant's responses are deemed inadequate, the naturalization request may be turned down. A similarly structured, albeit rather less blatant text, has also recently been introduced in the UK. Hence a recently published document entitled *The Path to Citizenship* (Home Office 2008) not only requires all migrants to *earn* the right to stay, not least by learning to speak English, obeying the law and contributing to the community, but also greatly extends what it describes as

3 <http://news.bbc.co.uk/nolpda/ukfs_news/hi/newsid_4655000/4655240.stm> [accessed 18 November 2008]

'the path to citizenship' to include a substantial period of 'provisional citizenship' during which applicants must prove the moral, linguistic and behavioural *bona fides* in an implicitly homogenous British socio-cultural order .

A Conclusion, Together with Some Vital Caveats

How best to move forward? In a world where processes of globalization are becoming steadily more powerful, such statutory efforts to turn back the clock seem likely to be ineffective. Our future, no less than our past, appears to be inescapably plural. In practical terms the unqualified promotion of methodological individualism within the context of an implicit assumption of methodological nationalism no longer holds water. However, there is no need to throw the baby out with the bathwater. There is much of value in the premises of the Enlightenment, just as there is in the more corporatist approach championed by Confucian and Indic traditions. The accommodation of plurality is likely to be less traumatic than the unilateralist champions of myopic universalism currently fear. All that is required (although the scale of the task should not be underestimated) is a systematic effort to re-contextualize crucial aspects of established expectations, in order to take more adequate cognizance of the ever more plural character of the contemporary global order. If such an exercise were to be undertaken, it would be foolish to set down the precise premises on which those subject to its provisions should order their lives, especially in domestic contexts. Rather in legal as in so many other contexts the central objective of such an initiative should be to maximize the capacity of judges and juries to take cognizance of all relevant dimensions of the context within which the events in question took place, in a conscious effort to enhance the prospect of precipitating equitable outcomes in the course of the delivery of justice. In an English context this would not be a revolutionary commitment; as the common law tradition has always recognized, one size will most definitely not fit all.

This would not entail the abandonment of all normative imperatives: social order is unsustainable unless all participants agree some basic rules. Homicide is in all circumstances a criminal offence, as is rape and other forms of physical assault; and if only to ensure the safety of our persons and our property, there must be sanctions against such criminally anti-social acts as theft. However, the common law tradition has always taken it for granted that justice cannot be done without taking careful cognizance of the context in which things were said and done and led to charges being laid against the defendant. Such context-setting is, and must be, an empirical business. Efforts to define it by statute are clumsy at best, and misleading at worst. Nor is 'common sense' of much utility in a society in which sub-sections of the population draw on differing conceptual premises to order their behaviour, and where members of the dominant majority readily apply stereotypical judgements to the behaviour of minorities.

For example, incidents of domestic homicide occur in all sections of the population, most usually because interpersonal relationships have got completely out of hand. The ultimate causes of those breakdowns (violent efforts of the powerful to impose their will, sexually grounded jealousies and betrayals, weaker members of families driven to the end of their tether) are more or less universal, and the outcome is tragic. But when such tragic incidents occur in South Asian families, why do they attract deeply pejorative labels such as 'honour killing', and in so doing lead to the invocation of statutory rules which insist that 'hate crimes' must of necessity attract exemplary punishment?

It is with such *humanitarian* considerations in mind that the tendency to uncritically entrench the premises of the contemporary discourse of human rights in statutory provisions must be regarded as double-edged. The discourse undoubtedly provides effective means whereby citizens of over-authoritarian states can mount legal challenges to tyranny. But however much this may promote individual liberty, it does nothing to prevent the launching of 'humanitarian initiatives' which nominally aim to introduce benighted others to the values of freedom and civilization. Likewise it provides committed libertarians with a ready means of condemning corporately oriented family structures as inherently oppressive patriarchies, with those trapped therein in urgent need of liberation. The issues unleashed in this context are far from purely legal in character; they are inescapably political, as is the double-edged sword of human rights. In such circumstance it is idle to assume that the discourse of human rights is everywhere and always an instrument of liberation: it can just as easily be deployed as a weapon of war.

References

Allen, S. 2008. *Launch of the ACPO Honour-based Violence Strategy*. Available at: <http://www.acpo.police.uk/pressrelease.asp?PR_GUID={3D5B8666-B246-4AA7-8AE6-031409519CC8> [accessed 28 October 2008].

Ballard, Roger. 2000. Panth, Kismet, Dharm te Qaum: Four Dimensions in Punjabi Religion. In *Punjabi Identity in a Global Context*, edited by Pritam Singh and Shinder Thandi. New Delhi: Oxford University Press, 7–38.

— 2003. The South Asian Presence in Britain and its Transnational Connections. In *Culture and Economy in the Indian Diaspora*, edited by H. Singh and S. Vertovec. London: Routledge, 197–222.

— 2005. Coalitions of Reciprocity and the Maintenance of Financial Integrity within Informal Value Transmission Systems: the Operational Dynamics of Contemporary *Hawala* Networks. *Journal of Banking Regulation*, 6(3), 319–52.

— 2007a. Common Law and Common Sense: Juries, Justice and the Challenge of Ethnic Plurality. In *Law and Ethnic Plurality: Socio-Legal Perspectives*, edited by Prakash Shah. Leiden: Brill/Martinus Nijhoff, 69–105.

— 2007b. Living with Difference: a Forgotten Art in Urgent Need of Revival? In *Religious Reconstruction in the South Asian Diasporas: From One Generation to Another*, edited by J. Hinnells. London: Palgrave Macmillan, 265–301.

— 2008. Inside and Outside: Contrasting Perspectives on the Dynamics of Kinship and Marriage in Contemporary South Asian Transnational Networks. In *The Family in Question: Immigrant and Ethnic Minorities in Multicultural Europe*, edited by R.D. Grillo. Amsterdam: Amsterdam University, 37–70.

Ballard, Roger and Tahirah Parveen. 2008. Minority Professionals' Experience of Marginalisation and Exclusion: the Rules of Ethnic Engagement. In *Advancing Multiculturalism, Post 7/7*, edited by John Eade, Martyn Barrett, Chris Flood and Richard Race. Cambridge: Scholar's Press, 73–96.

Beck, Ulrich. 2006. *Power in the Global Age: A New Global Political Economy.* Cambridge: Polity Press.

Bhagwati, Jagdish. 2003. Borders beyond Control. *Foreign Affairs*, 98(1), 98–106.

Bingham, Lord. 2006. *The Rule of Law, Sixth Sir David Williams Lecture.* Cambridge: Centre for Public Law.

Blackstone, Sir William. 1765. *Commentaries on the Laws of England.* Oxford: Clarendon Press.

Cantle Report. 2002. *Building Cohesive Communities: A Report of the Ministerial Group on Public Order and Community Cohesion.* London: Home Office.

Forced Marriage Unit. 2006. *Forced Marriage: A Wrong Not a Right. Summary of Responses to the Criminalisation of Forced Marriage.* London: Forced Marriage Unit.

Gray, J. 2000. *Two Faces of Liberalism.* Oxford: Polity Press.

Hagelund, A. 2008. 'For Women and Children!' The Family and Immigration Politics in Scandinavia. In *The Family in Question: Immigrant and Ethnic Minorities in Multicultural Europe*, edited by R.D. Grillo. Amsterdam: Amsterdam University Press, 71–88.

Home Office. 2008. *The Path to Citizenship: Next Steps in Reforming the Immigration System.* London: Border and Immigration Agency.

Hunt, Lynn. 2007. *Inventing Human Rights*. New York: Norton.

Hussain, Abdullah. 2000. *Émigré Journeys*. London: Serpent's Tail.

Lett, J.W. 1996 Emic/etic Distinctions. In *Encyclopaedia of Cultural Anthropology, Volume 2*. New York: Holt, 382–3.

Lewis, Ioan. 1971. *Ecstatic Religion: Anthropological Study of Spirit Possession and Shamanism*. London: Pelican.

Office of the High Commissioner on Human Rights. No date. *Fact Sheet No. 23, Harmful Traditional Practices Affecting the Health of Women and Children.* Geneva: OHCHR.

Oldenburg, Veena. 2002. *Dowry Murder: The Imperial Origins of a Cultural Crime.* Oxford: Oxford University Press.

Pennington, B.K. 2005. *Was Hinduism Invented? Britons, Indians, and the Colonial Construction of Religion*. New York/Oxford: Oxford University Press.

Poulter, Sebastian. 1998. *Ethnicity, Law and Human Rights: The English Experience*. Oxford: The Clarendon Press.

Raj, Dhooleka. 2003. *Where Are You From? Middle Class Migrants in the Modern World*. Berkeley: University of California Press.

Rousseau, Jean-Jacques. 1762 [2005]. *The Social Contract*. London: Penguin.

Sachdeva, Sanjiv. 1993. *The Primary Purpose Rule in British Immigration Law.* Stoke-on-Trent: Trentham Books.

Storhaug, H. and Human Rights Service. 2003. *Feminin integrering – utfordringer i et fleretnisk samfunn*. Oslo: Kolofon.

Wikan, Unni. 2002. *Generous Betrayal. Politics of Culture in the New Europe.* Chicago: University of Chicago Press.

Wimmer, Andreas. 2002. *Nationalist Exclusion and Ethnic Conflict: Shadows of Modernity.* Cambridge: Cambridge University Press.

Wollstonecraft, Mary. 1792 [1994]. *A Vindication of the Rights of Woman: with Strictures on Political and Moral Subjects*. Oxford: Oxford University Press.

Index

For Product Safety Concerns and Information please contact our EU representative GPSR@taylorandfrancis.com Taylor & Francis Verlag GmbH, Kaufingerstraße 24, 80331 München, Germany